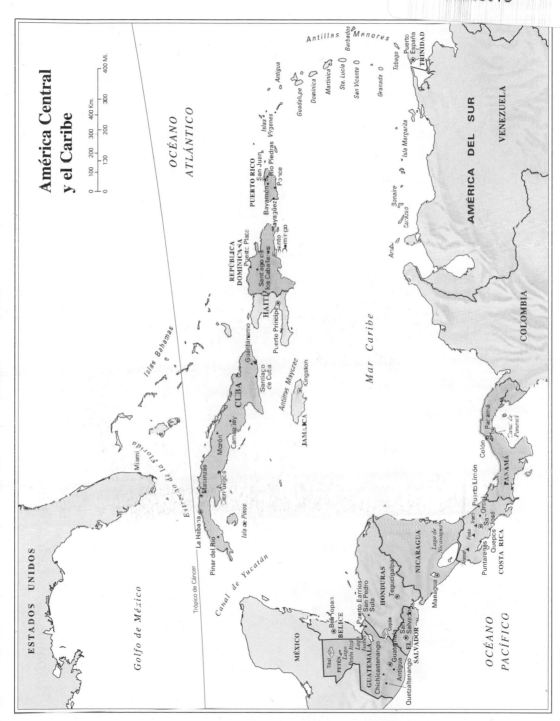

América Central y el Caribe

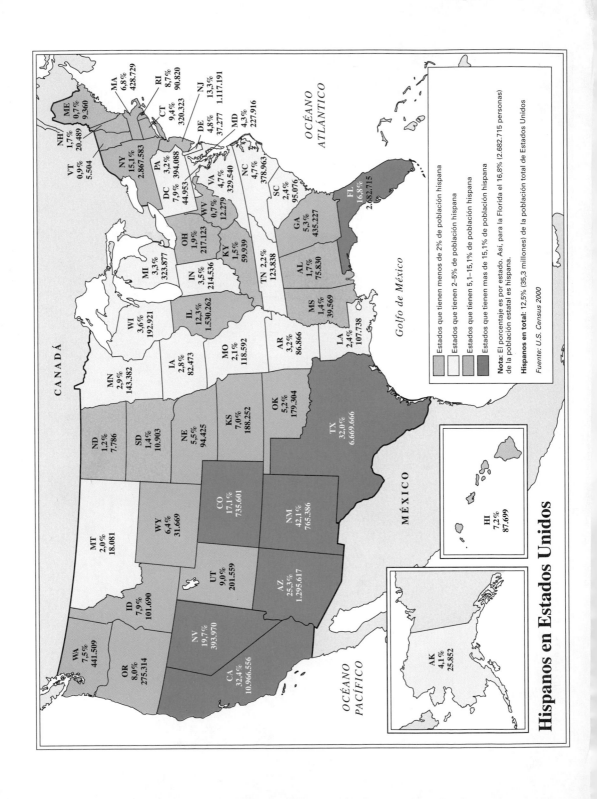

Hispanos en Estados Unidos

CANADÁ

OCÉANO ATLÁNTICO

OCÉANO PACÍFICO

MÉXICO

Golfo de México

ME
0,7%
9.360

NH
1,7%
20.489

VT
0,9%
5.504

MA
6,8%
428.729

RI
8,7%
90.820

CT
9,4%
320.323

NJ
13,3%
1.117.191

NY
15,1%
2.867.583

PA
3,2%
394.088

DC
7,9%
44.953

DE
4,8%
37.277

MD
4,3%
227.916

VA
4,7%
329.540

WV
0,7%
12.279

NC
4,7%
378.963

SC
2,4%
95.076

GA
5,3%
435.227

FL
16,8%
2.682.715

OH
1,9%
217.123

MI
3,3%
323.877

IN
3,5%
214.536

KY
1,5%
59.939

TN
2,2%
123.838

AL
1,7%
75.830

MS
1,4%
39.569

WI
3,6%
192.921

IL
12,3%
1.530.262

IA
2,8%
82.473

MO
2,1%
118.592

AR
3,2%
86.866

LA
2,4%
107.738

MN
2,9%
143.382

ND
1,2%
7.786

SD
1,4%
10.903

NE
5,5%
94.425

KS
7,0%
188.252

OK
5,2%
179.304

TX
32,0%
6.669.666

MT
2,0%
18.081

WY
6,4%
31.669

CO
17,1%
735.601

NM
42,1%
765.386

ID
7,9%
101.690

UT
9,0%
201.559

AZ
25,3%
1.295.617

NV
19,7%
393.970

CA
32,4%
10.966.556

OR
8,0%
275.314

WA
7,5%
441.509

HI
7,2%
87.699

AK
4,1%
25.852

Estados que tienen menos de 2% de población hispana

Estados que tienen 2–5% de población hispana

Estados que tienen 5,1–15,1% de población hispana

Estados que tienen mas de 15,1% de población hispana

Nota: El porcentaje es por estado. Así, para la Florida el 16,8% (2.682.715 personas) de la población estatal es hispana.

Hispanos en total: 12,5% (35,3 millones) de la población total de Estados Unidos

Fuente: U.S. Census 2000

THE BASIC SPANISH SERIES
BASIC SPANISH

THE BASIC SPANISH SERIES
BASIC SPANISH

ANA C. JARVIS
Chandler-Gilbert Community College

RAQUEL LEBREDO
California Baptist University

FRANCISCO MENA-AYLLÓN
University of Redlands

HOUGHTON MIFFLIN COMPANY
Boston   New York

Publisher: *Rolando Hernández*
Sponsoring Editor: *Van Strength*
Development Editor: *Judith Bach*
Senior Project Editor: *Tracy Patruno*
Manufacturing Manager: *Karen Banks*
Executive Marketing Director: *Eileen Bernadette Moran*
Associate Marketing Manager: *Claudia Martínez*

Cover image: Street in Red, © Ruby Aranguiz. Reprinted by arrangement with Mill Pond Press, Inc., Venice, Florida 34285

Photo credits: p. 2, Beryl Goldberg; p. 14, © Digital Vision/Getty Images; p. 26, © Owen Franken/Corbis; p. 42, Robert Fried; p. 54, © Susan Steinkamp/Corbis; p. 66, © Comstock Images/Alamy; p. 80, © Buddy Mays/Corbis; p. 100, © Danny Lehman/Corbis; p. 114, © John Neubauer/PhotoEdit; p. 128, © Andres Leighton/AP/Wide World Photos; p. 144, © Ulrike Welsch/PhotoEdit; p. 162, © ImageState Royalty Free/Alamy; p. 184, © Jeremy Horner/Corbis; p. 198, © 2005 Robert Frerck/Odyssey Productions, Inc.; p. 212, © Royalty-Free/Corbis; p. 222, David Simson/Stock Boston; p. 232, © Charles O'Rear/Corbis; p. 258, Peter Menzel; p. 272, ©Warren Morgan/Corbis; p. 284, © Jeff Greenberg/PhotoEdit; p. 296, © Larry Williams/Corbis; p. 308, © Ariel Skelley/Corbis.

Printed in the U.S.A.

Library of Congress Control Number: 2005924676

ISBN: 0-618-50569-5

123456789-MP-09 08 07 06 05

Contents

PREFACE

Drawn from the successful *Basic Spanish Grammar,* Sixth Edition, and career manuals, *The Basic Spanish Series* offers a flexible, concise introduction to Spanish grammar and communication in an updated series to better address the needs of today's students and professionals needing a working knowledge of Spanish.

Basic Spanish

The core text, **Basic Spanish,** provides the basic grammatical structures needed to communicate in Spanish. The organization of this central component of *The Basic Spanish Series* reflects its emphasis on the acquisition of Spanish fundamentals for practical use. The core text consists of two preliminary lessons, twenty regular lessons, and four self-tests. The preliminary lessons enable students to communicate in Spanish using basic, high-frequency language from the outset of the course.

The twenty regular lessons of *Basic Spanish* contain the following features:

- **Chapter-opening spreads** feature objectives (both structures and communication), a different Spanish-speaking country highlighted with a country profile in English, a map, and a legend of icons that indicate additional resources available with the program.

- Each **grammar presentation** lists the grammar topic in English and Spanish, followed by clear, concise grammar explanations in English, language models in Spanish with translations and charts, and *Vamos a practicar* exercises for reinforcement of the material.

- Chapter **vocabulary lists** are clearly divided into the following categories: Cognates, Verbs, Adjectives, and Other Words and Expressions.

- **Communicative activities** include situational role playing and group activities to encourage practice of the grammar points.

- **End-of-lesson activities** provide practice of the active vocabulary introduced in each lesson: *Palabras y más palabras,* followed by *En estas situaciones,* a pair/group activity, encourage students to apply structures and vocabulary learned in the lesson.

- Small **culture notes** throughout highlight customs, traditions, and Spanish language usage in everyday life.

■ ***Para escuchar y entender*** consists of two types of audio exercises: *Práctica* (grammar exercises) and *¿Qué dicen?* (listening comprehension).

■ ***¿Cuánto sabe usted ahora?*** self-tests appear after every five lessons, with answers on the HM ClassPrep CD, giving instructors the option to cover the answers in class or provide students the answers so they can monitor their own progress.

Other Components of *The Basic Spanish Series*

The Basic Spanish Series features a full range of components designed to meet the needs of students who wish to learn Spanish for specific purposes. To maximize students' exposure to natural spoken Spanish, each of the six companion worktexts is accompanied by its own audio program and website.

For Students and Instructors

Companion Worktexts

The six worktexts—***Basic Spanish for Getting Along, Basic Spanish for Medical Personnel, Basic Spanish for Business and Finance, Basic Spanish for Law Enforcement, Basic Spanish for Social Services, Basic Spanish for Teachers*** —are communication worktexts that take the grammar learned in *Basic Spanish* and put it to practical use. The worktexts present realistic situations students will encounter in everyday life and realistic situations professionals will encounter in their particular workplace with attention to specialized vocabulary for each profession. Students get the opportunity to practice through dialogue completions, role-plays, and realia-based activities. Each chapter also contains cultural notes that highlight Hispanic customs and traditions relevant to the subject matter of the lesson.

■ ***Basic Spanish for Getting Along*** is a communication manual designed to serve those students who seek to develop basic conversational skills in Spanish.

■ ***Basic Spanish for Medical Personnel*** provides key current medical vocabulary, practical reference information, and medical notes written from a cross-cultural perspective.

■ ***Basic Spanish for Business and Finance*** offers diversified business topics and vocabulary, technology-related terms, cultural notes, and activities on business culture and practices—correlated to the cultural notes—to check and reinforce students' business cross-cultural competency.

- ***Basic Spanish for Law Enforcement*** provides personnel in law enforcement with current, up-to-date vocabulary, situations, and role-plays preparing them to deal with job situations they will encounter on a daily basis.

- ***Basic Spanish for Social Services*** provides social workers and other staff in the social services field with model situations and current vocabulary to serve their non-English-speaking clients.

- ***Basic Spanish for Teachers*** provides teachers in a bilingual setting with the tools to communicate with students and parents in their native language.

For Students

Student In-Text Audio CDs

- Packaged automatically with the **core text**, this **five-CD set** contains audio files recorded by native speakers to accompany the *Para escuchar y entender* section of each chapter. The CDs also contain audio files for the *Práctica oral* questions from the four *Repaso* sections.

- Packaged automatically with each **worktext**, this **two-CD set** contains audio recordings of all lesson dialogues and *Lectura* conversations found in each of the six different worktexts, along with audio files to accompany *Práctica oral* sections of each *Repaso* self-test.

Student CD-ROM (video)

This CD-ROM contains 73 grammar presentations taught by a video instructor, covering the grammar topics presented in the core text. It provides additional support for those students who find the 20 grammar points taught on the student website helpful.

 **Student SMARTTHINKING™**

Online Tutoring

Using the Internet, SMARTTHINKING™ provides live learner support whenever and wherever students need it. SMARTTHINKING™ is a virtual learning assistance center that is staffed up to 24 hours a day, 7 days a week.

- Students work in real-time with an e-structor.
- Students can log on for live help during specified homework hours or submit a question at the time it arises and get a response within 24 hours. Students can also preschedule online appointments.

Student Website (www.college.hmco.com/students)

The student website for the **core text** contains the following:

- ACE practice tests for each grammar topic presented in the core text
- Audio Flashcards for vocabulary study and pronunciation practice
- 20 grammar presentations, one per lesson, taught by a video instructor
- Web search activities associated with the target country of each chapter
- Web links (to sites where students can explore additional information)

Completed activities can be printed or emailed directly to a course instructor.

The student website for the **worktexts** contains the following:

- Web search activities that coordinate with the culture notes in each of the individual worktexts
- ACE practice tests for each grammar point presented in the core text
- Audio flashcards for vocabulary study and pronunciation practice for each individual worktext
- Web links (to sites where students can explore additional information)

Student Blackboard™ Basic

The basic version of the BlackBoard™ course cartridge includes all that is found on the student website.

Student WebCT Basic

The student version of the WebCT course cartridge includes all that is found on the student website.

Spanish Phrasebooks

These pocket phrasebooks contain vocabulary and phrases arranged alphabetically to provide students and professionals with a handy reference for real-life and on-the-job situations.

- *Basic Spanish for Getting Along Phrasebook*
- *Basic Spanish for Law Enforcement and Social Services Phrasebook*
- *Basic Spanish for Business and Finance Phrasebook*
- *Basic Spanish for Medical Personnel and Social Services Phrasebook*

For Instructors

Instructor's HM ClassPrep CD

This **NEW** CD-ROM includes:

- Sample syllabi and sample lesson plans
- Transparency masters in PDF format
- Translation of worktext dialogues
- Test program available in PDF and Word files
- Audio and video scripts
- Answer keys for the core text and worktexts
- Situation cards

Instructor's Website (www.college.hmco.com/instructors)

The instructor's website contains all the resources that exist on the Instructor's ClassPrep CD minus the testing program and the answer key.

Instructor's Course Management powered by Blackboard™ and WebCT

Both components provide materials in an online format for those instructors or institutions moving to online instruction. They include all the resources included on the HM ClassPrep CD plus the Testing Program in Blackboard or WebCT format.

Feedback Welcome

We would like to hear your comments on and reactions to *The Basic Spanish Series.* Reports on your experiences using this program would be of great interest and value to us. Please write to us in care of:

Houghton Mifflin Company
College Division
222 Berkeley Street
Boston, MA 02116-3764

Acknowledgments

We wish to thank our colleagues who have used previous editions of *Basic Spanish Grammar* for their many constructive comments and recommendations. We especially appreciate the valuable suggestions of the following reviewers of *Basic Spanish:*

David Young, *Missouri Western State College*
Dianna Rodríguez-Lozano, *Mount Saint Mary's College*
Kirby Chadwick, *Scottsdale Community College*
Kathleen M Jiménez, *Miami-Dade Community College*
Robert L. Adler, *University of North Alabama*
Sally R. Brecher, *Buena Vista University*
Bárbara Villalonga, *San José State University*

We also extend our sincere appreciation to the World Languages staff at Houghton Mifflin Company, College Division: *Publisher,* Rolando Hernández; *Sponsoring Editor,* Van Strength; *Development Manager,* Glenn Wilson; *Development Editor,* Judith Bach; *Associate Marketing Manager,* Claudia Martínez; and *Executive Marketing Director,* Eileen Bernadette Moran.

Ana C. Jarvis
Raquel Lebredo
Francisco Mena-Ayllón

THE BASIC SPANISH SERIES
BASIC SPANISH

OBJECTIVES

Structures

1. Greetings and farewells
2. Cardinal numbers 0–39
3. The alphabet
4. Days of the week
5. Months of the year
6. Colors

Communication

You will learn to greet people and exchange some polite questions and answers, exchange phone numbers, talk about days and dates, and describe colors.

Countries highlighted: The Spanish-speaking World

There are twenty Spanish-speaking countries in Latin America, one in Europe (*España*) and one in Africa (*Guinea Ecuatorial*). There are 400 million people in the world whose first language is Spanish.

Spanish is one of the official languages of the United Nations.

RESOURCES

Wherever you see the following icons additional resources are available:

Internet

Go to **www.college.hmco.com/languages/spanish/students/** for additional practice on the topic.

Student CD-ROM

Go to the **Video Grammar Tutor** for help with understanding the grammar topic at hand.

Go to the **In-Text Audio CDs** for more practice.

EN LOS PAÍSES DE HABLA HISPANA
(In Spanish-speaking countries)

Look at the maps in the front and back of the book and complete the following:

1. La capital de España es _____.
2. España y _____ forman la Península Ibérica.
3. El Estrecho de _____ separa España de África.
4. Las Islas Baleares están (*are*) en el Mar _____.
5. Al sur (*south*) de México está (*is*) _____.
6. El país más pequeño (*smallest country*) de Centroamérica es (*is*) _____.
7. La capital de Honduras es _____, y la capital de _____ es Managua.
8. Haití y _____ comparten (*share*) una isla.
9. _____ conecta Centroamérica y la América del Sur.
10. La capital de Colombia es _____ con la capital de Ecuador es _____. Caracas es la capital de _____.
11. La Cordillera de los _____ separa Argentina de _____.
12. Montevideo, la capital de _____, está sobre el Océano _____.
13. Al norte (*north*) de Paraguay está _____.
14. Chile y _____ no limitan con (*don't border*) Brasil.
15. Las ruinas incas de Machu Picchu están en _____.
16. El Lago Titicaca está en _____.
17. Santiago es la capital de _____.
18. Buenos Aires es la capital de _____.

Did you know that . . . ?
Each student will select a Spanish-speaking country and will find one or two interesting facts having to do with that country. It may be the geography, the history, the music, the food, the arts, or the literature. Students will share the information with the rest of the class.

1 GREETINGS AND FAREWELLS
Saludos y despedidas

—**Buenos días, doctor Rivas.**   *"Good morning, Doctor Rivas.*
  ¿Cómo está usted?   *How are you?"*
—**Muy bien, gracias, Sra. Vega.**   *"Very well, thank you, Mrs. Vega.*
  ¿Y usted?   *And you?"*
—**Bien, gracias. Hasta luego.**   *"Fine, thank you. See you later."*
—**Adiós, señora.**   *"Good-bye, madam."*

—**Buenas tardes, señorita.**   *"Good afternoon, miss.*
  ¿Cómo está usted?   *How are you?"*
—**No muy bien, doctora.**   *"Not very well, doctor."*
—**¡Lo siento! Tome asiento,**   *"I'm sorry. Have a seat, please."*
  por favor.
—**Gracias.**   *"Thank you."*

—**Pase, señor Soto. ¿Cómo le va?**   *"Come in, Mr. Soto. How is it going for you?"*
—**Muy bien, profesora.**   *"Very well, professor."*
—**Señor Soto, el[1] señor Reyes.**   *"Mr. Soto, Mr. Reyes."*
—**Mucho gusto, señor Reyes.**   *"Pleased to meet you, Mr. Reyes."*
—**El gusto es mío, señor Soto.**   *"The pleasure is mine, Mr. Soto."*

—**Hola, Fernando. ¿Qué tal?**   *"Hi, Fernando. How is it going?"*
  Bien, gracias. ¿Y tú?   *"Fine, thank you. And you?"*
—**Muy bien. ¿Qué hay de nuevo?**   *"Just fine. What's new?"*
—**No mucho...**   *"Not much..."*

> When being introduced to a woman or to another man, a man might say "A sus órdenes." (*At your service*)

—**Buenas noches, señora.**   *"Good evening, madam."*
—**Buenas noches, señorita.**   *"Good evening, miss."*
—**¿Cómo se llama usted?**   *"What is your name?"*
—**Me llamo María Inés**   *"My name is María Inés*
  Díaz Peña.   *Díaz Peña."*

—**Muchas gracias, señor.**   *"Thank you very much, sir."*
—**De nada, señora.**   *"You're welcome, madam."*

> In Spanish-speaking countries, many people use their father's last name (in this case *Díaz*) and the mother's maiden name (in this case *Peña*) as in **María Inés Díaz Peña.**

---

[1]When speaking about or introducing a third person and a title is used with the name, the definite article is included.

VOCABULARIO
Audio

SALUDOS Y DESPEDIDAS (*GREETINGS AND FAREWELLS*)

Buenos días.	*Good morning. (Good day.)*
Buenas tardes.	*Good afternoon.*
Buenas noches.	*Good evening. (Good night.)*
Hola.	*Hi. (Hello.)*
Hasta luego.	*I'll see you later.* (lit., *until later*)
Hasta mañana.	*I'll see you tomorrow.*
Adiós.	*Good-bye.*

TÍTULOS (*TITLES*)

doctor (Dr.)[1]	*doctor* (masc.)
doctora (Dra.)	*doctor* (fem.)
profesor	*professor, teacher, instructor* (masc.)
profesora	*professor, teacher, instructor* (fem.)
señor (Sr.)	*Mr., sir, gentleman*
señora (Sra.)	*Mrs., madam, lady*
señorita (Srta.)	*Miss, young lady* (unmarried)

EXPRESIONES ÚTILES (*USEFUL EXPRESSIONS*)

¿Cómo está usted?	*How are you?*
Muy bien, ¿y usted?	*Very well, and you?*
¿Cómo le va?	*How is it going for you?*
¿Cómo se llama usted?	*What is your name?*
Me llamo...	*My name is . . .*
¿Qué hay de nuevo?	*What's new?*
No mucho.	*Not much.*
¿Qué tal?	*How is it going?*
Bien, ¿y tú?	*Fine (Well), and you?*
No muy bien.	*Not very well.*
Lo siento.	*I'm sorry.*
Mucho gusto.	*It's a pleasure (to meet you).*
El gusto es mío.	*The pleasure is mine.*
Pase.	*Come in.*
Por favor.	*Please.*
Tome asiento.	*Have a seat.*
Gracias.	*Thank you.*
Muchas gracias.	*Thank you very much.*
De nada.	*You're welcome.*

> Other titles are used: *arquitecto, ingeniero,* etc. Lawyers and members of some professions who hold the equivalent of a Ph.D. are addressed as **doctor** or **doctora.**

> Use the **tú** form when addressing a friend, a relative, or a very young person. If in doubt, use the **usted** form. Very young people call each other **tú** even if they have just met.

[1]Notice that in Spanish, titles are not capitalized except when they are abbreviated.

Vamos a practicar

Quiz

A Familiarize yourself with each of the dialogues on page 5, and then act them out with another student.

B What would you say in the following situations?

1. You meet your professor in the morning and ask him/her how he/she is.
2. You meet Miss Rojas in the afternoon and ask her how it's going for her.
3. You greet a good friend and ask him/her how it's going. You also ask what's new.
4. Someone tells you he/she is not feeling very well. You say you're sorry and offer a seat.
5. Somebody is introduced to you.
6. You thank Mr. Macías for a favor and tell him you'll see him later.
7. You greet Miss Burgos in the evening and ask her to come in.
8. Someone asks how you are. You are just fine. You ask him/her how he/she is.
9. Somebody says "Mucho gusto" to you.
10. Somebody thanks you for a favor.
11. Someone asks you what's new. You don't have much to report.
12. Someone asks you how you are. You are not feeling very well.
13. You are helping a Spanish speaking person to fill out an application. You ask what his/her name is.
14. You tell someone your name.

2 CARDINAL NUMBERS 0–39
Los números cardinales 0–39

0 cero	10 diez	20 veinte	30 treinta
1 uno[1]	11 once	21 veintiuno[1,2]	31 treinta y uno
2 dos	12 doce	22 veintidós	32 treinta y dos
3 tres	13 trece	23 veintitrés	33 treinta y tres
4 cuatro	14 catorce	24 veinticuatro	34 treinta y cuatro
5 cinco	15 quince	25 veinticinco	35 treinta y cinco
6 seis	16 dieciséis[2]	26 veintiséis	36 treinta y seis
7 siete	17 diecisiete	27 veintisiete	37 treinta y siete
8 ocho	18 dieciocho	28 veintiocho	38 treinta y ocho
9 nueve	19 diecinueve	29 veintinueve	39 treinta y nueve

---

[1] **Uno** changes to **un** before a masculine singular noun: *un* **libro** (*one book*). **Uno** changes to **una** before a feminine singular noun: *una* **silla** (*one chair*). All other numbers ending in -**uno** or -**una** follow the same pattern: *veintiún* **libros** (*twenty-one books*), *veintiuna* **sillas** (*twenty-one chairs*).

[2] The numbers 16 to 29 may also be written as separate words: **diez y seis, veinte y uno,** and so on. The most common spelling, however, is the single-word form used in this text.

Vamos a practicar

A Read the following numbers aloud in Spanish.

0	10	9	31	25	19	7	33
15	37	16	11	21	20	29	17
28	14	13	8	4	12	30	22

B Read the following telephone numbers in Spanish. Say each digit one by one.

383-5079	254-2675	792-5136	689-0275
985-0746	765-1032	985-7340	872-0695

C Find out the phone number of three classmates. Ask: **¿Cuál es tu número de teléfono?** (*What is your phone number?*)

③ THE ALPHABET
El alfabeto

Letter	Name	Letter	Name	Letter	Name	Letter	Name
a	a	h	hache	ñ	eñe	t	te
b	be	i	i	o	o	u	u
c	ce	j	jota	p	pe	v	ve
d	de	k	ca	q	cu	w	doble ve
e	e	l	ele	r	ere	x	equis
f	efe	m	eme	rr	erre	y	i griega
g	ge	n	ene	s	ese	z	zeta

Vamos a practicar

> Sometimes initials are used as a word. For example, TWA is called "Túa."

A Read the following in Spanish.

FBI   MIT   IBM   NFL   NBA   NHL

B A Spanish-speaking person may not know how to spell your name. He or she may ask: **¿Cómo se escribe?**[1] (*How do you spell it?*) Learn how to spell your name in Spanish and ask other members of the class how to spell theirs.

---

[1]Also: ¿Cómo se deletrea?

4 DAYS OF THE WEEK
Los días de la semana

SEPTIEMBRE						
LUNES	MARTES	MIÉRCOLES	JUEVES	VIERNES	SÁBADO	DOMINGO
		1	2	3	4	5
6	7	8	9	10	11	12
13	14	15	16	17	18	19
20	21	22	23	24	25	26
27	28	29	30			

—¿Qué día es hoy?   *"What day is it today?"*
—Hoy es lunes.   *"Today is Monday."*

—Hoy es martes, ¿no?   *"Today is Tuesday, isn't it?"*
—No, hoy es miércoles.   *"No, today is Wednesday."*

—¿Qué día es hoy?   *"What day is it today?*
¿Jueves?   *Thursday?"*
—No, hoy es viernes.   *"No, today is Friday."*

—Hoy es...sábado...   *"Today is...Saturday*
¡no! domingo...   *...no! Sunday..."*
—Sí, hoy es domingo.   *"Yes, today is Sunday."*

> In calendars in Spanish-speaking countries, the week starts on Monday.

ATENCIÓN: **The days of the week are not capitalized in Spanish. El and** los **are frequently used with the days of the week to express** *on:* el lunes *(on Monday)*, los sábados *(on Saturdays)*, **etc.**

Vamos a practicar

Quiz

Using the calendar of **septiembre** say what day of the week it is according to the date given.

MODELO   Hoy es el 13 de septiembre.
Hoy es lunes.

In Spanish-speaking countries, the equivalent of "a week from today" is **"de hoy en ocho,"** because *today* is counted as the first day.

1. Hoy es el 3 de septiembre.
2. Hoy es el 21 de septiembre.
3. Hoy es el 12 de septiembre.
4. Hoy es el 15 de septiembre.
5. Hoy es el 18 de septiembre.
6. Hoy es el 9 de septiembre.

⑤ MONTHS OF THE YEAR
Los meses del año

enero	*January*	**julio**	*July*
febrero	*February*	**agosto**	*August*
marzo	*March*	**septiembre**	*September*
abril	*April*	**octubre**	*October*
mayo	*May*	**noviembre**	*November*
junio	*June*	**diciembre**	*December*

 ATENCIÓN: **The names of the months are not capitalized in Spanish.**

■ To talk about the date, use the following expressions.

—¿**Qué fecha es hoy?**   *"What's the date today?"*
—**Hoy es el quince de enero.**   *"Today is January fifteenth."*

—¿**Hoy es el primero de mayo?**   *"Is today May first?"*
—**No, hoy es el dos de mayo.**   *"No, today is May second."*

 ATENCIÓN: **Spanish uses cardinal numbers to refer to dates. The only exception is** primero (*first*).

■ When telling the date, always begin with the expression **Hoy es el...**

Hoy es el veinte de mayo.   *Today is May twentieth.*

■ Complete the expression by saying the number followed by the preposition **de** (*of*), and then the month.

el **5 de mayo**	*May 5th*
el **12 de octubre**	*October 12th*

ATENCIÓN: In Spanish, the article el is usually included when giving the date orally, although it is sometimes omitted in writing. The article is also omitted if the *day* is mentioned: Hoy es lunes, 13 de septiembre.

> Since the day precedes the month, September 3rd, 2005 would be expressed thus: 3-9-05.

Vamos a practicar

Quiz

Say on what date the following events fall:

1. the first day of the year
2. Valentine's Day
3. Independence Day
4. Christmas
5. the first day of spring

6. April Fool's Day
7. Halloween
8. the first day of fall
9. the first day of winter
10. your birthday

6 COLORS
Los colores

amarillo	*yellow*	**morado**	*purple*
anaranjado	*orange*	**negro**	*black*
azul	*blue*	**rojo**	*red*
blanco	*white*	**rosado**	*pink*
gris	*gray*	**verde**	*green*
marrón (café)	*brown*		

> Sometimes "**verde**" can have the connotation of "dirty": **un chiste verde:** *a dirty joke.*

Vamos a practicar

Quiz

To ask a classmate whether he or she likes something, you say: **¿Te gusta**[1]**...?** To say that you like something say: **Me gusta...**
Conduct a survey of your classmates to find out which color is the most popular in class, following the model.

---
[1] When addressing someone as **usted,** use **¿Le gusta...?**

MODELO   —¿Qué color te gusta?
          —Me gusta el color rojo.

En estas situaciones What would you say in the following situations?

1. You are not sure about today's date. You also don't know what day today is. You ask someone.

2. You don't know how to spell a word. You ask someone.

3. You mention the days of the week when you have classes at the university.

4. Someone asks you when is your best friend's birthday.

5. Someone asks when you can meet to study. You reply: "A week from today."

6. A little child from Mexico wants to know what colors you can see when you look at the rainbow. You list all the colors.

PARA ESCUCHAR Y ENTENDER

The following material is to be used with the In-Text Audio CDs.

I. Práctica

A Saludos y despedidas
You find yourself in the following situations. What would you say? Repeat the correct answer after the speaker's confirmation. Listen to the model.

1–2

MODELO   You meet Mr. Vega in the morning.
          Buenos días, señor Vega.

B Números
Answer each of the addition problems you hear in Spanish. Repeat the correct answer after the speaker's confirmation. Listen to the model.

1–3

MODELO   tres y dos
          cinco

C El alfabeto

Say each of the acronyms you hear in Spanish. Repeat the correct answer after the speaker's confirmation. Listen to the model.

1-4

> MODELO USA
> **u-ese-a**

D Los días de la semana

The speaker will tell you what day of the week today is. Respond by saying what day tomorrow will be. Repeat the correct answer after the speaker's confirmation. Listen to the model.

1-5

> MODELO Hoy es lunes.
> **Mañana es martes.**

E Los meses del año

The speaker will name several holidays. Name the date on which each holiday falls. Repeat the correct answer after the speaker's confirmation. Listen to the model.

1-6

> MODELO Flag Day
> **el catorce de junio**

F Los colores

The speaker will name several familiar objects. State the color or colors of each object in Spanish. Repeat the correct answer after the speaker's confirmation. Listen to the model.

1-7

> MODELO a violet
> **morado**

LECCIÓN PRELIMINAR II

OBJECTIVES

Structures

1. Gender and number
2. The definite and indefinite articles
3. Subject pronouns
4. The present indicative of **ser**
5. Uses of **hay**
6. Cardinal numbers 40–299

Communication

You will learn about cognates and some simple vocabulary related to the classroom.

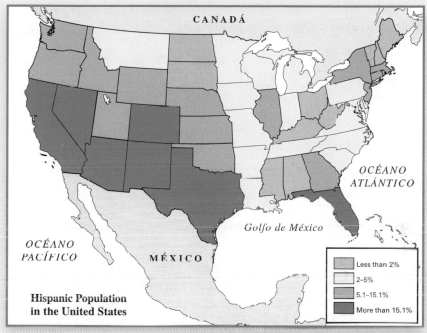

CANADÁ

OCÉANO
ATLÁNTICO

Golfo de México

OCÉANO
PACÍFICO

MÉXICO

	Less than 2%
	2–5%
	5.1–15.1%
	More than 15.1%

**Hispanic Population
in the United States**

The Hispanic influence in the United States is very important. Among the 39 million Hispanics living in this country, 67 percent come from Mexico, and most of them reside in the Southwest.

Puerto Ricans, who are American citizens, represent about 9 percent of Hispanics in the United States, and most of them live in New York and New Jersey. Cubans, who contribute about 4 percent of the Hispanic population, live mainly in Florida.

In addition to these three groups, millions of immigrants from other Latin American countries have arrived in recent years.

RESOURCES

Wherever you see the following icons additional resources are available:

Internet

Go to **www.college.hmco.com/languages/spanish/students/** for additional practice on the topic.

**Student
CD-ROM**

Go to the **Video Grammar Tutor** for help with understanding the grammar topic at hand.

Go to the **In-Text Audio CDs** for more practice.

VOCABULARIO

Audio

COGNADOS[1]

la conversación
la decisión
la idea
la lección
la libertad
el poema
el problema
el programa
el progreso
el (la) secretario(a)
el sistema
el teléfono
la televisión
la universidad

NOMBRES

la amistad *friendship*
la casa *house*
el clima *climate*
el día *day*
el dinero *money*
el español *Spanish (language)*
el hombre *man*
el idioma, la lengua *language*
la lámpara *lamp*
el lápiz *pencil*
el libro *book*
la luz *light*
la mano *hand*
el (la) médico(a), doctor(a)
   M.D., doctor

la mesa *table*
la mujer *woman*
la pluma *pen*
la puerta *door*
la silla *chair*

VERBO

ser *to be*

OTRAS PALABRAS Y EXPRESIONES

de *of, from*
¿de dónde? *from where?*
¿dónde? *where?*

---

[1] Cognates are words that resemble one another and have similar meanings in Spanish and English. Note that English cognates often have different spellings and always have different pronunciations than their Spanish counterparts.

① GENDER AND NUMBER
Género y número

Género

> **Gender** the classification of nouns, pronouns, and adjectives as masculine or feminine.

In Spanish, all nouns, including abstract nouns and those denoting non-living things, are either masculine or feminine.

masculine	*feminine*
año	puerta
señor	señora
teléfono	lámpara
progreso	idea

Here are some practical rules to use to determine the gender of Spanish nouns.

■ Nouns denoting females and most nouns ending in **-a** are feminine. Nouns referring to males and most nouns ending in **-o** are masculine.

masculine	*feminine*
hombre	mujer
teléf**o**no	silla
diner**o**	casa
libr**o**	mesa

ATENCIÓN: Two important exceptions to this rule are día (*day*), which is masculine, and mano (*hand*), which is feminine.

■ Some nouns that end in **-a** are masculine. These nouns are of Greek origin and have kept the gender they had in that language.

problem**a**	sistem**a**
program**a**	poem**a**
idiom**a**	clim**a**

■ Nouns ending in **-sión, -ción, -tad,** and **-dad** are feminine.

televi**sión**	lec**ción**
deci**sión**	conversa**ción**
liber**tad**	universi**dad**
amis**tad**	ciu**dad**

■ The gender of some nouns must be learned.

masculine   *feminine*
español   calle

■ Many masculine nouns ending in **-o** that refer to people have a corresponding feminine form ending in **-a.**

masculine   *feminine*
enfermer**o**   enfermer**a**
secretari**o**   secretari**a**

■ Certain masculine nouns ending in a consonant add **-a** to form the
corresponding feminine noun.

masculine   *feminine*
profesor   profesor**a**
doctor   doctor**a**

■ Colors, numbers, days of the week, and months of the year are
masculine.

Vamos a practicar
Quiz

Are the following nouns feminine (**femenino**) or masculine (**masculino**)?

1. teléfono	**6.** calle	**11.** silla	**16.** progreso
2. día	**7.** mesa	**12.** amistad	**17.** señor
3. televisión	**8.** universidad	**13.** mano	**18.** profesora
4. enfermera	**9.** dinero	**14.** ciudad	**19.** programa
5. problema	**10.** idioma	**15.** lección	**20.** clima

Número

> **Number** a term that identifies words as singular or plural: chair, chairs

Nouns are made plural in Spanish by adding **-s** to those ending in a vowel
and **-es** to those ending in a consonant. Nouns ending in **-z** are made plural by changing the **z** to **c** and adding **-es.**

teléfon**o**	teléfono**s**	lápi**z**	lápi**ces**
mes**a**	mesa**s**	lu**z**	lu**ces**
profeso**r**	profesor**es**	lecció**n**	leccio**nes**

ATENCIÓN: Accent marks that fall on the last syllable of singular words are omitted in the plural form: lección, lecciones.

 ## Vamos a practicar

Quiz

What are the plural forms of the following nouns?

1. silla	**5.** telegrama	**9.** clima	**13.** decisión
2. libro	**6.** ciudad	**10.** conversación	**14.** doctor
3. lápiz	**7.** lección	**11.** profesor	**15.** amistad
4. universidad	**8.** señor	**12.** luz	**16.** lámpara

 ## ② THE DEFINITE AND INDEFINITE ARTICLES
Los artículos definido e indefinido

El artículo definido

> **Definite article** a word used before a noun to indicate a definite person or thing. **the** woman, **the** money

Spanish has four forms that are equivalent to the English definite article *the*.

	Masculine	Feminine
Singular	el	la
Plural	los	las

el profesor	**la** profesora
los profesores	**las** profesoras
el lápiz	**la** lámpara
los lápices	**las** lámparas

 ATENCIÓN: Learning each noun's definite article will help you to remember the noun's gender.

Vamos a practicar

What are the definite articles for the following nouns?

1. universidades	**6.** señores	**11.** dinero
2. problema	**7.** día	**12.** profesores
3. profesor	**8.** televisión	**13.** idea
4. doctor	**9.** silla	**14.** sistema
5. señora	**10.** mujeres	**15.** libertad

El artículo indefinido

> **Indefinite article** a word used before a noun to indicate an indefinite person or object: **a** child, **an** apple, **some** students

The indefinite article in Spanish has four forms; they are equivalent to *a, an,* and *some.*

	Masculine	*Feminine*
Singular	un	una
Plural	unos	unas

un profesor	**una** profesora
unos profesores	**unas** profesoras
un lápiz	**una** pluma
unos lápices	**unas** plumas

Vamos a practicar

How would you name the following items in Spanish?

1. a pen	**5.** a problem	**9.** some pencils
2. a man	**6.** a house	**10.** a lesson
3. some days	**7.** a light	**11.** a friendship
4. some chairs	**8.** a program	**12.** a decision

③ SUBJECT PRONOUNS
Pronombres usados como sujetos

> **Subject** person or thing about which something is said in a sentence or phrase: **Mary** works. **The car** is new.
>
> **Pronoun** a word that replaces a noun: **she, them, us, it**
>
> **Subject pronoun** a personal pronoun that is used as a subject: **They** work. **It** is small.

Singular		Plural	
yo	I	**nosotros** we (*masculine*)	
		nosotras we (*feminine*)	
tú	you (*familiar*)	**vosotros** you (*masculine*)	
		vosotras you (*feminine*)	
usted[1]	you (*formal*)	**ustedes**[2] you	
él	he	**ellos**	they (*masculine*)
ella	she	**ellas**	they (*feminine*)

- The second person plural subject pronoun **vosotros(as)** is used only in Spain. In all other Spanish-speaking countries, **ustedes** is used for both the familiar and the formal plural form of *you*.

- The masculine plural pronoun may refer to the masculine gender alone or to both genders together.

Juan y Roberto: **ellos**   *Juan and Roberto:* **they**
Juan y María: **ellos**   *Juan and María:* **they**

> Use the **tú** form as the equivalent of *you* when addressing a close friend, a relative, or a child. Use the **usted** form in all other instances. Notice that **ustedes** is used for both familiar and polite plural. In Argentina, Paraguay, Guatemala, and Costa Rica **vos** is used instead of **tú**.

---

[1] Abbreviated **Ud.**

[2] Abbreviated **Uds.**

Vamos a practicar
Quiz

Complete the following sentences with the appropriate subject pronoun.

> **MODELO**   You refer to Mr. Gómez as...**él.**

1. You point to yourself and say...
2. You refer to Mrs. Gómez as...
3. You are talking to a little boy, and you call him...
4. You are talking to a woman you've just met, and you call her...
5. Your mother refers to herself and her sister as...
6. Your father refers to himself and his sister as...
7. You are talking to a few people, and you call them...
8. You refer to Mr. Gómez and his daughter as...
9. You refer to Mrs. Gómez and her daughter as...
10. You refer to Mr. and Mrs. Gómez as...
11. You are talking with one of your professors, and you call him...
12. You are talking with one of your friends, and you call her...

④ THE PRESENT INDICATIVE OF *SER*
El presente de indicativo del verbo *ser*

The verb **ser** (*to be*) is an irregular verb. It is one of the most frequently used verbs in the Spanish language. Learning its forms and the corresponding subject pronouns will help you express occupation, nationality, day and date, as well as many other useful facts.

ser (to be)		
yo	**soy**	I am
tú	**eres**	you are (*familiar*)
Ud.		you are (*formal*)
él	**es**	he is
ella		she is
nosotros	**somos**	we are
vosotros	**sois**	you are
Uds.		you are
ellos	**son**	they are (*masculine*)
ellas		they are (*feminine*)

—¿De dónde **son** Uds.?	*"Where are you from?"*
—Yo **soy** de México y Graciela **es** de Cuba. ¿De dónde **eres** tú?	*"I'm from Mexico and Graciela is from Cuba. Where are you from?"*
—Yo **soy** de Perú.	*"I'm from Peru."*
—¿**Son** Uds. norteamericanos?	*"Are you North American?"*
—Sí, nosotros **somos** norteamericanos.	*"Yes, we are North American."*
—¿Hoy **es** miércoles?	*"Is today Wednesday?"*
—No, hoy **es** martes.	*"No, today is Tuesday."*

> Americans are also called **americanos** and sometimes **yanquis.**

Vamos a practicar

A Use the verb **ser** to complete the following conversations. Then act them out with a partner.

1. —¿De dónde _____ tú, Anita?
   —Yo _____ de Buenos Aires. ¿De dónde _____ Ud., señora?
   —Yo _____ de Montevideo.
2. —¿Uds. _____ norteamericanos?
   —Sí, nosotros _____ de California.
3. —¿Elsa _____ profesora?
   —No, ella _____ enfermera.
4. —¿Qué día _____ hoy?
   —Hoy _____ viernes.

B Answer the following questions using complete sentences.
1. ¿Qué fecha es hoy?
2. ¿Qué día es hoy?
3. ¿Uds. son norteamericanos?
4. ¿De dónde es Ud.?
5. ¿De dónde es el profesor (la profesora) de español?

5 USES OF *HAY*
Usos de *hay*

The form **hay** means *there is* or *there are*. It has no subject and must not be confused with **es** (*it is*) and **son** (*they are*).

Hay un lápiz en la mesa.	***There is** a pencil on the table.*
Hay diez libros en la mesa.	***There are** ten books on the table.*

Vamos a practicar

Say how many of the following items there are in the classroom, using **hay.**

1. profesor(a)   **3.** mujeres   **5.** mesas
2. hombres   **4.** sillas   **6.** puertas

6 CARDINAL NUMBERS 40–299
Números cardinales 40–299

40 cuarenta   90 noventa
41 cuarenta y uno...   100 cien (ciento)
50 cincuenta   101 ciento uno...[1]
60 sesenta   150 ciento cincuenta
70 setenta   200 doscientos
80 ochenta   250 doscientos cincuenta...

ATENCIÓN: Ciento **becomes** cien **before a noun.**

cien días
cien casas

Remember that **uno** becomes **un** before a masculine noun and **una** before a feminine noun, even in compound numbers.

ciento **un** libros
ciento **una** sillas

Vamos a practicar

Read the following numbers aloud in Spanish.

86	48	57	123	42	69	74	214
80	91	100	65	111	234	200	261
197	136	115	175	169	185	101	299

---

[1]Notice that the word **y** (*and*) is not used after hundreds: **ciento uno, ciento dos, doscientos veinte,** and so on.

En estas situaciones What would you say in the following situations?

1. You ask a new student where he/she is from, and tell him/her where you are from.

2. You need to ask how many chairs there are in the classroom.

PARA ESCUCHAR Y ENTENDER

The following material is to be used with the In-Text Audio CDs.

I. Práctica

 A El artículo definido

1-8 You will hear some nouns. Repeat each noun, adding the appropriate singular or plural definite article. Repeat the correct answer after the speaker's confirmation. Listen to the model.

> **MODELO** silla
> **la silla**

 B El artículo indefinido

1-9 You will hear several singular nouns, each preceded by an indefinite article. Make the nouns and the articles plural. Repeat the correct answer after the speaker's confirmation. Listen to the model.

> **MODELO** un alumno
> **unos alumnos**

 C El verbo ser

1-10 Answer the questions, always using the second choice. Repeat the correct answer after the speaker's confirmation. Listen to the model.

> **MODELO** —¿Tú eres de Argentina o de los Estados Unidos?
> **—Yo soy de los Estados Unidos.**

 D Números

1-11 Say the numbers you hear in Spanish. Repeat the correct answer after the speaker's confirmation. Listen to the model.

> **MODELO** 157
> **ciento cincuenta y siete**

LECCIÓN

1

OBJECTIVES

Structures

1. The present indicative of regular **-ar** verbs
2. Interrogative and negative sentences
3. Forms and position of adjectives
4. Telling time
5. Cardinal numbers 300–1,000

Communication

You will learn vocabulary related to restaurants and cafeterias.

Country highlighted: España

Spain, which occupies most of the Iberian Peninsula, is separated from France by the Pyrenees Mountains. The country has an area of about 195,000 square miles, and a population of about 40 million.

Spain is a constitutional monarchy. The King, Juan Carlos, is the nation's symbol, but the true government is democratically chosen by the people.

Besides Spanish, several other languages are spoken in different regions: Catalan, Galician (*gallego*), and Basque (*vascuence*)

Spain has traditionally been an agricultural country and is still one of the largest producers of wine and olive oil, but from the mid-1950s, industrial growth was rapid. Nowadays tourism has become one of the most important sources of income, and in Madrid, the capital, as in Barcelona, Granada, Sevilla, and other Spanish cities, hotels, museums, and other places of interest are full of tourists from all over the world.

Spain has also produced great writers, musicians, and painters. One of the most important museums in the world is the **Museo del Prado,** in Madrid.

RESOURCES

Wherever you see the following icons, additional resources are available:

Internet Go to **www.college.hmco.com/languages/spanish/students/** for additional practice on the topic.

Student CD-ROM Go to the **Video Grammar Tutor** for help with understanding the grammar topic at hand.

Go to the **In-Text Audio CDs** for more practice.

 VOCABULARIO

Audio

COGNADOS

la cafetería
el champán
inteligente
el italiano
mexicano(a)
el restaurante

NOMBRES

el (la) camarero(a), mozo, mesero(a)
  (*Méx.*) *waiter, waitress*
la cerveza *beer*
la comida *meal, food*
la cuchara *spoon*
el cuchillo *knife*
la cuenta *bill, check*
el francés *French[1]* (*language*)
el inglés *English[1]* (*language*)
el mantel *tablecloth*
la mañana *morning*
la muchacha, la chica
  girl, young woman
el muchacho, el chico
  boy, young man
la noche *evening, night*
el refresco *soft drink, soda*
la servilleta *napkin*
la tarde *afternoon*
el tenedor *fork*
el vino *wine*
el vino tinto *red wine*

VERBOS

desear *to want, to wish*
estudiar *to study*
hablar *to speak, to talk*
necesitar *to need*
pagar *to pay (for)*
tomar *to drink*
trabajar *to work*

ADJETIVOS

alemán (alemana)[1] *German*
español(a) *Spanish*
feliz *happy*
francés (francesa) *French*
grande *big, large*
guapo(a) *handsome, attractive*
inglés (inglesa) *English*

OTRAS PALABRAS Y EXPRESIONES

¿a qué hora? *at what time?*
¿cuántos(as)? *how many?*
en *in, at*
mucho(a) *a lot, very much*
pero *but*
¿qué? *what?*
¿Qué hora es? *What time is it?*
sí *yes*
solamente, sólo *only*

---

[1]Names of languages and nationalities are not capitalized in Spanish.

1 THE PRESENT INDICATIVE OF REGULAR -AR VERBS
El presente de indicativo de los verbos regulares terminados en -ar

> **Verb** a word that expresses an action or a state: We **sleep.** The baby **is** sick.
>
> **Infinitive** the form of a verb showing no subject or number, preceded in English by the word *to:* **to do, to bring**

The infinitive of all Spanish verbs consists of a stem (such as **habl-**) and an ending (such as **-ar**). When looking up a verb in the dictionary, you will always find it listed under the infinitive (*e.g.,* **hablar:** *to speak*). Spanish verbs are classified according to their endings. There are three conjugations: **-ar, -er,** and **-ir.** The stem of regular verbs does not change; the endings change to agree with the subjects. Regular verbs ending in **-ar** are conjugated like **hablar,** as shown.

hablar *(to speak)*

	Stem Ending	Singular
yo	habl-**o**	Yo **hablo** español.
tú	habl-**as**	Tú **hablas** español.
Ud.	habl-**a**	Ud. **habla** español.
él	habl-**a**	Juan **habla** español. Él **habla** español.
ella	habl-**a**	Ana **habla** español. Ella **habla** español.
		Plural
nosotros	habl-**amos**	Nosotros **hablamos** español.
vosotros	habl-**áis**	Vosotros **habláis** español.
Uds.	habl-**an**	Uds. **hablan** español.
ellos	habl-**an**	Ellos **hablan** español.
ellas	habl-**an**	Ellas **hablan** español.

■ The present tense in Spanish is equivalent to three forms in English.

Yo **hablo** italiano.
{
  I speak Italian.
  I do speak Italian.
  I am speaking Italian.
}

■ Since the verb endings indicate who the speaker is, the subject pronouns are frequently omitted.

—**Hablas** inglés, ¿no?   *"You* (familiar) *speak English,*
                                     don't you?"
—Sí, **hablo** inglés.   *"Yes, I speak English."*

However, subject pronouns may be used for emphasis or clarification.

—**Ellos hablan** inglés, ¿no?   *"They speak English, don't they?"*
—**Ella habla** inglés. **Él habla** *"She speaks English. He speaks*
español.   *Spanish."*

■ Some common verbs that follow the regular -ar pattern are:

desear	to want, to wish	**pagar**	to pay
estudiar	to study	**tomar**	to drink
necesitar	to need	**trabajar**	to work

—Ud. **necesita** el mantel, ¿no?   *"You need the tablecloth, don't you?"*
—Sí, **necesito** el mantel y   *"Yes, I need the tablecloth and the*
las servilletas.   *napkins."*

—Uds. **estudian** francés en   *"You study French at the university,*
la universidad, ¿no?   *don't you?"*
—No, pero **estudiamos** inglés.   *"No, but we study English."*

—El Sr. Paz **trabaja** en una   *"Mr. Paz works at a cafeteria,*
cafetería, ¿no?   *doesn't he?"*
—No, él **trabaja** en un   *"No, he works at a restaurant."*
restaurante.

—Ud. **desea** una cerveza, ¿no?   *"You want a beer, don't you?"*
—Sí, y ella **desea** tomar[1] un   *"Yes, and she wants to drink a soda.*
refresco. Yo pago la cuenta.   *I'm paying the bill."*

The concept of "Dutch treat"
is not common in Spanish-
speaking countries. Usually
friends take turns in paying.
The one offering to pay might
say "**Yo invito**" (my treat).

 **ATENCIÓN: When speaking about a third person
(indirect address) and using a title with the last
name, the definite article is placed before the title.**
(*El* Sr. Paz habla español.) **It is not used when speaking
directly to someone** (Buenos días, Sr. Paz.).

---

[1]When two verbs are used together, the second verb is in the infinitive.

Vamos a practicar

A Form sentences that tell where these people work, what they study, what they need, and what they want.

1. trabajar:
yo / un restaurante
Eva / la cafetería
tú / Los Ángeles
nosotros / la universidad

3. necesitar:
Ana y Rosa / dinero
nosotras / una mesa
yo / pagar la cuenta
tú / una servilleta

2. estudiar:
Uds. / francés
Carlos / italiano
Ud. / la lección dos
él y yo / español

4. desear:
ellos / cerveza
nosotros / un refresco
yo / tomar Coca-Cola
Elsa / estudiar inglés

B Provide the missing information about yourself and other people.

1. Ella trabaja en Los Ángeles y yo...
2. Tú y yo trabajamos en la cafetería y ellos...
3. Carlos estudia italiano y nosotros...
4. Yo deseo estudiar francés y ellos...
5. Nosotros hablamos inglés y el profesor...
6. Ellos hablan francés y yo...
7. Yo necesito una pluma y tú...
8. María necesita sillas y nosotros...
9. Tú tomas refrescos y yo...
10. Ella toma cerveza y Uds....

② INTERROGATIVE AND NEGATIVE SENTENCES
Oraciones interrogativas y negativas

Interrogative sentences There are three ways of asking a question in Spanish to elicit a yes/no answer. These three questions ask for the same information and have the same meaning.

1. ¿**Uds.** necesitan el mantel?
2. ¿Necesitan **Uds.** el mantel?   } Sí, nosotros necesitamos el mantel.
3. ¿Necesitan el mantel **Uds.**?

■ Example 1 is a declarative sentence that is made interrogative by a change in intonation.

Uds. necesitan el mantel.   ¿Uds. necesitan el mantel?

- Example 2 is an interrogative sentence formed by placing the subject (**Uds.**) after the verb.

- Example 3, another interrogative sentence, is formed by placing the subject (**Uds.**) at the end of the sentence.

 ATENCIÓN: An auxiliary verb such as *do* or *does* is not used in Spanish to form an interrogative sentence.

In many Spanish-speaking countries, most restaurants have waiters, not waitresses.

¿El camarero habla francés?
(Does) the waiter speak French?
Notice that, in Spanish, interrogative sentences have a question mark at the end and an inverted question mark at the beginning.

 ## Vamos a practicar

Quiz

Ask the following questions in two other ways, using the model as an example.

MODELO   ¿**Elena** trabaja en Madrid?
¿Trabaja **Elena** en Madrid?
¿Trabaja en Madrid **Elena**?

1. ¿Tú tomas vino?
2. ¿Ella estudia inglés?
3. ¿Uds. hablan español?

4. ¿El camarero necesita el mantel?
5. ¿Tú pagas la cuenta?
6. ¿Ud. desea tomar un refresco?

Negative sentences   To make a sentence negative, simply place the word **no** in front of the verb.

Ella   habla inglés.   *She   speaks English.*
Ella **no** habla inglés.   *She **doesn't** speak English.*

 ATENCIÓN: Spanish does not use an auxiliary verb such as the English *do* or *does* in a negative sentence.

- If the answer to a question is negative, the word **no** appears twice: at the beginning of the sentence, as in English, and also in front of the verb.

—¿Necesitas las cucharas?   *"Do you need the spoons?"*
—**No,** (yo) **no** necesito las   *"No, I don't need the spoons,*
cucharas, pero necesito   *but I need the forks and the*
los tenedores y los cuchillos.   *knives."*

ATENCIÓN: The subject pronoun need not appear in the answer because the verb ending identifies the speaker.

Vamos a practicar

Quiz

Answer the following questions in the negative, using the information provided in parentheses. Then create two original questions to ask a classmate.

> **MODELO**   —¿Ud. trabaja en un restaurante? (cafetería)
> —**No, (yo) no trabajo en un restaurante; trabajo en una cafetería.**

1. ¿Uds. necesitan los tenedores? (cucharas, cuchillos)
2. ¿Ellos necesitan el mantel? (servilletas)
3. ¿Tú deseas tomar cerveza? (un refresco)
4. ¿Uds. toman Pepsi? (Sprite)
5. ¿Tú pagas la cerveza? (vino)

❸ FORMS AND POSITION OF ADJECTIVES
Formas y posición de los adjetivos

Formas

> Adjective a word that modifies a noun or pronoun: **tall** girl, **difficult** lesson

Adjectives whose masculine singular form ends in **-o** have four forms, ending in **-o, -a, -os, -as.** Most other adjectives have only two forms, a singular and a plural. Like nouns, adjectives are made plural by adding **-s, -es,** or by changing **z** to **c** and adding **-es.**

Singular		*Plural*	
Masculine	**Feminine**	**Masculine**	**Feminine**
negro	negra	negros	negras
inteligente	inteligente	inteligentes	inteligentes
feliz	feliz	felices	felices
azul	azul	azules	azules

- Adjectives of nationality that end in a consonant are made feminine by adding **-a** to the masculine singular form.

español	española
alemán	alemana
inglés	inglesa
francés	francesa

—¿Dónde trabaja Elsa?	*"Where does Elsa work?"*
—Trabaja en un restaurante **alemán**.	*"She works at a German restaurant."*
—¿Te gusta el champán **francés**?	*"Do you like French champagne?"*
—Sí, me gusta mucho.	*"Yes, I like it a lot."*
—¿Hay comida **española**?	*"Is there Spanish food?"*
—No, hay comida **francesa**.	*"No, there is French food."*

Posición

> The cuisine in Spanish-speaking countries has great variety. Each country has its own specialty, but international dishes are also very popular.

- Descriptive adjectives (such as adjectives of color, size, etc.) generally follow the noun in Spanish.

el mantel **rojo**	*the red tablecloth*
la casa **grande**	*the big house*
los muchachos **guapos**	*the handsome young men*
el hombre **soltero**	*the single man*

- Adjectives denoting nationality always follow the noun.

el chico **español**	*the Spanish young man*

- Other kinds of adjectives (possessive, demonstrative, numerical, etc.) precede the noun, as in English.

> In Spain and in some Latin American countries, wine is often served with meals. Some people drink water or soda, but never milk.

tres refrescos	*three sodas*	**mi** servilleta *my napkin*

—¿Cuántos tenedores necesitas?	*"How many forks do you need?"*
—Necesito solamente **un** tenedor.	*"I need only one fork."*
—¿Uds. toman vino **tinto**?	*"Do you drink red wine?"*
—No, tomamos vino **blanco**.	*"No, we drink white wine."*

Vamos a practicar

A Supply the three missing forms of the following adjectives.

1. blanco   _____   _____   _____
2. _____   _____   amarillos   _____
3. _____   guapa   _____   _____
4. _____   _____   _____   alemanas
5. feliz   _____   _____   _____

B Match the nouns in column **A** with the adjectives in column **B.**

A	B
1. hombre _____	**a.** rojo
2. mesa _____	**b.** inteligentes
3. chicas _____	**c.** feliz
4. libros _____	**d.** tinto
5. muchachos _____	**e.** mexicana
6. lápiz _____	**f.** verdes
7. vino _____	**g.** negra
8. comida _____	**h.** guapos

C How would you say the following in Spanish?

1. three married women
2. a handsome man
3. a big restaurant
4. a French girl
5. my spoon
6. twenty-five napkins
7. five German girls

4 TELLING TIME
La hora

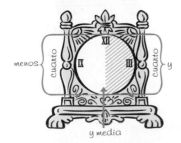

Here are some important points to remember when telling time in Spanish.

- **Es** is used with **una**, and **son** is used with all the other hours.

Es la **una** y cuarto.	*It is a quarter after one.*
Son las **cinco** y diez.	*It is ten after five.*

- The feminine definite article is always used before the hour, since it refers to **la hora**.

Es **la** una y veinte.	*It is twenty after one.*
Son **las** cuatro y media.	*It is four-thirty.*

- The hour is given first, then the minutes.

Son las **cuatro** y **diez.**	*It is ten after four* (lit., *four and ten*).

- The equivalent of *past* or *after* is **y**.

Son las doce **y** cinco.	*It's five after twelve.*

- The equivalent of *to* or *till* is **menos**.

Son las ocho **menos** veinte.	*It's twenty to eight.*

- When telling time, follow this order.
  - a. **Es** or **Son**
  - b. **la** or **las**
  - c. the hour
  - d. **y** or **menos**
  - e. the minutes

Es la una y veinte.

Son las cinco menos diez.

- The equivalent of *at + time* is **a + la(s) +** time.

A la una	*At one o'clock*
A las tres y media	*At three-thirty*

■ While both **por la** and **de la** mean *in the* when used with time, they are used differently and are not interchangeable. When a specific time is mentioned, **de la (mañana, tarde, noche)** should be used.

Yo estudio a las dos **de la** tarde.   *I study at two in the afternoon.*

■ When a specific time is *not* mentioned, **por la (mañana, tarde, noche)** should be used.

Yo estudio **por la** mañana.   *I study in the morning.*

—¿A qué hora estudias tú?   *"At what time do you study?"*
—Yo estudio a las dos **de la** tarde.   *"I study at two in the afternoon."*

—¿Trabajas **por la** noche?   *"Do you work in the evening?"*
—No, yo trabajo **por la** mañana.   *"No, I work in the morning."*

> The 24-hour system is often used in Spanish-speaking countries, especially for schedules and invitations. **"las 20 horas"** is the equivalent of eight o'clock P.M.

Vamos a practicar

A **¿Qué hora es?** (*What time is it?*) Say the time given on the following clocks, and then write the times in Spanish.

1.
2.
3.
4.

5.
6.
7.
8.

B   Complete the following dialogues with the Spanish equivalent of the words in parentheses.

    1. —¿Qué hora es?

       —Son _____ (*a quarter to six*).

    2. —¿A qué hora trabajas?

       —Trabajo _____ (*at two-thirty in the afternoon*).

    3. —¿Cuándo (*When*) estudian Uds.?

       —Estudiamos _____ (*in the evening*).

    4. —¿Es la una y media?

       —No, _____ (*it's twenty-five to two*).

C   Interview a classmate to find out the time of day at which he or she does the following things. When you have finished, switch roles.

    1. estudia   **2.** trabaja   **3.** habla español

⑤ CARDINAL NUMBERS 300–1,000
Números cardinales 300–1.000

300	trescientos	700	setecientos
400	cuatrocientos	800	ochocientos
500	quinientos	900	novecientos
600	seiscientos	1.000	mil[1]

In Spanish, one does not count in hundreds beyond 1,000; thus, 1,100 is expressed as **mil cien.** Note that a period is used instead of a comma to indicate thousands.

1.999	**mil novecientos noventa y nueve**
32.418	**treinta y dos mil cuatrocientos dieciocho**

Vamos a practicar

Read the following numbers aloud in Spanish.

896	380	519	937	722
1.305	451	978	643	504
1.000	15.893	11.906	27.567	565.736

---

[1]Notice that the indefinite article is not used before the word **mil.**

Palabras y más palabras Match the questions in column **A** with the answers in column **B.**

A	B
1. ¿Dónde trabaja Luis?	**a.** Vino tinto.
2. ¿Estudias por la mañana?	**b.** No, el Sr. Vargas.
3. ¿Qué desean tomar?	**c.** Los tenedores y los cuchillos.
4. ¿Necesitas el mantel?	**d.** A las cinco de la tarde.
5. ¿Tú pagas la cuenta?	**e.** No, las servilletas.
6. ¿Qué estudian los chicos?	**f.** Solamente dos.
7. ¿Qué necesitas?	**g.** Son las dos.
8. ¿Los manteles son rojos?	**h.** No, española.
9. ¿A qué hora estudiamos?	**i.** En un restaurante.
10. ¿Cuántas cucharas necesitas?	**j.** No, azules.
11. ¿Ana es mexicana?	**k.** Inglés y español.
12. ¿Qué hora es?	**l.** No, por la tarde.

En estas situaciones What would you say in the following situations?

1. There is no silverware on your table. Call the waiter and tell him the three things you need.
2. Ask a friend if he/she drinks red wine or white wine.
3. You ask two friends if they want to drink soda or beer.
4. You ask your friend if there is only one waiter at the restaurant.
5. Offer to pay the bill.
6. You ask someone what time it is. Ask also what time he/she studies French.

PARA ESCUCHAR Y ENTENDER

The following material is to be used with the In-Text Audio CDs.

I. Práctica

1–12

A Yo estudio...
Repeat each sentence, then substitute the new subject given by the speaker. Be sure the verb agrees with the new subject. Repeat the correct answer after the speaker's confirmation. Listen to the model.

Modelo   Yo estudio español. (nosotros)
Nosotros estudiamos español.

1. Yo estudio español. (nosotros / Ud. / ellos)
2. Ella trabaja en la cafetería. (yo / Uds. / tú)
3. Tú necesitas dinero. (él / nosotros / ellas)
4. Nosotros tomamos refrescos. (tú / Elsa / yo)
5. Él paga la cuenta. (nosotros / tú / Uds.)

B Preguntas (*Questions*)

1–13   Answer the questions in the negative. Repeat the correct answer after the speaker's confirmation. Listen to the model.

Modelo   ¿Tú necesitas dinero?
No, no necesito dinero.

C Género

1–14   Change each phrase you hear according to the new cue. Repeat the correct answer after the speaker's confirmation. Listen to the model.

Modelo   señor español (señorita)
señorita española

1. (manteles)
2. (servilletas)
3. (señora)
4. (mujeres)
5. (chicos)
6. (profesora)
7. (muchacho)
8. (comida)

D Números

1–15   Read the following numbers in Spanish. Repeat the correct answer after the speaker's confirmation. Listen to the model.

Modelo   1.581
mil quinientos ochenta y uno

1. 322
2. 430
3. 547
4. 659
5. 761
6. 878
7. 985
8. 1.000
9. 543
10. 2.715
11. 5.873
12. 9.108
13. 12.920
14. 15.008
15. 23.192

II. ¿Qué dicen?

1 ¿Lógico o ilógico?

1–16

The speaker will make some statements. Circle **L** (**lógico**) if the statement is logical and **I** (**ilógico**) if it is illogical. The speaker will verify your response.

1. L   I   **3.** L   I   **5.** L   I
2. L   I   **4.** L   I   **6.** L   I

2 ¿Verdadero o falso?

1–17

Listen carefully to the dialogue. Listen to it at least twice.

(Diálogo 1)

1–18   Now the speaker will make some statements about the dialogue you just heard. Tell whether each statement is true (**verdadero**) or false (**falso**). The speaker will confirm the correct answer.

3 Carmen y Andrés

1–19

Listen carefully to the dialogue. Listen to it at least twice.

(Diálogo 2)

1–20   Now the speaker will ask you some questions about the dialogue you just heard. Answer each question, omitting the subject. The speaker will confirm the correct answer. Repeat the correct answer.

LECCIÓN 2

OBJECTIVES

Structures

1. Agreement of articles, nouns, and adjectives
2. The present indicative of regular -**er** and -**ir** verbs
3. Possession with **de**
4. Possessive adjectives
5. The personal **a**

Communication

You will learn additional vocabulary pertaining to restaurants.

42

Country highlighted: México

With an area of over 760,000 square miles, Mexico has a population of about 96 million, of which over 23 million live in Mexico City, the capital, making it the most populated urban center in the world.

The ancient civilization that most influenced Mexico was that of the Aztecs, who understood about astronomy, had a very precise calendar, and built a great empire.

Today, Mexico is becoming an industrialized nation, and since the signing of NAFTA, foreign investment has increased rapidly. Tourism is one of the main sources of income of the Mexican economy. Cancún, Acapulco, Puerto Vallarta, and Ixtapa, among other tourists centers, receive millions of visitors every year, mainly from the United States.

Mexico has invaded the world with its music and its food, and the United States and the rest of the Hispanic world with its soap operas. Today there are Mexican restaurants in Paris, *mariachi* music is heard in Japan, and Televisa is the most powerful Spanish-speaking television enterprise in the world.

RESOURCES

Wherever you see the following icons additional resources are available:

Internet   Go to **www.college.hmco.com/languages/spanish/students/** for additional practice on the topic.

Student CD-ROM   Go to the **Video Grammar Tutor** for help with understanding the grammar topic at hand.

Go to the **In-Text Audio CDs** for more practice.

VOCABULARIO

COGNADOS

el chocolate
dominicano(a)
el menú
el museo
el taxi
el té

NOMBRES

el (la) amigo(a) *friend*
la bebida *drink*
la botella *bottle*
el café *coffee*
la fiesta *party*
el (la) hijo(a) *son, daughter*
los hijos *children*
   (sons and daughters)
el huevo, el blanquillo *(Méx.)* *egg*
la leche *milk*
el ómnibus, el autobús *bus*
la papa, la patata *(Esp.)* *potato*
el pastel[1] *pie*
el pescado *fish*
el pollo *chicken*

VERBOS

abrir *to open*
aprender *to learn*
beber *to drink*
comer *to eat*
deber (+ *inf.*) *must, to have to,*
   should

decidir *to decide*
escribir *to write*
esperar *to wait (for)*
leer *to read*
llamar *to call*
llevar *to take (something or someone*
someplace)
recibir *to receive*
tomar *to take (i.e., the bus)*
visitar *to visit*
vivir *to live*

ADJETIVOS

asado(a) *roasted, baked*
bueno(a) *good*
caliente *hot*
frío(a) *cold*
frito(a) *fried*
malo(a) *bad*

OTRAS PALABRAS Y EXPRESIONES

a menudo *often*
¿a quién? *to whom?*
aquí *here*
¿de quién? *whose?*
con *with*
¿con quién? *with whom?*
o *or*
¿quién(es)? *who?, whom?*
siempre *always*
tarde *late*
temprano *early*

---

[1] In Mexico, **pastel** is more commonly used for *cake* than for *pie*.

① AGREEMENT OF ARTICLES, NOUNS, AND ADJECTIVES
Concordancia de artículos, nombres y adjetivos

> **Agreement** the correspondence in number and gender between an article, a noun, and the adjective that modifies the noun

In Spanish, the article, the noun, and the adjective agree in number and gender.

la papa asa**da**	*the baked potato*
el poll**o** asa**do**	*the roasted chicken*
las papa**s** asada**s**	*the baked potatoes*
los poll**os** asad**os**	*the roasted chickens*

—¿Deseas huev**os** frit**os** o pescad**o** frit**o**?
"Do you want fried eggs or fried fish?"

—Pescad**o** frit**o** y **una** botell**a** de vino tint**o.**
"Fried fish and a bottle of red wine."

—¿La mesera es mexican**a**?
"Is the waitress Mexican?"

—No, es dominican**a**.
"No, she's Dominican."

—¿La comida es buen**a** aquí?
"Is the food good here?"

—No, es muy mal**a**.
"No, it's very bad."

—¿Qué deseas tomar?
"What do you want to drink?"

—Una Coca-Cola o una Pepsi.
"A Coke or a Pepsi."

> In Mexico, as in all Spanish-speaking countries, American products are very popular.

Vamos a practicar

Make the adjectives agree with the nouns in the list and add the corresponding definite article.

1. _____ pollo frito
   _____ papas _____

2. _____ servilletas blancas
   _____ vino _____

3. _____ muchacho alemán
   _____ mujeres _____

4. _____ champán francés
   _____ vinos _____

5. _____ mozos mexicanos
   _____ comida _____

6. _____ restaurante italiano
   _____ muchachas _____

7. _____ hombre feliz
   _____ hombres _____

8. _____ manteles azules
   _____ servilleta _____

2 THE PRESENT INDICATIVE OF REGULAR *-ER* AND *-IR* VERBS

El presente de indicativo de los verbos regulares terminados en *-er* e *-ir*

Regular verbs ending in **-er** are conjugated like **comer.** Regular verbs ending in **-ir** are conjugated like **vivir.**

comer *(to eat)*		vivir *(to live)*	
yo	com-**o**	yo	viv-**o**
tú	com-**es**	tú	viv-**es**
Ud.		Ud.	
él	com-**e**	él	viv-**e**
ella		ella	
nosotros	com-**emos**	nosotros	viv-**imos**
vosotros	com-**éis**	vosotros	viv-**ís**
Uds.		Uds.	
ellos	com-**en**	ellos	viv-**en**
ellas		ellas	

Some other common verbs that follow the **-er** and **-ir** patterns are:

aprender	to learn	**abrir**	to open
beber	to drink	**decidir**	to decide
deber	must, should	**escribir**	to write
leer	to read	**recibir**	to receive

—¿Qué **bebes** tú: leche fría, café o té?
—**Bebo** café o chocolate caliente.

"What do you drink: cold milk, coffee, or tea?"
"I drink coffee or hot chocolate."

—¿**Comen** Uds. temprano?
—No, **comemos** tarde.

"Do you eat early?"
"No, we eat late."

—¿Dónde **vive** Ud.?
—**Vivo** en la calle Unión.

"Where do you live?"
"I live on Union Street."

—¿Qué **leen** ellos?
—El menú.

"What are they reading?"
"The menu."

—¿A qué hora **abren** el restaurante?
—A las once.

"What time do they open the restaurant?"
"At eleven."

> In most Spanish-speaking countries, restaurants do not start serving dinner until 9:00 P.M. At 4:00, people have a **merienda,** an afternoon snack.

Vamos a practicar

A Provide the missing information about yourself and other people.

1. Nosotros bebemos leche fría y ellos...
2. Yo abro una botella de vino tinto y tú...
3. Elsa come en un restaurante y Uds....
4. Ellos aprenden inglés y yo...
5. Uds. escriben en español y nosotros...
6. Nosotros leemos libros en español y John...

 B Interview a classmate, using the following questions. When you have finished, switch roles.

1. ¿Qué bebes por la mañana: leche, café o chocolate caliente?
2. ¿Qué comes por la noche: pollo asado, pescado o huevos?
3. ¿Uds. comen temprano o tarde?
4. ¿En qué calle vives?
5. ¿Cuánto dinero recibes?
6. ¿Lees muchos libros?
7. ¿Aprendemos mucho en la clase (*class*)?
8. ¿Debes escribir en inglés o en español?

 ## ❸ POSSESSION WITH *DE*
El caso posesivo

De + *noun* is used to express possession or relationship. Unlike English, Spanish does not use the apostrophe.

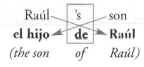

Raúl——'s——son
el hijo ◄ de ► Raúl
(the son   of   Raúl)

—¿**De quién** es la casa?   *"Whose house is it?"*
—Es la casa **de** Julio.   *"It's Julio's house."*
—¿Quién es Julio?   *"Who is Julio?"*
—Es el hijo **de** doña Ana.   *"He is doña Ana's son."*

—¿Dónde viven las hijas
  de don Antonio?   *"Where do don Antonio's daughters live?"*
—Viven en Guadalajara.   *"They live in Guadalajara."*

> **Don** (for men) and **doña** (for women) are titles used before a person's first name to show respect, especially when addressing or talking about an older person: **don** Antonio; **doña** Ana.

Vamos a practicar

Answer the following questions about Marisa, using the cues provided to show possession or relationship.

1. ¿Quién es Marisa?   (hija / doña Isabel)
2. ¿Qué necesita?   (dirección / Carlos)
3. ¿Dónde vive?   (casa / la familia Torres)
4. ¿Dónde trabaja?   (restaurante / don José)
5. ¿Qué lee?   (carta [*letter*] / Rodolfo)

4 POSSESSIVE ADJECTIVES
Los adjetivos posesivos

> **Possessive** a word that denotes ownership or possession: **our** house, **their** mother

Forms of the Possessive Adjectives

Singular	Plural	
mi	**mis**	my
tu	**tus**	your (*familiar*)
su	**sus**	his
		her
		its
		your (*formal*)
		their
nuestro(a)	**nuestros(as)**	our
vuestro(a)	**vuestros(as)**	your (*familiar*)

Possessive adjectives agree in number with the nouns they modify.

—¿Ud. necesita hablar con **mi** hijo?
"*Do you need to speak with my son?*"

—No, no necesito hablar con **su** hijo. Necesito hablar con **sus** hijas.
"*No, I don't need to speak with your son. I need to speak with your daughters.*"

—**Mis** hijas no viven aquí. Viven en la calle 5 de mayo.
"*My daughters don't live here. They live on 5 de Mayo Street.*"

ATENCIÓN: These forms of the possessive adjectives always precede the nouns they introduce and never take an accent.

- Since both **su** and **sus** may have different meanings, the form **de él (de ella, de ellos, de ellas, de Ud., de Uds.)** may be substituted to avoid confusion.

su hijo ⟨ el hijo **de Ud. (de Uds.)**
el hijo **de él (de ellos)**
el hijo **de ella (de ellas)**

—¿Ellas son **sus** hijas, señora?   *"Are they your daughters, madam?"*
—No, no son **mis** hijas;   *"No, they are not my daughters; they*
  son las hijas **de él.**   *are his daughters."*

- **Nuestro** and **vuestro** are the only possessive adjectives that have the feminine endings **-a, -as.** The others use the same endings for both the masculine and feminine genders.

—¿Con quién debemos hablar?   *"With whom should we speak?"*
—Deben hablar con **nuestras**   *"You should speak with our friends."*
  amigas.

Vamos a practicar

A Fill in the blanks with the appropriate form of the possessive adjective in Spanish. Whenever **su (sus)** is required, give the alternate form with **de.**

> MODELO   (*his*) _____ silla
>   **su** silla / **la** silla **de él**

1. (*my*) _____ amiga
2. (*his*) _____ hija / _____ hija _____ _____
3. (*our*) _____ casa
4. (*her*) _____ idioma / _____ idioma _____ _____
5. (*your*—**Ud.**) _____ dinero / _____ dinero _____ _____
6. (*my*) _____ hijos
7. (*our*) _____ mantel
8. (*your*—**tú**) _____ ocupación
9. (*your*—**Uds.**) _____ amigos / _____ amigos _____ _____
10. (*their*—*fem.*) _____ lecciones / _____ lecciones _____ _____

B Ask a classmate the following questions. When you have finished, switch roles.

1. ¿Dónde vive tu mejor (*best*) amigo(a)?
2. ¿Cuál es el número de teléfono de tu mejor amigo(a)?
3. ¿De dónde es nuestro(a) profesor(a)?
4. ¿A qué hora es nuestra clase de español?
5. ¿Tus otras (*other*) clases son por la mañana?
6. ¿Tú necesitas mi libro?

⑤ THE PERSONAL A
La *a* personal

In Spanish, as in English, a verb has a subject and may require one or more objects. The function of objects is to complete the idea expressed by the verb.

In English, the direct object cannot be separated from the verb by a preposition: *She killed **the burglar**. He sees **the nurse.*** In the preceding sentences, *the burglar* and *the nurse* are direct objects.

In Spanish, the preposition **a** is used before a direct object that refers to a specific person. This preposition is called "the personal **a**" and has no equivalent in English.

Yo visito **a** Carmen.

I visit   Carmen.

■ The personal **a** is not used when the direct object is not a person.

—¿**A** quién llevas a la fiesta?	*"Whom are you taking to the party?"*
—Llevo **a** mi amiga.	*"I'm taking my friend."*
—¿Ella lleva las bebidas?	*"Is she taking the drinks?"*
—No, lleva los pasteles.	*"No, she is taking the pies."*
—¿Tú visitas **a** tus hijos a menudo?	*"Do you visit your children often?"*
—Sí, yo visito **a** mis hijos los domingos.	*"Yes, I visit my children on Sundays."*
—¿Qué visitan los chicos hoy?	*"What are the boys visiting today?"*
—Visitan el museo.	*"They are visiting the museum."*
—¿**A** quién llama Ud.?	*"Whom are you calling?"*
—Llamo **a** la profesora.	*"I'm calling the professor."*

—¿Desea llamar un taxi?   *"Do you want to call a taxi?"*
—No, siempre tomo el ómnibus.   *"No, I always take the bus."*

—¿A quién esperas? ¿A Sergio?   *"Whom are you waiting for? Sergio?"*
—No, espero el autobús.   *"No, I'm waiting for the bus."*

Vamos a practicar

Quiz

Answer the following questions, using the cues provided.

1. ¿A quién visitas los domingos? (mi amigo Julio)
2. ¿Tú visitas museos de arte? (sí)
3. ¿A quién esperas? (la mesera)
4. ¿Qué esperas? (el menú)
5. ¿A quién deseas llamar? (mi hija)
6. ¿Deseas llamar un taxi? (sí)
7. ¿Qué llevas a la fiesta? (las bebidas)
8. ¿A quién llevas a la fiesta? (Ana)

Palabras y más palabras Circle the word or phrase that best completes each sentence.

1. Siempre comemos (huevos, café) por la mañana.
2. Bebo chocolate (asado, caliente) en la cafetería.
3. El mozo (abre, decide) una botella de vino.
4. Deseo comer pescado (feliz, frito).
5. Ellos (beben, leen) leche fría.
6. Diego (vive, escribe) en la calle Tercera.
7. Ellos visitan (el pollo, el museo) el sábado.
8. El restaurante Azteca no es bueno; es muy (malo, grande).
9. ¿Uds. comen temprano o (asado, tarde)?
10. Comen papas (asadas, felices).

En estas situaciones What would you say in the following situations? What might the other person say?

1. You are very hungry. At a restaurant, order a complete meal, including drinks and dessert.
2. You are having a guest for lunch. Ask if he/she wants fried fish and a baked potato.

3. Mention the person that you always take to parties. Ask someone if he/she takes his/her friends to parties.

4. You ask a friend if he/she visits Mrs. Vega's daughter on Sundays.

PARA ESCUCHAR Y ENTENDER

The following material is to be used with the In-Text Audio CDs.

I. Práctica

1-21

A Verbos terminados en **-er** e **-ir**
Answer the questions, always using the second choice. Omit the subject. Repeat the correct answer after the speaker's confirmation. Listen to the model.

> **MODELO** —¿Ana vive en la calle Cinco o en la calle Siete?
> **—Vive en la calle Siete.**

1-22

B ¿De quién es?
Using the cues provided, say to whom the following items belong. Repeat the correct answer after the speaker's confirmation. Listen to the model.

> **MODELO** el libro (Susana)
> **Es el libro de Susana.**

1. (Antonio)
2. (mi hijo)
3. (Juan)
4. (la profesora)
5. (Estela)

1-23

C La **a** personal
Answer the questions, using the cues provided. Remember to use the personal **a** when needed. Repeat the correct answer after the speaker's confirmation. Listen to the model.

> **MODELO** —¿A quién visitas? (Rosa)
> **—Visito a Rosa.**

1. (el museo)   **4.** (dinero)
2. (la Sra. Vega)   **5.** (la profesora)
3. (el ómnibus)

II. ¿Qué dicen?

1 ¿Lógico o ilógico?

1–24

The speaker will make some statements. Circle **L** (**lógico**) if the statement is logical and **I** (**ilógico**) if it is illogical. The speaker will verify your response.

1. L I	**5.** L I
2. L I	**6.** L I
3. L I	**7.** L I
4. L I	**8.** L I

2 ¿Verdadero o falso?

1–25

Listen carefully to the dialogue. Listen to it at least twice.

(Diálogo 1)

1–26   Now the speaker will make some statements about the dialogue you just heard. Tell whether each statement is true (**verdadero**) or false (**falso**). The speaker will confirm the correct answer.

3 Adela y Pedro

1–27

Listen carefully to the dialogue. Listen to it at least twice.

(Diálogo 2)

1–28   Now the speaker will ask you some questions about the dialogue you just heard. Answer each question, omitting the subject. The speaker will confirm the correct answer. Repeat the correct answer.

LECCIÓN 3

Objectives

Structures

1. The irregular verbs **ir, dar,** and **estar**
2. **Ir a** + infinitive
3. Uses of the verbs **ser** and **estar**
4. Contractions

Communication

You will learn vocabulary related to the family.

54

Country highlighted: Guatemala

Guatemala is one of the Central American countries whose territory was part of the Mayan Empire. The official language of the country is Spanish, but most of the indigenous people speak their own language.

Guatemala is a country of contrasts: In the capital itself, Guatemala City, luxury commercial centers and expensive mansions alternate with humble huts. The country's economy remains predominantly agricultural, although manufacturing has developed significantly since World War II.

Forty percent of the country's territory is covered by forest. In the northwest, the ruins of the Mayan city of Tikal are found. This is one of the most interesting archeological sites in America.

Guatemala is a country of volcanoes, mountains, and beautiful landscapes. Its climate is mild and very pleasant, and for that reason it is called the "country of eternal spring."

RESOURCES

Wherever you see the following icons additional resources are available:

Internet

Go to **www.college.hmco.com/languages/spanish/students/** for additional practice on the topic.

Student CD-ROM

Go to the **Video Grammar Tutor** for help with understanding the grammar topic at hand.

Go to the **In-Text Audio CDs** for more practice.

VOCABULARIO
Audio

COGNADOS

argentino(a)
el club
el dólar
el (la) estudiante
la familia
el hospital
el hotel
el metal
la profesión

NOMBRES

el (la) abuelo(a) *grandfather, grandmother*
el coche, el carro, el automóvil, el auto *car, automobile*
el (la) cuñado(a) *brother-in-law, sister-in-law*
los Estados Unidos *United States*
el (la) hermano(a) *brother, sister*
la madera *wood*
la mamá, la madre *mom, mother*
el (la) novio(a) *boyfriend, girlfriend*
los padres *parents*
el papá, el padre *dad, father*
el postre *dessert*
el (la) primo(a) *cousin*
la sala *living room*
el (la) sobrino(a) *nephew, niece*
el (la) suegro(a) *father-in-law, mother-in-law*
el (la) tío(a) *uncle, aunt*

VERBOS

dar *to give*
estar *to be*
ir *to go*
viajar *to travel*

ADJETIVOS

alto(a) *tall*
bonito(a) *pretty*
cansado(a) *tired*
enfermo(a) *sick*

OTRAS PALABRAS Y EXPRESIONES

a *to*
¿adónde? *where (to)?*
ahora *now*
¿cómo? *how?*
¿Cómo es? *What is he (she, it) like?*
¿cuál? *what?, which one?*
mañana *tomorrow*
¿por qué? *why?*
porque *because*
primero *first*

1 THE IRREGULAR VERBS *IR, DAR,* AND *ESTAR*
Los verbos irregulares *ir, dar* y *estar*

Irregular verbs do not follow the normal pattern of stem changes and endings that regular **-ar, -er,** and **-ir** verbs follow, and therefore must be learned by memory. One irregular verb that you have already learned is **ser.**

	ir (*to go*)	dar (*to give*)	estar (*to be*)
yo	**voy**	**doy**	**estoy**
tú	**vas**	**das**	**estás**
Ud. él ella	**va**	**da**	**está**
nosotros	**vamos**	**damos**	**estamos**
vosotros	**vais**	**dais**	**estáis**
Uds. ellos ellas	**van**	**dan**	**están**

—¿**Vas** a la fiesta que **dan**
  Rosa y David?
  No, no **voy** porque **estoy**
  muy cansada. ¿Con quién
  van Uds.?
—**Vamos** con Raúl. Él está
  aquí en Guatemala ahora.

"Are you going to the party that Rosa
and David are giving?"
"No, I'm not going because I'm very
tired. With whom are you going?"

"We are going with Raúl. He's here
in Guatemala now."

—¿Tú **das** dinero para la fiesta?
—No, yo no **doy** dinero, pero
  mi familia **da** 250 quetzales.[1]

"Are you giving money for the party?"
"No, I'm not giving money, but my
family is giving 250 quetzales."

> The term "**familia**" usually means the extended family, which is the most important social unit in Hispanic culture. It includes the nuclear family plus other relatives.

---

[1] Guatemala's currency

Vamos a practicar

Quiz

A Complete the following dialogues with the present indicative of **ir, dar,** and **estar.** Then act them out with a partner.

1. —Buenos días, ¿cómo _____ Ud., señora?
    —_____ muy bien, gracias.
    —¿Adónde _____ Ud.?
    —_____ a la fiesta que _____ la Dra. Sánchez.
2. —¿Cuánto dinero _____ Uds. para la fiesta?
    —Nosotros _____ diez dólares. ¿Cuánto _____ tú?
    —Yo _____ solamente cinco dólares.
3. —¿No _____ Uds. a la fiesta?
    —No, no _____ porque _____ muy cansados.
4. —¿Los chicos _____ aquí?
    —No, _____ en el museo.

B Interview a classmate, using the following questions. When you have finished, switch roles.

1. ¿Dónde estás ahora?
2. ¿Dónde están tus amigos?
3. ¿Dónde está tu familia?
4. ¿Adónde vas los viernes?
5. ¿Con quién vas?
6. ¿Vas a la biblioteca (*library*) los sábados?
7. ¿Van Uds. (tú y tus amigos) a la universidad los domingos?
8. ¿Das tu número de teléfono?

② *IR A* + INFINITIVE
Ir a + **infinitivo**

The construction **ir a** + *infinitive* is used to express future time. It is equivalent to the English expression *to be going to* + *infinitive*. The "formula" is:

ir	+	**a**	+	*infinitive*	
Yo voy		**a**		**viajar**	con mis abuelos.
I'm going				*to travel*	*with my grandparents.*

—¿Con quién **vas a comer?**   *"With whom are you going to eat?"*
—**Voy a comer** con mi primo.   *"I'm going to eat with my cousin."*

—¿Uds. van al restaurante ahora?   *"Are you going to the restaurant now?"*
—No, primero **vamos a llamar**   *"No, first we are going to call my mom."*
a mi mamá.

—¿Nora **va a viajar** con sus padres?   *"Is Nora going to travel with her parents?"*
—No, con su papá y su hermano.   *"No, with her dad and her brother."*

—¿Dónde **vamos a tomar** el café?   *"Where are we going to have coffee?"*

—En la sala, pero primero   *"In the living room, but first*
vamos a comer el postre.   *we are going to eat dessert."*

> Coffee is not usually drunk with dinner or supper but after the meal, and it is much stronger than coffee served in the United States. The coffee is generally served in a demitasse, a smaller cup.

Vamos a practicar
(Quiz)

A Use your imagination to describe what these people are going to do.

Modelo   yo / mañana por la mañana
         Yo voy a estudiar mañana por la mañana

1. mi hermano / por la noche
2. mi primo y yo / el lunes
3. tú / esta tarde
4. mis padres / el sábado
5. Ud. / el viernes
6. yo / el miércoles

B Interview a classmate, using the following questions and two of your own. When you have finished, switch roles.

1. ¿Qué vas a comer de postre?
2. ¿Qué van a beber Uds.?
3. ¿A qué hora vas a estudiar mañana?
4. ¿Qué van a hacer (*to do*) tú y tus amigos el sábado?
5. ¿Adónde vas a viajar en junio?
6. ¿Tus padres van a ir también (*also*)?

C With a partner, talk about what you and your friends and relatives are going to do tomorrow.

3 USES OF THE VERBS *SER* AND *ESTAR*
Usos de los verbos *ser* y *estar*

Although both **ser** and **estar** are equivalent to the English verb *to be,* they are not interchangeable. They are used to indicate the following.

ser	estar
1. Possession or relationship	1. Current condition (usually the product of a change)
2. Profession	2. Location
3. Nationality	
4. Origin	
5. Basic characteristics (color, shape, size, etc.)	
6. Marital status	
7. Expressions of time and dates	
8. Material (metal, wood, glass, etc.)	
9. Events taking place	

—El coche **es** de Pedro, ¿no?   *"The car is Pedro's, isn't it?"*
—No, **es** de mi sobrina.   *"No, it's my niece's."*

—¿Cuál **es** la profesión de tu tía?   *"What is your aunt's profession?"*
—**Es** profesora.   *"She is a professor."*

—Elena **es** muy inteligente.   *"Elena is very intelligent."*
—Ella **es** de Argentina, ¿no?   *"She's from Argentina, isn't she?"*
—Sí, **es** argentina, pero ahora   *"Yes, she's an Argentinian, but now*
  está en los Estados Unidos.   *she's in the United States."*

—¿Cómo **es** tu mamá?   *"What is your mom like?"*
—**Es** alta y muy bonita.   *"She's tall and very pretty."*

—¿**Es** Ud. casada?   *"Are you married?"*
—No, **soy** soltera.   *"No, I am single."*

—¿Qué día **es** hoy?   *"What day is today?"*
—Hoy **es** martes.   *"Today is Tuesday."*

—¿**Es** de madera la mesa?   *"Is the table made of wood?"*
—No, **es** de metal.   *"No, it is made of metal."*

—¿Dónde **es** la fiesta?   *"Where's the party?"*
—**Es** en el hotel Azteca.   *"It's at the Azteca Hotel."*

—¿Cómo **está** Ud.?   *"How are you?"*
—**Estoy** bien, gracias.   *"I am fine, thanks."*

—¿Dónde **está** tu novio?   *"Where is your boyfriend?"*
—**Está** en el hospital. **Está** enfermo. *"He is in the hospital. He is sick."*

Vamos a practicar

A Complete the following dialogues with **ser** or **estar,** as appropriate. Then act them out with a partner.

1. —¿Cómo _____ Amelia?
   —_____ muy inteligente y muy bonita.
   —¿De dónde _____ ella?
   —_____ argentina, pero ahora _____ en los Estados Unidos.
   —¿_____ soltera?
   —No, _____ casada.
   —¿Hoy no trabaja?
   —No, porque _____ enferma. _____ en el hospital.

2. —¿Las sillas _____ de metal?
   —No, _____ de madera.
   —¿_____ de tu novia?
   —No, _____ de mi sobrino.

3. ¿Cuál _____ su profesión, Sr. Paz?
   —_____ profesor.

4. —¿Cómo _____ sus hijos?
   —_____ altos y guapos.

5. —¿Qué fecha _____ hoy?
   —Hoy _____ el veinte de mayo.
   —¿_____ lunes?
   —No, hoy _____ martes.

6. —¿Dónde _____ las bebidas?
   —_____ en el auto de mi papá.

7. —¿La fiesta _____ en el hotel Guatemala?
   —No, _____ en el hotel Hilton.

B How would you describe Alberto to a Spanish-speaking friend?

Alberto is a very handsome young man. He's not an American; he's from Guatemala, but now he's in California. His father is a professor, and his mother is a doctor. He's single. Alberto studies at the University of California. Today he's at home (**en casa**); he is very sick.

C Use **ser** or **estar** to tell a classmate the following information.

1. nationality and origin
2. profession (student)
3. marital status
4. basic characteristics (i.e., appearance, qualities)
5. state of health
6. location

D Go the the map of South America at the back of this book and say what the capital of each Spanish-speaking country is.

MODELO   **Guatemala es la capital de Guatemala.**

4 CONTRACTIONS
Contracciones

> **Contraction** the combination of two or more words into one, with certain sounds or letters missing: **isn't, don't, can't, I'm**

In Spanish there are only two contractions: **al** and **del.**

■ The preposition **de** (*of, from*) plus the article **el** is contracted to form **del.**

Leen los libros **de + el** profesor.   Leen los libros **del** profesor.

■ The preposition **a** (*to, toward*) or the personal **a** plus the article **el** is contracted to form **al.**

Esperamos **a + el** profesor.   Esperamos **al** profesor.

ATENCIÓN: **None of the other combinations of prepositions and definite articles** (de la, de los, de las, a la, a los, a las) **is contracted.**

—¿Llaman Uds. **al** cuñado   *"Are you calling Julio's*
  de Julio?   *brother-in-law?"*
—No, llamamos a su suegra.   *"No, we're calling his mother-in-law."*

—¿Adónde vas mañana?   *"Where are you going tomorrow?*
  ¿**A la** fiesta?   *To the party?"*
—No, voy **al** club.   *"No, I'm going to the club."*

—¿Necesitan ellos el coche
  de la señora Villegas?
—Sí.

"Do they need
Mrs. Villegas's car?"
"Yes."

> In most Hispanic cities there
> are clubs that people can join
> to enjoy several types of
> activities: sports, dancing,
> and so on. Most of the time,
> all members of the family
> belong to the same club.

Quiz

Vamos a practicar

Complete the following dialogues, using one of the following: **de la, de
las, del, de los, a la, a las, al,** or **a los.** Then act them out with a partner.

1. —¿Por qué llamas _____ cuñado de Raúl?
   —Porque él va a llevar _____ hijas _____ Sr. López
   _____ fiesta _____ club.
2. —¿Uds. van _____ museo o _____ universidad mañana?
   —Vamos _____ restaurante.
3. —¿Dónde están los libros _____ estudiantes (*masc.*)?
   —Están en la casa _____ profesor.
4. —¿A quiénes llevas ___ fiesta? ¿_____ muchachos?
   —No, _____ muchachas.
5. —¿A quién esperan Uds.?
   —_____ suegro de Rita.
6. —¿Adónde llevas el café?
   —_____ sala.

Palabras y más palabras Complete the following exchanges, using
the vocabulary learned in this lesson.

1. —¿Gerardo es tu primo?
   —Sí, es el hijo de mi _____ Estela.
2. —¿Maribel es tu _____?
   —Sí, es la esposa de mi hermano.
3. —¿_____ vas?
   —Al club.
4. —¿La mesa es de metal?
   —No, es de _____.
5. —¿Aurora _____ en el hospital?
   —Sí, está muy _____.
6. —¿_____ es Alicia?
   —Es alta y bonita.
7. —¿Héctor es de Buenos Aires?
   —Sí, es _____.
8. —¿Uds. van a viajar en ómnibus?
   —No, vamos en mi _____.

9. —¿Doña Ana es tu abuela?
   —Sí, es la _____ de mi papá.
10. —¿Van a ir al club?
    —Sí, pero _____ vamos a comer.

 En estas situaciones   What would you say in the following situations?

1. Ask a friend where he/she goes on Saturdays and whether he/she is going to give a party on Friday.
2. You ask a foreign student where he/she is from.
3. Ask someone what his girlfriend (her boyfriend) is like.
4. Talk about your best (*mejor*) friend. Say where he/she is from, and give a description.

PARA ESCUCHAR Y ENTENDER

The following material is to be used with the In-Text Audio CDs.

I. Práctica

 A Ir, dar, estar

1-29
Answer the questions, always using the second choice. Omit the subject. Repeat the correct answer after the speaker's confirmation. Listen to the model.

> **MODELO**   —¿Vas a la cafetería o a la universidad?
> **—Voy a la universidad.**

 B ¿Adónde vas a ir?

1-30
Answer the questions, using the cues provided. Repeat the correct answer after the speaker's confirmation. Listen to the model.

> **MODELO**   —¿Con quién vas a ir tú? (con Elena)
> **—Voy a ir con Elena.**

1. (a la universidad)
2. (las bebidas)
3. (a las doce)
4. (la calle Victoria)

5. (con mi primo)
6. (a mi suegro)
7. (con mi hermano)
8. (a la fiesta de Eva)

 C ¿Ser o estar?

1-31
Answer the questions, using the cues provided. Repeat the correct answer after the speaker's confirmation. Listen to the model.

MODELO —¿Paula es argentina? (sí)
—**Sí, es argentina.**

1. (no)
2. (de Lima)
3. (alto y guapo)
4. (bien)

5. (en el club)
6. (en el hotel Hilton)
7. (viernes)

D Contracciones
Answer the questions, using the cues provided. Repeat the correct answer
1-32 after the speaker's confirmation. Listen to the model.

MODELO —¿Adónde vas? (club)
—**Voy al club.**

1. (Sr. López)
2. (profesor Mena)
3. (hijo de Marta)

4. (universidad)
5. (Dr. Barrios)
6. (cuñado de Ana)

II. ¿Qué dicen?

1 ¿Lógico o ilógico?
The speaker will make some statements. Circle **L** (**lógico**) if the statement
1-33 is logical and **I** (**ilógico**) if it is illogical. The speaker will verify your response.

1. L I   **3.** L I   **5.** L I   **7.** L I
2. L I   **4.** L I   **6.** L I   **8.** L I

2 ¿Verdadero o falso?
Listen carefully to the narration. Listen to it at least twice.
1-34
(Narración)

1-35 Now the speaker will make some statements about the narration you just
heard. Tell whether each statement is true (**verdadero**) or false (**falso**). The
speaker will confirm the correct answer.

3 Teresa y Pedro
Listen carefully to the dialogue. Listen to it at least twice.
1-36
(Diálogo)

1-37 Now the speaker will ask you some questions about the dialogue you just
heard. Answer each question, omitting the subject. The speaker will confirm the correct answer. Repeat the correct answer.

LECCIÓN 4

OBJECTIVES

Structures
1. The irregular verbs **tener** and **venir**
2. Expressions with **tener**
3. Comparative forms
4. Irregular comparative forms

Communication
You will learn vocabulary pertaining to hotels.

Countries highlighted: Honduras and El Salvador

Search

Honduras, with an area a little larger than the state of Tennessee, has a population of over five million people. Honduras is the most mountainous country in Central America, but it is the only one that has no volcanoes.

The country's economy is mostly based on agriculture, but it also exports lumber. In spite of the exploitation of its forest, Honduras has the largest pine forest in the world.

The capital of Honduras is Tegucigalpa, which in the Mayan language means "Silver Hill." The most important tourist attraction in the country is Copán, which was the center of Mayan civilization.

Southwest of Honduras is El Salvador, the smallest country in Central America but also the most densely populated. Over six million people live in an area the size of the state of Massachusetts. The capital of El Salvador, San Salvador, is the most industrialized city in Central America.

RESOURCES

Wherever you see the following icons additional resources are available:

Internet

Go to **www.college.hmco.com/languages/spanish/students/** for additional practice on the topic.

Student CD-ROM

Go to the **Video Grammar Tutor** for help with understanding the grammar topic at hand.

Go to the **In-Text Audio CDs** for more practice.

VOCABULARIO
Audio

COGNADOS

la clase
el (la) supervisor(a)

NOMBRES

el aire acondicionado   *air conditioning*
el (la) dueño(a)   *owner*
la esposa   *wife*
el esposo   *husband*
el (la) gerente   *manager*
el gimnasio   *gym*
la habitación, el cuarto   *room*
la hora   *hour*
la llave   *key*
la maleta, la valija   *suitcase*
el mercado   *market*
la piscina, la alberca (*Méx.*)   *swimming pool*
el televisor   *T.V. set*
la tienda   *store*
el ventilador   *fan*

VERBOS

creer   *to think, to believe*
llegar   *to arrive*
tener   *to have*
venir   *to come*

ADJETIVOS

barato(a)   *inexpensive*
caro(a)   *expensive*
mayor   *older; bigger*
mejor   *better*
menor   *younger; smaller*
peor   *worse*
pequeño(a)   *small, little (size)*
poco(a)   *little (quantity)*
solo(a)   *alone*

OTRAS PALABRAS Y EXPRESIONES

aquí está   *here it is*
mal   *badly*
más   *more*
menos   *less, fewer*
otro(a)   *other; another*
que   *than; that*
también   *also, too*
tan... como   *as . . . as*
tener que (+ *inf.*)   *to have to (+ inf.)*

① THE IRREGULAR VERBS *TENER* AND *VENIR*
Los verbos irregulares *tener* y *venir*

tener (*to have*)		venir (*to come*)	
yo	**tengo**	yo	**vengo**
tú	**tienes**	tú	**vienes**
Ud.		Ud.	
él	**tiene**	él	**viene**
ella		ella	
nosotros	**tenemos**	nosotros	**venimos**
vosotros	**tenéis**	vosotros	**venís**
Uds.		Uds.	
ellos	**tienen**	ellos	**vienen**
ellas		ellas	

—¿Con quién **viene** Ud. al
  gimnasio? ¿Con su hijo?
—No, **vengo** sola. Él tiene
  que trabajar.
—¿Cuántas horas **tiene**
  que trabajar?
—Ocho horas.

"With whom are you coming to the
* gym? With your son?"*
"No, I'm coming alone. He has
* to work."*
"How many hours does he have
* to work?"*
"Eight hours."

—¿Cuántos hijos **tiene** Ud.?
—**Tengo** tres hijos y una hija,
  que vive en Tegucigalpa.

"How many children does he have?"
"I have three sons and one daughter,
* who lives in Tegucigalpa."*

ATENCIÓN: The personal a is not used with the verb tener.

—Ana, ¿**tienes** novio?
—No, no **tengo** novio.

"Ana, do you have a boyfriend?"
"No, I don't have a boyfriend."

ATENCIÓN: Un and una are not used with the verb tener when the numerical concept is not emphasized.

No **tengo** novio.

I don't have a boyfriend.

—¿El hotel **tiene** piscina?   *"Does the hotel have a pool?"*
—Sí, y también **tiene** gimnasio   *"Yes, and it also has a gym, and all*
  y todos los cuartos **tienen**   *the rooms have T.V. sets."*
  televisor.
—¿**Tienes** la llave de la habitación?   *"Do you have the key to the room?"*
—Sí, aquí está.   *"Yes, here it is."*

> Hotels in a range of categories, including many owned by North American chains,
> exist in all Latin American cities and can usually be reserved through a travel agent.
> In choosing a hotel, remember that room rates quoted don't include taxes, which are
> very high in most countries.

Vamos a practicar

A Complete the dialogues with the present indicative of **tener** and
venir, as appropriate. Then act them out with a partner.

1. —Teresa, ¿tu hermano _____ a la universidad con su novia?
   —Él no _____ novia.
2. —¿A qué hora _____ Uds. mañana?
   —_____ a las cinco de la tarde. ¿A qué hora _____ Ud.?
   —Yo _____ a las cinco también.
3. —¿Cuántos hijos _____ Uds.?
   —_____ dos hijos. ¿Cuántos hijos _____ tú?
   —Yo _____ un hijo.
4. —¿Cuántas horas _____ que estudiar Uds.?
   —_____ que estudiar tres horas.

B Interview a classmate, using the following questions. When you have
finished, switch roles.

1. ¿A qué hora vienes a la universidad?
2. ¿Vienes solo(a)?
3. ¿Cuántas clases tienes?
4. ¿Tienes clases los sábados?
5. ¿Qué días tenemos la clase de español?
6. ¿Vienes a la universidad los domingos?
7. ¿Tú y tus amigos vienen a la universidad los sábados?
8. ¿La universidad tiene piscina? ¿Tiene gimnasio?
9. ¿Tú tienes televisor en tu cuarto?
10. ¿Tú tienes la llave de tu casa aquí?

② EXPRESSIONS WITH *TENER*
Las expresiones con *tener*

In Spanish, many useful idiomatic expressions are formed with the verb **tener** and a noun, while English uses *to be* and an adjective.

tener calor *to be hot*	**tener hambre** *to be hungry*
tener frío *to be cold*	**tener sed** *to be thirsty*
tener cuidado *to be careful*	**tener prisa** *to be in a hurry*
tener sueño *to be sleepy*	**tener razón** *to be right*
tener miedo *to be afraid*	**tener...años (de edad)** *to be...years old*

■ The equivalent of *I am very hungry,* for example, is **Tengo mucha hambre.**

—¿**Tienes hambre,** María?	*"Are you hungry, María?"*
—No, pero **tengo** mucha **sed.**	*"No, but I am very thirsty."*
—¿**Tienes calor,** Carlos?	*"Are you hot, Carlos?"*
—Sí, **tengo** mucho **calor.**	*"Yes, I'm very hot."*
—¿El hotel no **tiene** aire acondicionado?	*"Doesn't the hotel have air conditioning?"*
—No, pero **tiene** ventiladores.	*"No, but it has fans."*
—¿Cuántos **años tiene** su hija?	*"How old is your daughter?"*
—Mi hija **tiene** seis **años.**	*"My daughter is six years old."*
—Deseo hablar con el **dueño,** por favor.	*"I wish to speak with the owner, please."*
—Ahora no, lo siento. Él **tiene** mucha **prisa.**	*"Not now, I'm sorry. He's in a big hurry."*
—**Tiene razón.** Es tarde.	*"You're right. It's late."*

> Most houses in the Hispanic world don't have air conditioning. In hot climates, fans are very popular.

Vamos a practicar
Quiz

A Tell what is happening in each of the pictures. Follow the model.

MODELO

Ella ...
Ella tiene hambre.

1. Carlos...

3. Yo...

2. Él...

4. Ellas...

5. ¿Ud....?

6. Tú...

7. Nélida...

 B With a partner, take turns to indicate how these people feel according to each circumstance.

1. Daniel is in Alaska in January.
2. Rosa and Luis are in Phoenix in August.
3. Olga hasn't had a bite to eat all day.
4. Pablo is blowing out twenty candles on his birthday cake.
5. Marisol's throat is very dry.
6. Eva and Dora haven't slept the whole night.
7. Beto has to check out of the hotel in the next five minutes.
8. Tere is alone in the house and hears a strange noise.

C Interview a classmate, using the following questions. When you have finished, switch roles.

1. ¿Qué bebes cuando tienes sed? ¿Y cuando tienes frío?
2. ¿Qué comes cuando tienes hambre?
3. ¿Cuántos años tienes?
4. ¿Cuántos años tiene tu madre? ¿Y tu padre?
5. En tu familia, ¿quién tiene razón siempre? ¿Y en la clase?
6. ¿Tienes miedo a veces (*sometimes*)?

 ### 3 COMPARATIVE FORMS
Las formas comparativas

Comparisons of inequality

■ In Spanish, the comparative of most adjectives, adverbs, and nouns is formed by placing **más** (*more*) or **menos** (*less*) before the adjective, adverb, or noun and **que** after.

Honduras es	**más grande que**	El Salvador.
Honduras is	*bigger than*	*El Salvador.*

		adjective		
más	+	or adverb	+	**que**
menos		or noun		

In the construction shown in the chart, **que** is equivalent to *than*.

—El hotel Azteca es **barato.**
—Sí, pero creo que es **más caro que** el hotel Real.

"*The Azteca Hotel is inexpensive.*"
"*Yes, but I think it is more expensive than the Real Hotel.*"

—Yo tengo muy **poco** dinero.
—¡Yo tengo **menos dinero que** tú!

"*I have very little money.*"
"*I have less money than you!*"

—¿Quién llega **más tarde:** el gerente o el supervisor?
—El supervisor llega **más tarde que** el gerente.

"*Who arrives later? The manager or the supervisor?*"
"*The supervisor arrives later than the manager.*"

In most Hispanic cities, hotel guests must leave their room key at the registration desk every time they leave the hotel.

Comparisons of equality

- To form comparisons of equality with adjectives, adverbs, and nouns, use the adverb **tan** or the adjective **tanto (-a, -os, -as)** and **como.**

When comparing adjectives or adverbs:	When comparing nouns:
tan (*as*) < **bonita** **tarde** + **como**	**tanto** (*as much*) dinero **tanta** bebida **tantos** (*as many*) libros **tantas** plumas } + **como**

—¿Te gusta el hotel Tegucigalpa? *"Do you like the Tegucigalpa Hotel?"*
—Sí, pero no es **tan bonito como** el hotel Victoria. *"Yes, but it's not as pretty as the Victoria Hotel."*

—Tu casa es muy grande. *"Your house is very big."*
—Sí, pero no tiene **tantas habitaciones como** la casa de tus padres. *"Yes, but it doesn't have as many rooms as your parents' house."*

The superlative

- The superlative construction is similar to the comparative. It is formed by placing the definite article before the person or thing being compared.

definite article	+	*noun*	+	**más** or **menos**	+	*adjective*	+	**de**

—¿Cuál es **la habitación más grande del** hotel? *"Which is the biggest room in the hotel?"*
—La habitación número 5. *"Room number 5."*

ATENCIÓN: After a superlative construction, *in* is expressed by de in Spanish. In many instances, the noun may not be expressed in a superlative.

La habitación número 5 es **la más grande.** *Room number 5 is the biggest (one).*

Vamos a practicar

A Compare these people, places, or things to each other.

MODELO   Vermont / California (pequeño)
Vermont **es más pequeño que** California.

1. Texas / Rhode Island (grande)
2. tú / tu amigo (alto)
3. Tom Cruise (Meg Ryan) / tú (guapo/bonita)
4. Honduras / Brasil (pequeño)
5. un Rolls Royce / un Ford (caro)
6. el hotel Hilton / el Motel 6 (barato)

B With a partner, take turns asking each other the following questions.

1. ¿Tú eres más alto(a) que tu mejor amigo?
2. ¿Quién es la persona más inteligente de tu familia?
3. ¿Tú tienes tanto dinero como tus padres?
4. ¿Tú trabajas tanto como tu papá?
5. ¿Tú hablas español tan bien como el profesor (la profesora)?
6. ¿Quién crees tú que es más guapo: Leonardo diCaprio o Brad Pitt?
   ¿Quién es más bonita: Julia Roberts o Meg Ryan?
7. ¿Cuál es el hotel más grande de la ciudad donde tú vives? ¿Y el más caro?
8. ¿Cuál es el motel más barato de la ciudad donde vives?

4 IRREGULAR COMPARATIVE FORMS
Las formas comparativas irregulares

Adjectives	Adverbs	Comparative	Superlative
bueno	bien	mejor	el (la) mejor
malo	mal	peor	el (la) peor
grande		mayor	el (la) mayor
pequeño		menor	el (la) menor

- When the adjectives **grande** and **pequeño(a)** refer to size, their regular forms are generally used.

Tu maleta es **más grande**   *Your suitcase is bigger than Rita's.*
que la de Rita.

■ When these adjectives refer to age, the irregular forms are used.

—¿Felipe es **mayor** que tú?   *"Is Felipe older than you?"*
—No, es **menor** que yo.   *"No, he is younger than I (am)."*

—¿Quién es **mayor**? ¿Ud. o Elsa? *"Who is older? You or Elsa?"*
—Elsa. Ella es **la mayor** de la clase. *"Elsa. She is the oldest in the class."*

—Este hotel es muy malo.   *"This hotel is very bad."*
—Sí, pero el otro es **peor.**   *"Yes, but the other one is worse."*

—¿Su esposo habla español tan *"Does your husband speak Spanish*
 bien como Ud.?   *as well as you do?"*
—No, él habla español mucho *"No, he speaks Spanish much better*
 mejor que yo.   *than I."*

—¿El mercado es **más grande** *"Is the market bigger than the*
 que la tienda?   *store?"*
—No, el mercado es **más**   *"No, the market is smaller than the*
 pequeño que la tienda.   *store."*

Vamos a practicar

A Answer the following questions.

1. ¿Es Ud. menor o mayor que su mejor amigo o amiga?
2. ¿Tiene Ud. un hermano mayor (un hermano menor)?
3. ¿Cuál es la mejor universidad de los Estados Unidos?
4. ¿Quién habla mejor el español: Ud. o el profesor (la profesora)?
5. ¿Cuál cree Ud. que es el peor restaurante de la ciudad donde Ud. vive?
 ¿Y el mejor?

B With a partner, take turns comparing yourselves with other members of your families.

Palabras y más palabras Match the questions in column **A** with the answers in column **B**.

A	**B**
1. ¿Vas a hablar con el gerente?	**a.** Sí, y también tiene piscina.
_____	**b.** No, solo.
2. ¿Qué necesitas? _____	**c.** No, a la tienda.
3. ¿Necesitas las maletas? _____	**d.** No, tenemos ventiladores.

4. ¿El hotel tiene gimnasio? _____
5. ¿A qué hora llegan ellos? _____
6. ¿Vas al mercado? _____
7. ¿Eres mayor que tu esposo? _____
8. ¿Viene con su esposa? _____
9. ¿Tu casa tiene aire acondicionado? _____
10. ¿Tiene poco dinero? _____
11. ¿La habitación es grande? _____
12. ¿Con quién tienes que hablar? _____

e. Sí, porque voy a viajar.
f. No, es muy pequeña.
g. No, con la dueña.
h. Con el supervisor.
i. A las dos.
j. Sí, él es menor que yo.
k. La llave del cuarto.
l. Sí, pero tiene más que yo.

En estas situaciones What would you say in the following situations?

1. Compare yourself to some members of your family. Include height and age.
2. Mention three things that you have to do tomorrow.
3. Say what days you come to the university and what time you arrive.
4. You visit a city. Ask somebody which is the best restaurant. Ask also whether it's very expensive.
5. A friend of yours is staying at your house. Ask if he/she is hungry, thirsty, cold, etc.
6. You ask a little girl how old she is.

PARA ESCUCHAR Y ENTENDER

The following material is to be used with the In-Text Audio CDs.

I. Práctica

A Tener y venir

Answer the questions, using the cues provided. Omit the subject. Repeat the correct answer after the speaker's confirmation. Listen to the model.

1-38

| MODELO | —¿Cuántos hijos tienes? (tres) |
| | —**Tengo tres hijos.** |

1. (cuatro)
2. (no)
3. (los martes y los jueves)
4. (no)

5. (sí)
6. (cinco)
7. (los domingos)
8. (hoy)

B ¿Mucho o mucha?

1–39   Answer the questions in the affirmative, always using **mucho** or **mucha**, as appropriate. Repeat the correct answer after the speaker's confirmation. Listen to the model.

> MODELO   —¿Tienes hambre?
> —**Sí, tengo mucha hambre.**

C Las formas comparativas

1–40   Answer the questions, always using the second choice. Repeat the correct answer after the speaker's confirmation. Listen to the model.

> MODELO   —¿Quién es más bonita: Rosa o Ana?
> —**Ana es más bonita que Rosa.**

II. ¿Qué dicen?

1 ¿Lógico o ilógico?

1–41   The speaker will make some statements. Circle **L** (**lógico**) if the statement is logical and **I** (**ilógico**) if it is illogical. The speaker will verify your response.

1. L I	**3.** L I	**5.** L I	**7.** L I
2. L I	**4.** L I	**6.** L I	**8.** L I

2 ¿Verdadero o falso?

1–42   Listen carefully to the dialogue. Listen to it at least twice.

(Diálogo 1)

1–43   Now the speaker will make some statements about the dialogue you just heard. Tell whether each statement is true (**verdadero**) or false (**falso**). The speaker will confirm the correct answer.

3 La habitación de Rosa

Listen carefully to the dialogue. Listen to it at least twice.

1–44

(Diálogo 2)

1–45   Now the speaker will make some statements about the dialogue you just heard. Tell whether each statement is true (**verdadero**) or false (**falso**). The speaker will confirm the correct answer.

4 De viaje *(Traveling)*

Listen carefully to the dialogue. Listen to it at least twice.

1–46

(Diálogo 3)

1–47   Now the speaker will make some statements about the dialogue you just heard. Tell whether each statement is true (**verdadero**) or false (**falso**). The speaker will confirm the correct answer.

LECCIÓN 5

OBJECTIVES

Structures

1. Stem-changing verbs (**e:ie**)
2. Some uses of the definite article
3. The present progressive
4. Ordinal numbers

Communication

You will learn vocabulary about typical activities related to traveling in a foreign country.

Country highlighted: Nicaragua

With an area a little larger than the state of New York, Nicaragua is the largest country in Central America, but less than one tenth of its territory can be used as farmland.

Nicaragua is the land of lakes and volcanoes. Lake Nicaragua is one of the largest fresh-water lakes in the world, and in it there are sharks and other types of fish that normally are found only in the ocean in other regions.

The capital is Managua, and other important cities are León and Granada.

The economy of Nicaragua is based on agriculture, and almost half of its population works at this activity. Its main exports are coffee, cotton, beef, and wood.

Nicaragua has the natural conditions necessary to attract tourism, but this hasn't happened, due mainly to the lack of political stability.

RESOURCES

Wherever you see the following icons additional resources are available:

Internet

Go to **www.college.hmco.com/languages/spanish/students/** for additional practice on the topic.

Student CD-ROM

Go to the **Video Grammar Tutor** for help with understanding the grammar topic at hand.

Go to the **In-Text Audio CDs** for more practice.

VOCABULARIO

Audio

COGNADOS

el concierto
la discoteca
la educación
importante
la oficina
las vacaciones[1]

NOMBRES

el almuerzo   *lunch*
la cárcel   *jail*
la cena   *dinner*
el cine   *movie theater, movies*
el desayuno   *breakfast*
la escuela   *school*
la iglesia   *church*
el jabón   *soap*
el mes   *month*
la pensión   *boarding house*
el piso   *floor, story*
la primavera   *spring*
la revista   *magazine*
la semana   *week*
el teatro   *theater*
la toalla   *towel*

VERBOS

bailar   *to dance*
cerrar (e:ie)   *to close*
comenzar (e:ie)   *to begin, to start*

comprar   *to buy*
decir[2]   *to say*
desayunar   *to have breakfast*
dormir[3]   *to sleep*
empezar (e:ie)   *to begin, to start*
entender (e:ie)   *to understand*
hacer (yo hago)   *to do, to make*
pedir[2]   *to ask (for)*
pensar (e:ie)   *to think*
pensar + *infinitive*   *to plan*
perder (e:ie)   *to lose*
preferir (e:ie)   *to prefer*
querer (e:ie)   *to want*
servir[2]   *to serve*
traer (yo traigo)   *to bring*

ADJETIVO

próximo(a)   *next*

OTRAS PALABRAS Y EXPRESIONES

esta noche   *tonight*
todavía no   *not yet*
todos(as)   *all, everybody*
Ya lo creo.   *I'll say.*

---

[1]**Vacaciones** is always used in the plural.
[2]These verbs will be studied in **Lección 7.**
[3]This verb will be studied in **Lección 6.**

Resumen de las palabras interrogativas		
¿a quién?	*whom?*	¿A quién llamas?
¿adónde?	*where to?*	¿Adónde vas?
¿cuál(es)?	*which?*	¿Cuál prefieres?
¿cuándo?	*when?*	¿Cuándo vienen ellos?
¿cuánto(a)?	*how much?*	¿Cuánto dinero necesitas?
¿cuántos(as)?	*how many?*	¿Cuántas toallas quieres?
¿de dónde?	*from where?*	¿De dónde es Ud.?
¿de quién(es)?	*whose?*	¿De quién es la revista?
¿dónde?	*where?*	¿Dónde está el cine Rex?
¿por qué?	*why?*	¿Por qué no van al concierto?
¿qué?	*what?*	¿Qué desea comprar, señora?
¿quién(es)?	*who?*	¿Quiénes van a venir a la fiesta?

1 STEM-CHANGING VERBS (E:IE)
Verbos que cambian en la raíz (e:ie)

In Spanish, some verbs undergo a stem change in the present indicative. For these verbs, when **e** is the last stem vowel and it is stressed, it changes to **ie** as follows.

preferir (to prefer)	
prefiero	preferimos
prefieres	preferís
prefiere	prefieren

- Notice that the stem vowel is not stressed in the verb form corresponding to **nosotros,** and therefore the **e** does not change to **ie: nosotros preferimos.**

- Stem-changing verbs have regular endings like other **-ar, -er,** and **-ir** verbs.

- Some other verbs that undergo the same change are:

cerrar	*to close*	**pensar**	*to think, to plan*
comenzar[1]	*to start, to begin*	**perder**	*to lose*
empezar[1]	*to start, to begin*	**querer**	*to want*
entender	*to understand*		

---

[1]When **comenzar** and **empezar** are followed by an infinitive, the preposition **a** is used: **Yo comienzo (empiezo) a trabajar a las seis.** Notice that these two verbs are synonymous.

—¿**Quieres** ir al cine o al
teatro esta noche?

*"Do you want to go to the movies or
to the theater tonight?"*

—No, **prefiero** ir al concierto.

"No, I prefer to go to the concert."

—¿A qué hora **empieza?**

"At what time does it begin?"

—**Comienza** a las nueve.

"It starts at nine."

—¿A qué hora **cierran**
las tiendas?

"At what time do the stores close?"

—A las diez.

"At ten."

—¿Uds. **piensan** ir a
bailar esta noche? Aquí,
en Managua, **tienen**
buenas discotecas.

*"Do you plan to go dancing tonight?
Here in Managua they have good
discotheques."*

—Sí, todos **queremos** ir.

"Yes, we all want to go."

Discotheques are very
popular in Hispanic
countries. Young
people go dancing to
not only Latin rhythms
but also to American
music.

Vamos a practicar

Quiz

A Finish the following sentences in your own words, matching the verbs
to the new subjects.

1. Luis comienza a trabajar a las siete y nosotros...
2. Tú prefieres ir al cine y yo...
3. Nosotros cerramos a las nueve y ellos...
4. Yo empiezo a trabajar el lunes y Uds....
5. Rafael quiere aprender francés y nosotros...
6. Yo no entiendo inglés y Uds....
7. Nosotros pensamos ir a bailar y Eduardo...
8. Luis siempre pierde las llaves y tú...

B Interview a classmate, using the following questions and two of your
own. When you have finished, switch roles.

1. ¿Cuándo comienzan las clases en la universidad?
2. ¿A qué hora empieza la clase de español?
3. Cuando el profesor (la profesora) habla español, ¿tú entiendes?
4. ¿A qué hora cierran las tiendas?
5. Esta noche, ¿prefieres ir al cine, a un concierto o a una discoteca?
6. ¿Quieres ir al teatro el sábado?
7. ¿Quieres ir a un restaurante italiano o prefieres comer comida
   mexicana?
8. ¿Tú pierdes las llaves a menudo?

C With a partner, play the roles of two friends who cannot agree on anything. When one wants to do something, the other prefers to do something else.

② SOME USES OF THE DEFINITE ARTICLE
Algunos usos del artículo definido

The definite article is used in the following instances in Spanish.

- with expressions of time, the seasons, and the days of the week

—¿Cuándo es su clase de español?   *"When is your Spanish class?"*
—Tengo clase de español **los**[1]   *"I have a Spanish class on Mondays,*
lunes, miércoles y viernes,   *Wednesdays, and Fridays at nine."*
a **las** nueve.

The definite article is omitted with the seasons and days of the week when used after the verb **ser.**

—¿Es primavera ahora   *"Is it spring in Argentina now?"*
en Argentina?
—Sí, es primavera.   *"Yes, it is spring."*

—¿Qué día es hoy?   *"What day is today?"*
—Hoy es domingo.   *"Today is Sunday."*

> Seasons in the Southern Hemisphere are the reverse of those in the Northern Hemisphere. When it is fall in the United States, for example, it is spring in Argentina.

- before nouns used in a general sense

—¿Tomas **café**?   *"Do you drink coffee?"*
—Sí, pero prefiero **el té.**   *"Yes, but I prefer tea."*

- with abstract nouns

—**La educación** es muy importante.   *"Education is very important."*
—Ya lo creo.   *"I'll say."*

- before **próximo(a)** (*next*) with expressions of time

—¿Tus vacaciones comienzan   *"Does your vacation start*
la semana **próxima**?   *next week?"*
—Sí, comienzan el lunes.   *"Yes, it starts on Monday."*

---

[1]Notice that the definite article is used here as the equivalent of *on.*

- with the nouns **iglesia, escuela,** and **cárcel** when they are preceded by a preposition

—¿Vas a **la iglesia** los viernes?   *"Do you go to church on Fridays?"*
—No, los viernes voy a **la escuela.**   *"No, I go to school on Fridays."*

- before the words **desayuno, almuerzo,** and **cena**

—**¿El desayuno** es a las ocho?   *"Is breakfast at eight?"*
—Sí, y **el almuerzo** es a las doce.   *"Yes, and lunch is at twelve."*
—¿A qué hora es **la cena**?   *"What time is dinner?"*
—A las nueve.   *"At nine."*

Vamos a practicar

Quiz

A Is the definite article needed or not? Complete the following dialogues, then act them out with a partner.

1. —¿Tú vas a _____ iglesia hoy?
   —No, hoy es _____ sábado, y yo voy a _____ iglesia _____ domingos.
   —¿Vas a _____ escuela _____ lunes?
   —No, _____ lunes no tengo clases.
2. —¿A qué hora es _____ almuerzo?
   —_____ almuerzo es a _____ doce y _____ cena es a _____ ocho.
3. —_____ hombres son más inteligentes que _____ mujeres.
   —¡No! _____ mujeres somos tan inteligentes como _____ hombres.
4. —¿Adónde vas a ir _____ domingo próximo?
   —Voy a ir a visitar a Julio, que está en _____ cárcel.
5. —¿Qué es muy importante para ti?
   —_____ educación.

B Interview a classmate, using the following questions. When you have finished, switch roles.

1. ¿Qué días tienes clases en la universidad?
2. ¿A qué hora es tu primera (*first*) clase?
3. ¿A qué hora es la cena en tu casa? ¿Y el desayuno? ¿Y el almuerzo?
4. ¿Van a ir Uds. de vacaciones la semana próxima?
5. ¿Vas a la iglesia los domingos?
6. ¿Qué crees que es más importante, el amor (*love*) o el dinero?
7. ¿Quiénes crees tú que son más inteligentes, los hombres o las mujeres?
8. ¿Te gusta la comida mexicana o prefieres la comida italiana?

3 **THE PRESENT PROGRESSIVE**
El presente progresivo

The present progressive describes an action that is in process at the moment we are talking. In Spanish, it is formed with the present tense of **estar** and the Spanish equivalent of the present participle (*-ing* form)[1] of the main verb.

-ing Form Endings		
-ar: **hablar**	-er: **comer**	-ir: **escribir**
habl- **ando**	com- **iendo**	escrib- **iendo**

- Some irregular *-ing* forms:

pedir	**pidiendo**	servir	**sirviendo**
decir	**diciendo**	leer	**leyendo**[2]
dormir	**durmiendo**	traer	**trayendo**[2]

—¿Qué **están haciendo** tus hermanos?   *"What are your brothers doing?"*
—**Están desayunando.**   *"They're having breakfast."*

—¿**Están sirviendo** el almuerzo?   *"Are they serving lunch?"*
— Todavía no.   *"Not yet."*

—¿Qué **estás comiendo?**   *"What are you eating?"*
—**Estoy comiendo** pollo.   *"I'm eating chicken."*

—¿Qué **está leyendo** Ud.?   *"What are you reading?"*
—**Estoy leyendo** una revista.   *"I'm reading a magazine."*

 ATENCIÓN: Unlike in English, the present progressive is never used in Spanish to refer to a future action. Instead, the present indicative is used for actions that will occur in the near future.

Trabajo mañana.   *I'm working tomorrow.*

Verbs such as **ser, estar, ir (yendo),** and **venir (viniendo)** are rarely used in the progressive construction.

---

[1]The equivalent of the *-ing* form of the verb is called **el gerundio** in Spanish.
[2]Notice that the **-i** of **-iendo** becomes **y** between vowels.

Vamos a practicar

A Complete the following dialogues, using the present progressive of the verbs given. Then act them out with a partner.

1. —¿Qué _____ tú? (comer)
   —Yo _____ pollo y papa asada. (comer)
2. —¿Jorge _____? (dormir)
   —No, _____. (leer)
3. —¿Qué _____ Uds.? (servir)
   —_____ las bebidas. (servir)
4. —¿Qué _____ Gerardo ahora? (hacer)
   —_____ en la escuela. (trabajar)
   —¿Y Ana y Eva?
   —Ellas _____. (estudiar)
5. —¿Qué _____ los chicos? (pedir)
   —_____ el desayuno. (pedir)
6. —¿A quién _____ Uds.? (esperar)
   —_____ a mi suegra. (esperar)

B Imagine what these people are doing according to where they are.

MODELO   yo / en el hotel
Yo estoy hablando con el gerente.

1. Julia / en su cuarto
2. el mozo / en el restaurante
3. nosotros / en la discoteca
4. Ud. / en la cafetería
5. mis padres / en el hotel
6. los estudiantes / en la clase de español

❹ ORDINAL NUMBERS
Los números ordinales

primero(a)	*first*	**séptimo(a)**	*seventh*
segundo(a)	*second*	**octavo(a)**	*eighth*
tercero(a)	*third*	**noveno(a)**	*ninth*
cuarto(a)	*fourth*	**décimo(a)**	*tenth*
quinto(a)	*fifth*		
sexto(a)	*sixth*		

Ordinal numbers agree in gender and number with the nouns they modify.

—¿Qué oficina prefiere?   *"Which office do you prefer?"*
—Prefiero **la** quint**a** (oficin**a**).   *"I prefer the fifth (one)."*

■ The ordinal numbers **primero** and **tercero** drop the final **-o** before masculine, singular nouns.

—¿Qué día llegan Uds. a la pensión?
—Llegamos el **primer** día del mes.

"*What day are you arriving at the boarding house?*"
"*We're arriving the first day of the month.*"

—¿Dónde está Paco? ¿En el **tercer** piso?
—No, está en el **primer** piso, comprando toallas y jabón.

"*Where is Paco? On the third floor?*"
"*No, he's on the first floor, buying towels and soap.*"

> In Spanish-speaking countries, the first floor corresponds to the second floor in the United States. What Americans call the "first floor" is called the **"planta baja"** in Hispanic countries.

■ Ordinal numbers are seldom used after *the tenth*.

—¿En qué piso viven Uds.?
—Vivimos en el piso **doce.**

"*On which floor do you live?*"
"*We live on the twelfth floor.*"

■ Remember that cardinal numbers are used in Spanish for dates except for *the first*.

—¿Qué día es hoy?
—Hoy es el **treinta** de abril. Mañana es **el primero** de mayo. Es el Día del Trabajo.

"*What day is it today?*"
"*Today is April 30th. Tomorrow is the first (day) of May. It's Labor Day.*"

> In most Hispanic countries, Labor Day is celebrated on May first.

Vamos a practicar

Quiz

Complete the following dialogues with the correct ordinal numbers. Then act them out with a partner.

1. —¿La oficina de Alberto está en el _____ piso? (*third*)
   —No, está en el _____ piso. (*second*)
   —Yo quiero una en el _____ piso. (*fifth*)
2. —¿Uds. viajan la _____ semana? (*fourth*)
   —Sí, pero no viajamos el _____ día. (*first*)
3. —¿Septiembre es el _____ mes del año? (*tenth*)
   —No, es el _____ . (*ninth*)
4. —¿Ellos viven en el _____ piso o en el _____?
   (*sixth, seventh*)
   —No, viven en el _____. (*eighth*)

Palabras y más palabras Circle the word or phrase that best completes each sentence.

1. (El desayuno, La cena) es a las siete de la mañana.
2. Septiembre es el (octavo, noveno) mes del año.

3. La primavera comienza en (marzo, julio).
4. Mi familia y yo vamos a la (iglesia, escuela) los domingos.
5. Vamos a comprar jabón y (semanas, toallas).
6. ¿Qué está (diciendo, trabajando) Marcela?
7. ¿Quieres ir al cine o (al teatro, a la cárcel)?
8. Ellos (cierran, traen) a los chicos hoy.
9. Pablo está (durmiendo, pidiendo) la cuenta.
10. ¿Están trayendo (todas, próximas) las revistas?
11. Ellos todavía no están en la (toalla, pensión).
12. —María Inés es muy bonita.
    —¡Ya lo (creo, pierdo)!

 En estas situaciones What would you say in the following situations?

1. You ask a friend where he/she wants to go tonight. Suggest a few places, asking for preferences.
2. At a boarding house, you need to know what time they start serving meals.
3. You need to know what time stores close. Mention items that you want to buy.
4. You ask your friends what they are doing.
5. In a building, you ask whether an office you need to go to is on the third floor or on the fourth floor.

PARA ESCUCHAR Y ENTENDER

The following material is to be used with the In-Text Audio CDs.

I. Práctica

2–2

A Verbos que cambian en la raíz
Change the verb in each sentence according to the new subject. Repeat the correct answer after the speaker's confirmation. Listen to the model.

> **MODELO**   Nosotros comenzamos temprano. (yo)
> **Yo comienzo temprano.**

1. (Uds.)   3. (ella)   5. (Ud.)
2. (tú)   4. (ellos)   6. (él)

2–3

B El artículo definido
Answer the questions, using the cues provided. Repeat the correct answer after the speaker's confirmation. Listen to the model.

> **Modelo** —¿Qué día es hoy? (sábado)
> —**Hoy es sábado.**

1. (lunes y miércoles)   **3.** (mes próximo)   **5.** (mujeres)
2. (educación)   **4.** (iglesia)

C El presente progresivo

2–4 Change the verbs in each sentence to the present progressive. Repeat the correct answer after the speaker's confirmation. Listen to the model.

> **Modelo** —Yo tomo café.
> —**Yo estoy tomando café.**

D Los números ordinales

2–5 Say the ordinal number that corresponds to each cardinal number. Repeat the correct answer after the speaker's confirmation. Listen to the model.

> **Modelo** cuatro **cuarto**

II. ¿Qué dicen?

1 ¿Lógico o ilógico?

2–6 The speaker will make some statements. Circle **L** (**lógico**) if the statement is logical and **I** (**ilógico**) if it is illogical. The speaker will verify your response.

1. L I   **3.** L I   **5.** L I   **7.** L I
2. L I   **4.** L I   **6.** L I   **8.** L I

2 ¿Verdadero o falso?

2–7 Listen carefully to the dialogue. Listen to it at least twice.

(Diálogo 1)

2–8 Now the speaker will make some statements about the dialogue you just heard. Tell whether each statement is true (**verdadero**) or false (**falso**). The speaker will confirm the correct answer.

3 Alina y Delia

2–9 Listen carefully to the dialogue. Listen to it at least twice.

(Diálogo 2)

2–10 Now the speaker will ask you some questions about the dialogue you just heard. Answer each question, omitting the subject. The speaker will confirm the correct answer. Repeat the correct answer.

LECCIÓN 1

A The present indicative of regular -ar verbs

Complete the following exchanges, using the verbs given.

1. —¿Uds. _____ (hablar) inglés?
   —Sí, nosotros _____ (hablar) inglés y francés.
2. —¿Dónde _____ (trabajar) tú?
   —Yo _____ (trabajar) en el restaurante Miramar.
3. —¿Qué _____ (tomar) Uds.?
   —Yo _____ (desear) un refresco y Jorge
   _____ (desear) cerveza.
4. —¿Qué _____ (necesitar) ellos?
   —Ana _____ (necesitar) un mantel y Roberto
   _____ (necesitar) servilletas.
5. —¿Ud. _____ (estudiar) inglés?
   —No, yo _____ (estudiar) alemán.

B Interrogative and negative sentences

Give the Spanish equivalent of the following exchanges.

1. "Do they pay the bill?"
   "No, they don't pay the bill."
2. "At what time do you want to study, Anita?"
   "I don't want to study today."

C Forms and position of adjectives

Complete the following, using the Spanish equivalent of the words in parentheses.

1. Nosotros bebemos _____ (*French champagne*).
2. Ana necesita el _____ (*white tablecloth*) y las
   _____ (*red napkins*).
3. Sergio es _____ (*a very handsome young man*).

D Telling time

Complete the following, using the Spanish equivalent of the words in parentheses.

—¿Uds. estudian _____ ? (*in the morning*)

—Sí, estudiamos _____ . (*at eight-thirty in the morning*)

—¿Qué hora es?

—_____ . (*It's a quarter to seven.*)

E Cardinal numbers (300–1,000)

Write out the following numbers using Spanish words.

1. 1.578
2. 11.750
3. 23.380
4. 48.660
5. 420.200

F Vocabulary

Complete the following sentences, using vocabulary learned in **Lección 1.**

1. ¿A qué _____ estudian Uds.? ¿A las dos?
2. ¿Tú estudias por la mañana, por la tarde o por la _____?
3. Ella es ____; es de Berlín.
4. En Washington hablan _____ y en París hablan _____.
5. Sergio es un muchacho muy _____.
6. ¿_____ chicos hay? ¿Veinte?
7. Yo no necesito mucho. Necesito _____ diez dólares.
8. ¿Uds. toman vino o _____ cerveza?
9. Necesito un mantel y seis _____.
10. Ella necesita un tenedor, una _____ y un _____.
11. Yo no _____ tomar cerveza.
12. Yo pago la _____.

LECCIÓN 2

A Agreement of articles, nouns, and adjectives

Change the following according to each new noun.

1. la papa asada (pollos)
2. los huevos fritos (papa)
3. el muchacho mexicano (muchachas)
4. el hombre francés (mujeres)
5. el café frío (leche)

B **The present indicative of regular *-er* and *-ir* verbs**

Complete the following exchanges, using the verbs given.

1. —¿Qué _____ (beber) Uds.?
   —Nosotros _____ (beber) chocolate caliente.
2. —¿Eva _____ (escribir) en inglés?
   —Sí, y nosotros _____ (escribir) en español.
3. —¿Dónde _____ (vivir) los chicos?
   —Marisa _____ (vivir) en Quito y Rafael _____ (vivir) en Guayaquil.
4. —¿Tú _____ (comer) en la cafetería?
   —No, yo _____ (comer) en un restaurante.
5. —¿A qué hora _____ (abrir) (ellos)?
   —A las once.
6. —¿Qué _____ (leer) Ud.?
   —_____ (leer) el menú.

C **Possession with *de***

Give the Spanish equivalent of the following exchanges.

1. "Is she Sergio's sister?"
   "No, she is Mario's cousin."
2. "Do you need Luisa's address, Miss Fuentes?"
   "No, I need María's phone number."

D **Possessive adjectives**

Answer the following questions in the negative.

1. ¿Uds. necesitan sus libros?
2. ¿La profesora de Uds. es de Venezuela?
3. ¿Ud. vive con su madre?
4. ¿Los amigos de Uds. son de Colombia?
5. ¿El profesor necesita su coche hoy?

E **The personal *a***

Give the Spanish equivalent of the following exchanges.

1. "Whom are you calling, Mr. Viñas?"
   "My niece."
2. "Do you take Mrs. Mena's daughter to the university, Miss Soto?"
   "No, I take Mr. Villalba's son."

F **Vocabulary**

Circle the word or phrase that does not belong in each group.

1. pollo   pescado   leche
2. botella   mozo   camarero
3. leer   escribir   esperar
4. caliente   frito   frío
5. papa   amiga   patata
6. malo   temprano   tarde
7. siempre   de quién   a menudo
8. bueno   frito   asado

LECCIÓN 3

A **The irregular verbs** *ir, dar,* **and** *estar*

Write sentences using the subjects and the items given and the present indicative of **ir, dar,** or **estar,** as appropriate. Add any necessary words.

1. Yo / a la universidad / lunes
2. Nosotros / no / número de teléfono
3. Los chicos / la cafetería / ahora
4. ¿Tú / a la fiesta / Nora?
5. Elena / solamente / cinco dólares
6. Yo / cansado / enfermo

B *Ir a* **+ infinitive**

Answer the following questions, using the cues provided.

1. ¿Qué van a comer Uds.? (el postre)
2. ¿A qué hora va a estar Ud. en el hotel? (a las seis)
3. ¿A quién va a esperar su amiga? (a su mamá)
4. ¿Con quién van a viajar ellos? (con Alberto)
5. ¿A quién va a visitar su papá? (a la Srta. Mejía)

C **Uses of the verbs** *ser* **and** *estar*

What would you say in the following situations?

1. You want to know where Teresa is from and where she is now. You also want to know whether she is married or single.
2. You don't know what day of the week it is. You are also wondering where Ana's party is taking place.
3. You ask Carlos if he's tired.
4. You are wondering whether Eva is Mario's friend or girlfriend. You also want to know whether she's French or English.

D Contractions

Complete the following, adding **al, a la, a los, a las, del, de la, de los,** or **de las,** as appropriate.

1. Elsa lleva _____ hijo _____ Sra. Goytisolo _____ universidad.
2. Nosotros llamamos _____ amigos _____ Sr. Villegas y _____ sobrino _____ Sra. Torres.
3. Ellos van _____ hotel con los padres _____ Srta. Barrios.
4. Vamos a llamar _____ sobrinas _____ Dr. Aranda.
5. Ellos llevan _____ cuñado de Marta _____ sala.

E Vocabulary

Match the questions in column **A** with the answers in column **B.**

A	B
1. ¿Es tu abuelo?	a. No, de madera.
2. ¿Cómo es tu novio?	b. A mi novia.
3. ¿La mesa es de metal?	c. Sí, es de Buenos Aires.
4. ¿Elena es tu tía?	d. En el hospital.
5. ¿Es argentina?	e. Sí, es el hijo de mi hermana Eva.
6. ¿A quién esperas?	f. Sí, es la hija de mi tía Beatriz.
7. ¿Paquito es tu sobrino?	g. Vino tinto.
8. ¿Qué bebida deseas?	h. Sí, es el padre de mi mamá.
9. ¿Dónde están ellos?	i. A México.
10. ¿Carolina es tu prima?	j. Sí, son mis suegros.
11. ¿Son los padres de tu esposo?	k. Sí, es la hermana de mi papá.
12. ¿Adónde vas primero?	l. Alto y guapo.

LECCIÓN 4

A The irregular verbs *tener* and *venir*

Change the sentence given according to each new subject.

Carlos viene a la universidad con Mirta porque no tiene coche.

1. Yo
2. Nosotras
3. Los chicos
4. Tú

B Expressions with *tener*

Use expressions with **tener** to say how these people feel, according to each situation.

1. I am in the Sahara desert in the summer. (Yo...)
2. We are in North Dakota in the winter. (Nosotros...)

3. A big dog is chasing Carlos. (Carlos...)
4. Marisa hasn't had anything to eat for 12 hours. (Marisa...)
5. Luis and Beto have a class in two minutes and they are five minutes away from the classroom. (Luis y Beto...)
6. My throat is truly dry. (Yo...)
7. You haven't slept for two days. (Tú...)
8. Liliana is blowing out ten candles on her birthday cake. (Liliana...)

C Comparative forms

Give the Spanish equivalent of the following exchanges.

1. "Are you as tall as your sister, Anita?"
   "No, she's much taller than I. She's the tallest in the family."
2. "Is your house big, Mr. Varela?"
   "Yes, but it doesn't have as many rooms as your grandparents' house, Rosita."

D Irregular comparative forms

Say who is oldest and youngest among the girls and which hotels are the best and the worst.

1. Amelia tiene quince años, Laura tiene dieciocho años y Marisol tiene veinte años.
   a.
   b.
2. El hotel Azteca es bueno; el hotel Mirasol no es muy bueno; el hotel Sandoval es muy malo.
   a.
   b.

E Vocabulary

Circle the word or phrase that best completes each sentence.

1. Tengo que hablar con el (gerente, esposo) del hotel.
2. Olivia (cree, llega) a las dos de la tarde.
3. Tú tienes (más, mal) de cien dólares.
4. No es caro; es (mayor, barato).
5. Los cuartos tienen (televisor, gimnasio).
6. Yo (creo, tengo) que ella es una chica muy inteligente.
7. Colorado es más (grande, pequeño) que Rhode Island.
8. ¿Carlos viene con los chicos o viene (mejor, solo)?
9. ¿Tú tienes (el mercado, la llave) del cuarto?

10. Vamos a viajar. Necesitamos las (tiendas, valijas).
11. Aquí (está, da) el ventilador.
12. El hotel tiene (piscina, esposo).

LECCIÓN 5

A Stem-changing verbs (*e:ie*)

Complete the following exchanges, using the present indicative of the verbs given.

  1. —¿Tú _____ (querer) ir a Madrid?
    —No, _____ (preferir) ir a Buenos Aires.
  2. —¿A qué hora _____ (empezar) a trabajar Uds.?
    —Nosotros _____ (empezar) a las ocho.
  3. —¿Elsa _____ (perder) mucho dinero cuando va a Las Vegas?
    —Sí.
  4. —¿Ud. _____ (entender) la lección dos?
    —Sí, pero (yo) no _____ (entender) la lección tres.
  5. —¿Cuándo _____ (comenzar) las clases?
    —En agosto.

B Some uses of the definite article

Complete the following, using the Spanish equivalent of the words in parentheses.

  1. Tenemos clases _____. (*on Mondays*)
  2. ¿A qué hora es _____? (*dinner*)
  3. Ellos van a _____ y yo voy a _____. (*school/church*)
  4. Mis vacaciones comienzan _____. (*next Friday*)
  5. Eusebio está en _____. (*jail*)
  6. Yo creo que _____ es muy importante. (*education*)
  7. _____ es una bebida (*drink*) alcohólica. (*Champagne*)

C The present progressive

Change the following from the present indicative to the present progressive.

  1. Yo leo y él duerme.
  2. Ella trabaja y ellos estudian.
  3. ¿Tú comes pollo?
  4. Nosotros esperamos al profesor.
  5. ¿Uds. beben vino o cerveza?

D Ordinal numbers

Complete the following appropriately.

1. Enero es el _____ mes del año.
2. _____ es el sexto mes del año.
3. Septiembre es el _____ mes del año.
4. _____ es el tercer mes del año.
5. Febrero es el _____ mes del año.
6. _____ es el cuarto mes del año.
7. Octubre es el _____ mes del año.
8. _____ es el quinto mes del año.
9. Agosto es el _____ mes del año.
10. Julio es el _____ mes del año.

E Vocabulary

Circle the word or phrase that does not belong in each group.

1. cine   teatro   iglesia
2. toalla   cárcel   jabón
3. almuerzo   cena   piso
4. cerrar   comenzar   empezar
5. desear   perder   querer
6. semana   desayuno   mes
7. ¡Ya lo creo!   primero   próximo
8. discoteca   bailan   año
9. hotel   pensión   escuela

LECCIÓN

6

OBJECTIVES

Structures

1. Stem-changing verbs (**o:ue**)
2. Affirmative and negative expressions
3. Pronouns as object of a preposition
4. Direct object pronouns

Communication

You will learn more vocabulary related to situations encountered while traveling.

Countries highlighted: Costa Rica and Panamá

Costa Rica is a very small country. Its area is half that of the state of Virginia. Sixty percent of its territory is covered by forest, including rain forest, which the government tries to protect with very strict laws. Costa Rica has 24 national parks and ecological reserves that are open to the public. Therefore, ecotourism is increasingly important in this country.

Costa Rica is a democracy and has no army. The country has been called "America's Switzerland." The capital of Costa Rica is San José, a small city with a population of about 300,000.

Panamá is situated on the isthmus that joins the two Americas. Its territory is bisected by the famous Panamá Canal, which is the main source of income for the country. Panamá has developed very few of its natural resources. The two most important Panamanian cities are Panamá, the capital, and Colón.

RESOURCES

Wherever you see the following icons additional resources are available:

Internet
Go to **www.college.hmco.com/languages/spanish/students/** for additional practice on the topic.

Student CD-ROM
Go to the **Video Grammar Tutor** for help with understanding the grammar topic at hand.

Go to the **In-Text Audio CDs** for more practice.

VOCABULARIO
Audio

COGNADOS

el banco
el cheque
la excursión
la farmacia

NOMBRES

la cama   *bed*
la carta   *letter*
el colchón   *mattress*
la estampilla, el sello, el timbre
   (*Méx.*)   *stamp*
la frazada, la manta, la cobija
   blanket
la librería   *bookstore*
los lugares de interés
   places of interest
el mar   *ocean*
la oficina de correos   *post office*
los padrinos   *godparents*[1]
el periódico, el diario   *newspaper*
la playa   *beach*
el regalo   *present, gift*
el tiempo   *time*
el zoológico   *zoo*

VERBOS

almorzar (o:ue)   *to have lunch*
costar (o:ue)   *to cost*
poder (o:ue)   *to be able*
recordar (o:ue)   *to remember*
volar (o:ue)   *to fly*
volver (o:ue)   *to return, to come*
   (go) back

ADJETIVOS

abierto(a)   *open*
este(a)   *this*

OTRAS PALABRAS Y EXPRESIONES

a casa   *home*
allí   *there*
cerca de   *near to*
con vista al mar   *with an ocean view*
más tarde, después   *later*
para   *for*
por noche   *per night*
que viene   *next*

---

[1]**padrino:** *godfather,* **madrina:** *godmother*

1 STEM-CHANGING VERBS (O:UE)

Verbos que cambian en la raíz (*o:ue*)

As you learned in **Lección 5,** certain verbs undergo a change in the stem in the present indicative. When the last stem vowel is a stressed **o,** it changes to **ue.**

volver (*to return*)	
vuelvo	volvemos
vuelves	volvéis
vuelve	**vue**lven

- Notice that the stem vowel is not stressed in the verb form corresponding to **nosotros;** therefore, the **o** does not change to **ue.**

—¿Cuándo **vuelven** Uds. de la excursión al Volcán Arenal?
—**Volvemos** a las siete. ¿A qué hora **vuelves** tú?
—**Vuelvo** a las nueve.

"When are you coming back from the excursion to the Arenal Volcano?"
"We are coming back at seven. What time are you coming back?"
"I'm coming back at nine."

Some other common verbs that undergo the same change in the stem are:

almorzar	*to have lunch*	**poder**	*to be able*
costar	*to cost*	**recordar**	*to remember*
dormir	*to sleep*	**volar**	*to fly*

—¿Cuánto **cuesta** una habitación con vista al mar?
—10.500 colones[1] por noche.

"How much does a room with an ocean view cost?"
"10,500 colones per night."

—¿**Puede** Ud. comprar el colchón mañana?
—Sí. ¡Ah!, no, ahora **recuerdo** que no tengo tiempo.

"Can you buy the mattress tomorrow?"
"Yes. Oh!, no, now I remember that I don't have time."

—¿Cuándo **vuela** Eva a San José?
—**Vuela** la semana que viene.

"When is Eva flying to San José?"
"She is flying next week."

---

[1]Costa Rica's currency.

—No **duermo** bien.   *"I don't sleep well."*
—¿Cuántas horas **duermes?**   *"How many hours do you sleep?"*
—**Duermo** solamente tres   *"I sleep only three or four hours."*
o cuatro horas.

—¿Cuándo **pueden** ir Uds.   *"When can you go to the*
a la farmacia?   *pharmacy?"*
—**Podemos** ir más tarde.   *"We can go later. There is a*
Hay una farmacia de   *pharmacy that is open near here."*
turno cerca de aquí.

In Spain and in Latin American countries there is always a pharmacy in each neighborhood that stays open all night. Since they take turns staying open, they are called **"farmacias de turno."**

Vamos a practicar

A Complete the following dialogues with the correct verb forms. Then act them out with a partner.

1. *almorzar*   —¿Dónde _____ Uds.?
    —Nosotros _____ en la cafetería y mis hijos _____
    en la escuela.

2. *volver*   —¿Cuándo _____ tú de la excursión?
    —Yo _____ a las ocho. ¿Y Uds.?
    —Nosotros _____ mañana a las diez.

3. *costar /*   —¿Cuánto _____ un cuarto con vista al mar en el
    hotel Calinda? ¿Ochenta dólares por noche?
   recordar   —Yo no _____.

4. *poder*   —¿Uds. _____ ir a la farmacia ahora?
    —No, no _____. ¿Tú _____ ir más tarde?
    —Sí, yo _____ ir más tarde con Daniel.

5. *dormir /*   —¿Tú _____ cuando _____?
   volar   —No, porque tengo miedo.

B Interview a classmate, using the following questions. When you have finished, switch roles.

1. Cuando viajas, ¿vuelas o vas en ómnibus?
2. ¿Cuánto cuestan tus libros para la universidad?
3. ¿A qué hora vuelves a tu casa?
4. ¿Cuántas horas duermes?
5. ¿Puedes venir a clase la semana que viene?

6. ¿Recuerdas el número de teléfono de tu mejor amigo o amiga? ¿Cuál es?
7. ¿A qué hora almuerzan Uds. en su casa?
8. ¿Puedes estudiar esta noche o no tienes tiempo?

C With a classmate, discuss your daily routine: when and where you have lunch, about how much it costs, what you can and cannot do every day, what time you return home, and how many hours you sleep. Compare notes!

② AFFIRMATIVE AND NEGATIVE EXPRESSIONS
Expresiones afirmativas y negativas

Affirmative		Negative	
algo	something, anything	nada	nothing
alguien	someone, anyone	nadie	nobody, no one
alguno(a)		ninguno(a)	none, not any
algún	any, some	ningún	
algunos(as)			
siempre	always	nunca	never
alguna vez	ever	jamás	
algunas veces, a veces	sometimes		
también	also, too	tampoco	neither
o...o	either... or	ni... ni	neither... nor

- A double negative is frequently used in Spanish. In this construction, the adverb **no** is placed immediately before the verb. The second negative word may either precede the verb, follow the verb, or come at the end of the sentence. If the negative word precedes the verb, **no** is not used.

—¿Uds. van a la playa **algunas veces**?   *"Do you go to the beach sometimes?"*
—No, **no** vamos **nunca.**   *"No, we never go."*
  (**Nunca** vamos.)

—¿Compra Ud. **algo** allí?   *"Do you buy anything there?"*
—No, allí **no** compro **nada nunca.**   *"No, I never buy anything there."*
  (**Nunca** compro **nada** allí.)

In most Spanish cities, stores are closed on Sundays. Small stores have great freedom in opening and closing times. It is not uncommon to see signs such as "**cerrado hoy.**" (*closed today*)

—¿Están abiertas las tiendas hoy?

—No, en San José las tiendas **siempre** cierran los domingos.

"Are stores open today?"

"No, in San José stores always close on Sundays."

Vamos a practicar
Quiz

A Answer the following questions in the negative.

1. ¿Necesita Ud. algo?
2. ¿Hay alguien allí?
3. ¿Estudia Ud. siempre por la noche?
4. ¿Quiere té o café?
5. ¿Hay algunos lugares de interés cerca de aquí?
6. Su amigo no va a la excursión. ¿Va Ud.?
7. ¿Va Ud. a la playa algunas veces?
8. ¿Hay alguna tienda abierta hoy?

B David always contradicts everyone. Play the part of David and say the opposite of the following statements.

1. Raquel siempre va a la playa con Jorge o con Rafael.
2. Las tiendas nunca están abiertas los jueves.
3. Mauricio tiene algunos amigos de Costa Rica.
4. Ana siempre almuerza con alguien en la cafetería.
5. Graciela necesita comprar algo en la farmacia.
6. Pablo viaja en autobús a veces.
7. Los chicos van a la discoteca y las chicas van también.

C With a classmate, talk about the things that you always do, you sometimes do, and you never do. Compare notes!

❸ PRONOUNS AS OBJECT OF A PREPOSITION
Pronombres usados como objetos de preposición

> **Preposition** a word that introduces a noun, pronoun, adverb, or verb and indicates its function in the sentence. They were **with** us. She is **from** Lima.

Prepositional Pronouns			
Singular		*Plural*	
mí	*me*	**nosotros(as)**	*us*
ti	*you (fam.)*	**vosotros(as)**	*you (fam.)*
Ud.	*you (formal)*	**Uds.**	*you (formal, pl.)*
él	*him*	**ellos**	*them (masc.)*
ella	*her*	**ellas**	*them (fem.)*

■ Notice that only the first and the second persons singular (**mí, ti**) have special forms. The other persons use the forms of the subject pronouns.

■ When used with the preposition **con,** the first and second person singular forms become **conmigo** and **contigo.**

—¿Vas a casa **conmigo**?　　　　*"Are you going home with me?"*
—No, no voy **contigo**.　　　　　*"No, I'm not going with you. I'm*
　Voy **con ella** a la librería.　　*going with her to the bookstore."*

—¿Es **para nosotros** el regalo?　*"Is the present for us?"*
—Sí, es **para Uds**.　　　　　　*"Yes, it's for you."*
—¿Y la frazada?　　　　　　　　*"And the blanket?"*
—Es **para mí**.　　　　　　　　*"It's for me."*

—¿Hablan **de ti**?　　　　　　　*"Are they talking about you?"*
—No, no hablan **de mí**.　　　　*"No, they're not talking*
　　　　　　　　　　　　　　　about me."

—¿Tú vas al zoológico　　　　　*"Are you going to the zoo*
　con tus padrinos?　　　　　　　*with your godparents?"*
—Sí, yo voy **con ellos**.　　　　*"Yes, I'm going with them."*

> When most Spanish children are baptized, their parents ask two people to be **padrinos** (*godparents*) to serve as religious sponsors and to act as guardians in case of the death of the parents.

Vamos a practicar

Quiz

A Complete the following sentences with the correct form of the pronoun.

1. Mi hermana va al zoológico con _____. (*us*)
2. El regalo es para _____. (*him*)
3. Ellos siempre hablan de _____, no de _____. (*you, fam./me*)
4. La cama es para _____ y el colchón es para _____, señor. (*her/you*)
5. Mis padrinos vienen con _____; no vienen con _____. (*you, sing., fam./me*)

B Interview a classmate, using the following questions and two questions of your own. When you have finished, switch roles. Use the appropriate prepositions and pronouns in your responses.

1. ¿Hablas con tus amigos en la clase?
2. ¿Puedes estudiar español conmigo?
3. ¿Trabajas para tus padres?
4. ¿Vives cerca de tus abuelos?
5. ¿Hablas mucho con tus amigos por teléfono?
6. ¿Vas de vacaciones con tu familia?

4 DIRECT OBJECT PRONOUNS
Los pronombres de complemento directo

> **Direct object** generally a noun or a pronoun that is the receiver of a verb's action and answers the question *"what?"* or *"whom?"*. Take **it**. We know **her**. I call **Mary**.

The forms of the direct object pronouns are as follows.

Subject	Direct Object	
yo	**me** (*me*)	Ella **me** visita.
tú	**te** (*you, fam.*)	Yo **te** espero.
Ud.	**lo** (*you, masc., formal*)	Yo **lo** llamo. (a Ud.)[1]
	la (*you, fem., formal*)	Yo **la** llamo. (a Ud.)[1]
él	**lo** (*him, it*)	Él **lo** visita. (a él)[1]
ella	**la** (*her, it*)	Él **la** visita. (a ella)[1]
nosotros nosotras	**nos** (*us, masc. and fem.*)	Tú **nos** llamas.
vosotros vosotras	**os** (*you, masc. and fem. fam.*)	Él **os** espera.
Uds.	**los** (*you, masc., pl., formal*)	Nosotros **los** llevamos. (a Uds.)[1]
	las (*you, fem., pl., formal*)	Nosotros **las** llevamos. (a Uds.)[1]
ellos	**los** (*them, masc.*)	Él **los** trae. (a ellos)[1]
ellas	**las** (*them, fem.*)	Él **las** trae. (a ellas)

---

[1]Used for clarification to avoid confusion between **Ud.** and **él** or **ella,** or between **Uds.** and **ellos** or **ellas.**

The direct object pronoun replaces the direct object noun and is placed *before* the conjugated verb.

Yo espero **al Sr. Lima.**
Yo   **lo**   espero.

Ella escribe **la carta.**
Ella   **la**   escribe.

Nosotros llevamos **a nuestros amigos.**
Nosotros   **los**   llevamos.

—¿**Me** llamas hoy?   *"Will you call me today?"*
—Sí, **te** llamo después.   *"Yes, I'll call you later."*

—¿Tu lees el periódico?   *"Do you read the paper?"*
—Sí, **lo** leo.   *"Yes, I read it."*

—¿Cuándo traes   *"When are you bringing*
las estampillas?   *the stamps?"*
—**Las** traigo por la tarde.   *"I'm bringing them in the*
                                        afternoon."

¿Dónde **las** compras?   *"Where do you buy them?"*
—**Las** compro en la oficina   *"I buy them at the post office."*
de correos.

> In most Spanish-speaking countries, stamps can only be purchased at the post office or at some specialized stores that have the authorization to sell them.

■ In a negative sentence, the **no** must precede the object pronoun.

Yo   leo   **las revistas.**
Yo   **las**   leo.
Yo   **no**   **las**   leo.

—¿Tú llevas los cheques al banco?   *"Do you take the checks to the bank?"*
—No, yo **no los** llevo.   *"No, I don't take them."*

■ If a conjugated verb and an infinitive appear together, the direct object pronoun may be placed before the conjugated verb or attached to the infinitive.

Yo **te** voy a llamar. }   *I'm going to call* **you.**
Yo   voy a llamar**te.** }

—¿Vas a traer las mantas?   *"Are you going to bring the blankets?"*
—Sí, **las** voy a traer.   *"Yes, I'm going to bring them."*
—¿Vas a traer**las** hoy?   *"Are you going to bring them today?"*
—Sí.   *"Yes."*

■ In the present progressive, the direct object pronoun can be placed either before the verb **estar** or after the present participle.

Lo está leyendo.   *He's reading **it.***
Está leyéndo**lo.**

Note that when the direct object pronoun is attached to the present participle, a written accent is added to preserve the original stress.[1]

Vamos a practicar

A Complete the following dialogues by supplying the missing direct object pronouns.

1. —¿Tú puedes llevar _____ al banco? No tengo coche.
—Sí, yo _____ puedo llevar.
2. —¿Uds. van a traer los periódicos?
—No, nosotros no vamos a traer_____.
3. —¿Cuándo llevas las cartas al correo?
— _____ llevo esta tarde.
4. —¿Cuándo los visitan a Uds. sus amigos?
— _____ visitan los domingos.
5. —¿Tú llamas a Sergio hoy?
—No, _____ llamo mañana.
6. —¿A qué hora cierran la librería?
— _____ cierran a las ocho.

B Tell the person asking you these questions that you are the one who does everything. Follow the model.

MODELO   —¿Quién trae los periódicos?
—Yo los traigo.

1. ¿Quién compra las frazadas?
2. ¿Quién hace la cena?
3. ¿Quién trae las revistas?
4. ¿Quién llama al gerente?
5. ¿Quién compra las estampillas?
6. ¿Quién lleva los cheques al banco?
7. ¿Quién lleva a las chicas a San José?
8. ¿Quién escribe las cartas?

---

[1]See Appendix A for rules governing the use of accent marks in Spanish.

C You are planning a trip to Costa Rica. How are you getting ready for it? What is going to happen there? Answer the following questions, always using the direct object pronouns.

1. ¿Habla Ud. bien el español?
2. ¿Sus amigos van a esperarlo (esperarla)?
3. ¿Va a ver (*to see*) a sus profesores allí?
4. ¿Va a visitar los museos?
5. ¿Ud. va a llamarnos?
6. ¿Va a llevarme a Costa Rica con Ud.?
7. ¿Tiene Ud. sus maletas?
8. ¿Va a llevar a sus padres?

Palabras y más palabras   Match the questions in column **A** with the answers in column **B**.

A	B
1. ¿Qué lees?	a. Cerca de la pensión.
2. ¿Dónde compras los sellos?	b. No, al zoológico.
3. ¿Vas con tus padrinos?	c. En la cafetería.
4. ¿Cuánto cuesta este colchón?	d. A casa.
5. ¿Dónde está la farmacia?	e. La semana que viene.
6. ¿Adónde vas?	f. Trescientos dólares.
7. ¿Para quién es la carta?	g. No, no hay ninguno.
8. ¿La vas a llevar a la playa?	h. En la oficina de correos.
9. ¿Hay algunos lugares de interés allí?	i. Una con vista al mar.
10. ¿Dónde almuerzan Uds.?	j. El periódico.
11. ¿Cuándo llega Rafael?	k. Para ti.
12. ¿Qué habitación quiere?	l. No, no tengo tiempo.

En estas situaciones   What would you say in the following situations?

1. You ask a friend if he/she can take you home. Ask also if he/she is going to call you tonight.
2. You need to find out how much a room with an ocean view costs.
3. You have your first apartment. Mention three things you have to buy for your bedroom.
4. You need stamps. Ask somebody if the post office is open.
5. You feel like eating Mexican food. Ask if there is a Mexican restaurant near the hotel.

PARA ESCUCHAR Y ENTENDER

The following material is to be used with the In-Text Audio CDs.

I. Práctica

A Verbos que cambian en la raíz

2–11

Answer the questions, using the cues provided. Repeat the correct answer after the speaker's confirmation. Listen to the model.

> **MODELO** —¿Cuándo puede volver Ud.? (mañana)
> —**Puedo volver mañana.**

1. (a las dos y cuarto)
2. (el lunes)
3. (ocho horas)
4. (los sábados)
5. (con Raúl)

B Expresiones afirmativas y negativas

2–12

Change the following negative statements to the affirmative. Repeat the correct answer after the speaker's confirmation. Listen to the model.

> **MODELO** Ellos nunca van al teatro.
> **Ellos siempre van al teatro.**

C ¡No!

2–13

Answer the questions in the negative. Replace the direct objects with the appropriate direct object pronouns. Repeat the correct answer after the speaker's confirmation. Listen to the model.

> **MODELO** —¿Ud. llama a Carlos?
> —**No, no lo llamo.**

II. ¿Qué dicen?

1 ¿Lógico o ilógico?

2–14

The speaker will make some statements. Circle **L (lógico)** if the statement is logical and **I (ilógico)** if it is illogical. The speaker will confirm your response.

1. L I	**3.** L I	**5.** L I	**7.** L I
2. L I	**4.** L I	**6.** L I	**8.** L I

2 ¿Verdadero o falso?

Listen carefully to the narration. Listen to it at least twice.

2–15

(Narración)

2–16 Now the speaker will make statements about the narration you just heard. Tell whether each statement is true (**verdadero**) or false (**falso**). The speaker will confirm the correct answer.

3 Gustavo y Beatriz

Listen carefully to the dialogue. Listen to it at least twice.

2–17

(Diálogo)

2–18 Now the speaker will ask you some questions about the dialogue you just heard. Answer each question, omitting the subject. The speaker will confirm the correct answer. Repeat the correct answer.

Structures

1 Stem-changing verbs (**e:i**)
2 Irregular first-person forms
3 **Saber** contrasted with **conocer**
4 Indirect object pronouns

Communication

You will learn vocabulary related to travel arrangements.

Country highlighted: Puerto Rico

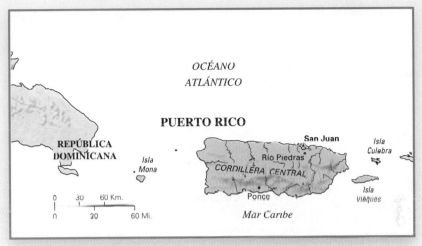

Puerto Rico is one of the islands of the **Antillas Mayores** in the Caribbean Sea. It is about one hundred miles long, and its area is similar to that of New Hampshire. In Puerto Rico, which is a Free State Associated to the United States, the Hispanic-American culture coincides with the American culture, government, and economics.

The country has two official languages: Spanish and English. Puerto Ricans are American citizens and don't need a visa or passport to enter the United States.

The African influence as well as the Spanish influence can be seen in the art and music of Puerto Rico. Among young people, one can also see the influence of the United States.

San Juan, the capital, is the largest city and the most populated. The old section of town, called **El Viejo San Juan,** is visited by many tourists throughout the year.

RESOURCES

Wherever you see the following icons additional resources are available:

Internet

Go to **www.college.hmco.com/languages/spanish/students/** for additional practice on the topic.

Student
CD-ROM

Go to the **Video Grammar Tutor** for help with understanding the grammar topic at hand.

Go to the **In-Text Audio CDs** for more practice.

VOCABULARIO
Audio

COGNADOS

la información
el Internet
la licencia
la novela
el pasaporte
la reservación

NOMBRES

la agencia de viajes   *travel agency*
el (la) agente de viajes   *travel agent*
la avenida   *avenue*
el avión   *plane*
la carne   *meat*
la embajada   *embassy*
la ensalada   *salad*
España   *Spain*
los folletos turísticos
   tourist brochures
el (la) guía   *guide*
la oficina de turismo   *tourist office*
el país   *country*
el pasaje, el billete   *ticket*
el postre   *dessert*
la sopa   *soup*
la suerte   *luck*
la verdad   *truth*
el viaje   *trip*
el vuelo   *flight*

VERBOS

buscar   *to look up*
cancelar   *to cancel*
conducir (yo conduzco),
   manejar   *to drive*
confirmar   to confirm
conocer (yo conozco)   *to know, to be
   familiar with*
conseguir (e:i)   *to obtain, to get*
nadar   to swim
poner (yo pongo)   *to put, to place*
quedar   *to be located*
saber (yo sé)   *to know how,
   to know a fact*
salir (yo salgo)   *to go out, to leave*
seguir (e:i)   *to follow, to continue*
traducir (yo traduzco)   *to translate*
ver   *to see*

ADJETIVOS

extranjero(a)   *foreign*
helado(a)   *iced*

OTRAS PALABRAS Y EXPRESIONES

¡Buen viaje!   *Have a nice trip!,
   Bon voyage!*
de memoria   *by heart*
entonces   *then, in that case*
sobre   *about*
tener suerte   *to be lucky*

① STEM-CHANGING VERBS (*E:I*)
Verbos que cambian en la raíz (*e:i*)

Some **-ir** verbs undergo a special stem change in the present indicative. For these verbs, when **e** is the last stem vowel and it is stressed, it changes to **i**.

servir (*to serve*)	
sirvo	servimos
sirves	servís
sirve	sirven

■ Notice that the stem vowel is not stressed in the verb form corresponding to **nosotros;** therefore, the **e** does not change to **i**.

—¿Qué **sirven** Uds.?   "*What do you serve?*"
—**Servimos** té helado.   "*We serve iced tea.*"

—¿Qué **sirven** en la cafetería?   "*What do they serve at the cafeteria?*"
—**Sirven** sopa, ensalada,   "*They serve soup, salad, meat, and*
carne y postre.   *dessert.*"

■ Some other common verbs that undergo the same **e** to **i** change in the stem are **pedir** (*to ask for, to request, to order*), **seguir** (*to follow, to continue*), and **repetir** (*to repeat*). Verbs like **seguir** (such as **conseguir,** *to obtain*) contain a **u** to preserve the hard **g** sound before an **e** or an **i**. Verbs that follow this pattern drop the **u** before an **a** or an **o: yo sigo, yo consigo.**

—¿**Pide** Enrique información   "*Does Enrique request information*
en la agencia de viajes?   *at the travel agency?*"
—No, la busca en el Internet.   "*No, he looks it up on the Internet.*"
—¿Dónde **consiguen** Uds.   "*Where do you get tourist*
folletos turísticos sobre   *brochures*
Puerto Rico?   *about Puerto Rico?*"
—En la oficina de turismo.   "*At the tourist office.*"

—¿A quién **siguen** Uds.?   "*Whom are you following?*"
—**Seguimos** al guía.   "*We are following the guide.*"

> All Hispanic countries have their own Web pages on the Internet. All sorts of information may be found through these sources.

■ The verb **decir** (*to say, to tell*) undergoes the same **e** to **i** stem change, but in addition it is irregular in the first person singular: **yo digo.**

—¿Qué **dice** Fernando?
—**Dice** que podemos confirmar la reservación en el hotel porque no van a cancelar el vuelo.

"What does Fernando say?"
"He says that we can confirm the reservation at the hotel because they are not going to cancel the flight."

—Yo siempre **digo** que Él tiene suerte.
—Es verdad.

"I always say that he is lucky."

"That's the truth." or *"That's true."*

Quiz

Vamos a practicar

A Complete the following dialogues with the correct verb forms. Then act them out with a partner.

1. —En este restaurante mexicano _____ una sopa muy buena. (servir)
   —Cuando yo vengo aquí, siempre _____ tacos. (pedir)
   —Yo siempre _____ que los tacos de aquí son los mejores. (decir)
2. —Carlos, ¿dónde _____ tú folletos en español? (conseguir)
   —Yo _____ algunos en San Juan y algunos en la oficina de turismo. (conseguir)
   —¿Tú _____ en la clase de la Dra. Peña? (seguir)
   —Sí, y ella siempre _____ que yo soy su mejor estudiante. (decir)
3. —Los chicos _____ que tú sólo _____ carne y ensalada. (decir/servir)
   —No es verdad; algunas veces también _____ sopa y postre. (servir)

B Tell about yourself by answering the following questions.

1. ¿Dónde consigue Ud. libros de español?
2. ¿Sigue Ud. en la clase de español?
3. En un restaurante mexicano, ¿qué pide Ud.?
4. ¿A qué hora sirven Uds. la cena?
5. ¿Sirve Ud. té helado con la comida?
6. ¿Dice Ud. siempre la verdad?

C With a classmate, discuss your favorite restaurants. Tell what you say about those restaurants, what type of food they serve, and what you order when you go there. Compare notes!

The Three Types of Stem-Changing Verbs

Here is a list of stem-changing verbs studied up to now. Every time you learn a new one, add it to the list.

e:ie	o:ue	e:i
cerrar	almorzar	conseguir
comenzar	costar	decir
empezar	dormir	pedir
entender	poder	repetir
pensar	recordar	seguir
perder	volar	servir
preferir	volver	
querer		

② IRREGULAR FIRST-PERSON FORMS
Verbos irregulares en la primera persona

Some common verbs are irregular in the present indicative only in the first person singular. The other persons are regular.

Verb	First-person (yo) form	Regular forms
salir (*to go out, to leave*)	**salgo**	sales, sale, salimos, salís, salen
hacer (*to do, to make*)	**hago**	haces, hace, hacemos, hacéis, hacen
poner (*to put, to place*)	**pongo**	pones, pone, ponemos, ponéis, ponen
traer (*to bring*)	**traigo**	traes, trae, traemos, traéis, traen
conducir (*to drive*)	**conduzco**	conduces, conduce, conducimos, conducís, conducen
traducir (*to translate*)	**traduzco**	traduces, traduce, traducimos, traducís, traducen
conocer (*to know*)	**conozco**	conoces, conoce, conocemos, conocéis, conocen
ver (*to see*)	**veo**	ves, ve, vemos, veis, ven
saber (*to know*)	**sé**	sabes, sabe, sabemos, sabéis, saben

—¿Tú **sabes** conducir?   *"Do you know how to drive?"*
—Sí, yo **sé** conducir, pero   *"Yes, I know how to drive,*
   no **conduzco** porque   *but I don't drive because*
   no tengo licencia.   *I don't have a license."*

—Mañana **salgo** para   *"I'm leaving for Puerto Rico*
   Puerto Rico.   *tomorrow."*
—¿A qué hora **sale** el avión?   *"What time does the plane leave?"*
—A las siete.   *"At seven."*
—¡Buen viaje!   *"Have a nice trip!"*

—¿Qué **haces** los domingos?   *"What do you do on Sundays?"*
—No **hago** nada.   *"I don't do anything."*
—Entonces, ¿no **ves** a   *"Then, you don't see*
   tus amigos?   *your friends?"*
—No, no **veo** a nadie.   *"No, I don't see anybody."*

> An American tourist can drive in most Spanish-speaking countries using a driver's license from the United States. It is advisable, however, to take out car insurance from the host country.

Vamos a practicar

Quiz

A Interview a classmate, using the following questions. When you have finished, switch roles.

1. ¿Sales a menudo? ¿Con quién?
2. ¿Ves a tus amigos los sábados? ¿Y los domingos?
3. ¿Haces algo los domingos?
4. ¿Conoces la ciudad de Nueva York? ¿Qué otras ciudades grandes conoces?
5. ¿Conduces bien? ¿Qué coche conduces?
6. ¿Sabes francés? ¿Sabes algún otro idioma?
7. ¿Traduces del español al inglés?
8. ¿Traes tus libros a clase?
9. ¿Dónde pones tus libros?
10. ¿Conoces a alguien de Puerto Rico? ¿A quién?

❸ *SABER* CONTRASTED WITH *CONOCER*
Saber contrastado con *conocer*

There are two verbs in Spanish that mean *to know:* **saber** and **conocer.**
These verbs are not interchangeable.

- **Saber** means to know something by heart, to know how to do something, or to know a fact.

—¿**Sabe** Ud. algunos poemas
de memoria?

"Do you know any poems by heart?"

—No, no **sé** ninguno.

"No, I don't know any."

—¿**Saben** ellos nadar?

"Do they know how to swim?"

—Sí, ellos **saben** nadar.

"Yes, they know how to swim."

—¿**Sabes** dónde queda la
embajada norteamericana?

*"Do you know where the American
Embassy is located?"*

—Sí, queda en la avenida Ponce.

"Yes, it's located on Ponce Avenue."

- **Conocer** means to be familiar or acquainted with a person, a thing, or a place.

—¿**Conoces** al agente de viajes?

"Do you know the travel agent?"

—¿Al Sr. Paz? Sí.

"Mr. Paz? Yes."

—¿**Conocen** Uds. las novelas
de Cervantes?

*"Are you familiar with Cervantes's
novels?"*

—Sí, **conocemos** algunas.

*"Yes, we are familiar with some
(of them)."*

—¿Qué país extranjero
conoces tú?

*"What foreign country are you
familiar with (do you know)?"*

—**Conozco** Cuba.

"I'm familiar with Cuba."

Vamos a practicar

Quiz

Tell what these people know or don't know, using **saber** or **conocer**.

1. Ellos / San Juan
2. Ud. / a mi madre
3. Tú / el poema de memoria
4. Él / al agente de viajes
5. Yo no / nadar
6. ¿Uds. / las novelas de Hemingway?
7. Yo no / qué día es hoy
8. Yo no / ningún país extranjero
9. Nosotras no / dónde queda la embajada
10. Ellas / al hijo del profesor

4 INDIRECT OBJECT PRONOUNS
Los pronombres de complemento indirecto

> **Indirect object** a word or phrase that tells *to whom* or *for whom* something is done. An indirect object pronoun can be used in place of the indirect object. In Spanish, the indirect object pronoun includes the meaning *to* or *for:* Yo **les** mando los libros (*a los estudiantes*). I send the books **to them** (*to the students*).

The forms of the indirect object pronouns are as follows.

Subject	Indirect Object	
yo	**me** (*to / for me*)	Él **me** da las revistas.
tú	**te** (*to / for you, fam.*)	Yo **te** doy el periódico.
Ud. ⎱		Ella **le** compra un pasaje.
él ⎬	**le** (*to / for you, formal, masc. and fem.*)	Yo **le** hablo en inglés.
ella ⎰	**le** (*to / for him / her*)	
nosotros ⎱		
nosotras ⎰	**nos** (*to / for us, masc. and fem.*)	Ella **nos** da la lección.
vosotros ⎱		
vosotras ⎰	**os** (*to / for us, masc. and fem.*)	Él **os** trae los billetes.
Uds. ⎱		Yo **les** digo la dirección.
ellos ⎬	**les** (*to / for you, formal pl., masc. and fem.*)	El agente **les** da el dinero.
ellas ⎰	**les** (*to / for them, masc. and fem.*)	

The forms of the indirect object pronouns are the same as the forms of the direct object pronouns, except in the third person. Indirect object pronouns are usually placed *in front* of a conjugated verb.

> Many Spanish-speaking people don't refer to the Spanish language as **español** but as **castellano.** This term is also used to refer to Spanish as a subject matter in school.

—¿Quién **les** compra a Uds. los pasajes?

"Who buys you the tickets?"

—Mi padre **nos** compra los pasajes.

"My father buys us the tickets."

—¿En qué idioma **le** hablas?

"In which language do you speak to him (to her)?"

—**Le** hablo en castellano.

"I speak to him (to her) in Spanish."

- When an infinitive follows the conjugated verb, the indirect object pronoun may be placed in front of the conjugated verb or attached to the infinitive.[1]

Te voy a comprar   una maleta.
  Voy a compra**rte**   una maleta.

- With the present progressive forms, the indirect object pronoun can be placed in front of the conjugated verb, or it can be attached to the end of the progressive construction.[1]

Le estoy escribiendo   al agente de viajes.
  Estoy escribiéndo**le**[2]   al agente de viajes.

ATENCIÓN: The indirect object pronouns le **and** les **require clarification when the person to whom they refer is not specified. Spanish provides clarification by using the preposition** a+ *noun or personal (subject) pronoun.*

Le doy la información.   *I give the information...*(to whom? to him? to her? to you?)

but: **Le** doy la información   *I give the information to her*
a ella (a Rosa).   *(to Rosa).*

- This prepositional form is also used to express emphasis.

Me da el pasaporte **a mí.**   *He gives the passport to me*
                                          (and to nobody else)

- Although the prepositional form provides clarification, it is not a substitute for the indirect object pronoun. The prepositional form may be omitted, but the indirect object pronoun must always be used.

—¿Qué **le** vas a traer (a Roberto)?
—**Le** voy a traer unas novelas.

> When registering at a hotel in most Hispanic cities, the traveler must include his/her passport number in the register. This information may be provided to the local police.

---

[1]This is also true of direct object pronouns.
[2]See Appendix A for rules governing the use of accent marks in Spanish.

Vamos a practicar

Quiz

A Add the missing indirect object pronouns to express for whom the following are being done.

> **MODELO**   Ella va a traer los billetes. (**para él;** *both ways*)
> Ella **le** va a traer (va a traer**le**) los billetes.

1. Yo compro el regalo. (**para ti**)
2. Nosotros vamos a traer los postres. (**para Uds.;** *both ways*)
3. Ada compra las bebidas. (**para mí**)
4. Ellos están escribiendo una carta. (**para ella;** *both ways*)
5. Yo voy a traer los pasajes. (**para Ud.;** *both ways*)
6. Fernando compra los sellos. (**para nosotros**)

B Answer the following questions, using the information in parentheses.

1. ¿Qué vas a comprarle a tu hermano? (un pasaje para España; *both ways*)
2. ¿Qué les da a Uds. el agente? (folletos turísticos)
3. ¿Quién te escribe? (mi novio / mi novia)
4. ¿Qué vas a traerme? (un regalo; *both ways*)
5. ¿Qué les vas a comprar a las chicas? (refrescos; *both ways*)
6. ¿Cuándo nos va a escribir Ud.? (mañana; *both ways*)

C Answer the following questions.

1. ¿Ud. les pide dinero a sus padres?
2. ¿El profesor le va a dar a Ud. una A en español?
3. ¿Puede Ud. darme el periódico?
4. ¿Uds. pueden traernos unos refrescos?
5. ¿El profesor les trae a Uds. revistas en español?
6. ¿Tú les hablas a tus amigos en inglés o en español?

D Marcos is going to Puerto Rico and is planning to bring gifts for everybody. Use your imagination and say what he's bringing to each person listed.

> **MODELO**   a su mamá
> Yo sé que **le** va a traer una novela.

1. a su papá
2. a mí
3. a ti

4. a usted
5. a nosotros
6. a sus hermanos

Palabras y más palabras Circle the word or phrase that best completes each sentence.

1. Van a cancelar los (aviones, vuelos).
2. Va a llamar a la agencia de viajes para (confirmar, cancelar) la reservación porque no puede viajar.
3. ¿Vas a España? ¡Buen (viaje, billete)!
4. Viven en la (alberca, avenida) Victoria.
5. La (embajada, ensalada) americana queda en la avenida Morelos.
6. Ellos no saben (traducir, manejar) al español.
7. Te deseamos buena (sopa, suerte).
8. Vamos a servir té (helado, frito).
9. ¿No tienes pasaporte? (Entonces, Sobre) no puedes viajar.
10. Alicia no dice la (verdad, suerte).

En estas situaciones What would you say in the following situations?

1. You are at a travel agency. Ask pertinent questions to arrange a trip to a foreign country.
2. In San José, Costa Rica, you ask where the American Embassy is located.
3. At a hotel, find out whether or not they serve certain types of food and beverage that you like.
4. You and a friend are talking about interesting places that you are acquainted with. Tell him/her about the places that you know.
5. Your friend is leaving for Puerto Rico. Ask him/her what things he/she is going to see, and wish him/her a nice trip.

PARA ESCUCHAR Y ENTENDER

The following material is to be used with In-Text Audio CDs.

I. Práctica

A Verbos que cambian en la raíz
Change each sentence, using the verb provided. Repeat the correct answer after the speaker's confirmation. Listen to the model.

2–19

MODELO	Yo quiero carne. (pedir)
	Yo pido carne.

B Verbos irregulares

2–20   Answer the questions, always using the first choice. Omit the subject. Repeat the correct answer after the speaker's confirmation. Listen to the model.

> **MODELO**   —¿Conduces un Ford o un Chevrolet?
> —**Conduzco un Ford.**

C Los pronombres de complemento indirecto

2–21   Answer the questions, using the cues provided. Repeat the correct answer after the speaker's confirmation. Listen to the model.

> **MODELO**   —¿Qué me vas a traer? (los folletos turísticos)
> —**Te voy a traer los folletos turísticos.**

1. (el agente de viajes)
2. (que es tarde)
3. (inglés)
4. (las maletas)
5. (sopa y ensalada)
6. (revistas)

II. ¿Qué dicen?

1 ¿Lógico o ilógico?

2–22   The speaker will make some statements. Circle **L (lógico)** if the statement is logical and **I (ilógico)** if it is illogical. The speaker will verify your response.

1. L I	**3.** L I	**5.** L I	**7.** L I
2. L I	**4.** L I	**6.** L I	**8.** L I

2 El viaje de Ana

2–23   Listen carefully to the narration, in which Ana will tell you about her plans. Listen to it at least twice.

(Narración)

2–24   Now the speaker will ask you some questions about the narration you just heard. Answer each question, omitting the subject. The speaker will confirm the correct answer. Repeat the correct answer.

3 Eva y Paquito
Listen carefully to the dialogue. Listen to it at least twice.

2–25

(Diálogo)

2–26   Now the speaker will ask you some questions about the dialogue you just heard. Answer each question, omitting the subject. The speaker will confirm the correct answer. Repeat the correct answer.

OBJECTIVES

Structures

1. **Pedir** contrasted with **preguntar**
2. Special construction with **gustar, doler,** and **hacer falta**
3. Demonstrative adjectives and pronouns
4. Direct and indirect object pronouns used together

Communication

You will learn vocabulary related to sports and other outdoor activities.

Countries highlighted: Cuba and República Dominicana

Cuba is the largest island of the Antilles. The country has extensive coasts with beautiful beaches. Cuba has been called "The pearl of the Antilles." Cuba's capital is La Habana, the largest city in the Caribbean. Its old section, "La Habana Vieja", has wonderful colonial buildings like the Cathedral, and the fortresses "El Morro" and "La Cabaña." Cuba is the only communist country in this hemisphere.

The Dominican Republic occupies two thirds of the island that Christopher Columbus named La Española. The rest of the island belongs to Haiti, a French-speaking country. The Dominican Republic has an area of about half that of the state of Kentucky, and it is very mountainous. In fact, the highest mountain in the Caribbean region, Pico Duarte, with a height of 10,000 feet, is located in this country.

The capital and main port is Santo Domingo, the first city founded by Europeans in the New World.

RESOURCES

Wherever you see the following icons additional resources are available:

Internet

Go to **www.college.hmco.com/languages/spanish/students/** for additional practice on the topic.

Student CD-ROM

Go to the **Video Grammar Tutor** for help with understanding the grammar topic at hand.

Go to the **In-Text Audio CDs** for more practice.

VOCABULARIO
Audio

COGNADOS

la aspirina
el básquetbol
el béisbol
la bicicleta
el (la) presidente(a)
la raqueta
el tenis

NOMBRES

la bolsa de dormir   *sleeping bag*
el caballo   *horse*
la cabeza   *head*
la entrada   *ticket (for an event)*
el (la) entrenador(a)   *trainer, coach*
los esquíes, los esquís   *skis*
el fútbol[1]   *soccer*
la mochila   *backpack*
el (la) niño(a)   *child, kid*
la página deportiva   *sports page*
el partido   *game, match*
los patines   *skates*
la pelota   *ball*
el pie   *foot*
la raqueta de tenis   *tennis racket*
la tienda de campaña   *tent*

VERBOS

bucear   *to scuba dive*
doler (o:ue)   *to hurt, to ache*
esquiar   *to ski*
gustar   *to like, to be pleasing*
jugar[2]   *to play (e.g., a game)*
mandar, enviar   *to send*
patinar   *to skate*
preguntar   *to ask (a question)*
prestar   *to lend*
regalar   *to give (a gift)*

OTRAS PALABRAS Y EXPRESIONES

allá   *over there*
hacer falta   *to lack, to need*
ir a esquiar   *to go skiing*
montar a caballo   *to ride a horse*
montar en bicicleta   *to ride a bike*
¿para quién?   *for whom?*
que   *that, which*
si   *if*

---

1 *PEDIR* CONTRASTED WITH *PREGUNTAR*
Pedir contrastado con *preguntar*

■ Pedir means *to ask for* or *to request something*

—¿Qué le **piden** los muchachos   *"What do the boys ask the coach for?"*
al entrenador?

---

[1] *Football* is called "fútbol americano".
[2] Present tense: **juego, juegas, juega, jugamos, jugáis, juegan**

—Le **piden** entradas para el partido de béisbol. Aquí, en Santo Domingo, es nuestro deporte favorito.	*"They ask him for tickets for the baseball game. Here, in Santo Domingo, it's our favorite sport."*
—¿Le vas a **pedir** dinero a tu tío?	*"Are you going to ask your uncle for money?"*
—Sí, le voy a **pedir** dos mil pesos[1] para comprar una bicicleta.	*"Yes, I'm going to ask him for two thousand pesos to buy a bicycle."*

■ **Preguntar** means *to ask a question*

—¿Qué vas a **preguntarle** a René? —Voy a **preguntarle** si quiere ir a Chile a esquiar.	*"What are you going to ask René?"* *"I'm going to ask him if he wants to go to Chile to ski."*
—¿Qué le vas a **preguntar** a Ana? —Si quiere jugar al tenis, patinar, montar a caballo o montar en bicicleta.	*"What are you going to ask Ana?"* *"If she wants to play tennis, skate, ride a horse, or ride a bicycle."*

> While soccer is the favorite sport in most Hispanic countries, baseball is very popular in the Dominican Republic and other countries in the Caribbean region. Many American recruiters from the major leagues go to those countries in search of new baseball players.

Vamos a practicar

Complete the following dialogues, using **pedir** and **preguntar** as appropriate. Then act them out with a partner.

1. —¿Qué le vas a _____ al entrenador?
   —Si vamos a jugar al béisbol mañana.

2. —¿Cuánto dinero le vas a _____ a tu tía?
   —Cien dólares, para comprar una bicicleta.

3. —¿Qué te está _____ Elsa?
   —Me está _____ adónde voy a ir a esquiar.

4. —¿Qué están haciendo los chicos?
   —Están _____ información sobre el partido.

_____

[1]currency in the Dominican Republic

5. —¿Tú siempre les _____ consejo (*advice*) a tus padres?
   —No, nunca les _____ consejo.
6. —¿Qué le quiere _____ a Ester?
   —Le quiero _____ si vamos al cine hoy.

2 SPECIAL CONSTRUCTION WITH *GUSTAR, DOLER,* AND *HACER FALTA*

Construcción especial con *gustar, doler* y *hacer falta*

The verb **gustar** means *to like.* A special construction is required in Spanish to translate the English structure *to like.* This is done by making the English direct object the subject of the Spanish sentence. The English subject then becomes the indirect object of the Spanish sentence.

English:	*I like Spain.*
	subj. d.o.
Spanish:	**Me** gusta España.
	i.o. subj.
Literally:	*Spain appeals to me.*

The two most commonly used forms of **gustar** are: (1) the third person singular **gusta** if the subject is singular or if **gustar** is followed by one or more infinitives; and (2) the third person plural **gustan** if the subject is plural.

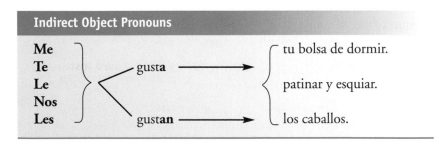

Indirect Object Pronouns

Me
Te
Le   gusta ——————→ tu bolsa de dormir.
Nos   patinar y esquiar.
Les   gustan ——————→ los caballos.

■ Note that the verb **gustar** agrees with the subject of the sentence, that is, the person or thing *being liked.*

Me gusta **el café.**   Le gust**an los patines.**

■ Note that the person who does the liking is the *indirect object.*

Me gusta el café.   **Le** gustan las chicas inteligentes.
I.O.   I.O.

—**¿Les gusta** el básquetbol?   *"Do you like basketball?"*
—Sí, **nos gusta** mucho, pero   *"Yes, we like it very much, but we*
   nos gusta más el fútbol.   *like soccer better."*

 ATENCIÓN: Note that the words más **(***better***) and** mucho **immediately follow** gustar.

■ The preposition **a** + *noun or pronoun* is used to clarify meaning or to emphasize the indirect object.

A Aurora (A ella) le gusta ese   *Aurora likes that place,*
lugar, pero **a mí** no me gusta.   *but I don't like it.*

A Roberto y **a Rosa** les   *Roberto and Rosa like my tent.*
gusta mi tienda de campaña.

A nosotros nos gusta bucear.   *We like to scuba dive.*

■ The verb **doler** (*to hurt, to ache*) and the expression **hacer falta** (*to need*) use the same construction as **gustar.**

—¿Qué **les hace falta,** señoras?   *"What do you need, ladies?"*
—**Nos hacen falta** las entradas.   *"We need the tickets."*

—¿Por qué estás tomando aspirinas?   *"Why are you taking aspirin?"*
—Porque **me duele** la cabeza.   *"Because my head hurts."*
—¿A ti **te duele** la cabeza?   *"Your head hurts?"*
   A mí **me duelen** los pies.   *My feet hurt."*

 ATENCIÓN: In Spanish, the definite article is generally used instead of the possessive adjective with parts of the body as in *Me duele la cabeza.*

 ## Vamos a practicar

Quiz

A Use **gustar** to say what you and the people named like.

MODELO   José / el café
             (A José) **Le gusta** el café.

Many outdoor activities are popular in the Dominican Republic, but swimming and scuba diving are among the most popular, due to the magnificent beaches and the abundance of sea life.

1. Elsa / tu caballo
2. nosotros / la bolsa de dormir
3. yo / la tienda de campaña
4. ellos / patinar y esquiar
5. tú / jugar al básquetbol y al fútbol
6. Uds. / la comida dominicana

B Indicate what everybody needs, using **hacer falta.**

1. Yo tengo mil pesos y necesito mil quinientos.
2. Las chicas tienen tres raquetas y necesitan seis.
3. Tú tienes una entrada y necesitas dos.
4. El entrenador tiene cuatro pasajes y necesita diez.
5. Nosotros tenemos noventa y nueve dólares y necesitamos cien.

C Interview a classmate, using the following questions. When you have finished, switch roles.

1. ¿Cuándo tomas aspirinas?
2. ¿Te duele la cabeza a menudo? ¿Te duelen los pies?
3. ¿Qué te duele hoy?
4. ¿Qué te hace falta?
5. ¿Les hace falta más dinero a tu familia y a ti?
6. ¿Les gusta a tus amigos y a ti el español?
7. ¿Te gusta esquiar?
8. ¿Qué te gusta más: el básquetbol o el tenis? ¿El béisbol o el fútbol?

D With a classmate discuss your likes and dislikes as well as those of your family and friends.

❸ DEMONSTRATIVE ADJECTIVES AND PRONOUNS

Los adjetivos y pronombres demonstrativos

> **Demonstrative** a word that points out a definite person or object: **this, that, these, those**

Demonstrative adjectives   Demonstrative adjectives point out persons or things. They agree in gender and number with the nouns they modify or point out. The forms of the demonstrative adjectives are as follows.

Masculine		*Feminine*		
Singular	**Plural**	**Singular**	**Plural**	
este	estos	esta	estas	*this, these*
ese	esos	esa	esas	*that, those*
aquel	aquellos	aquella	aquellas	*that, those* (*at a distance*)

—¿Para quién es **esta** raqueta de tenis?
—**Esta** raqueta es para Marta y **esa** pelota es para Rita.

"Whom is this tennis racket for?"
"This racket is for Marta and that ball is for Rita."

—¿Te gusta **este** caballo?
—No, me gusta **aquel** caballo blanco que está allá.

"Do you like this horse?"
"No, I like that white horse over there."

Vamos a practicar

Quiz

Change the demonstrative adjectives so that they agree with the new nouns.

1. Este caballo, _____ raqueta, _____ revistas, _____ programas.
2. Esas ciudades, _____ teatros, _____ librería, _____ museo.
3. Aquella mesa, _____ sillas, _____ hombre, _____ coches.
4. Esta lección, _____ idioma, _____ problemas, _____ universidades.
5. Ese jabón, _____ frazadas, _____ cuartos, _____ toalla.

Demonstrative pronouns The demonstrative pronouns are the
same as the demonstrative adjectives, except that the pronouns have a
written accent mark. The forms of the demonstrative pronouns are as
follows.

Masculine		Feminine		Neuter	
Singular	**Plural**	**Singular**	**Plural**		
éste	éstos	ésta	éstas	esto	*this* (*one*), *these*
ése	ésos	ésa	ésas	eso	*that* (*one*), *those*
aquél	aquéllos	aquélla	aquéllas	aquello	*that* (*one*), *those* (*at a distance*)

—¿Qué patines quiere Ud.?   *"Which skates do you want?*
 ¿Éstos o **aquéllos**?   *These or those* (over there)?"
—Quiero **aquéllos.**   *"I want those* (over there)."

—¿Qué mochilas van a llevar   *"Which backpacks are the children*
 los niños, **éstas** o **ésas**?   *going to take, these or those?"*
—**Éstas.**   *"These."*

■ Each demonstrative pronoun has a neuter form. The neuter pronoun
 has no accent, because there are no corresponding demonstrative
 adjectives.

■ The neuter forms are used to refer to situations, ideas, or things that
 are abstract, general, or unidentified. The neuter pronouns are equivalent to the English *this* or *that* (*matter, business; thing, stuff*).

—¿Qué crees de **eso**?   *"What do you think about that*
      (matter, issue)?"
—Creo que es un problema   *"I think it is a problem for the*
 para el presidente del   *president of the Club Atlético."*
 Club Atlético.

—¿Qué es **esto**?   *"What is this* (thing, stuff)?"
—No sé.   *"I don't know."*

In Spanish-speaking
countries, athletic
clubs sponsor teams
of all different types
of sports for both
men and women.

Vamos a practicar

Complete the following sentences with the Spanish equivalent of the pronouns in parentheses.

1. El presidente del club quiere este coche y _____ (*that one*).
2. Necesitamos esa pelota y _____ (*that one [over there]*).
3. Compramos esos patines y _____ (*these*).
4. Recibimos este periódico y _____ (*those*).
5. ¿Estudia Ud. esta lección o _____ (*that one*)?
6. ¿Habla Ud. con este señor o con _____ (*that one [over there]*)?
7. ¿Prefieren ellos estas mesas de madera o _____ (*those [over there]*)?
8. ¿Va Ud. a leer este libro o _____ (*those*)?
9. Deseo aquellas mochilas y _____ (*these*).
10. ¿Van Uds. a comprar esa raqueta o _____ (*this one*)?
11. Ellas no saben qué es _____ (*this*).
12. ¿Para quién es _____ (*that*)?

④ DIRECT AND INDIRECT OBJECT PRONOUNS USED TOGETHER

Pronombres de complemento directo e indirecto usados juntos

When both an indirect object pronoun and a direct object pronoun are used in the same sentence, the indirect object pronoun always appears first.

D.O.

Ana   me   da   la pluma.   Ana   me   la   da.

I.O.

—¿Cuándo me das el dinero?   *"When are you giving me the money?"*
—**Te lo** doy[1] mañana.   *"I'll give it to you tomorrow."*

■ With an infinitive, the pronouns may be placed either before the main verb or attached to the infinitive.

I.O. D.O.

Ana   me   la   va a dar.

Ana   va a **dármela**.[2]

I.O. D.O.

---

[1]Remember that the present indicative is frequently used in Spanish to express future time.
[2]See Appendix A for rules governing the use of accent marks in Spanish.

—Necesito la página deportiva   *"I need the sports page that*
que tiene el artículo sobre   *has the article about **jai alai.***
el jai alai. ¿Puedes prestár**mela**?   *Can you lend it to me?"*
—Sí, **te la** puedo prestar.   *"Yes, I can lend it to you."*

Jai alai, of Basque origin, is a very fast, dynamic, and dangerous sport. The players use a very hard ball, which they throw against the wall, using a glove which has a long, curved basket.

■ With the present progressive, the pronouns can be placed either before the conjugated verb or attached to the present participle.

I.O. D.O.

Ana   te   lo   está diciendo.
Ana   está diciéndotelo. [1]
                I.O.   D.O.

■ If both pronouns begin with **l,** the indirect object pronoun (**le** or **les**) is changed to **se.**

D.O.

Ana   le   da   la pluma.   Ana   se   la   da.
                I.O.

■ For clarification, it is sometimes necessary to specify the person(s) to whom the indirect object pronoun refers: **a él, a ella, a Ud., a Uds., a ellos, a ellas, a José,** etc.

—¿**Le** vas a regalar los   *"Are you going to give the skis*
esquíes **a él** o **a ella**?   *to him or to her?"*
—**Se los** voy a regalar **a ella.**   *"I'm going to give them to her."*

—¿Uds. **les** mandan las cartas   *"Do you send the letters to them*
a ellas o **a ellos**?   *(fem.) or to them (masc.)?"*
—**Se las** mandamos **a ellos.**   *"We send them to them (masc.)."*

Vamos a practicar

Quiz

A Mom is always doing things for the family. Explain what she does, using the information provided.

MODELO   **Yo** quiero **una mochila.** (comprar)
Mamá **me la** compra.

---

[1]See Appendix A for rules governing the use of accent marks in Spanish.

1. **Papá** quiere **café.** (servir)
2. **Nosotros** necesitamos **dinero.** (dar)
3. **Tú** quieres **los periódicos.** (traer)
4. **Yo** quiero **una raqueta.** (prestar)
5. **Mis hijos** necesitan **toallas.** (comprar)
6. **Papá** quiere **la página deportiva.** (traer)
7. **Uds.** necesitan **la bolsa de dormir.** (dar)
8. **Ud.** quiere comer **comida mexicana.** (hacer)

B You keep changing your mind when someone asks you a question. First you say "yes" and then you say "no." Substitute pronouns for the boldface nouns.

MODELO   —¿Me compra Ud. **la mochila?**
       —Sí, se la compro.
       —No, no se la compro.

1. ¿Me presta Ud. **sus patines?**
2. ¿Me compra Ud. **la tienda de campaña?**
3. ¿Les paga Ud. **los pasajes** a ellos?
4. ¿Está Ud. pidiéndole **el periódico** a Inés?
5. ¿Nos va a traer Ud. **los esquíes?**
6. ¿Le vas a regalar **la raqueta de tenis** a tu tía?

C With a partner, take turns volunteering to do everything for everybody. Follow the model.

MODELO   Tú no puedes comprar los patines.
       Yo te los compro.

1. Mario no tiene tiempo para buscar la información.
2. Mi padre no puede traer el periódico.
3. Los chicos no pueden mandarle la mochila a Pepe.
4. Elba no puede prestarle la tienda de campaña a Carlos.
5. Tú no puedes conseguir las entradas para el partido de jai alai.

Palabras y más palabras   Complete the following dialogues with words from the lesson vocabulary.

1. —¿Quieres ir a _____ con nosotros?
   —Sí, pero no tengo esquíes.
   —¿Quieres ir a patinar?
   —Sí, pero no tengo _____.

2. —¿Qué te _____ falta para jugar al tenis?

—Una _____ y una _____.

3. —¿Qué está leyendo el entrenador?

—La _____ deportiva.

4. —¿Quieres montar a _____?

—No, prefiero montar en _____.

5. —¿Por qué tomas aspirinas?

—Porque me _____ la cabeza.

6. —Necesito tu mochila. ¿Me la puedes _____?

—No te la presto. Te la _____.

7. —¿Quién es ese _____?

—Es mi hijo Carlitos.

8. —¿Qué le vas a _____ a Sergio?

—_____ prefiere ir a bucear o ir a _____ al tenis.

En estas situaciones What would you say in the following situations? What might the other person say?

1. You and a friend are planning to go camping and to go play tennis. Mention what items you need.

2. You are telling your new roommate what outdoor activities you like. Mention at least four.

3. You are interviewing a student from the Dominican Republic. Mention several sports and ask him/her if he/she likes them.

4. Mention to a friend several items that you need and ask him/her if he/she can lend each one of them to you.

PARA ESCUCHAR Y ENTENDER

The following material is to be used with the In-Text Audio CDs.

I. Práctica

2–27

A ¿Pedir o preguntar?

Answer the questions, using the cues provided. Repeat the correct answer after the speaker's confirmation. Listen to the model.

MODELO   —¿Qué te pide Jorge? (la pelota)

—Me pide la pelota.

1. (mi dirección)

2. (500 dólares)

3. (no, a mi papá)
4. (si pueden ir al cine)
5. (la página deportiva)

B Me gusta más...
Repeat each statement or question, replacing **preferir** with **gusta más** or
gustan más and the appropriate indirect object pronoun. Repeat the correct answer after the speaker's confirmation. Listen to the model.

2–28

> **MODELO** Yo prefiero la bicicleta gris.
> **Me gusta más la bicicleta gris.**

C Los adjetivos demostrativos
Give the Spanish equivalent of the demonstrative adjective that agrees
with each noun mentioned by the speaker. Repeat the correct answer after
the speaker's confirmation. Listen to the model.

2–29

> **MODELO** this / these
> **esta raqueta**

1. this / these
2. that / those
3. that (*over there*) / those (*over there*)

D Cambia las frases
Repeat each sentence, changing the direct object to the corresponding
direct object pronoun. Make all the necessary changes in the sentence.
Repeat the correct answer after the speaker's confirmation. Listen to
the model.

2–30

> **MODELO** Le traen **el periódico.**
> **Se lo traen.**

II. ¿Qué dicen?

1 ¿Lógico o ilógico?
The speaker will make some statements. Circle **L (lógico)** if the statement
is logical and **I (ilógico)** if it is illogical. The speaker will verify your
response.

2–31

1. L   I   3. L   I   5. L   I   7. L   I
2. L   I   4. L   I   6. L   I   8. L   I

2 ¿Verdadero o falso?
Listen carefully to the dialogue. Listen to it at least twice.

2–32

(Diálogo 1)

2–33   Now the speaker will make some statements about the dialogue you just heard. Tell whether each statement is true (**verdadero**) or false (**falso**). The speaker will confirm the correct answer.

3 Rodolfo y Graciela
Listen carefully to the dialogue. Listen to it at least twice.

2–34

(Diálogo 2)

2–35   Now the speaker will ask you some questions about the dialogue you just heard. Answer each question, omitting the subject. The speaker will confirm the correct answer. Repeat the correct answer.

OBJECTIVES

Structures
1 Possessive pronouns
2 Reflexive constructions
3 Command forms: **Ud.** and **Uds.**
4 Uses of object pronouns with command forms

Communication
You will learn vocabulary related to daily routine and personal grooming.

Country highlighted: Venezuela

Mar Caribe

TRINIDAD
Y TOBAGO

Maracaibo   Caracas

Lago   Barquisimeto
Maracaibo

Río Orinoco

VENEZUELA   GUYANA

COLOMBIA

Maroa

0   150   300 Km.

0   150   300 Mi.

BRASIL

The name of this country means "little Venecia" because the Spaniards were reminded of Venice by the way the Indians built their houses on stakes on the shores of Lake Maracaibo.

Venezuela is a tropical country situated in the north of South America. Its territory, as big as the states of Texas and Utah, is divided into four geographic regions: the west, which has the Andes Mountains; the northern zone, where the larger cities are found; the east, which is a great plain, and the south, with high plateaus and jungles. In this last region are the famous Angel Falls, which are the highest waterfalls in the world, and the major tourist attraction in the country.

Venezuela's main export is oil, which represents 70 percent of the country's revenue.

Caracas, Venezuela's capital, is a city of contrasts where the ultra-modern mixes with the old, and luxury mixes with poverty. Simón Bolívar, the Liberator of five South American countries, was born in Caracas.

RESOURCES

Wherever you see the following icons additional resources are available:

 Go to **www.college.hmco.com/languages/spanish/students/** for additional
Internet practice on the topic.

 Go to the **Video Grammar Tutor** for help with understanding the grammar
Student CD-ROM topic at hand.

 Go to the **In-Text Audio CDs** for more practice.

VOCABULARIO

Audio

COGNADOS

el champú
generalmente
impaciente
el momento
el parque
el perfume
la terraza

NOMBRES

el baño   *bathroom*
el botiquín   *medicine cabinet*
el cepillo   *brush*
el dormitorio   *bedroom*
el espejo   *mirror*
la máquina de afeitar   *razor*
la medianoche   *midnight*
el pantalón, los pantalones   *pants*
el peine   *comb*
el pelo   *hair*
la peluquería   *beauty salon,*
   beauty parlor
el (la) peluquero(a)   *hairdresser*
la tarjeta   *card*
la tarjeta de crédito   *credit card*
la tintorería   *dry cleaners*
la ventana   *window*
el vestido   *dress*

VERBOS

acordarse (o:ue) (de)   *to remember*
acostarse (o:ue)   *to go to bed*
atender (e:ie)   *to wait on, to attend to*
bañar(se)   *to bathe (oneself)*
cortar(se)   *to cut (oneself)*
doblar   *to turn*
lavar(se)   *to wash (oneself)*
levantarse   *to get up*
llamarse   *to be named*
probarse (o:ue)   *to try on*
sentarse (e:ie)   *to sit down*

ADJETIVOS

corto(a)   *short*
querido(a)   *dear*

OTRAS PALABRAS Y EXPRESIONES

a la derecha   *to the right*
a la izquierda   *to the left*
ahora mismo   *right now*
antes de   *before*
lavarse la cabeza   *to wash one's hair*
seguir derecho   *to continue straight*
   ahead

1 POSSESSIVE PRONOUNS
Los pronombres posesivos

Singular		Plural		
Masculine	**Feminine**	**Masculine**	**Feminine**	
el mío	**la mía**	**los míos**	**las mías**	*mine*
				yours (familiar)
el tuyo	**la tuya**	**los tuyos**	**las tuyas**	*his*
el suyo	**la suya**	**los suyos**	**las suyas**	*hers*
				yours (formal)
el nuestro	**la nuestra**	**los nuestros**	**las nuestras**	*ours*
el vuestro	**la vuestra**	**los vuestros**	**las vuestras**	*yours (fam.)*
el suyo	**la suya**	**los suyos**	**las suyas**	*theirs, yours (formal)*

The possessive pronouns in Spanish agree in gender and number with the thing possessed. They are generally used with the definite article.

—Aquí están las máquinas de afeitar de ellos. ¿Dónde están **las nuestras**?
—**Las nuestras** están en el dormitorio.

"Here are their razors. Where are ours?"

"Ours are in the bedroom."

—Tus pantalones están aquí. ¿Dónde están **los míos**?
—**Los tuyos** están en la tintorería.

"Your trousers are here. Where are mine?"
"Yours are at the dry cleaners."

—Mi peine está aquí. ¿Dónde está **el suyo**?
—**El mío** está en el baño.

"My comb is here. Where is yours?"

"Mine is in the bathroom."

—Mi peluquero es de Caracas. ¿De dónde es **el tuyo**?
—**El mío** es de Maracaibo.

"My hairdresser is from Caracas. Where is yours from?"
"Mine is from Maracaibo."

■ After the verb **ser,** the definite article is frequently omitted.

—¿Es **tuyo** este perfume?
—Sí, este perfume es **mío,** pero ése es **tuyo.**

"Is this perfume yours?"
"Yes, this perfume is mine, but that one is yours."

American credit cards such as Visa, MasterCard, or American Express are accepted in most big hotels, stores, and restaurants in Hispanic cities.

—¿Esta tarjeta de crédito **es suya,** Sr. Smith?
—Sí, **es mía,** gracias.

"Is this credit card yours, Mr. Smith?"
"Yes, it's mine, thanks."

- Since the third person forms of the possessive pronouns (**el suyo, la suya, los suyos, las suyas**) could be ambiguous, they may be replaced for clarification by the following.

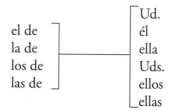

el de
la de
los de
las de

Ud.
él
ella
Uds.
ellos
ellas

—Estos cepillos y estos peines son de Marta y de Arturo, ¿no?
—Bueno, los cepillos son **de ella,** pero los peines son **de él.**

"These brushes and these combs are Marta's and Arturo's, right?"
"Well, the brushes are hers, but the combs are his."

Quiz

Vamos a practicar

A Supply the correct possessive pronouns and read the sentences aloud. Follow the models.

MODELO Yo tengo una tarjeta. Es _____.
Yo tengo una tarjeta. Es **mía.**

Juan tiene una tarjeta. Es _____. (Es _____.)
Juan tiene una tarjeta. Es **suya.** (Es **de él.**)

1. Tú tienes un cepillo. Es _____.

2. Juan tiene una entrada. Es _____. (Es _____.)

3. Nosotros tenemos una tarjeta de crédito. Es _____.

4. Ud. tiene unos peines. Son _____. (Son _____.)

5. Yo tengo una máquina de afeitar. Es _____.

6. Uds. tienen dos bicicletas. Son _____. (Son _____.)

7. Yo tengo unos pantalones. Son _____.

8. Lucía tiene tres hijos. Son _____. (Son _____.)

B Interview a classmate, using the following questions. When you have finished, switch roles.

1. Mi mejor amigo vive en _____. ¿Dónde vive el tuyo?

2. Mis padres son de _____. ¿De dónde son los tuyos?

3. Nuestros abuelos son de _____. ¿De dónde son los de Uds.?

4. Yo tengo mis tarjetas de crédito en el dormitorio. ¿Tú tienes las tuyas?

5. Mis libros de español están aquí. ¿Dónde están los del (de la) profesor(a)? ¿Dónde están los tuyos?

6. Tu pantalón (vestido) es _____. ¿De qué color es el mío?

2 REFLEXIVE CONSTRUCTIONS
Las construcciones reflexivas

Reflexive pronouns

> A **reflexive construction**, such as *I introduce myself*, consists of a reflexive pronoun and a verb. Reflexive pronouns refer to the same person who is the subject of the sentence.

Subjects	Reflexive Pronouns	
yo	**me**	*myself, to / for myself*
tú	**te**	*yourself, to / for yourself* (**tú** form)
nosotros	**nos**	*ourselves, to / for ourselves*
vosotros	**os**	*yourselves, to / for yourselves*
Ud.		*yourself, to / for yourself*
Uds.		*yourselves, to / for yourselves*
él		*himself, to / for himself*
ella	**se**	*herself, to / for herself*
		itself, to / for itself
ellos, ellas		*themselves, to / for themselves*

- Note that, with the exception of **se,** reflexive pronouns have the same forms as the direct and indirect object pronouns.

- The third person singular and plural **se** is invariable.

■ Reflexive pronouns are positioned in the sentence in the same manner as object pronouns. They are placed in front of a conjugated verb.

Yo **me** baño a las ocho.   *I bathe at eight.*

They may be attached to an infinitive or to a present participle.

Yo voy a bañar**me** a las ocho.   *I'm going to bathe at eight.*
Yo estoy bañándo**me**.[1]   *I'm bathing.*

■ In Spanish most verbs can be made reflexive with the aid of a reflexive pronoun to indicate that they act upon the subject.

Julia le prueba el
vestido a su hija.

Julia se prueba
el vestido.

Reflexive verbs

■ Reflexive verbs are conjugated in the following manner.

lavarse *(to wash oneself, to wash up)*	
Yo **me lavo.**	*I wash (myself).*
Tú **te lavas.**	*You wash (yourself—fam.).*
Ud. **se lava.**	*You wash (yourself—formal).*
Él **se lava.**	*He washes (himself).*
Ella **se lava.**	*She washes (herself).*
Nosotros **nos lavamos.**	*We wash (ourselves).*
Vosotros **os laváis.**	*You wash (yourselves).*
Uds. **se lavan.**	*You wash (yourselves).*
Ellos **se lavan.**	*They (masc.) wash (themselves).*
Ellas **se lavan.**	*They (fem.) wash (themselves).*

[1]See Appendix A for rules governing the use of accent marks in Spanish.

■ Some commonly used reflexive verbs are listed below.

acostarse (o:ue)   *to go to bed, to lie down*
afeitarse   *to shave*
bañarse   *to bathe*
despertarse (e:ie)   *to wake up*
levantarse   *to get up*
sentarse (e:ie)   *to sit down*
vestirse (e:i)   *to get dressed*

—¿A qué hora **se levanta**
Ud., Srta. López?
—Generalmente **me levanto** a
las ocho, pero no **me
acuesto** hasta la medianoche.

*"At what time do you get up,
Miss López?"*
*"I generally get up at eight o'clock,
but I don't go to bed until
midnight."*

■ Some verbs change their meaning when they are used with reflexive
pronouns.

acostar (o:ue) *to put to bed*	**acostarse** *to go to bed*
dormir (o:ue) *to sleep*	**dormirse** *to fall asleep*
ir *to go*	**irse** *to leave, to go away*
levantar *to lift, to raise*	**levantarse** *to get up*
llamar *to call*	**llamarse** *to be named*
probar (o:ue) *to try, to taste*	**probarse** *to try on*
poner *to put*	**ponerse** *to put on (e.g., clothing)*
quitar *to take away, to remove*	**quitarse** *to take off (e.g., clothing)*

■ Notice the use of the reflexive in the following sentences.

—¿Por qué no **te acuestas,** querido?
—Primero voy a **acostar** a los chicos.

"Why don't you go to bed, dear?"
*"First I'm going to put the children
to bed."*

—Voy a **llamar** al hermano
de Teresa antes de salir.[1]
—¿Cómo **se llama** él?
—**Se llama** Enrique,
pero le dicen Quique.

*"I'm going to call Teresa's
brother before going out."*
"What's his name?"
*"His name is Enrique, but
they call him Quique."*

Nicknames are very
popular in Hispanic
countries. Some names
have specific nick-
names: Francisco: **Paco;**
José: **Pepe;** Dolores:
Lola; Guadalupe: **Lupe.**

---

[1]The infinitive, not the *-ing* form, is used after a preposition in Spanish.

■ Some verbs are *always* used with reflexive pronouns in Spanish.

acordarse (o:ue) (de)   *to remember*
quejarse (de)   *to complain*

Notice that the use of a reflexive pronoun does not necessarily imply a reflexive action.

—¿**Se acuerda** Ud. de Rosita?   *"Do you remember Rosita?"*
—Sí, **me acuerdo** de ella.   *"Yes, I remember her."*

Vamos a practicar

Quiz

A Describe what these people do, using the present indicative or the infinitive of the verbs in parentheses.

1. Elena _____ (probarse) el vestido.
2. Ella _____ (acostarse) y Ud. _____ (acostar) a los niños.
3. Carlos _____ (bañarse) y Luis _____ (vestirse).
4. Tú siempre _____ (dormirse) en la clase.
5. Nosotros nunca _____ (quejarse) de nada.
6. Yo voy a _____ (probarse) los pantalones.
7. Debes _____ (bañarse) antes de _____ (vestirse).
8. Nosotros vamos a _____ (sentarse) aquí.
9. ¿Por qué no _____ (afeitarse), querido?
10. Pepito, tienes que _____ (lavarse) las manos.

B Interview a classmate, using the following questions. When you are finished, switch roles.

1. ¿A qué hora te acuestas generalmente?
2. ¿Te duermes en la clase?
3. ¿A qué hora te levantas?
4. ¿Siempre te despiertas temprano?
5. ¿Qué te vas a poner para salir mañana?
6. ¿Te acuerdas del número de teléfono de tus amigos?
7. ¿Siempre pruebas la comida antes de servirla?
8. ¿Uds. se quejan de sus profesores?

C Describe what you do during a typical day from the time you wake up to the time you go to bed.

Summary of Personal Pronouns

Subject	Direct Object	Indirect Object	Reflexive	Object of Prepositions
yo	me	me	me	mí
tú	te	te	te	ti
Ud. (*fem.*)	la			Ud.
Ud. (*masc.*)	lo	le	se	Ud.
él	lo			él
ella	la			ella
nosotros	nos	nos	nos	nosotros
vosotros	os	os	os	vosotros
Uds. (*fem.*)	las			Uds.
Uds. (*masc.*)	los	les	se	Uds.
ellos	los			ellos
ellas	las			ellas

③ COMMAND FORMS: *Ud.* AND *Uds.*

El imperativo: *Ud.* y *Uds.*

> Command form the form of a verb used to give an order or a direction: **Go! Come back! Turn to the right.**

To form the command for **Ud.** and **Uds.**,[1] drop the **-o** of the first person singular of the present indicative and add the following endings to the stem.

-ar verbs: **-e** (Ud.) and **-en** (Uds.)

-er verbs: **-a** (Ud.) and **-an** (Uds.)

-ir verbs: **-a** (Ud.) and **-an** (Uds.)

ATENCIÓN: Notice that the endings for the -er **and** -ir **verbs are the same.**

---

[1]The **tú** form will be studied in **Lección 11.**

Infinitive	First Person Present Ind.	Stem	Commands Ud.	Uds.
hablar	Yo hablo	habl-	hable	hablen
comer	Yo como	com-	coma	coman
abrir	Yo abro	abr-	abra	abran
cerrar	Yo cierro	cierr-	cierre	cierren
volver	Yo vuelvo	vuelv-	vuelva	vuelvan
pedir	Yo pido	pid-	pida	pidan
decir	Yo digo	dig-	diga	digan
hacer	Yo hago	hag-	haga	hagan
traducir	Yo traduzco	traduzc-	traduzca	traduzcan

—¿Con quién debo hablar? "With whom must I speak?"
—**Hable** con el peluquero. "Speak with the hairdresser."

—¿Vengo por la mañana o por la tarde? "Shall I come in the morning or in the afternoon?"
—**Venga** por la mañana y **traiga** a su hija. "Come in the morning and bring your daughter."

—¿Cierro la puerta? "Shall I close the door?"
—No, no **cierre** la puerta. "No, don't close the door. Close the window, please."
Cierre la ventana, por favor.

—Para ir a la peluquería, ¿sigo derecho o doblo a la derecha? "To go to the beauty parlor, shall I continue straight ahead or shall I turn right?"
—**Doble** a la izquierda. La peluquería está en el edificio Bolívar, en la planta baja. "Turn left. The beauty parlor is in the Bolívar Building, on the first (ground) floor."

In Caracas, as in most Hispanic cities, buildings with offices, stores or other types of businesses on the ground floor often have apartments above.

■ The command forms of the following verbs are irregular.

	dar	estar	ser	ir
Ud.	dé	esté	sea	vaya
Uds.	den	estén	sean	vayan

—¿Podemos ir solas al parque?	*"Can we go to the park alone?"*
—No, no **vayan** solas.	*"No, don't go alone. Go with your*
Vayan con sus padres.	*parents."*
—¡Tiene que atenderme	*"You must wait on me right now!"*
ahora mismo!	
—Un momento, señora.	*"One moment, madam. Don't be*
¡No **sea** impaciente!	*impatient!"*

Vamos a practicar

A Answer the questions, using the cues provided.

MODELO ¿Hablo con el peluquero? (no, dueño)
—No, **hable** con el dueño.

—¿Tenemos que hablar con el peluquero? (no, dueño)
—No, **hablen** con el dueño.

1. ¿Vamos a la peluquería mañana? (no, hoy)
2. ¿Tenemos que estar allí a las diez? (no, a las nueve)
3. Para ir a la peluquería, ¿tengo que seguir derecho? (no, doblar en la calle Lima)
4. ¿Doblo a la derecha? (no, izquierda)
5. ¿Desayunamos antes de salir? (no, en la cafetería)
6. ¿Qué perfume compro para Estela? (Chanel número cinco)
7. ¿Qué traemos para la cena? (pollo frito)
8. ¿A qué hora volvemos? (a las tres)
9. ¿Cerramos las ventanas antes de salir? (no, la puerta)

B With a partner, prepare a list of ten commands (five affirmative and five negative) that a professor would give to students.

4 USES OF OBJECT PRONOUNS WITH COMMAND FORMS
Uso de los pronombres con el imperativo

Affirmative commands With all direct *affirmative* commands, the object pronouns are placed *after* the verb and are attached to it, forming a single word.

—¿Dónde pongo el champú?	*"Where shall I put the shampoo?"*
—**Póngalo**[1] en el botiquín.	*"Put it in the medicine cabinet."*

---

[1]See Appendix A for rules governing the use of accent marks in Spanish.

—¿Dónde sirvo el café?	*"Where shall I serve the coffee?"*
—**Sírvalo** en la terraza.	*"Serve it on the terrace."*
—¿Qué le doy a la chica?	*"What shall I give the girl?"*
—**Déle** el espejo.	*"Give her the mirror."*
—¿Abrimos la puerta?	*"Shall we open the door?"*
—Sí, **ábranla.**	*"Yes, open it."*
—¿Se lo digo a Ana?	*"Shall I tell (it to) Ana?"*
—Sí, **dígaselo** a Ana.	*"Yes, tell (it to) Ana."*
—¿Dónde me siento?	*"Where shall I sit?"*
—**Siéntese** aquí.	*"Sit here."*
—¿Le corto el pelo?	*"Shall I cut your hair (for you)?"*
—Sí, **córtemelo,** por favor.	*"Yes, cut it (for me), please."*
—¿Adónde llevamos a las chicas?	*"Where shall we take the girls?"*
—**Llévenlas** a la plaza. Hoy hay un concierto.	*"Take them to the plaza. There is a concert today."*

Generally Hispanic cities and towns are built around a plaza, which is the social and geographic center of the city. Important government buildings, restaurants, stores, and so on are found around the plaza.

Vamos a practicar

A Answer the following questions, using affirmative commands.

MODELO   —El peluquero necesita el champú. ¿Lo traigo ahora?
           —Sí, **tráigalo.**

1. Mi amiga quiere ir a la peluquería. ¿La llevo?
2. Las ventanas están abiertas (*open*). ¿Las cierro?
3. Tienen un disco compacto (*CD*) que me gusta. ¿Lo compro?
4. Los niños están durmiendo. ¿Los despierto?
5. La señora quiere el espejo. ¿Se lo doy?
6. Mi hermana quiere un perfume. ¿Se lo compro?
7. La peluquera necesita los peines. ¿Se los traigo?
8. Mis amigos necesitan mis cintas (*tapes*). ¿Se las presto?

B Answer the following questions, using the appropriate pronouns and the cues provided.

MODELO   —¿Cuándo traemos las maletas? (ahora mismo)
          —**Tráiganlas** ahora mismo.

1. ¿Dónde servimos el desayuno? (en la terraza)
2. ¿Compramos pescado para el almuerzo? (sí)
3. ¿Cuándo llamamos a nuestros amigos? (esta tarde)
4. ¿A qué hora nos levantamos? (a las siete)
5. ¿Dónde nos bañamos? (en este baño)
6. ¿Nos ponemos los pantalones blancos? (sí)
7. ¿Nos lavamos las manos antes de comer? (sí)
8. ¿A qué hora nos acostamos hoy? (a la medianoche)

Negative commands With all *negative* commands, the object pronouns are placed in front of the verb.

—¿Nos levantamos ahora?	*"Shall we get up now?"*
—No, **no se levanten** todavía.	*"No, don't get up yet."*
—¿Sirvo los refrescos?	*"Shall I serve the sodas?"*
—No, **no los sirva** todavía.	*"No, don't serve them yet."*
—¿Me lavo la cabeza con este champú?	*"Shall I wash my hair with this shampoo?"*
—No, no **se la lave** con ese champú. No es muy bueno.	*"No, don't wash it with that shampoo. It's not very good."*
—¿Le corto el pelo?	*"Shall I cut your hair (for you)?"*
—No, **no me lo corte.** No me gusta el pelo corto.	*"No, don't cut it (for me). I don't like short hair."*

Quiz

Vamos a practicar

A Answer the following questions with negative commands. Use the appropriate pronouns.

MODELO   —¿Atiendo **a la señora** ahora?
          —No, no **la atienda** todavía.

1. ¿Traemos **el champú**?
2. ¿Llevamos **a Mirta** a la peluquería?
3. ¿**Me** lavo **la cabeza** ahora?

4. ¿Pongo **el perfume** en el botiquín?
5. ¿Le traigo **el espejo** a Ud.?
6. ¿Le doy **el peine** a Roberto?
7. ¿Llevamos **los pantalones** a la tintorería?
8. ¿Esperamos **a Rosa** un momento?
9. **¿Les** decimos que son muy impacientes?
10. **¿Nos** acostamos ahora?

B Say what Mrs. Rodríguez asked her hairdresser to do by transforming the infinitives in the following instructions to command forms.

Lavarle la cabeza, pero **no usar** el champú que usa siempre. **Cortarle** el pelo, pero **no cortárselo** muy corto. **Traerle** una revista y **darle** una taza (*cup*) de café pero **no ponerle** leche al café.

C You and a partner have a group of teenagers coming to stay with you for a few days. Use **Uds.** commands to prepare a list of ten to fifteen things they should and shouldn't do.

Palabras y más palabras Match the questions in column **A** with the answers in column **B**.

A	B
1. ¿Cómo vas a pagar? _____	a. Sí, y me acuesto a la medianoche.
2. ¿Eva está en su dormitorio? _____	b. Ahora mismo.
3. ¿Cómo te llamas? _____	c. Sí, cuando me baño.
4. ¿Doblo a la derecha o a la izquierda? _____	d. Sí, necesito cortarme el pelo.
5. ¿Cuándo salen? _____	e. Marisol Villalobos.
6. ¿Dónde está el champú? _____	f. No, los voy a llevar a la tintorería.
7. ¿Te levantas temprano? _____	g. El pantalón negro.
8. ¿Vas a la peluquería? _____	h. Sí, está durmiendo.
9. ¿Qué vas a hacer antes de comer? _____	i. No, no le gusta el pelo corto.
10. ¿Te lavas la cabeza? _____	j. Con tarjeta de crédito.
11. ¿Vas a lavar los pantalones? _____	k. En la terraza.
12. ¿Qué te vas a poner? _____	l. Siga derecho.
13. ¿Dónde sirven el almuerzo? _____	m. Un momento. ¡No sea impaciente!
14. ¡Tengo mucha prisa! ¿Puede venir? _____	n. Me voy a lavar las manos.
15. ¿Le vas a cortar el pelo a Rita? _____	o. En el botiquín.

En estas situaciones What would you say in the following situations?

1. You have a new roommate. Ask him/her what time he/she gets up and goes to bed, and whether he/she bathes in the morning or in the evening.
2. Tell your hairdresser (barber) to cut your hair and shampoo (wash) it (for you).
3. You tell a group of people to call the supervisor right now and to be at your office at ten.
4. You are asking for directions. Ask if you should turn to the right or to the left or if you should continue straight ahead.

PARA ESCUCHAR Y ENTENDER

The following material is to be used with the In-Text Audio CDs.

I. Práctica

A Los pronombres posesivos
Answer the questions, using the cues provided. Repeat the correct answer after the speaker's confirmation. Listen to the model.

2-36

> **MODELO** —Mi maleta es verde. ¿Y la de Eva? (blanca)
> —**La suya es blanca.**

1. (grande)
2. (aquí)
3. (azules)

4. (también)
5. (en Honduras)
6. (de Guatemala)

B Las construcciones reflexivas
Answer the questions, using the cues provided. Repeat the correct answer after the speaker's confirmation. Listen to the model.

2-37

> **MODELO** —¿A qué hora te levantas tú? (a las seis)
> —**Me levanto a las seis.**

1. (no, tarde)
2. (en el dormitorio)
3. (no, por la noche)

4. (aquí)
5. (no, de nada)
6. (sí)

C El imperativo: **Ud.** y **Uds.**

Change the following statements to commands. Repeat the correct answer after the speaker's confirmation. Listen to the model.

MODELO   **Debe hablar** con el peluquero.
Hable con el peluquero.

II. ¿Qué dicen?

1 ¿Lógico o ilógico?

The speaker will make some statements. Circle **L (lógico)** if the statement is logical and **I (ilógico)** if it is illogical. The speaker will verify your response.

1. L I   3. L I   5. L I   7. L I   9. L I
2. L I   4. L I   6. L I   8. L I   10. L I

2 El día de Carlos

Listen carefully to the narration, in which Carlos will tell you what he does every day. Listen to it at least twice.

(Narración)

Now the speaker will make some statements about the narration you just heard. Tell whether each statement is true (**verdadero**) or false (**falso**). The speaker will confirm the correct answer.

3 En la oficina

Listen carefully to the dialogue. Listen to it at least twice.

(Diálogo 1)

Now the speaker will make some statements about the dialogue you just heard. Tell whether each statement is true (**verdadero**) or false (**falso**). The speaker will confirm the correct answer.

4 Pilar y Nora

Listen carefully to the dialogue. Listen to it at least twice.

2–44

(Diálogo 2)

2-45   Now the speaker will ask you some questions about the dialogue you just heard. Answer each question, omitting the subject. The speaker will confirm the correct answer. Repeat the correct answer.

LECCIÓN
10

OBJECTIVES

Structures
1. The preterit of regular verbs
2. The preterit of **ser, ir,** and **dar**
3. Uses of **por** and **para**
4. Seasons of the year and weather expressions

Communication
You will learn vocabulary pertaining to housework, shopping, and the weather.

Country highlighted: Colombia

Colombia, the only nation named in honor of Christopher Columbus, is the fourth-largest South American country. Its area is a little larger than that of California and Texas combined.

The cultural heritage of colonial Spain is more noticeable in Colombia than in any other Latin American country. It's said that the best Spanish is spoken in this country.

As in many other Latin American countries, soccer is the favorite sport, but bullfights are also popular.

Agriculture plays a very important role in the economy of Colombia. Among its main exports are flowers, bananas, and coffee. Colombian coffee is one of the best in the world. Another important export is emeralds. More than 90 percent of the world's emeralds come from Colombia.

Bogotá, the capital, is known as the "Athens of America" due to its many cultural institutions.

RESOURCES

Wherever you see the following icons additional resources are available:

Internet

Go to **www.college.hmco.com/languages/spanish/students/** for additional practice on the topic.

Student CD-ROM

Go to the **Video Grammar Tutor** for help with understanding the grammar topic at hand.

Go to the **In-Text Audio CDs** for more practice.

VOCABULARIO

COGNADOS

el límite
la milla
el suéter
el tomate
la velocidad

NOMBRES

el abrigo   *coat*
la aspiradora   *vacuum cleaner*
la carnicería   *meat market*
la cocina   *kitchen*
el (la) criado(a)   *servant*
la escoba   *broom*
el impermeable   *raincoat*
el invierno   *winter*
la lata, el bote *(Méx.)*   *can*
la lavadora   *washing machine*
la lluvia   *rain*
la niebla   *fog*
el otoño   *fall, autumn*
el paraguas   *umbrella*
la puerta de atrás   *back door*
la ropa   *clothes, clothing*
la salsa   *sauce*
el supermercado   *supermarket*
los tallarines, los espaguetis   *spaghetti*
el verano   *summer*

VERBOS

ayudar   *to help*
barrer   *to sweep*
cocinar   *to cook*
entrar   *to enter, to come in*
limpiar   *to clean*
llover (o:ue)   *to rain*
nevar (e:ie)   *to snow*
pasar (por)   *to go by*
preparar   *to prepare*

ADJETIVOS

nublado(a)   *cloudy*
pasado(a)   *past, last*

OTRAS PALABRAS Y EXPRESIONES

además   *besides*
anoche   *last night*
ayer   *yesterday*
¿Cuál es el límite de velocidad?
   What's the speed limit?
por hora   *per hour*
los (las) dos   *both*
¿Qué tiempo hace hoy?   *What's the*
   weather like today?

 ❶ THE PRETERIT OF REGULAR VERBS
El pretérito de los verbos regulares

Spanish has two simple past tenses: the preterit and the imperfect. (The imperfect will be studied in **Lección 12.**) The preterit of regular verbs is formed by dropping the infinitive ending and adding the appropriate preterit ending to the verb stem, as follows. Note that the endings for **-er** and **-ir** verbs are identical.

-ar *Verbs*	-er *Verbs*	-ir *Verbs*
entrar (*to enter*)	**comer** (*to eat*)	**escribir** (*to write*)
stem: entr-	com-	escrib-
entré	comí	escribí
entraste	comiste	escribiste
entró	comió	escribió
entramos	comimos	escribimos
entrasteis	comisteis	escribísteis
entrasteis	comisteis	escribisteis

yo **entré**   *I entered; I did enter*
Ud. **comió**   *you ate; you did eat*
ellos **escribieron**   *they wrote; they did write*

- The preterit tense is used to refer to actions or states that the speaker views as completed in the past. Note that Spanish has no equivalent for the English auxiliary verb *did* in questions and negative sentences.

—¿Quién **cocinó** ayer?　　　　　"*Who cooked yesterday?*"
—Yo **cociné** y Pablo me **ayudó.**　"*I cooked, and Pablo helped me.*"
—¿Qué **comieron**?　　　　　　　"*What did you eat?*"
—**Comimos** tallarines.　　　　　"*We ate spaghetti.*"
—¿Uds. **prepararon** la salsa?　　"*Did you prepare the sauce?*"
—No, **abrimos** dos latas　　　　"*No, we opened two cans of tomato*
de salsa de tomate.　　　　　　*sauce.*"

—¿A qué hora **volvieron** tus　　"*What time did your parents come*
padres de Bogotá anoche?　　　*back from Bogotá last night?*"
—**Volvieron** a las once.　　　　"*They came back at eleven.*"

—¿A qué hora **llegaste** de la　　"*What time did you arrive from the*
universidad hoy?　　　　　　　*university today?*"
—**Llegué** a las ocho y　　　　　"*I arrived at eight and cleaned*
limpié mi cuarto.　　　　　　*my room.*"

Although certain activities and responsibilities are still considered by some to be performed exclusively by males or females, traditional patterns of behavior have changed in Latin America and Spain. Now most men and women work outside the home and share household tasks.

ATENCIÓN: -ar **and** -er **stem-changing verbs do not change stems in the preterit:** Yo *volví* anoche y *cerré* la puerta. **Verbs ending in** -gar, -car, **and** -zar **change** g **to** gu, c **to** qu, **and** z **to** c **before** é **in the first person of the preterit:** *pagar* → *pagué   buscar* → *busqué   empezar* → empecé.[1]

Vamos a practicar

Quiz

A Change the following description of Carmen's daily routine to say what happened yesterday, changing all verbs to the preterit.

Yo me <u>levanto</u> a las seis y me <u>baño</u>. <u>Salgo</u> de casa a las siete. Mi hermano y yo <u>desayunamos</u> en la cafetería. <u>Comemos</u> huevos y <u>bebemos</u> café. Mi hermano <u>trabaja</u> en la oficina y yo <u>estudio</u> en la biblioteca. Mis amigos <u>estudian</u> conmigo. Yo <u>vuelvo</u> a casa a las cinco y mi hermano <u>vuelve</u> a las seis. Yo me <u>acuesto</u> a las diez.

B Complete the following sentences with the preterit of the verbs in parentheses.

1. ¿Dónde _____ (aprender) Ud. a hablar español?

2. ¿Qué _____ (decidir) Uds. anoche? ¿Ir al concierto?

3. Yo no _____ (entender) su carta.

4. ¿Dónde _____ (comprar) tú esa bicicleta?

5. ¿_____ (Abrir) Ud. las puertas?

6. ¿Qué le _____ (preguntar) Ud. a su suegra?

7. ¿A qué hora _____ (pasar) tú por mi casa ayer?

8. Carmen y yo _____ (ayudar) a preparar la cena.

9. ¿Cuántas horas lo _____ (esperar) Uds.?

10. Yo _____ (llegar) al supermercado a las seis.

C Interview a classmate, using the following questions. When you have finished, switch roles.

1. ¿A qué hora te levantaste hoy?

2. ¿Desayunaste en tu casa?

3. ¿Quién preparó el desayuno?

4. ¿Qué bebiste en el desayuno?

---

[1]For other verbs with spelling changes, see Appendix B.

5. ¿Viste a tus amigos ayer?
6. ¿Tus amigos almorzaron contigo?
7. ¿Quién cocinó anoche en tu casa?
8. ¿Le escribiste a alguien ayer?
9. ¿A qué hora volviste a tu casa?
10. ¿A qué hora cenaron Uds.?
11. ¿Comieron tallarines con salsa de tomate?
12. ¿A qué hora te acostaste?

2 THE PRETERIT OF *SER, IR,* AND *DAR*
El pretérito de los verbos *ser, ir* y *dar*

The preterit forms of **ser, ir,** and **dar** are irregular. Note that **ser** and **ir** have the same forms.

ser (*to be*)	ir (*to go*)	dar (*to give*)
fui	fui	di
fuiste	fuiste	diste
fue	fue	dio
fuimos	fuimos	dimos
fuisteis	fuisteis	disteis
fueron	fueron	dieron

—¿Uds. **fueron** estudiantes del profesor Vargas el año pasado?
—Yo **fui** estudiante suyo pero mi hermano **fue** estudiante de la profesora Rojas.

"Were you professor Vargas's students last year?"
"I was his student, but my brother was professor Rojas's student."

—¿Tú **fuiste** a la **carnicería** anoche?
—No, Teresa y yo **fuimos** al supermercado.
—¡Ah, **viste** a Teresa! ¿Le **diste** la ropa para su hija?

—Sí, se la **di.**

"Did you go to the meat market last night?"
"No, Teresa and I went to the supermarket."
"Oh, you saw Teresa! Did you give her the clothing for her daughter?"
"Yes, I gave it to her."

Although nowadays, supermarkets are very popular in Spanish countries, it is still a custom to shop at small stores that specialize in one or two products: **carnicería** (*meat market*), **panadería** (*bakery*), **pescadería** (*fish market*), and so on.

Vamos a practicar

A Complete the following dialogues, using the preterit of **ser, ir,** or **dar** as appropriate. Then act them out with a partner.

1. —¿Adónde _____ tú ayer?
   —Por la tarde _____ a una tienda con mi suegro. Él me _____ dinero para comprar ropa.
   —¿_____ Uds. a casa de tía Eva por la noche?
   —Sí, _____ y le _____ el regalo que tú le mandaste.

2. —¿Adónde _____ Uds. anoche?
   —_____ a un concierto. Los padres de Dora nos _____ las entradas.

3. —¿Tú _____ estudiante del profesor Vega el año pasado?
   —No, yo _____ estudiante de la profesora Soto.

B Answer the following questions.

1. ¿Dieron Ud. y sus amigos una fiesta el viernes pasado?
2. ¿Dio Ud. dinero para la fiesta?
3. ¿Adónde fue Ud. el sábado pasado?
4. ¿Sus amigos fueron con Ud.?
5. ¿Fue Ud. al supermercado la semana pasada?
6. ¿Fue Ud. estudiante en esta universidad el año pasado?

C Write a short paragraph describing what you did yesterday. Give as many details as possible.

③ USES OF *POR* AND *PARA*
Usos de *por* y *para*

■ The preposition **por** is used to express the following concepts.

1. Motion (*through, along, by*)

—¿**Por** dónde entró **Juan?**	"*How (Through where) did Juan come in?*"
—Entró **por** la puerta de atrás.	"*He came in through the back door.*"
—¿A qué hora pasaste **por** mi casa ayer?	"*At what time did you go by my house yesterday?*"
—Pasé **por** tu casa a las tres.	"*I went by your house at three o'clock.*"

2. Cause or motive of an action (*because of, on account of, on behalf of*)

—¿Por qué no fueron Uds.
a la playa ayer?

—No fuimos **por** la lluvia.

"*Why didn't you go to the beach
yesterday?*"

"*We didn't go because of the rain.*"

3. Agency, means, manner, unit of measure (*by, for, per*)

—¿Vas a Bogotá **por** avión?

—No, llevo el coche.

—¿Cuál es el límite de
velocidad en Venezuela?

—Noventa kilómetros **por** hora.

"*Are you going to Bogotá
by plane?*"

"*No, I'm taking the car.*"

"*What's the speed limit in
Venezuela?*"

"*Ninety kilometers per hour.*"

> The metric system is
> used in all Hispanic
> countries. The basic unit
> of the metric system is
> the meter, which is
> equivalent to 3.28 feet.
> One mile is equivalent
> to 1.6 kilometers.

4. *In exchange for*

—¿Cuánto pagaste **por** el abrigo
y **por** el suéter?

—Pagué cien dólares **por** los dos.

"*How much did you pay for the
coat and the sweater?*"

"*I paid one hundred dollars
for both.*"

5. Period of time during which an action takes place (*during, in, for*)

—¿**Por** cuánto tiempo vas
a estar en Puerto Rico?

—Voy a estar allí **por** un mes.

"*How long are you going to be in
Puerto Rico?*"

"*I'm going to be there for a month.*"

■ The preposition **para** is used to express the following concepts.

1. Destination in space (*to*)

—¿A qué hora hay vuelos
para Colombia?

—A las ocho y a las diez
de la noche.

"*What time are there flights to
Colombia?*"

"*At eight and at ten P.M.*"

2. Goal for a point in the future (*by, for*)

—¿Cuándo necesita Ud.
la aspiradora?

—La necesito **para** mañana.

"*When do you need the vacuum
cleaner?*"

"*I need it by tomorrow.*"

3. Whom or what something is for

—¿**Para** quién es la lavadora?   "*Whom is the washing machine for?*"
—Es **para** mi suegra.   "*It's for my mother-in-law.*"

4. Purpose (*in order to*)

—¿**Para** qué necesitas la escoba?   "*What do you need the broom for?*"
—La necesito **para** barrer la cocina.   "*I need it (in order) to sweep the kitchen.*"

Vamos a practicar

A Complete the following paragraph, using **por** or **para** as appropriate.

Mañana _____ la mañana salimos _____ Chile. Vamos _____ avión y pensamos estar allí _____ tres semanas. Pagamos quinientos dólares _____ el pasaje y vamos a viajar _____ todo el país. En Santiago voy a comprar regalos _____ todos mis amigos. Tengo que estar aquí _____ el veinte de agosto _____ poder comenzar las clases en septiembre.

B With a partner, take turns answering the following questions about Sergio, using the clues provided.

1. ¿Cómo viajó él? (avión)
2. ¿Cuánto pagó por el pasaje? (mil dólares)
3. ¿Por cuánto tiempo piensa estar en Bogotá? (dos semanas)
4. ¿Cuándo sale para Medellín? (mañana)
5. ¿Para cuándo necesita la ropa? (el sábado)
6. ¿Para quién es el abrigo que compró? (su esposa)
7. ¿Para qué necesita dos latas de salsa de tomate? (hacer tallarines)
8. ¿Por qué no fue a la playa ayer? (la lluvia)
9. ¿Por dónde entró en su casa anoche? (la puerta de atrás)
10. ¿A qué hora pasó por nuestra casa? (a las diez)

④ SEASONS OF THE YEAR AND WEATHER EXPRESSIONS
Las estaciones del año y las expresiones para describir el tiempo

Las estaciones del año

la primavera	*spring*	**el verano**	*summer*
el otoño	*fall*	**el invierno**	*winter*

Expresiones para describir el tiempo

■ In the following weather expressions, the verb **hacer** (*to make*) followed by a noun is used in Spanish, whereas the verb *to be* followed by an adjective is used in English.

Hace (mucho) frío.	*It is (very) cold.*
Hace (mucho) calor.	*It is (very) hot.*
Hace (mucho) viento.[1]	*It is (very) windy.*
Hace sol.[1]	*It is sunny.*
Hace buen (mal) tiempo.[2]	*The weather is good (bad).*

—¿Cómo es el clima de Phoenix?   *"What is the weather like in Phoenix?"*

—**Hace** mucho **calor** en el **verano,** pero en el **invierno** no **hace** mucho **frío.**   *It is very hot in the summer, but in winter it's not very cold."*

—¿Cuándo vienes a Chicago? ¿En octubre?   *"When are you coming to Chicago? In October?"*

—Sí. ¿Voy a necesitar un abrigo?   *"Yes. Am I going to need a coat?"*

—No, en el **otoño** no **hace** mucho **frío. Hace** mucho **viento.**   *"No, it is not very cold in the fall. It is very windy."*

■ **Hacer** is not used in weather expressions with **llover (o:ue)** (*to rain*) or **nevar (e:ie)** (*to snow*).

Llueve.	*It rains (It's raining).*
Está lloviendo.	*It's raining.*
Nieva.	*It snows (It's snowing).*
Está nevando.	*It's snowing.*

—¿En Oregón **llueve** mucho en la **primavera**?   *"Does it rain a lot in the spring in Oregon?"*

—¡En Oregón **llueve** siempre!   *"In Oregon it always rains!"*

■ Other words and expressions related to the weather are:

la lluvia	*rain*
la niebla	*fog*
Está nublado.	*It's cloudy.*

---

[1] It is also correct to say **hay viento, hay sol.**

[2] **Bueno** and **malo** drop the final -o before a masculine singular noun.

Many families in Spain and Latin America still have maids. Some live in the house where they work and often are treated as part of the family.

■ As in English, the Spanish impersonal verbs use third person singular forms only.

—¿Vas a limpiar la terraza?
—No, porque **hace** mucho **viento** y **va** a **llover.** Además la criada la limpió ayer.

"Are you going to clean the terrace?"
"No, because it's very windy and it's going to rain. Besides, the maid cleaned it yesterday."

Vamos a practicar

Quiz

A Complete the following sentences, using a word from the list or an appropriate weather expression.

el paraguas
el impermeable

el suéter
el abrigo

1. ¿Necesitas un paraguas? Sí, porque _____.
2. ¿No necesitas un abrigo? No, porque _____.
3. ¿Quieres un impermeable? No, no está _____.
4. ¿Necesitas un suéter? No, hoy _____.
5. Está nevando. Lleve el _____.
6. Va a llover. Está _____.

B **¿Qué tiempo hace?** (*How is the weather?*) **¿Qué estación del año es?**

1.

2.

3.

4.

5.

6.

Palabras y más palabras Circle the word or phrase that best completes each sentence.

1. Aquí hace mucho frío en el (verano, invierno).
2. Fui al supermercado para comprar una (aspiradora, lata de salsa).
3. Necesito un paraguas y un impermeable porque (está lloviendo, hace calor).
4. La criada necesita la escoba para (cocinar, barrer) la cocina.
5. El límite de velocidad es de 65 millas por (minuto, hora).
6. Nosotras (preparamos, entramos) por la puerta de atrás.
7. Está nublado. Va a (hacer sol, llover).
8. No hay vuelos porque hay (niebla, ropa).
9. Fuimos a México el verano (pasado, que viene).
10. Necesitamos salsa de tomate para los (tallarines, abrigos).
11. La criada (preparó, limpió) la cocina.
12. Voy a poner la ropa en la (escoba, lavadora).

En estas situaciones What would you say in the following situations?

1. You are driving in Caracas. Ask someone what the speed limit is in Venezuela, and tell him/her what the speed limit is in your state.
2. Tell an exchange student from Colombia how the weather is where you live in summer and in winter.
3. You want to know what the weather is like today and whether you're going to need a coat, a raincoat, or an umbrella.
4. Talk about all the chores you have to do this weekend.

PARA ESCUCHAR Y ENTENDER

The following material is to be used with the In-Text Audio CDs.

I. Práctica

3–2

A El pretérito

Answer the questions, using the cues provided. Repeat the correct answer after the speaker's confirmation. Listen to the model.

> **MODELO**   —¿Quién te ayudó ayer? (Roberto)
> **—Me ayudó Roberto.**

1. (ayer)	6. (a las nueve)
2. (por la puerta de atrás)	7. (la puerta)
3. (anoche)	8. (al supermercado)
4. (tallarines)	9. (a Esteban)
5. (a Teresa)	10. (el Dr. Mena)

3–3

B ¿Por o para?

Answer the questions, always using the first choice. Omit the subject. Repeat the correct answer after the speaker's confirmation. Listen to the model.

> **MODELO**   —¿Entraron Uds. por la ventana o por la puerta?
> **—Entramos por la ventana.**

C ¿Cómo es el clima?
Answer the questions, using the cues provided. Repeat the correct answer
after the speaker's confirmation. Listen to the model.

3–4

MODELO   —¿Dónde hace mucho frío? (Alaska)
—**Hace mucho frío en Alaska.**

1. (Oregón)   4. (Chicago)
2. (Arizona)   5. (sí)
3. (otoño)

II. ¿Qué dicen?

 1 ¿Lógico o ilógico?
The speaker will make some statements. Circle **L (lógico)** if the statement
is logical and **I (ilógico)** if it is illogical. The speaker will verify your
response.

3–5

1. L I   4. L I
2. L I   5. L I
3. L I   6. L I

 2 ¿Verdadero o falso?
Listen carefully to the dialogue. Listen to it at least twice.

3–6

 (Diálogo 1)

3–7   Now the speaker will make some statements about the dialogue you just
heard. Tell whether each statement is true (**verdadero**) or false (**falso**). The
speaker will confirm the correct answer.

 3 Madre e hijo
Listen carefully to the dialogue. Listen to it at least twice.

3–8

(Diálogo 2)

3–9   Now the speaker will ask you some questions about the dialogue you just
heard. Answer each question, omitting the subject. The speaker will confirm the correct answer. Repeat the correct answer.

LECCIÓN 6

A Stem-changing verbs (*o:ue*)

Answer the following questions.

1. ¿A qué hora vuelve Ud. a casa?
2. Cuando Uds. van a México, ¿vuelan o van en auto?
3. ¿Recuerdan Uds. los verbos irregulares?
4. ¿Cuántas horas duerme Ud.?
5. ¿Pueden Uds. ir a la playa?

B Affirmative and negative expressions

Change the following sentences to the affirmative.

1. Ellos no recuerdan nada.
2. No hay nadie en el cuarto.
3. Yo no quiero volar tampoco.
4. No recibimos ningún regalo.
5. Nunca tiene fiestas en su casa.

C Pronouns as object of a preposition

Complete the following with the Spanish equivalent of the words in parentheses.

1. ¿Puedes venir _____ (*with me*)?
2. ¿Vas a trabajar _____ (*with them*)?
3. El dinero es _____, Anita (*for you*).
4. El regalo no es _____; es _____ (*for me / for her*).
5. No, Paco, no puedo ir _____ (*with you*).

D Direct object pronouns

Complete the following sentences with the Spanish equivalent of the direct object pronouns in parentheses. Follow the models.

MODELO   Yo llamo (*him*)
        Yo lo llamo.

        Yo quiero llamar (*him*)
        Yo quiero llamarlo.

1. Yo espero (*them*, fem.)
2. Uds. van a comprar (*it*, masc.)
3. Nosotros no queremos visitar (*you*, fam.)
4. Ella lee (*it*, fem.)
5. ¿Ud. llama? (*me*)
6. Él escribe (*them*, masc.)
7. Mi padrino va a visitar (*us*)
8. Nosotros no esperamos (*you*, formal, sing., masc.)

E Vocabulary

Complete the following sentences, using words learned in **Lección 6.**

1. Una habitación con _____ al _____ cuesta más.
2. Ellos _____ dos días a la semana en la cafetería.
3. El _____ de esta cama es muy malo.
4. ¿Cuánto _____ el libro de español?
5. Los Ángeles tiene muchos _____ de interés.
6. No puedo ir porque no tengo _____.
7. Él _____ siete horas todas las noches.
8. ¿Está abierta la _____ de _____? Necesito comprar estampillas.

LECCIÓN 7

A Stem-changing verbs (*e:i*)

Answer the following questions.

1. ¿Qué sirven Uds., sopa o ensalada?
2. ¿Qué pide Ud. para beber cuando va a un restaurante?
3. ¿Dice Ud. su edad?
4. ¿Sigue Ud. en la universidad?
5. ¿Uds. siempre piden postre?

B Irregular first-person forms

Complete the sentences with the present indicative of the verbs in the following list. Use each verb once.

traer	conocer	traducir	hacer	saber
ver	salir	poner	conducir	

1. Yo _____ mi coche.
2. Yo siempre _____ con ella.
3. Yo _____ la carne en la mesa.

4. Yo _____ del inglés al español.
5. Yo no _____ al profesor de mi hijo.
6. Yo _____ los folletos turísticos.
7. Yo _____ el postre.
8. Yo no _____ el regalo. ¿Dónde está?
9. Yo no _____ nadar.

C *Saber* contrasted with *conocer*

Use the present indicative of **saber** or **conocer** to complete the following sentences.

1. Yo _____ al hijo de doña Marta.
2. Nosotros _____ hablar inglés, pero no _____ Washington.
3. ¿Ud. _____ nadar, señorita?
4. ¿Tú _____ las novelas de Cervantes?
5. Yo _____ la verdad.

D Indirect object pronouns

Answer the following questions according to the model.

MODELO   —¿Qué me vas a traer de México?
                (un regalo)
         —**Te voy a traer un regalo.**

1. ¿Qué te va a dar Carlos? (dinero)
2. ¿Qué le das tú a Luis? (una revista)
3. ¿En qué idioma les habla a Uds. el profesor? (en español)
4. ¿Qué va a decirles Ud. a los niños? (que es tarde)
5. ¿Qué nos pregunta Ud.? (la dirección de la oficina)
6. ¿A quién están escribiéndole Uds.? (a nuestro padre)
7. ¿Cuándo le escribe Ud. a su abuelo? (los lunes)
8. ¿A quién le da Ud. la información? (al agente de viajes)
9. ¿En qué idioma me hablas tú? (en inglés)
10. ¿Qué te compran tus hijos? (nada)

E Vocabulary

Complete the following sentences, using the words learned in **Lección 7.**

1. Compré el pasaje en la _____ de viajes.
2. Ellos van a _____ en la piscina.
3. Mi hijo sabe de _____ todos los verbos.

4. Necesita confirmar la _____ hoy.
5. ¿Necesitamos los _____ para entrar en México?
6. No podemos viajar hoy porque van a _____ los vuelos.
7. La embajada de Estados Unidos _____ en la _____ Paz.
8. ¿Dónde _____ ellos libros en español?
9. El guía tiene los folletos _____.
10. ¿Vas a Puerto Rico? ¡Buen _____!

LECCIÓN 8

A *Pedir* contrasted with *preguntar*

Tell what these people are asking or asking for, using **pedir** or **preguntar.**

1. yo / dónde vive
2. Rosa / las entradas
3. nosotros / la hora
4. los niños / las pelotas
5. tú / la raqueta
6. el entrenador / tu edad

B Special construction with *gustar, doler,* and *hacer falta*

Complete the following sentences with the appropriate forms of **gustar, doler,** and **hacer falta.**

1. No _____ esas mochilas. Prefiero aquéllas.
2. ¿Qué _____, Jorge? ¿La tienda de campaña?
3. A Marta _____ la cabeza. ¿Tienes aspirinas?
4. A nosotros no _____ dinero. No necesitamos comprar nada.
5. ¿ _____ a Ud. esta bicicleta, o prefiere la otra?
6. A Rodolfo _____ unos esquíes. ¿Puedes comprárselos?
7. A mí _____ los pies.
8. A nosotros no _____ caminar (*to walk*). ¿Podemos ir en coche?

C Demonstrative adjectives and pronouns

Complete the following sentences with the Spanish equivalent of the words in parentheses.

1. Necesito _____ (*these*) pelotas y _____ (*those over there*).
2. ¿Quieres _____ (*this*) caballo o _____ (*that one*)?
3. Yo prefiero _____ (*these*) patines, no _____ (*those over there*).

4. Papá, ¿tú quieres comprar _____ (*that*) raqueta o _____ (*this one*)?

5. Yo no entiendo _____ (*that,* neuter form).

D **Direct and indirect object pronouns used together**

Complete with the Spanish equivalent of the words in parentheses.

1. Necesito el dinero. ¿Ud. puede _____, señora? (*lend it to me*)

2. Cuando Raúl necesita libros, su mamá _____. (*buy them for him*)

3. ¿Necesitas la mochila? Yo puedo _____ esta tarde. (*bring it to you*)

4. Cuando nosotros necesitamos las entradas, Jorge _____. (*give them to us*)

E **Vocabulary**

Complete the following sentences, using words learned in **Lección 8.**

1. Quiero leer la página _____.

2. ¿Para _____ son esos patines? ¿Para tu hijo?

3. Para jugar al tenis, los niños necesitan una _____ y una _____ de tenis.

4. Tengo dos _____ de dormir. Te presto una.

5. Voy a comprar las _____ para el partido del domingo.

6. Me _____ mucho la cabeza.

7. Necesito la tienda de _____ este fin de semana.

8. Me _____ falta diez dólares para comprar el libro.

LECCIÓN 9

A **Possessive pronouns**

Answer the following questions in the negative, according to the model.

MODELO   —¿Estos pantalones son **de Juan**?
            —No, no son **de él.**

1. ¿Son **tuyas** estas tarjetas?

2. ¿Estos cepillos son **de Julia**?

3. ¿El vestido es **suyo,** señora?

4. ¿Es **de Uds.** esta cama?
5. ¿Esta tarjeta de crédito es **de tus padres**?
6. ¿Son **tuyos** estos espejos?
7. ¿Es **de Uds.** esta máquina de afeitar?
8. ¿Es **nuestro** este dormitorio?

B **Reflexive constructions**

Answer the following questions using the cues provided.

1. ¿A qué hora te levantas? (a las seis)
2. ¿Uds. se bañan por la mañana? (no, por la noche)
3. ¿A qué hora se despiertan los niños? (a las siete)
4. ¿Dónde te sientas tú? (aquí)
5. ¿Uds. se acuerdan de sus profesores? (sí)
6. ¿Quieres probarte los pantalones ahora? (no)

C **Command forms:** *Ud.* and *Uds.*

Complete the sentences with the command forms of the verbs in the following list, as appropriate, and read each sentence aloud. Use each verb once.

escribir	venir	dar	hablar	doblar
servir	cerrar	volver	seguir	ser
estar	poner	ir	abrir	traer

1. _____ la puerta, Sr. Benítez.
2. _____ español, señores.
3. _____ a su hija, señora.
4. _____ mañana por la mañana, señoras.
5. No _____ la ventana, señorita. Tengo calor.
6. _____ a la izquierda, señores.
7. _____ derecho, señorita.
8. _____ su nombre y dirección, señores.
9. _____ en la oficina mañana por la tarde, señores.
10. ¡No _____ tan impacientes, señoritas!
11. Sr. Vega, _____ a la casa del director.
12. _____ el martes, señora. El doctor no está hoy.
13. _____ el café en la terraza, señorita.
14. _____ los libros aquí, señorita.
15. _____ las cartas mañana, señoras.

D Uses of object pronouns with command forms

Give the Spanish equivalent of the words in parentheses.

1. _____ mi dirección, Sr. Mena. (*Tell them*)
2. ¿El vestido? _____ ahora, Srta. Ruiz. (*Don't bring it to me*)
3. _____ mi peluquero, por favor. (*Don't tell it to*)
4. _____, Sra. Miño. (*Don't get up*)
5. _____ las bebidas, señores. _____ a la terraza.
   (*Bring / Bring them*)
6. ¿El té? _____. (*Bring it to her*)

E Vocabulary

Complete the following sentences, using words learned in **Lección 9.**

1. No tengo máquina de _____.
2. Mañana voy a la _____. Necesito _____ la cabeza y cor-
   tarme el _____.
3. Lleve los pantalones a la _____, señorita.
4. No tengo dinero; voy a pagar con la _____.
5. No está a la derecha; está a la _____.
6. Ponga el botiquín en el baño ahora _____.
7. Voy a _____ a los niños; ya son las nueve de la noche.
8. Para llegar a la universidad, siga Ud. _____.

LECCIÓN 10

A The preterit of regular verbs / preterit of *ser, ir,* and *dar*

Rewrite the following sentences according to the new beginnings. Follow
the model.

> **MODELO**   Voy al cine. (Ayer...)
> **Ayer fui al cine.**

1. Ella entra en la cafetería y come tallarines. (Ayer...)
2. María le escribe a su suegra. (Ayer...)
3. Ella me presta su abrigo. (El viernes pasado...)
4. Ellos son los mejores estudiantes. (El año pasado...)
5. Ellos te esperan cerca del supermercado. (El sábado pasado...)
6. Mi hijo va a Cuba. (El verano pasado...)
7. Le doy el impermeable. (Ayer por la mañana...)
8. Nosotros decidimos comprar la aspiradora. (El lunes pasado...)

9. Le pregunto la hora. (Anoche...)
10. Tú no pagas por la ropa. (Anoche...)
11. Somos los primeros. (El jueves pasado...)
12. Me dan muchos problemas. (Ayer...)
13. Mi suegro no bebe café. (Anoche...)
14. Yo no voy a esquiar. (Ayer...)
15. Te damos el suéter. (La semana pasada...)

B Uses of *por* and *para*

Complete the following sentences, using **por** or **para.**

1. La criada entró _____ la puerta de atrás.
2. Ella pasó _____ la carnicería anoche a las nueve.
3. Ellos no vienen _____ la lluvia.
4. No hay viajes _____ Ecuador los sábados.
5. Vamos _____ avión y necesitamos el dinero _____ pagar los pasajes.
6. El límite de velocidad en California es 65 millas _____ hora.
7. ¿ _____ quién es el paraguas?
8. Eva pagó doscientos dólares _____ la aspiradora.
9. Necesito la lavadora _____ mañana _____ la mañana.

C Seasons of the year and weather expressions

Say what the weather is like, according to the place and time of year.

1. Phoenix / agosto
2. Alaska / invierno
3. Oregón / octubre
4. Chicago / otoño
5. San Francisco / invierno
6. Florida / verano

D Vocabulary

Complete the following sentences, using words learned in **Lección 10.**

1. Necesito el _____ porque hace frío.
2. ¿Cuál es el _____ de velocidad?
3. Ella quiere ponerse el _____ porque va a llover.
4. ¿Dónde compraste la _____ de tomate? ¿En el supermercado?
5. Ponga el vestido en la _____, señorita.
6. Adela siempre _____ unos tallarines muy buenos.
7. ¿Quién barrió la cocina? ¿La _____?
8. ¿Qué _____ hace hoy? ¿Hace frío?

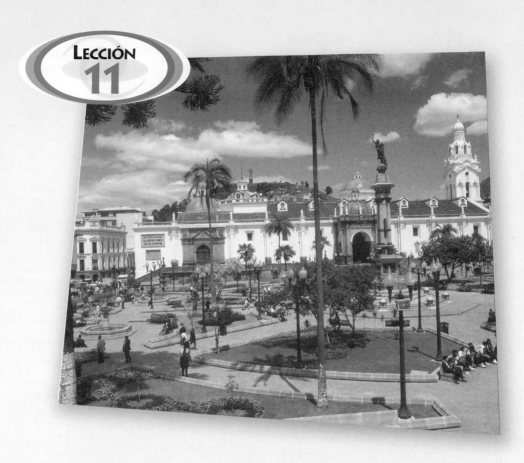

OBJECTIVES

Structures

1. Time expressions with **hacer**
2. Irregular preterits
3. The preterit of stem-changing verbs (**e:i** and **o:u**)
4. Command forms: **tú**

Communication

You will continue to learn vocabulary related to everyday life.

Country highlighted: Ecuador

E cuador es un país un poco más pequeño que el estado de Nevada, y se encuentra exactamente en la línea del ecuador. A pesar de esto (*in spite of this*), su clima varía de acuerdo con la altura de cada región.

Como en otros países cuyo territorio formó parte del imperio inca, en Ecuador se habla, además del español, el quechua, lengua original de los incas. La influencia de esta cultura se nota, además, en las costumbres y tradiciones populares y especialmente en las prácticas religiosas.

A 600 millas de la costa de Ecuador están las Islas Galápagos, llamadas así debido a (*due to*) las enormes tortugas que allí viven. Estas islas están consideradas como un centro ecológico de primer orden.

Quito, la capital de Ecuador, está situada en la ladera (*side*) del volcán Pichincha, a más de 9.000 pies de altura sobre el nivel del mar (*above sea level*). Es la capital más antigua de América del Sur y todavía hoy mantiene un aspecto colonial.

RESOURCES

Wherever you see the following icons additional resources are available:

Internet

Go to **www.college.hmco.com/languages/spanish/students/** for additional practice on the topic.

Student
CD-ROM

Go to the **Video Grammar Tutor** for help with understanding the grammar topic at hand.

Go to the **In-Text Audio CDs** for more practice.

VOCABULARIO

Audio

COGNADOS

el accidente
el favor
interesante
la paciencia

NOMBRES

el **arroz**   *rice*
la **basura**   *trash, garbage*
la **cafetera**   *coffeepot*
el (la) **cocinero(a)**   *cook*
la **cosa**   *thing*
la **facultad**   *college*
la **facultad de derecho**   *law school*
el **fregadero**   *sink*
el (la) **invitado(a)**   *guest*
la **licuadora**   *blender*
la **liquidación, la venta**   *sale*
la **marca**   *brand*
el **piso**   *floor*
la **reunión, la junta**   *meeting*
la **secadora**   *dryer*
la **tostadora**   *toaster*
los **trabajos de la casa**   *household chores*

VERBOS

apagar   *to turn off*
caminar   *to walk*
despedirse (e:i)   *to say good-bye*
divertirse (e:ie)   *to have a good time*
elegir (e:i)   *to choose, to select*
enseñar   *to teach*
mentir (e:ie)   *to lie*
morir (o:ue)   *to die*

ADJETIVOS

aburrido(a)   *boring, bored*
todo(a)   *all*
todos(as)   *every*

OTRAS PALABRAS Y EXPRESIONES

arroz con pollo   *chicken with rice*
¿cuánto tiempo?   *how long?*
debajo (de)   *underneath*
ir caminando, ir a pie   *to walk, to go on foot*
ir de compras   *to go shopping*
media hora   *half an hour*
otra vez   *again*
¡Rápido!   *Quick!*
según   *according to*
Ten paciencia.   *Be patient.*

① TIME EXPRESSIONS WITH *HACER*
Expresiones de tiempo con *hacer*

Spanish uses the following formula to express how long something has been going on.

> **Hace** + length of time + **que** + verb (in present tense)
> **Hace**   quince años   **que**   vivo en esta ciudad.
> *I have been living in this city for fifteen years.*

—¿Tienes hambre?   *"Are you hungry?"*
—Sí, **hace** ocho horas **que**   *"Yes, I haven't eaten in eight hours."*
no como.

—¿Cuánto tiempo **hace** que Ud.   *"How long have you been teaching*
enseña en la Universidad   *at the Universidad Central de*
Central de Ecuador?   *Ecuador?"*
—**Hace** tres años. Enseño en   *"Three years. I teach at the School*
la Facultad de Derecho.   *of Law."*

—¿Cuánto tiempo **hace que** Uds.   *"How long have you been walking?"*
están caminando?
—**Hace** media hora **que** estamos   *"We have been walking for a half*
caminando.   *hour."*

ATENCIÓN: **To ask how long something has been going on, use the expression** ¿Cuánto tiempo hace que...?

> Las universidades hispanas se dividen en facultades. Los estudiantes van directamente de la escuela secundaria a la facultad de su especialización. Generalmente es gratis (*free*) o la matrícula (*tuition*) es muy baja (*low*). Los estudiantes deben pasar un examen de ingreso (*entrance*) bastante riguroso.

Quiz

Vamos a practicar

A Use the expression **hace**... **que**... to say how long each action has been taking place.

Modelo   Estamos en enero. / Él empezó a trabajar en octubre.
Hace tres meses **que** él trabaja.

1. Son las tres de la tarde. / Ellos están aquí desde (*since*) las dos y media.
2. Estamos en el año 2006. El Dr. Paz empezó a enseñar en la facultad de derecho en 1998.

3. Hoy es viernes. / Empezamos a trabajar el lunes.
4. Son las cuatro. / Graciela empezó a hablar por teléfono a las cuatro menos cuarto.
5. Son las cinco. / Empezaste a caminar a las cuatro y media.

B Interview a classmate, using the following questions. When you have finished, switch roles.

1. ¿Cuánto tiempo hace que estudias español?
2. ¿Cuánto tiempo hace que conoces a tu mejor amigo o amiga?
3. ¿Cuánto tiempo hace que no comes?
4. ¿Cuánto tiempo hace que vives en esta ciudad?
5. ¿Cuánto tiempo hace que no ves a tus padres?
6. ¿Cuánto tiempo hace que Uds. no van de vacaciones?
7. ¿Cuánto tiempo hace que no llueve aquí?

2 IRREGULAR PRETERITS
Pretéritos irregulares

The following Spanish verbs are irregular in the preterit.

tener:	tuve, tuviste, tuvo, tuvimos, tuvisteis, tuvieron
estar:	estuve, estuviste, estuvo, estuvimos, estuvisteis, estuvieron
poder:	pude, pudiste, pudo, pudimos, pudisteis, pudieron
poner:	puse, pusiste, puso, pusimos, pusisteis, pusieron
saber:	supe, supiste, supo, supimos, supisteis, supieron
hacer:	hice, hiciste, hizo, hicimos, hicisteis, hicieron
venir:	vine, viniste, vino, vinimos, vinisteis, vinieron
querer:	quise, quisiste, quiso, quisimos, quisisteis, quisieron
decir:	dije, dijiste, dijo, dijimos, dijisteis, dijeron[1]
traer:	traje, trajiste, trajo, trajimos, trajisteis, trajeron[1]
conducir:	conduje, condujiste, condujo, condujimos, condujisteis, condujeron[1]
traducir:	traduje, tradujiste, tradujo, tradujimos, tradujisteis, tradujeron[1]

---

[1]Note that the **-i** is omitted in the third person plural ending of these verbs.

—¿Dónde **pusieron** Uds. la lata de la basura?   *"Where did you put the garbage can?"*

—La **pusimos** debajo del fregadero.   *"We put it underneath the sink."*

—¿No **vino** la criada?   *"Didn't the maid come?"*

—Sí, pero **trajo** a su hijo y no **pudo** hacer los trabajos de la casa.   *"Yes, but she brought her son and she couldn't do the household chores."*

—¿**Vinieron** caminando?   *"Did they walk?"*

—Sí, **vinieron** a pie.   *"Yes, they came on foot."*

—¿Qué te **dijeron** de la reunión?   *"What did they tell you about the meeting?"*

—Me **dijeron** muchas cosas interesantes.   *"They told me many interesting things."*

ATENCIÓN: Notice that the third person singular form of the verb hacer **changes the** c **to** z **in order to maintain the soft sound of the** c **in the infinitive.**

—¿**Hizo** el arroz con pollo la cocinera?   *"Did the cook make the chicken and rice?"*

—No, no **pudo** hacerlo porque **tuvo** que limpiar el piso de la cocina.   *"No, she wasn't able to do it because she had to clean the kitchen floor."*

> En todos los países hispanos, se come comida internacional. La comida española y la comida italiana, por ejemplo, son muy populares. Sin embargo (*However*), cada país y cada región tiene sus platos típicos. Un plato típico de Ecuador es *el locro,* una sopa de vegetales y pollo.

■ The preterit of **hay** (from the verb **haber**) is **hubo,** which is used with singular and plural subjects.

Ayer **hubo** una reunión en la universidad.   *Yesterday there was a meeting at the university.*

Hubo dos accidentes la semana pasada.   *There were two accidents last week.*

Vamos a practicar

A Complete the following letter with the preterit of the verbs in parentheses.

Isabel le escribe una carta a Teresa.   Guayaquil, 15 de julio de 20...

Querida Teresa:

Ayer yo _____ (estar) en Quito, pero no _____ (poder) ir a verte. Salí de Guayaquil por la mañana y _____ (conducir) por cinco horas hasta llegar a Quito. Allí _____ (tener) que ir al hospital para ver a Gustavo. Caminé por la ciudad y _____ (querer) llamarte por teléfono, pero no _____ (poder) encontrar tu número.

_____ (Venir) de Quito muy cansada. Esta tarde hablé por teléfono con Ramón. Él me _____ (decir) muchas cosas interesantes. ¡Ah...! Me _____ (poner) el vestido que compré en Quito y salí con Jorge. El sábado vuelvo a Quito para verte.

Tu amiga,
Isabel

B Complete the following dialogue, using appropriate irregular verbs in the preterit. Then act it out with a partner.

—¿Dónde _____ Uds. anoche? ¿Adónde fueron?
—_____ en casa de Julio. _____ una cena en su casa.
—¿Tú _____ tu coche o fueron caminando?
—Yo _____ mi coche.
—¿Tus primos fueron a la cena?
—No, ellos no _____ ir porque _____ que trabajar.
—¿Quién _____ la comida?
—La _____ Julio y su esposa.
—¿Qué vestido te _____ para ir a la cena?
—Me _____ el vestido negro.

C Answer the following questions, using complete sentences.

1. ¿A qué hora vino Ud. a la universidad hoy?
2. ¿Condujo su coche o vino a pie?
3. ¿Trajo sus libros de español?
4. ¿Pudo Ud. venir a clase la semana pasada?
5. ¿Tuvo que trabajar ayer?

6. ¿Dónde estuvo Ud. anoche? ¿Con quién?
7. ¿Qué hizo anoche para la cena?
8. ¿En qué banco puso Ud. su dinero?

D Interview a classmate, using the questions in **Práctica C** in the **tú** form. When you have finished, switch roles.

3 THE PRETERIT OF STEM-CHANGING VERBS (E:I AND O:U)

El pretérito de verbos de cambio radical *e:i* y *o:u*

e:i verbs Stem-changing verbs of the **-ir** conjugation, whether they change **e** to **ie** or **e** to **i** in the present indicative, change **e** to **i** in the third person singular and plural of the preterit.

sentir		pedir	
sentí	sentimos	pedí	pedimos
sentiste	sentisteis	pediste	pedisteis
sintió	sintieron	pidió	pidieron

■ The following verbs follow the same e to i pattern.

conseguir	**preferir**
despedirse (*to say good-bye*)	**repetir**
divertirse (*to have a good time*)	**seguir**
elegir (*to choose*)	**servir**
mentir (*to lie*)	

—¿Daniel compró la licuadora?   *"Did Daniel buy the blender?"*
—No, **prefirió** comprar   *"No, he preferred to buy a coffeepot."*
una cafetera.
—¿Qué marca **eligió**?   *"What brand did he choose?"*
—Mr. Coffee.   *"Mr. Coffee."*

> En los países de habla hispana, las marcas (*brands*) norteamericanas son muy populares, especialmente en lo que se refiere a los autos y a los aparatos electrodomésticos como refrigeradores, lavadoras (*washers*), etc.

—Según Juan, todos **se
divirtieron** mucho
en la fiesta.

*"According to Juan, everybody had
a good time at the party."*

—¡Te **mintió!** La fiesta estuvo
muy aburrida y no **sirvieron**
nada para comer. Los invitados
se **despidieron** muy temprano.

*"He lied to you! The party was very
boring and they didn't serve
anything to eat. The guests said
good-bye very early."* (i.e., They left
very early.)

o:u verbs   Stem-changing verbs of the **-ir** conjugation that change **o** to
ue in the present indicative change **o** to **u** in the third person singular and
plural of the preterit.

dormir	
dormí	dormimos
dormiste	dormisteis
d**u**rmió	d**u**rmieron

■   Another verb that follows the same **o** to **u** pattern is **morir** (*to die*).

—¿Cuántas horas **durmió**
Ud. anoche?

*"How many hours did you sleep
last night?"*

—Yo dormí seis horas, pero Ana
y Luis sólo **durmieron** tres.

*"I slept six hours, but Ana and Luis
slept only three."*

—¿Cuántas personas **murieron**
en el accidente?

*"How many people died in the
accident?"*

—Por suerte, no **murió** nadie.

"Luckily, nobody died."

Quiz

Vamos a practicar

Complete the following dialogues, using the preterit of the verbs in parentheses. Then act them out with a partner.

1. —¿Doblaron ellos?
   —No, _____ (seguir) derecho.
2. —¿Dónde _____ (dormir) Uds. anoche?
   —Yo _____ (dormir) en la casa de Ana, pero Carlos
   _____ (dormir) en un hotel.

3. —¿ _____ (Conseguir) Uds. la licuadora?
   —Sí, por suerte la _____ (conseguir) ayer. También
   _____ (elegir) dos cafeteras de una marca muy buena.

4. —¿Uds. _____ (despedirse) de los chicos?
   —No, porque no se fueron. No _____ (conseguir) pasaje.
   —¿Entonces todos fueron a la fiesta?
   —Sí, y _____ (divertirse) mucho.

5. —¿Gerardo te _____ (mentir)?
   —Sí.

6. —¿ _____ (Haber) un accidente aquí ayer?
   —Sí, y según Ada, _____ (morir) dos personas.

Now create two original exchanges using stem-changing verbs in the preterit.

④ COMMAND FORMS: *TÚ*
Las formas imperativas: *tú*

The affirmative command The affirmative command for **tú** has
exactly the same form as the third person singular of the present indicative.

Verb	Present Indicative Third Person Singular	Familiar Command (tú Form)
hablar	él habla	**habla**
comer	él come	**come**
abrir	él abre	**abre**
cerrar	él cierra	**cierra**
volver	él vuelve	**vuelve**
pedir	él pide	**pide**
traer	él trae	**trae**

—**Cierra** las ventanas y **apaga**
las luces antes de salir.[1]

"*Close the windows and turn off the
lights before going out.*"

_____

[1]The infinitive, not the *-ing* form, is used after a preposition in Spanish.

—Muy bien. **Espérame** en el
coche. ¿Vamos a llevarle la
tostadora a Inés?
—Sí, **tráela,** por favor.

"Very well. Wait for me in the car.
Are we going to take the toaster
to Inés?"
"Yes, bring it, please."

ATENCIÓN: **Remember that direct, indirect, and reflexive pronouns are**
always attached to an affirmative command.

■ Eight Spanish verbs have irregular affirmative familiar command forms.

decir:	**di** (*say, tell*)	salir:	**sal** (*go out, leave*)
hacer:	**haz** (*do, make*)	ser:	**sé** (*be*)
ir:	**ve** (*go*)	tener:	**ten** (*have*)
poner:	**pon** (*put*)	venir:	**ven** (*come*)

—Carlitos, **ven** aquí. **Hazme**
un favor. **Ve** y **dile** a tía Eva
que necesito la escoba. ¡Rápido!
—¡**Ten** paciencia! Voy a ver
si está en su cuarto.

"Carlitos, come here. Do me a favor.
Go tell Aunt Eva that I need the
broom. Quick!"
"Be patient! I'll go see if she's in
her room."

> En los países hispanos, las
> personas mayores (*elderly*)
> generalmente viven en
> casa de un pariente, espe-
> cialmente las mujeres que
> no tienen esposo. Una tía
> soltera, por ejemplo,
> puede vivir con un her-
> mano y su familia.

The negative command   The negative command for
tú is formed by adding **-s** to the command form for **Ud.**

hable	no hable**s**	*don't talk*
vuelva	no vuelva**s**	*don't return*
venga	no venga**s**	*don't come*
salga	no salga**s**	*don't leave*

—Voy a la tienda porque
tienen una liquidación.
—**No** me **digas** que quieres ir
de compras otra vez.
—Sí, porque necesito una secadora.
—Bueno, pero **no vayas** hoy;
ve mañana.

"I'm going to the store because they
are having a sale."
"Don't tell me (that) you want to
go shopping again."
"Yes, because I need a dryer."
"Okay, but don't go today; go
tomorrow."

ATENCIÓN: **Remember that all object pronouns are placed** *before* **a nega-**
tive command: No *me lo* traigas hoy.

Quiz

Vamos a practicar

A You and a partner are doing household chores. Take turns asking each other what to do, answering in the affirmative. Follow the model.

MODELO   —¿Traigo la escoba?
—Sí, **tráela,** por favor.

1. ¿Pongo el pan (*bread*) en la tostadora?
2. ¿Compro la cafetera?
3. ¿Lo pongo en la mesa?
4. ¿Limpio el piso?
5. ¿Pongo la lata de la basura debajo del fregadero?
6. ¿Preparo el arroz con pollo?
7. ¿Lavo el mantel?
8. ¿Lo pongo en la secadora después (*afterwards*)?
9. ¿Llamo a Estrella otra vez?
10. ¿Cierro las ventanas?
11. ¿Apago la luz?
12. ¿Me voy?

B Now answer the questions in **Práctica A** in the negative. Follow the model.

MODELO   —¿Traigo la escoba?
—No, **no la traigas** ahora

C You are leaving a child home alone for a few hours. Using the **tú** form, tell the child what to do and what not to do. Give at least ten commands.

Palabras y más palabras   Say the following in another way, using the vocabulary learned in this lesson.

1. treinta minutos
2. venta
3. reunión
4. ir caminando
5. lo que hace un profesor en la clase
6. la uso para hacer café

7. persona que cocina
8. limpiar, barrer, cocinar
9. persona a quien invitamos
10. decir adiós
11. ir a comprar
12. opuesto de vivir

En estas situaciones What would you say in the following situations? What might the other person say?

1. You tell your roommate, who is very lazy, all the things you had to do yesterday. You had to cook, you did all the household chores, and then had to walk to the supermarket and go shopping.
2. Ask a friend whether he/she had fun at the party or whether the party was boring.
3. Your friend is rushing you. Tell him/her to be patient.
4. You want to know how long your professor has been teaching.
5. You give your roommate instructions about what to do and what not to do while you're gone for the day.

PARA ESCUCHAR Y ENTENDER

The following material is to be used with the In-Text Audio CDs.

I. Práctica

3–10

A ¿Cuánto tiempo hace...?

Answer the questions, using the cues provided. Repeat the correct answer after the speaker's confirmation. Listen to the model.

MODELO   —¿Cuánto tiempo hace que vives en La Habana? (tres años)
             —**Hace tres años que vivo en La Habana.**

1. (veinte años)
2. (tres meses)
3. (una hora)
4. (cuatro años)
5. (media hora)
6. (dos semanas)
7. (cinco días)
8. (quince minutos)

3–11

B Pretéritos irregulares

Answer the questions, using the cues provided. Repeat the correct answer after the speaker's confirmation. Listen to the model.

MODELO   —¿Qué tuviste que hacer ayer? (estudiar español)
             —**Tuve que estudiar español.**

1. (una secadora)
2. (anoche)
3. (los estudiantes)
4. (a las siete)
5. (debajo del fregadero)
6. (nada)
7. (el arroz con pollo)
8. (sí, otra vez)

C El pretérito de verbos de cambio radical

3–12
The speaker will read some sentences in the present tense. Restate each one, changing the verb to the preterit. Repeat the correct answer after the speaker's confirmation. Listen to the model.

> MODELO   Ellos piden café.
> **Ellos pidieron café.**

D Las formas imperativas (**tú**)

3–13
Change the following commands from the negative to the affirmative. Repeat the correct answer after the speaker's confirmation. Listen to the model.

> MODELO   **No hables** inglés.
> **Habla inglés.**

II. ¿Qué dicen?

1 ¿Lógico o ilógico?

3–14
The speaker will make some statements. Circle **L (lógico)** if the statement is logical and **I (ilógico)** if it is illogical. The speaker will verify your response.

1. L I	**3.** L I	**5.** L I	**7.** L I
2. L I	**4.** L I	**6.** L I	**8.** L I

2 ¿Verdadero o falso?

3–15
Listen carefully to the dialogue. Listen to it at least twice.

(Diálogo)

3–16
Now the speaker will make some statements about the dialogue you just heard. Tell whether each statement is true (**verdadero**) or false (**falso**). The speaker will confirm the correct answer.

3 Teresa va de compras

3–17
Listen carefully to the narration. Listen to it at least twice.

(Narración)

3–18
Now the speaker will ask some questions about the narration you just heard. Answer each question, omitting the subject. The speaker will confirm the correct answer. Repeat the correct answer.

OBJECTIVES

Structures

1. **En** and **a** as equivalents of *at*
2. The imperfect tense
3. The past progressive
4. The preterit contrasted with the imperfect

Communication

You will learn vocabulary related to things found at a shopping mall.

Country highlighted: Perú

Perú es una tierra (*land*) de contrastes: junto (*next*) a las altas montañas y a las espesas (*dense*) junglas se encuentran áridos desiertos. Es el tercer país más grande de la América del Sur; su territorio es casi tan extenso como el de Alaska. La capital de Perú es Lima, que es la ciudad más grande del país, y su centro urbano más importante. Allí se encuentra la Universidad Nacional de San Marcos, la más antigua de la América del Sur.

Dos grandes atracciones turísticas de Perú son Cuzco, capital del imperio inca, y las ruinas de Machu Picchu, descubiertas en 1911. En realidad, la civilización inca todavía marca, en cierto grado, la cultura peruana actual.

Las riquezas naturales de Perú incluyen el cobre (*copper*), la plata (*silver*), el oro, el petróleo, la industria maderera (*timber*) y la industria pesquera (*fishing*), que es una de las más importantes del mundo.

RESOURCES

Wherever you see the following icons additional resources are available:

Internet

Go to **www.college.hmco.com/languages/spanish/students/** for additional practice on the topic.

Student CD-ROM

Go to the **Video Grammar Tutor** for help with understanding the grammar topic at hand.

Go to the **In-Text Audio CDs** for more practice.

VOCABULARIO
Audio

COGNADOS

el aeropuerto
el catálogo
la computadora
el par

NOMBRES

el (la) adolescente   *teenager*
la cartera   *purse*
el centro comercial   *mall*
el departamento de ropa para
   señoras (caballeros)
   ladies' (men's) department
la joyería   *jewelry store*
el mensaje electrónico   *email*
la modista   *dressmaker*
el probador   *fitting room*
el sastre   *tailor*
el sombrero   *hat*
el traje de baño   *bathing suit*
la vidriera, el escaparate   *store window*
la zapatería   *shoe store*
los zapatos   *shoes*

VERBOS

celebrar   *to celebrate*
encontrarse (con) (o:ue)   *to meet*
   (for an appointment)
mirar   *to look at*
quedarse   *to stay, to remain*
sentir(se) (e:ie)   *to feel*

ADJETIVOS

magnífico(a)   *great*
nuevo(a)   *new*
preocupado(a)   *worried*

OTRAS PALABRAS Y EXPRESIONES

anteayer   *the day before yesterday*
casi nunca   *hardly ever*
cumplir ... años   *to turn ... (years old)*
de vez en cuando   *once in a while*
en casa   *at home*
en esa época   *in those days*
escribir a máquina   *to type*
ir de vacaciones   *to go on vacation*
juntos(as)   *together*
mirar vidrieras   *to window shop*
pues   *well*
todo el día   *all day long*

1 *EN* **AND** *A* **AS EQUIVALENTS OF** *AT*
En y *a* como equivalentes de *at*

■ **En** is used in Spanish as the equivalent of *at* to indicate a certain place or location.

—¿Dónde están los chicos? ¿No están **en** casa?   "*Where are the boys? Aren't they at home?*"

—No, están **en** el centro comercial, mirando vidrieras.   "*No, they're at the mall, window shopping.*"

■ **A** is used in Spanish as the equivalent of *at*.

1. to refer to a specific moment in time.

—¿Cuándo se encontraron Uds.?   "*When did you meet?*"

—Ayer **a** las once, en la joyería.   "*Yesterday at eleven, at the jewelry store.*"

2. to indicate direction towards a point after the verb **llegar.**

—¿A qué hora llegaron **al** aeropuerto de Lima?   "*What time did they arrive at the Lima airport?*"

—**A** las cinco.   "*At five.*"

> En Lima, como en todas las grandes ciudades hispanas, existen centros comerciales muy modernos. En contraste con esto todavía hay vendedores ambulantes por las calles, que se dedican a vender toda clase de artículos a precios más económicos.

Vamos a practicar

Complete the following dialogues, using **en** or **a,** as appropriate. Then act them out with a partner.

1. —¿ _____ qué hora llegaron Uds. _____ Cuzco?
—Llegamos _____ las seis.
—¿Dónde comieron?
—_____ un restaurante mexicano que hay _____ el aeropuerto.

2. —¿Dónde está tu esposa ahora? ¿_____ casa?
—No, está _____ el centro comercial, mirando vidrieras.

3. —¿Carlos está _____ la joyería?
—Sí, él trabaja allí todo el día.
—¿_____ qué hora te vas a encontrar con él _____ el restaurante?
—_____ las ocho y media.

2 THE IMPERFECT TENSE
El imperfecto de indicativo

There are two simple past tenses in Spanish: the preterit, which you have studied in **Lecciones 10** and **11,** and the imperfect.

Regular imperfect forms To form the imperfect tense, add these endings to the verb stem.

The Imperfect Tense		
-ar *Verbs*	**-er *and* -ir *Verbs***	
hablar	**comer**	**vivir**
habl**aba**	com**ía**	viv**ía**
habl**abas**	com**ías**	viv**ías**
habl**aba**	com**ía**	viv**ía**
habl**ábamos**	com**íamos**	viv**íamos**
habl**abais**	com**íais**	viv**íais**
habl**aban**	com**ían**	viv**ían**

- Notice that the endings of **-er** and **-ir** verbs are the same. Notice also that there is a written accent mark on the final **í** of **-er** and **-ir** verbs.

- Depending on the context, the imperfect tense in Spanish is equivalent to three forms in English.

Yo **vivía** en Lima.

{ *I used to live* in Lima.
I was living in Lima.
I lived in Lima.

- The imperfect is used to refer to habitual or repeated actions in the past, with no reference to when they began or ended.

—¿Tú **llamabas** a tu suegra? "*Did you use to call your mother-in-law?*"

—Sí, la **llamaba** de vez en cuando. "*Yes, I used to call her once in a while.*"

—¿Dónde **vivías** en esa época? "*Where did you live in those days?*"
—Yo **vivía** en Arequipa. "*I lived (was living) in Arequipa.*"

- The imperfect is also used to describe actions or events that the speaker views as in the process of happening in the past.

Yo **empezaba** a probarme la ropa cuando ella vino.

I was beginning to try on the clothes when she came.

- The imperfect is also used to describe physical, mental, or emotional conditions in the past.

El probador **era** muy grande.
Ella **estaba** enferma.
Nosotros **estábamos** preocupados.

The fitting room was very big.
She was sick.
We were worried.

- The imperfect tense of **hay** (from the verb **haber**) is **había.**

En la tienda **había** un departamento de ropa para señoras.

In the store there was a women's clothing department.

Irregular imperfect forms   There are only three irregular verbs in the imperfect tense: ser, ir, and ver.

ser	ir	ver
era	iba	veía
eras	ibas	veías
era	iba	veía
éramos	íbamos	veíamos
erais	ibais	veíais
eran	iban	veían

—¿Dónde vivían Uds. cuando **eran** adolescentes?
—En Perú, pero **íbamos** a Chile todos los años para celebrar el santo de mi abuela.
—Yo casi nunca **veía** a mis abuelos cuando era niña.

"Where did you live when you were teenagers?"
*"In Perú, but we went to Chile every year to celebrate my grand-mother's **santo**."*
"I hardly ever saw my grandparents when I was a child."

Los hispanos generalmente celebran el cumpleaños y también el día de su "santo", que corresponde al santo de su nombre en el calendario católico. Por ejemplo, si un niño nace (*is born*) en junio y sus padres lo llaman Miguel, celebra su cumpleaños en junio y celebra el día de su "santo" el 29 de septiembre, que es el día de San Miguel.

Quiz

Vamos a practicar

A Complete the following dialogues, using the imperfect tense of the verbs in parentheses. Then act them out with a partner.

1. —¿Uds. _____ (ir) al centro comercial cuando _____ (ser) adolescentes?
   —Sí, _____ (ir) de vez en cuando, pero generalmente sólo _____ (mirar) vidrieras.
2. —¿Viste a tu tía ayer?
   —Sí, y me dijo que _____ (necesitar) ir a la joyería.
3. —¿Tú _____ (ver) a tus abuelos en esa época?
   —No, casi nunca los _____ (ver) porque nosotros no _____ (vivir) cerca de ellos.
4. —¿Tus padres _____ (celebrar) el día de tu santo todos los años?
   —Sí, y todos mis parientes (*relatives*) _____ (venir) a la fiesta.

B Interview a classmate, using the following questions. When you have finished, switch roles.

1. ¿Dónde vivías cuando eras niño(a)?
2. ¿A qué escuela ibas?
3. ¿Iban Uds. al cine a veces?
4. ¿Veías a tus abuelos en esa época?
5. ¿Cocinaban tú y tus hermanos cuando eran niños? ¿Qué preparaban?
6. Cuando eras chico(a), ¿qué hacías los domingos?

C With a classmate, talk about what you used to do when you were children.

❸ THE PAST PROGRESSIVE
El pasado progresivo

The past progressive indicates an action in progress in the past. It is formed with the imperfect tense of the verb **estar** and the Spanish equivalent of the present participle (the **gerundio**).

—¿Qué **estabas haciendo** cuando te llamé?
—**Estaba escribiendo** un mensaje electrónico. Tengo una computadorqa nueva en casa.

"*What were you doing when I called you?*"
"*I was writing an email. I have a new computer at home.*"

—Pues ahora me puedes
  mandar uno a mí.

"Well, now you can send me one.

—¿Qué **estaban haciendo**
  las chicas?

"What were the girls doing?"

—**Estaban mirando** un catálogo.
  Ana **me estaba diciendo** que
  quería un traje de baño nuevo.

*"They were looking at a catalogue.
Ana was telling me that she
wanted a new bathing suit."*

—¿Dónde estaba Eva cuando
  tú la viste?

*"Where was Eva when you
saw her?"*

—**Estaba** en casa de la modista
  probándose el vestido.

*"She was at the dressmaker's
house, trying on the dress."*

> En las ciudades his-
> panas hay excelentes
> tiendas donde se
> puede comprar ropa
> hecha (*ready-to-wear*),
> pero muchas personas
> prefieren utilizar los
> servicios de un sastre
> o de una modista.

Note that direct and indirect object pronouns, as with other verb
tenses, preceed the conjugated verb (**estar**) or are attached to the
end of the **gerundio: estaba diciéndome.**

Vamos a practicar

A Tell what the following people were doing when a friend came to
visit. Use the cues provided.

MODELO   Elsa / hablar con Jorge
             Elsa **estaba hablando** con Jorge.

1. yo / hablar con la modista
2. Uds. / mirar un catálogo
3. tu mamá / limpiar la cocina
4. Isabel / probarse el traje de baño nuevo
5. los niños / dormir
6. Marta / usar la computadora
7. Carlos y papá / jugar al tenis
8. tu hermana / escribir un mensaje electrónico

B With a classmate, talk about what everybody was doing when the professor arrived.

④ THE PRETERIT CONTRASTED WITH THE IMPERFECT
El pretérito contrastado con el imperfecto

There are two simple past tenses in Spanish: the imperfect and the preterit.
The difference between the two can be visualized in the following way.

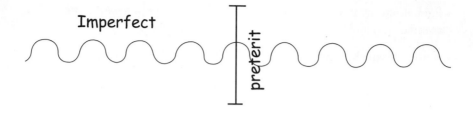

The continuous moving line of the imperfect represents an action or state that was taking place in the past. We don't know when the action started or ended. The vertical line of the preterit represents a completed or finished event in the past.

The following table summarizes the uses of the preterit and the imperfect.

Preterit	Imperfect
1. Records, narrates, and reports an independent past act or event as a completed and undivided whole, regardless of its duration. 2. Sums up a past condition or state viewed as a whole.	1. Describes an action in progress in the past. 2. Indicates a continuous and habitual action: *used to ...*[1] 3. Describes a physical, mental, or emotional state or condition in the past. 4. Expresses time in the past. 5. Indicates age in the past. 6. Is generally used in indirect discourse.[2]

---

[1]Note that this use of the imperfect also corresponds to the English *would,* when used to describe a repeated action in the past: **Cuando yo era niña,** *comía* **pollo todos los domingos.** *When I was a child, I* used to eat *chicken every Sunday. (When I was a child, I* would eat *chicken every Sunday.)*

[2]Amanda dijo que **estaba** cansada.

The preterit

—¿Qué **compró** Ud. ayer?

—**Compré** un sombrero y una cartera.

—¿Su esposo **fue** a la tienda también?

—No, él **estuvo** enfermo todo el día. **Se quedó** en casa.

—¿Qué **hicieron** tus padres cuando **cumpliste** 15 años?

—Me **dieron** una fiesta magnífica.

"*What did you buy yesterday?*"

"*I bought a hat and a purse.*"

"*Did your husband go to the store too?*"

"*No, he was sick all day long. He stayed home.*"

"*What did your parents do when you turned fifteen?*"

"*They gave me a great party.*"

> Para las muchachas latinoamericanas, es muy importante la celebración de los 15 años. En México la fiesta recibe el nombre de "quiceañera"; en otros países se llama la celebración de "los quince"

The imperfect

—Anteayer, cuando **íbamos** a la zapatería, vimos a María Ortiz mirando vidrieras.

—¿Sí? Ella y yo siempre **íbamos** juntas de vacaciones.

¿Cuántos años **tenías** tú cuando viniste a Lima?

—**Tenía** quince años.

—¿Por qué te fuiste tan temprano? **Eran** sólo las ocho de la noche.

—Me fui porque no **me sentía** muy bien.

—¿Qué dijo Eva ayer?

—Dijo que **necesitaba** dinero.

"*The day before yesterday as (when) we were going to the shoe store, we saw María Ortiz window shopping.*"

"*Really? She and I always used to go on vacation together.*"

"*How old were you when you came to Lima?*"

"*I was fifteen years old.*"

"*Why did you leave so early? It was only eight o'clock in the evening.*"

"*I left because I wasn't feeling very well.*"

"*What did Eva say yesterday?*"

"*She said she needed money.*"

ATENCIÓN: In the first exchange, íbamos **describes an action in progress, while in the third exchange,** me sentía **describes a physical state. These verbs in the imperfect act as background for completed actions in the past, which are expressed by the preterit verbs** vimos **and** me fui.

Vamos a practicar

A Complete the following paragraph with the preterit or the imperfect of the verbs in parentheses, as appropriate.

_____ (Ser) las cuatro de la tarde cuando yo _____ (llegar) a casa ayer. _____ (Preparar) la cena y _____ (escribir) hasta las ocho. Roberto _____ (venir) a comer conmigo y después (*afterwards*) _____ (mirar) la televisión juntos. Roberto y yo _____ (vivir) en Lima cuando _____ (ser) niños, pero él _____ (irse) a Colombia cuando _____ (tener) quince años. A las diez, Roberto _____(decidir) irse y yo _____ (acostarse) porque no _____ (sentirse) muy bien.

B Complete the following in an original manner, saying what everybody did differently. Use the preterit or the imperfect as appropriate.

1. Hoy voy a ir a la zapatería, pero anteayer _____.

2. Ahora nosotros vamos de vacaciones a Chile, pero cuando éramos adolescentes _____.

3. Ahora no uso sombrero, pero cuando tenía cuatro años _____.

4. Ahora tú te quedas en casa todo el día, pero cuando eras chico _____.

5. Hoy Elena va a escribir a máquina, pero ayer _____.

6. Ahora ellos viven en Cuzco, pero en esa época _____.

7. Ahora casi nunca veo a mis primos, pero cuando vivía en Lima _____.

8. Hoy Elba se va a encontrar con su novio, pero ayer _____.

C Interview a classmate, using the following questions. When you have finished, switch roles.

1. ¿Dónde vivías cuando tenías diez años?
2. ¿Hablabas inglés o español con tus amigos?
3. ¿Adónde ibas de vacaciones?
4. ¿Veías a tus abuelos a menudo?
5. ¿Adónde fuiste anoche?
6. ¿A quién viste?

7. ¿Qué hora era cuando volviste a tu casa?

8. ¿Estuviste enfermo(a) ayer?

9. ¿Cómo te sentías hoy cuando saliste de tu casa ayer?

10. Cuando fuiste de compras, ¿estuviste en el departamento de ropa para caballeros o en el departamento de ropa para señoras?

 D With a partner, prepare a list of ten questions you would like to ask your teacher about his or her childhood and youth.

Palabras y más palabras Match the questions in column **A** with the answers in column **B**.

A	B
1. ¿Dónde está el probador? _____	**a.** En la zapatería.
2. ¿Cuántos años cumpliste? _____	**b.** En mi cartera.
3. ¿Qué vas a comprar? _____	**c.** No, solamente la mañana.
4. ¿Por qué te quedaste en tu casa? _____	**d.** Un par de zapatos.
5. ¿Dónde se van a encontrar Uds.? _____	**e.** Sí, lo compré ayer.
6. ¿Pasaron todo el día juntos? _____	**f.** Veinte.
7. ¿Qué estaban haciendo en el centro comercial? _____	**g.** A la playa.
8. ¿Dónde pusiste el dinero? _____	**h.** En Perú.
9. ¿Tu traje de baño es nuevo? _____	**i.** No, solamente de vez en cuando.
10. ¿Dónde vivías tú en esa época? _____	**j.** A la izquierda.
11. ¿Adónde ibas de vacaciones? _____	**k.** Mirando vidrieras.
12. ¿Veías a tus amigos a menudo? _____	**l.** No me sentía bien.

 En estas situaciones What would you say in the following situations?

1. You ask an acquaintance where he/she lived when he/she was a child, and what he/she liked to do.

2. Describe what your first boyfriend (girlfriend) was like.

3. Say what you were doing when someone called you on the phone last night.

4. You ask a friend what time it was when he/she got home yesterday.

5. Mention several things that you did last week.

PARA ESCUCHAR Y ENTENDER

The following material is to be used with the In-Text Audio CDs.

I. Práctica

A El imperfecto

3–19   Explain what these people used to do by changing the following sentences to the imperfect. Listen to the model.

> **MODELO**   —Mis abuelos hablan en español.
> **Mis abuelos hablaban en español.**

B El pasado progresivo

3–20   Answer the questions, using the cues provided. Repeat the correct answer after the speaker's confirmation. Listen to the model.

> **MODELO**   —¿Qué estabas haciendo tú cuando yo llamé? (almorzar)
> —**Estaba almorzando.**

1. (mirar vidrieras)
2. (leer los catálogos)
3. (escribir en la computadora)
4. (comprar zapatos)
5. (probarse el traje de baño)

C ¿Pretérito o imperfecto?

3–21   Answer the questions, using the cues provided. Notice the use of the preterit or the imperfect. Repeat the correct answer after the speaker's confirmation. Listen to the model.

> **MODELO**   —¿Qué hora era cuando él llegó? (las nueve)
> —**Eran las nueve cuando él llegó.**

1. (en casa)   6. (que no podían venir)
2. (en México)   7. (sí)
3. (esta mañana)   8. (no, pero vine)
4. (en una fiesta)   9. (no)
5. (sí)   10. (a Luisa)

II. ¿Qué dicen?

1 ¿Lógico o ilógico?

3–22 The speaker will make some statements. Circle **L (lógico)** if the statement is logical and **I (ilógico)** if it is illogical. The speaker will verify your response.

1. L I	**3.** L I	**5.** L I	**7.** L I
2. L I	**4.** L I	**6.** L I	**8.** L I

2 ¿Verdadero o falso?

3–23 Listen carefully to the dialogue. Listen to it at least twice.

(Diálogo 1)

3–24 Now the speaker will make some statements about the dialogue you just heard. Tell whether each statement is true (**verdadero**) or false (**falso**). The speaker will confirm the correct answer.

3 Ester y Hugo

3–25 Listen carefully to the dialogue. Listen to it at least twice.

(Diálogo 2)

3–26 Now the speaker will ask you some questions about the dialogue you just heard. Answer each question, omitting the subject. The speaker will confirm the correct answer. Repeat the correct answer.

Structures

1 Changes in meaning with the imperfect and preterit of **conocer, saber,** and **querer**
2 **Hace** meaning *ago*
3 Uses of **se**
4 **¿Qué?** and **¿cuál?** used with **ser**

Communication

You will learn vocabulary related to shopping.

Country highlighted: Bolivia

Bolivia tiene una superficie de 424.165 millas cuadradas (*square miles*) y es tan grande como California y Texas unidos. Su población es de unos ocho millones de habitantes.

Se ha dicho que Bolivia es un país de superlativos. Tiene el lago navegable más alto del mundo: el Titicaca; el aeropuerto más alto; la capital más alta; una de las ruinas más antiguas del mundo, y la mayor concentración de rayos cósmicos que existe en la Tierra (*Earth*). Una característica que diferencia a Bolivia de otros países es el hecho (*fact*) de tener dos capitales: La Paz, que es la capital administrativa, y Sucre, que es la capital política. Aunque el país tiene muchas riquezas naturales, es difícil explotarlas debido (*due*) a la dificultad en las comunicaciones, y al hecho de que no tiene salida al mar (*is land-locked*).

La música boliviana es una muestra del carácter desigual (*different*) de las tres grandes regiones del país: los ritmos rápidos caracterizan la música del este y del noroeste; los lentos y melancólicos marcan la región andina, y los alegres (*happy*) ritmos de los valles centrales marcan la vida de esta región.

RESOURCES

Wherever you see the following icons additional resources are available:

Internet
Go to **www.college.hmco.com/languages/spanish/students/** for additional practice on the topic.

Student CD-ROM
Go to the **Video Grammar Tutor** for help with understanding the grammar topic at hand.

Go to the **In-Text Audio CDs** for more practice.

VOCABULARIO

Audio

COGNADOS

elegante
el portugués
el tipo

NOMBRES

el anillo, la sortija *ring*
el anillo de compromiso
  engagement ring
el ascensor *elevator*
la boda *wedding*
el camisón *nightgown*
la chaqueta *jacket*
el collar *necklace*
la corbata *tie*
la escalera *stairs*
la escalera mecánica *escalator*
la ferretería *hardware store*
la galería de arte *art gallery*
la moda *fashion*
la mueblería *furniture store*
el (la) nieto(a) *grandson,*
  granddaughter
el oro *gold*
la panadería *bakery*
la talla *size*
el traje *suit, outfit*

VERBOS

casarse (con) *to get married (to)*
conocer *to meet (for the first time)*
funcionar *to work (i.e., a machine,*
  a motor, etc.)
usar *to wear, to use*

ADJETIVO

mediano(a) *medium*

OTRAS PALABRAS Y EXPRESIONES

¿Cómo se dice...? *How do you say...?*
¿Cuánto tiempo hace que...? *How*
  long ago...?
no tener nada que ponerse *to have*
  nothing to wear

---

1 CHANGES IN MEANING WITH THE IMPERFECT AND PRETERIT OF *CONOCER, SABER,* AND *QUERER*

Cambios de significado del imperfecto y del pretérito de *conocer, saber* y *querer*

In Spanish, a few verbs have different meanings when used in the preterit or the imperfect.

	Preterit		Imperfect	
conocer	conocí	I met	conocía	I knew, I was acquainted with
saber	supe	I found out, I learned	sabía	I knew (a fact, how to)
querer	no quise	I refused	no quería	I didn't want to

—Mario, ¿**conocías** a la nieta de Luisa?
—No, la **conocí** ayer en la mueblería.

"*Mario, did you know Luisa's granddaughter?*"
"*No, I met her yesterday at the furniture store.*"

—¿**Sabes** que ella es de Bolivia?

—Sí, lo **supe** anoche cuando me dijo que era de La Paz.

"*Do you know that she's from Bolivia?*"
"*Yes, I found out last night when she told me that she was from La Paz.*"

—Rita, ¿**sabías** que la escalera mecánica no funcionaba?
—No, lo **supe** esta mañana. Tuve que tomar el ascensor.

"*Rita, did you know that the escalator wasn't working?*"
"*No, I found out this morning. I had to take the elevator.*"

—¿Por qué no fuiste a la galería de arte?
—Porque mi hermano **no quiso** llevarme. Tuve que quedarme en casa.

"*Why didn't you go to the art gallery?*"
"*Because my brother refused to take me. I had to stay home.*"

—Ada **no quería** ir a la boda porque no tenía nada que ponerse.
—¿Y qué hiciste tú?
—Le compré un vestido muy elegante y fuimos.

"*Ada didn't want to go to the wedding because she didn't have anything to wear.*"
"*And what did you do?*"
"*I bought her a very elegant dress and we went.*"

En los países hispanos para que el matrimonio sea reconocido legalmente, los novios deben casarse por lo civil. Luego pueden casarse por la iglesia si lo desean.

Vamos a practicar

A Complete the following dialogue, using the preterit or the imperfect of **saber, conocer,** or **querer,** as appropriate. Then act it out with a partner.

—¿Tú _____ a la nieta de doña Elsa?

—No, la _____ anteayer.

—¿Tú _____ que ella era la esposa de Roberto?

—No, lo _____ anoche. Me lo dijo Raquel.

—¿Alberto fue a la galería de arte ayer?

—Sí, fue. Él no _____ ir, pero su hermano lo llevó.

—¿Y Rosa? ¿Por qué no fue?

—Rosa no fue porque no _____.

B Use the following questions to interview a partner. When you have finished switch roles.

1. ¿Cuándo conociste a tu mejor amigo(a)?
2. ¿Conocías al profesor (a la profesora) antes de empezar esta clase?
3. ¿Tú querías o no querías venir a clase hoy?
4. La última vez (*Last time*) que no viniste a clase, ¿fue porque no pudiste o porque no quisiste?
5. ¿Tú sabías que el español era difícil?
6. Cuando tú supiste que había un examen, ¿qué hiciste?

② *HACE* MEANING *AGO*
Hace como equivalente de *ago*

In sentences in the preterit and in some cases the imperfect, **hace** + *period of time* is equivalent to the English *ago*.

Llegué **hace dos años.**   *I arrived two years ago.*

When **hace** is placed at the beginning of the sentence, the construction is as follows.

Hace	+	*period of time*	+	**que**	+	*verb (preterit)*
Hace		**dos años**		**que**		**llegué.**

—¿Cuánto tiempo **hace que** Luis
  te dio el anillo de compromiso?
—**Hace dos meses que** me lo dio.
  Pensamos casarnos en tres años.

"*How long ago did Luis give
  you the engagement ring?*"
"*He gave it to me two months ago.
  We are planning to get married
  in three years.*"

—¿Cuánto tiempo **hace que**
  compraste esa corbata y
  esa chaqueta?
—**Hace tres semanas que**
  las compré.

"*How long ago did you buy
  that tie and that jacket?*"

"*I bought them three
  weeks ago.*"

> Cuando una pareja
> (*couple*) se compro-
> mete, generalmente
> no se casan en segui-
> da. Los novios espe-
> ran hasta completar
> su educación y
> encontrar trabajo.

Vamos a practicar

A Interview a classmate, using the following questions. When you have
finished, switch roles.

1. ¿Cuánto tiempo hace que empezaste a estudiar en esta universidad?
2. ¿Cuánto tiempo hace que comiste?
3. ¿Cuánto tiempo hace que tomaste un examen en una de tus clases?
4. ¿Cuánto tiempo hace que conociste a tu mejor amigo o amiga?
5. ¿Cuánto tiempo hace que fuiste a una fiesta?
6. ¿Cuánto tiempo hace que aprendiste a conducir?

B With a partner, prepare six questions to ask your instructor. Use **hace**
to mean *ago* in each question.

3 USES OF SE
Usos de se

In Spanish, the pronoun **se** is used before the third person of the verb
(either singular or plural, depending on the subject) when the person
performing the action is not mentioned or is not known.

La panadería **se abre** a las ocho.   *The bakery opens (is opened) at eight.*
Las oficinas **se cierran** a las cinco. *The offices close (are closed) at five.*

■ Notice the use of **se** in the following impersonal constructions,
announcements, and general directions.

—Quiero comprar un traje y un
  camisón. ¿A qué hora **se abren**
  las tiendas?
—**Se abren** a las diez.

"*I want to buy a suit and a nightgown. What time do the stores
  open?*"
"*They open at ten.*"

—¿A qué hora **se cierra**
la ferretería?

"*What time does the hardware
store close?*"

—La ferretería **se cierra** a las
nueve de la noche.

"*The hardware store closes
at 9 P.M.*"

A las personas del mundo hispánico les gusta vestirse bien y usar ropa que está a la moda. Cuando salen a la calle tratan de estar siempre bien vestidos.

—¿En Brasil **se habla** español?

"*Is Spanish spoken in Brazil?*"

—No, **se habla** portugués.

"*No, Portuguese is spoken (there).*"

—¿Te gusta el tipo de ropa
que **se usa** ahora?

"*Do you like the type of clothes
that is used (worn) today?*"

—No, no me gusta.
No es muy elegante.

"*No, I don't like it. It isn't very
elegant.*"

■ **Se** is also used with the third person singular of the verb as the equivalent of *one, they,* or *people,* when the subject of the verb is not definite.

—¿Cómo **se dice** "necklace"
en español?

"*How does one say* necklace *in
Spanish?*"

—**Se dice** "collar".

"*One says* collar."

Vamos a practicar

Quiz

Luis Otero, a student from Chile, is visiting your hometown and needs some information. Answer his questions, using a construction with **se**.

1. ¿A qué hora se abre la librería de la universidad?
2. ¿Se habla español aquí?
3. ¿Cómo se dice "ferretería" en inglés?
4. ¿A qué hora se cierra la cafetería?
5. ¿Se abren las oficinas de la universidad los sábados?
6. ¿A qué hora se cierra la oficina de correos?
7. ¿Se abren los bancos los sábados aquí?
8. ¿A qué hora se abre la biblioteca? ¿A qué hora se cierra?

4 ¿QUÉ? AND ¿CUÁL? USED WITH SER
¿Qué? y ¿cuál? usados con el verbo ser

■ When asking for a definition, use **¿qué?** to translate *what.*

—¿**Qué** es el oro?

"*What is gold?*"

—Es un metal amarillo.

"*It is a yellow metal.*"

■ When asking for a choice, use **¿cuál?** (plural **¿cuáles?**) to translate as *what* (*which*). **¿Cuál?** implies selection from among many objects or ideas.

—¿**Cuál** es su talla?   "*What is your size?*"
—Mediana.   "*Medium.*"

—¿**Cuáles** son sus ideas sobre   "*What are your ideas*
la moda?   *about fashion?*"
—Yo no sé nada de moda.   "*I don't know anything
                                           about fashion.*"

> Algunos de los diseñadores (*designers*) más famosos de la moda Internacional son hispanos. Por ejemplo: Carolina Herrera, de Venezuela; Oscar de la Renta, de la República Dominicana y Adolfo, de Cuba.

Vamos a practicar

Quiz

Write the questions that correspond to the following answers, using **qué** or **cuál (cuáles).**

1. —¿ _____?
   —348–5490.

2. —¿ _____?
   —Calle Victoria, número 1542.

3. —¿ _____?
   —Es un metal amarillo.

4. —¿ _____?
   —Una enchilada es un tipo de comida mexicana.

5. —¿ _____?
   — ¿Mis ideas sobre la educación? ¡Creo que es muy importante y necesaria!

6. —¿ _____?
   — Rodríguez.

7. —¿ _____?
   — Es un lugar donde hay muchas tiendas.

8. —¿ _____?
   —Mediana.

Palabras y más palabras Circle the word or phrase that best completes each sentence.

1. ¿Usaste la escalera mecánica o (el ascensor, la corbata)?
2. Me voy a acostar. ¿Dónde está mi (chaqueta, camisón)?
3. Pedro le dio a Raquel un (anillo, collar) de compromiso.

4. Vamos a la (ferretería, panadería) para comprar un pastel.
5. El ascensor no (trabaja, funciona).
6. Ernesto se va a poner el (traje, camisón) nuevo para ir a la galería de arte.
7. Le voy a regalar una (sortija, corbata) de oro.
8. Uso (talla, boda) mediana.
9. En Brasil se habla (español, portugués).
10. (La talla, El tipo) de ropa que ella usa es muy elegante.
11. Estaban hablando sobre la (escalera, moda) francesa.
12. Compré la cama en la (ferretería, mueblería).

 En estas situaciones What would you say in the following situations?

1. You ask your professor how to say "ring" in Spanish.
2. Your friend just got engaged. Ask him/her when he/she is going to get married.
3. You complain about not having anything to wear and ask your friend if he/she wants to go shopping with you.
4. You ask a classmate how long ago he/she started studying Spanish.

PARA ESCUCHAR Y ENTENDER

The following material is to be used with the In-Text Audio CDs.

I. Práctica

A ¿Hace cuánto...?

3–27   The speaker will give you information that you will use to say how long ago everything took place. Repeat the correct answer after the speaker's confirmation. Listen to the model.

> **MODELO**   Son las cinco. Nora llegó a las cuatro y media.
> **Hace media hora que Nora llegó.**

B Quiero saber...

3–28   Answer the questions, using the cues provided. Repeat the correct answer after the speaker's confirmation. Listen to the model.

> **MODELO**   —¿A qué hora se abre el banco? (a las diez)
> **—El banco se abre a las diez.**

1. (a las nueve)	4. (no)
2. (portugués)	5. (a las doce)
3. (oro)	6. (un traje de baño)

II. ¿Qué dicen?

1 ¿Lógico o ilógico?

3–29

The speaker will make some statements. Circle **L (lógico)** if the statement is logical and **I (ilógico)** if it is illogical. The speaker will verify your response.

1. L I	**3.** L I	**5.** L I	**7.** L I
2. L I	**4.** L I	**6.** L I	**8.** L I

2 ¿Verdadero o falso?

Listen carefully to the dialogue. Listen to it at least twice.

3–30

(Diálogo 1)

3–31 Now the speaker will make some statements about the dialogue you just heard. Tell whether each statement is true (**verdadero**) or false (**falso**). The speaker will confirm the correct answer.

3 Silvia y Miguel

Listen carefully to the dialogue. Listen to it at least twice.

3–32

(Diálogo 2)

3 33 Now the speaker will ask you some questions about the dialogue you just heard. Answer each question, omitting the subject. The speaker will confirm the correct answer. Repeat the correct answer.

OBJECTIVES

Structures

1. The past participle
2. The present perfect tense
3. The past perfect (pluperfect) tense

Communication

You will learn vocabulary related to automobiles.

Country highlighted: Paraguay

Paraguay es un país que tiene más o menos el tamaño de California. Paraguay y Bolivia son los únicos países que no tienen salida al mar.

Paraguay exporta algodón (*cotton*), ganado (*cattle*), tabaco, madera y frutas cítricas, pero ahora es el principal exportador de energía eléctrica del mundo. La represa (*dam*) de Itaipú tiene la capacidad de producir seis veces la electricidad que produce la represa de Asuán, en Egipto.

El idioma oficial de Paraguay es el español, pero también se habla guaraní, una lengua indígena que aún se conserva y se enseña en las escuelas. La moneda (*currency*) nacional es el guaraní.

En Asunción, la capital, se ve un gran contraste entre edificios muy modernos y casas coloniales.

RESOURCES

Wherever you see the following icons additional resources are available:

Internet

Go to **www.college.hmco.com/languages/spanish/students/** for additional practice on the topic.

Student CD-ROM

Go to the **Video Grammar Tutor** for help with understanding the grammar topic at hand.

Go to the **In-Text Audio CDs** for more practice.

VOCABULARIO

Audio

COGNADOS

la gasolina, nafta *(Paraguay)*
imposible
el mecánico
el tanque

NOMBRES

el aceite *oil*
el acumulador, la batería *battery*
el club automovilístico *auto club*
  (e.g., AAA)
el (la) empleado(a) *clerk, attendant*
el freno *brake*
la gasolinera, la estación
  de servicio *gas station*
la goma, la llanta, el neumático *tire*
la goma pinchada *flat tire*
el limpiaparabrisas *windshield wiper*
el parabrisas *windshield*
la pieza de repuesto *spare part*
el remolcador, la grúa *tow truck*
el seguro, la aseguranza *(Méx.)*
  insurance
el taller *(repair) shop*

VERBOS

arrancar *to start (e.g. a motor)*
arreglar *to fix*
cambiar *to change*
cubrir *to cover*
llenar *to fill*
romper *to break*
sacar *to take out*

ADJETIVOS

cerrado(a) *closed*
descompuesto(a)[1] *out of order,*
  broken
listo(a) *ready*
vacío(a) *empty*

OTRAS PALABRAS Y EXPRESIONES

casi *almost*
en seguida *right away*
recientemente *recently*
sacar seguro *to take out insurance*
últimamente *lately*

 1 THE PAST PARTICIPLE
El participio pasado

> **Past participle** a past form of a verb that may be used in conjunction with
> another (auxiliary) verb in certain past tenses. The past participle may also be
> used as an adjective: *gone, worked, written*

---

[1]from the verb **descomponerse** (*to break*, i. e. mechanical things)

The past participle of regular verbs is formed by adding the following endings to the stem of the verb.

Past Participle Endings		
-ar *Verbs*	**-er** *Verbs*	**-ir** *Verbs*
habl- **ado**	ten- **ido**	ven- **ido**

- The following verbs have irregular past participles in Spanish.

abrir	**abierto**	morir	**muerto**
cubrir	**cubierto**	poner	**puesto**
decir	**dicho**	ver	**visto**
escribir	**escrito**	volver	**vuelto**
hacer	**hecho**	romper	**roto**

- In Spanish, most past participles may be used as adjectives. As such, they agree in number and gender with the nouns they modify.

—¿La gasolinera está **abierta?**   "*Is the gas station open?*"
—No, está **cerrada.**   "*No, it's closed. Do you need gas?*"
 ¿Necesitas gasolina?
—No, tengo una goma **pinchada**   "*No, I have a flat tire and the*
 y el parabrisas está **roto.**   *windshield is broken.*"

—¿Por qué viniste en ómnibus?   "*Why did you come by bus?*"
—Porque mi coche está   "*Because my car is broken.*"
 descompuesto.

—Entonces, ¿cómo vas a   "*Then, how are you going*
 volver a Asunción?   *to return to Asunción?*"
—Voy a ir por tren.   "*I'm going to go by train.*"

> En las ciudades hispanas hay mejor transporte público que en la mayoría de las ciudades norteamericanas. Por eso los hispanos dependen menos del automóvil.

Vamos a practicar

A What are the past participles of the following verbs?

1. dormir	**6.** cubrir	**11.** caminar	**16.** abrir
2. romper	**7.** recibir	**12.** pedir	**17.** ver
3. estar	**8.** hacer	**13.** decir	**18.** volver
4. comer	**9.** cerrar	**14.** comprar	**19.** aprender
5. poner	**10.** ser	**15.** morir	**20.** escribir

B Using the elements from the columns below and the verb **estar,** create ten descriptive sentences. You may use a verb more than once.

> **MODELO**   ventanas / cerrar
> Las ventanas **están cerradas.**

los hombres	las puertas	pinchar	escribir (en español)
Pedro	el neumático	descomponer	hacer (de madera)
la gasolinera	la mesa	cerrar	abrir
la carta	el parabrisas	morir	romper
el coche		dormir	

❷ THE PRESENT PERFECT TENSE
El pretérito perfecto

The present perfect tense is formed by using the present tense of the auxiliary verb **haber** and the past participle of the verb to be conjugated.

This tense is equivalent to the use in English of the auxiliary verb *have* + past participle, as in *I have spoken.*

Present of haber[1] *(to have)*	
he	hemos
has	habéis
ha	han

The Present Perfect Tense

	hablar	tener	venir
yo	**he** hablado	**he** tenido	**he** venido
tú	**has** hablado	**has** tenido	**has** venido
Ud. él ella	**ha** hablado	**ha** tenido	**ha** venido
nosotros	**hemos** hablado	**hemos** tenido	**hemos** venido
vosotros	**habéis** hablado	**habéis** tenido	**habéis** venido
Uds. ellos ellas	**han** hablado	**han** tenido	**han** venido

---

[1]Note that the English verb *to have* has two equivalents in Spanish: **haber** (used only as an auxiliary verb) and **tener.**

—¿Está listo el coche?

"*Is the car ready?*"

—No, porque el mecánico todavía no **ha conseguido** las piezas de repuesto.

"*No, because the mechanic still hasn't obtained the spare parts.*"

—¿Le **ha puesto** un acumulador nuevo?

"*Has he put a new battery in it?*"

—Sí, y también **ha cambiado** los limpiaparabrisas y **ha arreglado** los frenos.

"*Yes, and he has also changed the windshield wipers and has fixed the brakes.*"

—El coche no arranca.

"*The car won't start.*"

—¿**Han llamado** al club automovilístico?

"*Have you called the auto club?*"

—Sí, y el empleado **dice** que el remolcador viene en seguida.

"*Yes, and the clerk says that the tow truck is coming right away.*"

> En algunos países latinoamericanos no es obligatorio sacar seguro de automóvil, por lo que muchos no lo consideran necesario.

—¿Ya **ha sacado** seguro para su coche, Sr. Vega?

"*Have you taken out insurance on your car, Mr. Vega?*"

—No, porque es muy caro y, además, no es necesario.

"*No, because it is very expensive and, besides, it's not necessary.*"

—¿**Han comprado** alguna vez esta marca de aceite?

"*Have you ever bought this brand of oil?*"

—No, nunca la **hemos comprado.**

"*No, we have never bought it.*"

—¿**Has tenido** que llevar tu coche al taller recientemente?

"*Have you had to take your car to the repair shop recently?*"

—No, últimamente no **he tenido** problemas con el coche.

"*No, lately I have not had problems with my car.*"

ATENCIÓN: Note that when the past participle is part of a perfect tense, it is invariable and cannot be separated from the auxiliary verb haber.

Vamos a practicar

Quiz

A Say what the subjects given have or haven't done.

1. yo / comprar / un limpiaparabrisas nuevo
2. el mecánico / arreglar / los frenos
3. tú / no llamar / al club automovilístico
4. ellos / venir / en seguida
5. nosotros / no ver / al empleado
6. Uds. / cambiar / las llantas

B Interview a classmate, using the following questions. When you have finished, switch roles.

1. ¿Has comprado un coche alguna vez? (¿Cuánto te ha costado?)
2. ¿Cuántas veces (*times*) has cambiado el aceite de tu coche este año?
3. ¿Has tenido una goma pinchada alguna vez?
4. ¿Has cambiado una llanta alguna vez?
5. ¿Has cambiado los frenos de tu coche últimamente?
6. ¿Han tenido tú y tus amigos un accidente alguna vez?
7. ¿Han llamado una grúa alguna vez?
8. ¿Has tenido que comprar un acumulador últimamente?
9. ¿Has llevado tu coche al mecánico recientemente?
10. ¿Has sacado seguro para tu coche? ¿Es muy caro?

3 THE PAST PERFECT (PLUPERFECT) TENSE
El pluscuamperfecto

The past perfect tense is formed by using the imperfect tense of the auxiliary verb **haber** and the past participle of the verb to be conjugated.

This tense is equivalent to the use, in English, of the auxiliary verb *had* + past participle, as in *I had spoken*. As in English, the past perfect tense in Spanish describes an action or event completed before some other past action or event.

Imperfect of haber	
había	habíamos
habías	habíais
había	habían

The Past Perfect Tense

	estudiar	beber	ir
yo	**había** estudi**ado**	**había** beb**ido**	**había ido**
tú	**habías** estudi**ado**	**habías** beb**ido**	**habías ido**
Ud. él ella	**había** estudi**ado**	**había** beb**ido**	**había ido**
nosotros	**habíamos** estudi**ado**	**habíamos** beb**ido**	**habíamos ido**
vosotros	**habíais** estu**diado**	**habíais** beb**ido**	**habíais ido**
Uds. ellos ellas	**habían** estudi**ado**	**habían** beb**ido**	**habían ido**

—Tengo que comprar nafta.
El tanque está casi vacío.

—Eso es imposible. Carlos me
dijo que lo **había llenado.**

"*I have to buy gas. The tank is
almost empty.*"

"*That's impossible. Carlos told
me that he had filled it.*"

—Nosotros nunca **habíamos
usado** esa marca de aceite.

—¿Por qué la compraron?

—Porque el mecánico nos
había dicho que era
muy buena.

"*We had never used that
brand of oil.*"

"*Why did you buy it?*"

"*Because the mechanic
had told us that it was
very good.*"

> Como (*Since*) la gasolina
> es muy cara en los países
> hispanos, los coches
> pequeños y las motoci-
> cletas, que usan poca
> gasolina, son muy popu-
> lares, especialmente
> entre la gente joven.

Vamos a practicar

Quiz

A Complete the following dialogues, using the pluperfect of the verbs in parentheses. Then act them out with a partner.

1. —¿Por qué no le pusiste gasolina al coche?
   —Porque Javier ya _____ (llenar) el tanque.

2. —¿Hablaste con los empleados del taller?
   —No, porque cuando yo llegué, (ellos) ya _____ (irse).

3. —¿Uds. _____ (viajar) a México en coche antes?
   —No, siempre _____ (ir) en avión.

4. —¿Tú _____ (usar) esta marca de gasolina?
   —No, nunca la _____ (usar).

5. —Cuando tú llegaste a casa, ¿tus padres ya _____ (venir)?
   —No, no _____ (llegar) todavía.

6. —¿Ya estaba listo el coche cuando llegaste?
   —No, porque ellos no _____ (traer) las piezas de repuesto.
   —¿Por qué _____ (ir) ellos a la gasolinera?
   —Porque el tanque estaba casi vacío.

B Say what the subjects given had done to prepare for a car trip across the country.

1. el mecánico / los frenos
2. tú / el tanque
3. yo / la goma pinchada
4. mis padres / una batería nueva
5. mi hermano y yo / el coche

C Tell a partner five things you had already done today by the time you arrived at Spanish class.

Cuando llegué a la clase de español, ya (*already*) **había tomado** cuatro tazas de café...

Palabras y más palabras Say the following in a different way, using the vocabulary that you have learned in this lesson.

1. lo que se pone en el tanque de un coche
2. batería
3. gasolinera
4. lo que se usa para limpiar el parabrisas
5. llanta
6. grúa
7. lo que se usa para parar (*to stop*) el coche
8. persona que arregla coches
9. opuesto de posible
10. *Penzoil,* por ejemplo (*for example*)
11. opuesto de abierto
12. la AAA, por ejemplo

En estas situaciones What would you say in the following situations? What might the other person say?

1. You mention to somebody that your car won't start and ask if he/she can call a tow truck.
2. You have problems with your car. Tell the mechanic what they are. Mention three things.
3. You are traveling with a friend. You tell him/her that the tank is almost empty and that you need to get gas.
4. You ask the mechanic if the spare parts for your car have arrived.
5. In Asunción, you ask if all the service stations are closed on Sundays.

PARA ESCUCHAR Y ENTENDER

The following material is to be used with the In-Text Audio CDs.

I. Práctica

3–34

A El participio pasado

Answer the questions in the affirmative, using the past participle of the verb in the question as an adjective in your response. Repeat the correct answer after the speaker's confirmation. Listen to the model.

MODELO   —¿Terminaste la carta?
          —Sí, ya **está terminada.**

B El pretérito perfecto

Change each sentence to the present perfect tense. Repeat the correct
answer after the speaker's confirmation. Listen to the model.

3–35

MODELO   Yo llamo al club automovilístico.
Yo he llamado al club automovilístico.

 C El pluscuamperfecto

Restate the model sentence according to the new subjects. Repeat the correct answer after the speaker's confirmation. Listen to the model.

3–36

MODELO   Yo no lo había hecho todavía.

1. (Uds.)   4. (Eva)
2. (nosotras)   5. (ellos)
3. (tú)   6. (Ud.)

II. ¿Qué dicen?

 1 ¿Lógico o ilógico?

The speaker will make some statements. Circle **L (lógico)** if the statement
is logical and **I (ilógico)** if it is illogical. The speaker will verify your
response.

3–37

1. L I   3. L I   5. L I   7. L I
2. L I   4. L I   6. L I   8. L I

 2 ¿Verdadero o falso?

Listen carefully to the narration. Listen to it at least twice.

3–38

(Narración)

3–39   Now the speaker will make some statements about the narration you just
heard. Tell whether each statement is true (**verdadero**) or false (**falso**). The
speaker will confirm the correct answer.

 3 Celia y Luis

Listen carefully to the dialogue. Listen to it at least twice.

3–40

(Diálogo)

3–41   Now the speaker will ask you some questions about the dialogue you just
heard. Answer each question, omitting the subject. The speaker will confirm the correct answer. Repeat the correct answer.

LECCIÓN
15

OBJECTIVES

Structures

1 The future tense
2 The conditional tense
3 Some uses of the prepositions **a, de,** and **en**

Communication

You will learn more vocabulary related to transportation.

Country highlighted: Chile

Separado de Argentina por la cordillera (*mountain range*) de los Andes, se encuentra Chile, un país largo y estrecho (*narrow*) con variadas zonas climáticas. Algunos llaman a este país "la Suiza de América del Sur" por su espléndida belleza natural. La base de su economía está en la explotación de sus productos minerales y en la exportación de sus productos agrícolas. Exporta tanta (*so much*) fruta que se le considera "la frutería del mundo". Chile es también uno de los más importantes productores de cobre (*copper*) del mundo.

En cuanto a la educación, este país está muy adelantado (*advanced*), casi el 95 por ciento de los chilenos saben leer y escribir.

Santiago, que tiene una población de más de cuatro millones y medio de habitantes, es la capital de Chile, y es el centro industrial y cultural del país. Es una ciudad cosmopolita que refleja la influencia de Europa y de Norteamérica.

Las hermosas playas de Chile—como la de Viña del Mar, un centro turístico internacional—son visitadas anualmente por miles de turistas.

RESOURCES

Wherever you see the following icons additional resources are available:

Internet

Go to **www.college.hmco.com/languages/spanish/students/** for additional practice on the topic.

Student CD-ROM

Go to the **Video Grammar Tutor** for help with understanding the grammar topic at hand.

Go to the **In-Text Audio CDs** for more practice.

233

VOCABULARIO

Audio

COGNADOS

automático(a)
el (la) veterinario(a)
el examen

NOMBRES

la agencia de alquiler de automóviles
   car rental agency
el barco   *ship*
el (la) cajero(a)   *cashier*
el cajero automático   *automatic*
   teller machine (ATM)
la cuenta   *account*
la motocicleta, la moto   *motorcycle*
el motor   *engine*
el perro   *dog*
la plata   *silver*
el precio   *price*
el reloj   *clock, watch*
el tren   *train*
la vez   *time (in a series;*
   as equivalent of occasion)

VERBOS

alquilar   *to rent*
cobrar   *to charge*
depositar   *to deposit*
revisar, chequear   *to check*
terminar   *to finish*

ADJETIVOS

hermoso(a)   *beautiful*
peligroso(a)   *dangerous*

OTRAS PALABRAS Y EXPRESIONES

cambiar un cheque   *to cash a check*
de cambios mecánicos   *with a stan-*
dard shift
hasta   *until*
lejos (de)   *far (from)*
sin falta   *without fail*

---

① THE FUTURE TENSE
El futuro

The English equivalent of the Spanish future is *will* or *shall* + *verb*. As
you have already learned, Spanish also uses the construction **ir a** + *infinitive* or the present tense with a time expression to express future actions or
states, very much like the English present tense or the expression *going to.*

Vamos a usar el cajero automático.	*We're going to use (We'll use) the ATM.*
or: **Usaremos** el cajero automático.	

Anita **toma** el examen mañana.	*Anita is taking (will take) the exam tomorrow.*
or: Anita **tomará** el examen mañana.	

ATENCIÓN: The Spanish future is *not* used to make requests, as is the English future. In Spanish, requests are expressed with the verb querer.

¿Quieres llamar a Tomás?	*Will you call Tomás?*

Regular future forms Most Spanish verbs are regular in the future. The infinitive serves as the stem of almost all Spanish verbs. The endings are the same for all three conjugations.

The Future Tense

Infinitive		Stem	Endings
trabajar	yo	trabajar-	é
aprender	tú	aprender-	ás
escribir	Ud.	escribir-	á
hablar	él	hablar-	á
decidir	ella	decidir-	á
entender	nosotros	entender-	**emos**
viajar	vosotros	viajar-	éis
caminar	Uds.	caminar-	án
perder	ellos	perder-	án
recibir	ellas	recibir-	án

ATENCIÓN: Notice that all the endings, except the one for the nosotros form, have written accent marks.

—¿Cómo **viajarán** Uds. de Concepción Santiago?	*"How will you travel from Concepción to Santiago?"*
—**Alquilaremos** un coche o **viajaremos** en tren.	*"We will rent a car or we will travel by train."*
—¿Cuánto tiempo **estarán** en Santiago?	*"How long will you be in Santiago?"*
—Ana y yo **estaremos** allí por una semana y Jorge **se quedará** un mes. ¿Y adónde **irás** tú?	*"Ana and I will be there for a week and Jorge will stay for a month. And where will you go?"*

—Iré a Viña del Mar. Dicen que es una hermosa ciudad.

"I'll go to Viña del Mar. They say it's a beautiful city."

—¿**Irás** al banco a pie?

"Will you go to the bank on foot?"

—No, **tomaré** un taxi porque el banco queda lejos.

"No, I'll take a taxi because the bank is far from here."

> En la mayor parte de las ciudades de España y de Latinoamérica se pueden encontrar taxis en la calle o se pueden pedir por teléfono. En algunas ciudades hay taxis llamados colectivos. Estos taxis tienen una ruta fija y pueden llevar hasta diez pasajeros.

Vamos a practicar

Quiz

The following sentences say what everybody did. Rephrase them using the future tense to say what everyone will do.

1. Nosotros viajamos en tren.
2. Tú alquilaste un coche.
3. Yo fui a Chile.
4. Juan tomó un taxi.
5. El empleado cambió el aceite.
6. Mis padres fueron al banco.
7. Ud. consiguió las piezas de repuesto.
8. Estela cubrió el coche.
9. El mecánico volvió a la gasolinera.
10. Uds. llenaron el tanque.

Irregular future forms A few verbs are irregular in the future tense. These verbs use a modified form of the infinitive as a stem. The endings are the same as the ones for regular verbs.

Infinitive	Stem		Future Tense	
decir	dir-	yo	**dir-**	é
hacer	har-	tú	**har-**	ás
saber	sabr-	Ud.	**sabr-**	á
querer	querr-	él, ella	**querr-**	á
poder	podr-	nosotros	**podr-**	emos
poner	pondr-	vosotros	**pondr-**	éis
venir	vendr-	Uds.	**vendr-**	án
tener	tendr-	ellos	**tendr-**	án
salir	saldr-	ellas	**saldr-**	án

- The future of **hay** (from the verb **haber**) is **habrá.**

—Mañana **tendré** que ir al banco
para depositar un cheque.
¿Tú **podrás** llevarme esta vez?
—Sí, pero no **vendré** por ti hasta
las once porque tengo que
trabajar.

"*Tomorrow I'll have to go to the
bank to deposit a check. Will you be
able to take me this time?*"
"*Yes, but I won't come for you until
eleven because I have to work.*"

—¿Qué le **dirán** Uds. a Roberto?
—Le **diremos** que **saldremos** de
la agencia de alquiler de
automóviles a las once.
—¿Qué **harán** después?
—**Iremos** al banco para cambiar
un cheque.

"*What will you tell Roberto?*"
"*We will tell him that we'll be
leaving the car rental agency at
eleven.*"
"*What will you do afterwards?*"
"*We will go to the bank to cash a
check.*"

Vamos a practicar

Quiz

A Complete the following dialogues, using the future tense of the verbs
in parentheses. Then act them out with a partner.

1. —¿Qué le _____ (decir) Uds. al empleado?
   —Le _____ (decir) que (nosotros) _____ (tener) que venir
   mañana.
   —¿Cuándo _____ (estar) listo el coche?
   —Nosotros lo _____ (saber) esta tarde.

2. —¿_____ (Poder) el mecánico traer el coche?
   —Sí, él me ha dicho que _____ (venir) mañana.
   —Muy bien, porque nosotros _____ (salir) para Valparaíso por
   la noche.

3. —¿Cuándo _____ (poder) Uds. depositar el cheque?
   —Lo _____ (hacer) esta tarde después de salir de la agencia de
   alquiler de automóviles.

4. —¿Qué _____ (hacer) Uds. el domingo?
   —_____ (Ir) a la fiesta que _____ (haber) en el club.
   —¿Qué te _____ (poner) para ir a la fiesta?
   —Esta vez me _____ (poner) el traje azul.

B Interview a classmate, using the following questions. When you have finished, switch roles.

1. ¿A qué hora llegarás a tu casa hoy?
2. ¿Vendrán tú y tus amigos a una fiesta en la universidad esta noche? (¿A cuál?)
3. ¿Habrá mucha gente (*people*)?
4. ¿A qué hora llegarás a tu casa hoy?
5. ¿Podrás venir a clase mañana?
6. ¿Qué más tendrás que hacer mañana?
7. ¿Qué harán tú y tus amigos el domingo?
8. ¿Adónde irás el verano próximo?

C With a classmate, talk about your plans for the coming month. Use the future tense.

❷ THE CONDITIONAL TENSE
El condicional

The conditional tense in Spanish is equivalent to the conditional in English, expressed by *would* + *verb*.[1] Like the future tense, the conditional uses the infinitive as the stem and has only one set of endings for all three conjugations.

Regular conditional forms

The Conditional Tense			
Infinitive		*Stem*	*Endings*
trabajar	yo	trabajar-	**ía**
aprender	tú	aprender-	**ías**
escribir	Ud.	escribir-	**ía**
ir	él	ir-	**ía**
ser	ella	ser-	**ía**
dar	nosotros	dar-	**íamos**
ver	vosotros	ver-	**íais**
servir	Uds.	servir-	**ían**
estar	ellos	estar-	**ían**
preferir	ellas	preferir-	**ían**

---

[1]The imperfect, not the conditional, is used in Spanish as an equivalent of *used to*: **Cuando era pequeño siempre *iba* a la playa.** *When I was little* ***I would always go*** *to the beach.*

—¿**Vendería** Ud. su coche por cinco mil dólares?

—No, yo no lo **vendería** por ese precio. **Preferiría** regalárselo a mi hijo.

"Would you sell your car for five thousand dollars?"

"No, I wouldn't sell it at that price. I would prefer to give it (as a gift) to my son."

■ The conditional is also used to express the future of a past action; that is, the conditional describes an event that in the past was perceived as occurring in the future. In these cases, *would* in English carries the meaning *was going to.*

—¿Qué te dijo el mecánico ayer?

—Me dijo que **revisaría** el motor.

—¿Te dijo cuánto te **cobraría**?

—No, pero me dijo que no **costaría** mucho.

"What did the mechanic tell you yesterday?"

"He told me that he would (was going to) check the motor."

"Did he tell you how much he would charge you?"

"No, but he told me it wouldn't cost very much."

Quiz

Vamos a practicar

Most people don't agree with Eduardo's ideas. Use the cues in parentheses to explain what the people named wouldn't do.

> **MODELO**   Eduardo va a vender su coche. (yo)
> **Yo no lo vendería.**

1. Eduardo va a revisar el motor del coche. (tú)
2. Eduardo va a ponerle una batería nueva al coche. (ellos)
3. Eduardo va a cobrar diez mil dólares por su coche. (Elsa)
4. Eduardo no va a regalarle el coche a su hija. (yo)
5. Eduardo va a comprar un coche nuevo por veinte mil dólares. (nosotros)
6. Eduardo va a trabajar en la agencia de alquiler de automóviles. (Uds.)

Irregular conditional forms   The same verbs that are irregular in the future are also irregular in the conditional. The conditional endings are added to the modified form of the infinitive.

Infinitive	Stem		Conditional Tense	
decir	dir-	yo	**dir-**	ía
hacer	har-	tú	**har-**	ías
saber	sabr-	Ud.	**sabr-**	ía
querer	querr-	él, ella	**querr-**	ía
poder	podr-	nosotros	**podr-**	íamos
poner	pondr-	vosotros	**pondr-**	íais
venir	vendr-	Uds.	**vendr-**	ían
tener	tendr-	ellos	**tendr-**	ían
salir	saldr-	ellas	**saldr-**	ían

ATENCIÓN: The conditional of hay **(from the verb** haber**) is** habría.

—Mi coche no es automático.
¿Tú **podrías** manejarlo?
—Sí, pero primero **tendría** que
aprender a manejar coches
de cambios mecánicos.

*"My car is not automatic. Would
you be able to drive it?"*
*"Yes, but first I would have to learn
to drive cars with a standard shift."*

—Mi hijo quiere comprar
una motocicleta.
—Yo le **diría** que las motocicletas
son muy peligrosas.

*"My son wants to buy a motor-
cycle."*
*"I would tell him that motorcycles
are very dangerous."*

—Voy a abrir una cuenta en
el Banco Nacional.
—Yo no **pondría** mi dinero
en ese banco.

*"I'm going to open an account at the
National Bank."*
*"I wouldn't put my money in that
bank."*

Abrir una cuenta bancaria en Latinoamérica no es tan fácil como en Estados Unidos,
especialmente si es una cuenta corriente (*checking account*). En muchos países solamente las personas de clase media y de clase alta tienen cuentas bancarias.

Vamos a practicar

Quiz

A Complete the following dialogues, using the conditional of the verbs
in parentheses. Then act them out with a partner.

1.   —¿A qué hora _____ (salir) Uds.?
   —No _____ (salir) hasta las ocho.

—Pero, entonces Uds. no _____ (poder) llegar a la agencia a las ocho y media.

—Bueno, entonces nosotros _____ (tener) que salir antes.

2. —Teresa va a venir en autobús.

—Yo no _____ (hacer) eso. Yo _____ (venir) en coche.

3. —¿Tú _____ (saber) arreglar el coche?

—No, yo _____ (tener) que llevarlo al mecánico. Él lo _____ (poder) revisar.

4. —Quiero comprar una moto. ¿Qué crees tú que me _____ (decir) mamá?

—Probablemente te _____ (decir) que las motocicletas son muy peligrosas.

5. —¿Tú _____ (poder) vender tu coche por diez mil dólares?

—No, yo no _____ (poder) cobrar diez mil dólares. Mi coche es automático, pero no es nuevo.

6. —¿En qué banco _____ (depositar) tú el dinero?

—Yo lo _____ (poner) en el Banco Nacional. Allí tengo yo mi cuenta.

B With a partner, take turns telling each other what you would do if you won a million dollars in the lottery. Say at least five things each, and then compare your responses with those of other classmates.

③ SOME USES OF THE PREPOSITIONS *A, DE,* AND *EN*
Algunos usos de las preposiciones *a, de* y *en*

■ The preposition **a** (*to, at, in*) is used in the following ways.

1. To introduce the direct object when it is a person,[1] animal, or anything that is given personal characteristics

Esperamos **a** la cajera.	*We're waiting for the cashier.*
Llevé **a** mi perro al veterinario.	*I took my dog to the vet.*

2. To indicate the time (hour) of day

El coche estará listo **a** las cinco.	*The car will be ready at five.*

---

[1]When the direct object is not a definite person, the personal **a** is not used: **Busco un buen maestro.**

3. To express destination or result after verbs of motion when they are
followed by an infinitive, a noun, or a pronoun

Siempre venimos **a** alquilar
coches aquí.

We always come to rent cars here.

4. After the verb **llegar,** when it expresses destination

Llegaremos **a** Lima mañana
sin falta.

*We will arrive in Lima
tomorrow without fail.*

5. After the verbs **enseñar, aprender, comenzar,** and **empezar** when
they are followed by an infinitive

Voy **a empezar** a
arreglar el carro.

*I'm going to start fixing
the car.*

Él dijo que su hijo
aprendería a manejar.

*He said that his son would
learn how to drive.*

> En los países hispanos
> una persona debe tener
> por lo menos 18 años
> para empezar a manejar.
> Para recibir la licencia de
> conducir tiene que pasar
> un examen muy difícil.

■ The preposition **de** (*of, from, about*) is used in the following
ways.

1. To refer to a specific time of the day or night

Dijeron que terminarían a
las ocho **de** la noche.

*They said that they would finish
at eight in the evening.*

2. To distinguish one from a group when using superlatives

Mi sobrina es la más inteligente
de la familia.

*My niece is the most intelligent
in the family.*

3. To indicate possession or relationship

Ésta es la motocicleta **de**
mi esposo.

This is my husband's motorcycle.

Carlos es el hijo **del** veterinario.

Carlos is the vet's son.

4. To indicate the material something is made of

El reloj es **de** plata.

The watch is made of silver.

5. To indicate origin

Ellos son **de** La Habana.

They are from Havana.

6. As a synonym of **sobre** or **acerca de** (*about*)

Hablaban **de** los precios
de las casas.

*They were speaking about
the prices of houses.*

■ The preposition **en** (*at, in, on, inside, over*) is used in the following
ways.

1. To refer to a definite place

Mi coche está **en** la gasolinera.   *My car is at the service station.*

2. To indicate means of transportation

Muchas veces viajábamos
en barco.

We traveled by ship many times.

3. As a synonym of **sobre** (*on*)

Los libros están **en** la mesa.   *The books are on the table.*

ATENCIÓN: In Mexico and in most Spanish-speaking countries of Latin
America, por **(by)** is used with certain means of transportation, whereas
en is used with other means.

Vamos **por** barco. (*or* Vamos **en** barco.)
Vamos **por** avión. (*or* Vamos **en** avión.)
Vamos **por** tren. (*or* Vamos **en** tren.)

but

Vamos **en** autobús.
Vamos **en** automóvil.
Vamos **en** motocicleta.

Vamos a practicar

Complete the following dialogues, using **a, de,** or **en** as appropriate. Then
act them out with a partner.

1. —¿ _____ qué hora llegarán Uds. _____ la agencia _____ viajes?
—Llegaremos _____ las ocho y media _____ la mañana sin falta.

2. —¿ _____ quién esperan Uds.?

   —Esperamos _____ la cajera.

   —¿Dónde está ella ahora?

   —Está _____ la oficina _____ la agencia.

3. —¿No trajiste _____ tu perro?

   —No, está enfermo. Lo llevé _____ la veterinaria ayer.

4. —¿Para qué fueron Uds. _____ la agencia?

   —Fuimos _____ alquilar un coche _____ cambios mecánicos.

   —¿Tú sabes manejar ese tipo de coche?

   —No, pero mi hermano me va _____ enseñar _____ manejarlo.

5. —¿Quién es esa chica? ¡Es muy hermosa!

   —Es la hermana _____ Raúl. Es la chica más inteligente _____ la clase.

   —¿ _____ dónde es Raúl?

   —Creo que es _____ Perú.

6. —¿ _____ quién es el reloj que está _____ la mesa?

   —Es _____ Aurelio.

   —¿Es _____ plata?

   —No, es _____ oro blanco.

7. —¿ _____ qué estaban hablando Uds.?

   —Estábamos hablando _____ nuestras vacaciones.

   —¿Adónde fueron?

   —Fuimos _____ San Antonio.

   —¿Fueron _____ autobús?

   —No, fuimos _____ automóvil.

8. —¿Dónde está Teresa?

   —Está _____ el banco. Fue _____ cambiar un cheque.

   —¿Para qué necesitaba el dinero?

   —Para pagarle _____ un mecánico que arregló el motor _____ su coche.

Palabras y más palabras Complete the following dialogues, using the vocabulary learned in this lesson. Then act them out with a partner.

1. —¿Cuál es el _____ de esa moto?
    —Cuesta doce mil dólares.

2. —Tengo que ir al banco para _____ un cheque.
    —Pues ve hoy sin _____, porque el banco estará cerrado mañana.

3. —¿A qué hora comienza la clase?
    —Empieza a las dos y _____ a las tres.

4. —¿Cuánto dinero tenemos en nuestra _____?
    —Mil dólares, y hoy voy a depositar doscientos.

5. —¿Tu coche es automático?
    —No, es de _____ mecánicos.

6. —¿Le vas a comprar una motocicleta a tu hijo?
    —No, porque son muy _____.

7. —Quiero alquilar un coche. ¿Quieres ir a la agencia de _____ de automóviles conmigo?
    —Si puedes esperar _____ las tres, voy contigo.

8. —¿Cuánto te _____ el mecánico por _____ el motor del coche?
    —Cincuenta dólares, pero dice que no puede arreglarlo.

9. —¿Tu casa queda cerca?
    —No, queda muy _____.

10. —¿Van de Nueva York a Madrid en avión?
    —No, van en _____.

En estas situaciones What would you say in the following situations?

1. Mention three things that you will have to do tomorrow.
2. Someone wants to sell you his car. Ask whether it is an automatic or standard shift.
3. Your professor wants to see you in his/her office. Tell him/her that you will come tomorrow without fail.
4. Your friend Nora needs money, but the bank is closed. Tell her that she can take money out from the ATM.
5. You are making plans to visit another state. Say how you would like to travel.

PARA ESCUCHAR Y ENTENDER

The following material is to be used with the In-Text Audio CDs.

I. Práctica

 A El futuro

4–2   Rephrase each sentence, using the future tense instead of the expression **ir a + *infinitive*.** Repeat the correct answer after the speaker's confirmation. Listen to the model.

> **MODELO**   Vamos a salir muy tarde.
> **Saldremos muy tarde.**

 B El condicional

4–3   Answer the questions, always using the second choice. Repeat the correct answer after the speaker's confirmation. Listen to the model.

> **MODELO**   —¿Comprarías un coche o una casa?
> —**Compraría una casa.**

 C ¿A, de, o en?

4–4   Answer the questions in complete sentences, using the cues provided. Repeat the correct answer after the speaker's confirmation. Listen to the model.

> **MODELO**   —¿Cómo van ellos? (coche)
> —**Van en coche.**

1. (la cajera)
2. (las ocho)
3. (autobús)
4. (la mesa)
5. (las vacaciones)
6. (la agencia)
7. (Carlos)
8. (sí)

II. ¿Qué dicen?

 1 ¿Lógico o ilógico?

4–5   The speaker will make some statements. Circle **L (lógico)** if the statement is logical and **I (ilógico)** if it is illogical. The speaker will verify your response.

1. L I
2. L I
3. L I
4. L I
5. L I
6. L I
7. L I
8. L I
9. L I
10. L I

2 ¿Verdadero o falso?

4-6   Listen carefully to the dialogue. Listen to it at least twice.

(Diálogo 1)

4-7   Now the speaker will make some statements about the dialogue you just heard. Tell whether each statement is true **(verdadero)** or false **(falso).** The speaker will confirm the correct answer.

3 Rosa y José

4-8   Listen carefully to the dialogue. Listen to it at least twice.

(Diálogo 2)

4-9   Now the speaker will ask you some questions about the dialogue you just heard. Answer each question, omitting the subject. The speaker will confirm the correct answer. Repeat the correct answer.

 **¿Cuánto sabe usted ahora?**

Lección 11

A Time expressions with *hacer*

Give the Spanish equivalent of the words in parentheses.

1. _____ en la Facultad de Derecho.
   (*I have studied for two years*)
2. ¿_____ Sra. Sanz? (*How long have you been waiting*)

B Irregular preterits

Rewrite the sentences, beginning with the expressions provided. Follow the model.

Modelo   Tenemos que salir. (Ayer)
   Ayer tuvimos que salir.

1. María no está en la clase. (Ayer)
2. No pueden venir. (Anoche)
3. Pongo el dinero en el banco. (El mes pasado)
4. No haces nada. (El domingo pasado)
5. Ella viene con Juan. (Ayer)
6. No queremos venir a clase. (El lunes pasado)
7. Yo no digo nada. (Anoche)
8. Traemos la tostadora. (Ayer)
9. Yo conduzco mi coche. (Anoche)
10. Ellos traducen las lecciones. (Ayer)

C The preterit of stem-changing verbs (*e:i* and *o:u*)

Rewrite the sentences, beginning with the expressions provided. Follow the model.

Modelo   Él no pide dinero. (Ayer)
   Ayer él no **pidió** dinero.

1. Ella elige la secadora. (Ayer)
2. Marta no duerme bien. (Anoche)
3. No le pido nada. (Ayer)

4. Ella te miente. (La semana pasada)
5. Ellos sirven los refrescos. (El sábado pasado)
6. No lo repito. (Ayer)
7. Ella sigue estudiando. (Anoche)
8. Tú no consigues nada. (El lunes pasado)

D The affirmative familiar command (*tú* form)

Change the commands from the **Ud.** (*formal*) form to the **tú** (*informal*) form. Follow the model.

MODELO   Salga con los niños.
            Sal con los niños.

1. Venga acá, por favor.
2. Hable con la profesora.
3. Dígame su dirección.
4. Lávese las manos.
5. Póngase el abrigo.
6. Tráiganos el arroz con pollo.
7. Compre los libros.
8. Hágame un favor.
9. Apague la luz.
10. Vaya de compras hoy.
11. Salga temprano.
12. Aféitese aquí.
13. Tenga paciencia.
14. Sea buena.
15. Coma con nosotros.

E The negative familiar command (*tú* form)

Give the Spanish equivalent of the words in parentheses.

1. _____ esta tarde. (*Don't wait for me*)
2. _____ muy temprano. (*Don't get up*)
3. _____ ahora, Marta. (*Don't leave*)
4. _____ en inglés. (*Don't speak to them*)
5. _____ al club con él. (*Don't go*)
6. _____ ese vestido. (*Don't put on*)
7. _____ eso. (*Don't do*)
8. _____ mañana. (*Don't come back*)

F **Vocabulary**

Complete the following sentences, using words learned in **Lección 11.**

1. Ayer fui de _____ porque necesitaba un vestido.
2. Ana, _____ la luz, por favor.
3. Los domingos nosotros siempre comíamos _____ con pollo.
4. No me gusta hacer los _____ de la casa.
5. Ayer hubo una gran _____ en Sears. Todo estaba muy barato.
6. En _____ hora estamos en tu casa.
7. Vamos a tomar un taxi porque ella no quiere _____.
8. Él estudia en la _____ de Derecho.
9. Me voy a _____ del invitado porque se va.
10. ¿Vas a salir otra _____?

LECCIÓN 12

A *En* and *a* as equivalents of *at*

Write sentences using the words provided with **en** or **a,** as appropriate. Follow the model.

MODELO   Yo / estar / universidad

        Yo estoy en la universidad.

1. Nosotros / llegar / aeropuerto / seis y media
2. Mi cuñada / estar / casa
3. Ellos / estar / joyería
4. La fiesta / ser / las doce
5. ¿Raúl / estar / clase?

B **The imperfect tense**

Answer the following questions using the model as a guide.

MODELO   —¿Qué querían ellos? (arroz con pollo)
        —Querían arroz con pollo.

1. ¿Donde vivían Uds. cuando eran chicos? (en Alaska)
2. ¿Qué idioma hablabas tú cuando eras chico(a)? (alemán)
3. ¿A quién veías siempre cuando eras chico(a)? (a mi abuela)

4. ¿En qué banco ponían Uds. el dinero? (en el Banco Nacional)
5. ¿A qué hora se acostaban ellos? (a las nueve)
6. ¿Adónde iba Rosa? (a la universidad)
7. ¿Qué compraba Ud.? (arroz)
8. ¿Qué enseñaba Elsa? (español)

C The past progressive

Complete the sentences with the past progressive of **hacer, hablar, estudiar, comer, leer, trabajar, escribir,** or **comprar** as appropriate. Use each verb once.

1. Nosotros _____ arroz con pollo cuando llegó Elsa.
2. ¿Qué _____ tú cuando yo llamé?
3. Elena _____ en la computadora cuando llegó el Dr. Vargas.
4. Yo _____ por teléfono (*on the phone*) con mi cuñado.
5. ¿Uds. _____ el reloj (*watch*) en la joyería?
6. Ud. _____ el periódico cuando yo vine.
7. Los niños _____ la lección.
8. Roberto _____ en la zapatería cuando yo lo vi.

D The preterit contrasted with the imperfect

Complete the sentences, using the preterit or the imperfect of the verbs given.

1. Teresa _____ (cumplir) veinte años ayer.
2. Ella _____ (estar) en el departamento de señoras cuando yo la _____ (ver).
3. Cuando nosotros _____ (ser) niños, _____ (ir) a Lima todos los veranos y _____ (celebrar) el cumpleaños de mi abuelo.
4. Cuando ellos _____ (ser) adolescentes, casi nunca _____ (estudiar).
5. Ayer la modista me _____ (decir) que _____ (necesitar) más dinero.
6. _____ (ser) las once cuando yo _____ (llegar) a casa anoche. Mis padres _____ (estar) muy preocupados.

E Vocabulary

Complete the following sentences, using words learned in **Lección 12.**

1. Mi hija compró ayer un _____ de baño nuevo.
2. Ellos vieron el sombrero en el _____ de JC Penney.
3. No podemos irnos. Tenemos que _____ aquí _____ el día.
4. Puse el dinero en mi _____.
5. Voy a _____ con Rosa a las cinco.
6. El mes pasado fuimos de _____ a México. Fue un viaje _____.
7. No quiero ir sola. ¿Por qué no vamos _____ tú y yo?
8. Tengo que estar en el _____ a las ocho porque el avión sale a las ocho y media.
9. Voy a probarme los _____ nuevos.
10. Nos gusta ir al centro _____ a mirar _____.

LECCIÓN 13

A Changes in meaning with imperfect and preterit of *conocer, saber,* and *querer*

Complete the sentences with the preterit or the imperfect of the verbs **conocer, saber,** and **querer,** as appropriate.

1. Yo no _____ a los abuelos de María. Los _____ ayer.
2. Nosotros no _____ que ella era casada. Lo _____ anoche.
3. Mamá no fue a la fiesta porque no _____ ir.
4. Yo no _____ ir a la fiesta, pero cuando _____ que Carlos iba a ir, decidí ir también.

B *Hace* meaning *ago*

Write two sentences for each set of items. Follow the model.

MODELO   Un año / yo / conocer / él
Hace un año que yo lo conocí.
Yo lo conocí hace un año.

1. tres meses / nosotros / llegar / a California
2. dos horas / el chico / tomar / café
3. dos días / ellos / terminar / la lección
4. veinte años / ella / venir / a esta ciudad
5. dos días / tú / ver / a tu nieta

C Uses of *se*

Answer the following questions.

1. ¿Qué idiomas se hablan en los Estados Unidos?
2. ¿Cómo se dice *mattress* en español?
3. ¿A qué hora se cierra la oficina de correos?
4. ¿Cómo se escribe su nombre?
5. ¿A qué hora se abren las bibliotecas?

D ¿*Qué?* and ¿*cuál?* used with *ser*

Complete the following, using **cuál** or **qué**.

1. ¿ _____ es su dirección?
2. ¿_____ es una enchilada? ¿Una comida mexicana?
3. ¿_____ es tu número de teléfono?
4. ¿_____ es tu opinión sobre eso?
5. ¿ _____ es el fútbol?

E Vocabulary

Complete the following sentences, using words learned in **Lección 13**.

1. Compré la mesa en la _____.
2. ¿Cómo se _____ corbata en portugués?
3. No voy a subir por la escalera; voy a usar el _____.
4. Carlos me llevó a la _____ de arte.
5. El anillo es de _____.
6. La escalera _____ no funciona.
7. Me voy a poner la _____ porque tengo frío.
8. Elena es mi _____. Es la hija de mi hijo.
9. Otro nombre para anillo es _____.
10. Teresa usa _____ mediana.
11. Luis y Olga se casan mañana. ¿Tú vas a la _____?
12. Yo no tengo _____ que ponerme.

LECCIÓN 14

A The past participle

Complete the following chart.

Infinitive	Past Participle
1. trabajar	1. trabajado
2. recibir	2. _____
3. _____	3. vuelto
4. usar	4. _____
5. escribir	5. _____
6. _____	6. ido
7. aprender	7. _____
8. _____	8. abierto
9. cubrir	9. _____
10. comer	10. _____
11. _____	11. visto
12. hacer	12. _____
13. ser	13. _____
14. _____	14. dicho
15. cerrar	15. _____
16. _____	16. muerto
17. _____	17. roto
18. dormir	18. _____
19. estar	19. _____
20. _____	20. puesto

B Past participles used as adjectives

Write sentences using **estar** and the past participle of the verbs given.

1. ventana / romper
2. libros / abrir
3. puertas / cerrar
4. mesa / cubrir
5. cartas / escribir

C The present perfect tense

Complete the sentences with the present perfect of **hablar, hacer, abrir, venir, decir, estudiar, escribir, tener, poner, romper,** or **comer,** as appropriate. Use each verb once.

1. Yo _____ muchas veces a este lugar.

2. ¿_____ Uds. la lección?

3. Nosotros todavía no _____ con el mecánico.

4. Ella me _____ que tengo que venir el sábado y el domingo.

5. ¿No _____ (tú) las cartas todavía?

6. Hoy nosotros no _____ nada porque no _____ tiempo.

7. ¿Quién _____ las puertas?

8. ¿Dónde _____ Ud. las sillas?

9. Elena y Carlos no _____ todavía.

10. Ellos _____ el parabrisas.

D The past perfect (pluperfect) tense

Give the Spanish equivalent of the words in parentheses.

1. Ella me dijo que él ya _____ la batería. (*had bought*)

2. Los niños _____ la ventana. (*had broken*)

3. Yo _____ seguro. (*had taken out*)

4. ¿Tú _____ con el empleado? (*had spoken*)

5. Nosotros le _____ que el coche estaba estropeado. (*had told*)

E Vocabulary

Complete the following sentences, using words learned in **Lección 14.**

1. Voy a la estación de _____ porque necesito comprar _____.

2. Otro nombre para batería es _____.

3. Tengo que llenar el tanque porque está casi _____.

4. Tengo que cambiar la _____ porque está _____.

5. Voy a llamar al club _____ porque necesito una grúa. Mi coche no _____.

6. ¿Qué marca de _____ usa Ud.? ¿Penzoil?

7. La gasolinera no está abierta; está _____.

8. El coche no está listo todavía porque necesita varias piezas de _____.

LECCIÓN 15

A The future tense

Complete the following sentences, using the future tense of the verb in parentheses.

1. ¿Cuándo _____ (ir) Uds. a la agencia de alquiler de automóviles?

2. El cajero _____ (venir) mañana a las ocho.

3. Ellos _____ (pagar) la cuenta el viernes.

4. ¿Tú _____ (llevar) al perro al veterinario?

5. El examen _____ (ser) mañana.

6. ¿Dónde _____ (poner) tú la moto?

7. Ellos _____ (manejar) mi coche.

8. El mecánico _____ (revisar) los frenos.

9. ¿Qué _____ (hacer) Uds. el domingo por la tarde?

10. Yo _____ (alquilar) un coche el próximo sábado.

B The conditional tense

Complete the sentences with the conditional tense of **servir, poner, haber, trabajar, seguir, vender, levantarse, preferir,** or **ir.** Use each verb once.

1. Él dijo que nosotros _____ a Europa el verano próximo.

2. ¿Ellos _____ su casa a ese precio? Yo creo que sí.

3. ¿Dijo Ud. que no _____ clases esta tarde?

4. Yo no _____ el café en la terraza.

5. Tú no _____ en una gasolinera.

6. ¿_____ Ud. su dinero en ese banco?

7. ¿Qué _____ Uds.: ir a México o ir a Guatemala?

8. ¿_____ Uds. estudiando español?

9. ¿_____ tú a las tres de la mañana?

C **Some uses of the prepositions *a, de,* and *en***

Give the Spanish equivalent of the words in parentheses.

1. Nosotros _____ la universidad a las seis. (*will arrive at*)

2. ¿Llevaste _____ al veterinario? (*your dog*)

3. Ella está _____ de alquiler de automóviles. (*at the agency*)

4. Nosotros viajaremos _____. (*by plane*)

5. ¿_____ están hablando ellos? (*About what*)

D **Vocabulary**

Complete the following sentences, using words learned in **Lección 15.**

1. Necesito alquilar un coche. Voy a la _____ de alquiler de automóviles.

2. Mi mamá dice que las motocicletas son muy _____.

3. Yo no sé manejar coches de cambios _____; sólo sé manejar coches _____.

4. Voy al banco para _____ cien dólares en mi cuenta.

5. Los aretes (*earrings*) de Rosalía no son de oro; son de _____.

6. El mecánico va a _____ el motor del auto.

7. Mañana sin _____ voy a llevar a mi perro al veterinario.

8. El _____ de español fue ayer.

9. No vive cerca de la universidad, vive muy _____.

10. Saqué dinero del _____ automático.

OBJECTIVES

Structures
1. The present subjunctive
2. The subjunctive with verbs of volition
3. The absolute superlative

Communication
You will learn vocabulary related to traveling by train.

Country highlighted: Argentina

Search

Argentina, con un área un poco menor de la cuarta parte de los Estados Unidos, es uno de los países menos densamente poblados de América, y uno de los más urbanizados del mundo. Su variado paisaje (*landscape*) incluye las maravillosas cataratas (*waterfalls*) de Iguazú (mucho más altas que las del Niágara) en el norte, y el Glaciar Perito Moreno en el sur.

Buenos Aires, la capital de Argentina, es la ciudad más grande del hemisferio sur. Es el centro nacional de la cultura, el comercio (*business*), la industria y la política. Su población es casi enteramente de origen europeo. Predominan los españoles y los italianos, pero hay también gran número de ingleses, franceses y alemanes. A las personas de Buenos Aires se las llama **porteños,** que significa "gente del puerto (*port*)".

En Buenos Aires hay más de cuarenta universidades y la ciudad tiene una vida cultural muy activa. Hay numerosos museos y teatros muy importantes; el teatro Colón es uno de los más famosos del mundo. La ciudad tiene muchos parques muy hermosos y la Avenida 9 de Julio es una de las más anchas (*wide*) del mundo.

RESOURCES

Wherever you see the following icons additional resources are available:

 Internet

Go to **www.college.hmco.com/languages/spanish/students/** for additional practice on the topic.

 Student CD-ROM

Go to the **Video Grammar Tutor** for help with understanding the grammar topic at hand.

Go to the **In-Text Audio CDs** for more practice.

VOCABULARIO
Audio

COGNADOS

la polución
el tráfico

NOMBRES

el asiento   *seat*
el boleto[1]   *ticket*
el descuento   *discount*
el despacho de boletos   *ticket window*
la estación de trenes   *train station*
el fin de semana   *weekend*
el itinerario, el horario   *schedule*
el rápido, el expreso   *express train*
el subterráneo, el metro   *subway*

VERBOS

acompañar   *to go with, to accompany*
aconsejar   *to advise*
buscar   *to look for, to pick up, to get*
esperar   *to hope*
mandar   *to order*
negar (e:ie)   *to deny*
perder (e:ie)   *to miss (i.e., a train)*

recomendar (e:ie)   *to recommend*
reservar   *to reserve*
rogar (o:ue)   *to beg*
sugerir (e:ie)   *to suggest*

ADJETIVOS

bello(a)   *beautiful*
bueno(a)   *kind*
difícil   *difficult*
fácil   *easy*
largo(a)   *long*
lento(a)   *slow*
mareado(a)   *dizzy*
ocupado(a)   *busy*
rápido(a)   *fast*

OTRAS PALABRAS Y EXPRESIONES

cuanto antes   *as soon as possible*
hacer las maletas   *to pack*
por ciento   *percent*
por eso   *that's why*
sumamente   *extremely*

---

 1 THE PRESENT SUBJUNCTIVE
El presente de subjuntivo

Uses of the subjunctive While the indicative mood is used to express events that are factual and definite, the subjunctive mood is used to refer to events or conditions that the speaker views as uncertain, unreal, or hypothetical. Since the subjunctive mood reflects feelings or attitudes toward events or conditions, certain expressions of volition, doubt, surprise, fear, and so forth are followed by the subjunctive.

---

[1]Used when traveling by train or by bus.

Except for its use in main clauses to express commands, the Spanish subjunctive is most often used in subordinate or dependent clauses.

The subjunctive is also used in English, although not as often as in Spanish. For example:

I suggest that he arrive tomorrow.

The expression that requires the use of the subjunctive is in the main clause, *I suggest.* The subjunctive appears in the subordinate clause, *that he arrive tomorrow.* The subjunctive mood is used because the action of arriving is not yet realized; it is only what is *suggested* that he do.

There are four major concepts that require the use of the subjunctive in Spanish.

1. *Volition:* demands, wishes, advice, persuasion, and other impositions of will

Ella **quiere** que yo **compre** los boletos.	*She wants me to buy the tickets.*
Te **aconsejo** que **vayas** en el rápido.	*I advise you to go on the express train.*
No quiero que **pierdas** el tren.	*I don't want you to miss the train.*

2. *Emotion:* pity, joy, fear, surprise, hope, regret, etc.

Espero que Uds. **puedan** hacer las maletas.	*I hope that you can pack.*
Siento mucho que Luisa **esté** mareada.	*I'm very sorry that Luisa is dizzy.*

3. *Doubt, disbelief,* and *denial:* uncertainty, negated facts

Dudo que nos **den** un diez por ciento de descuento.	*I doubt that they'll give us a ten percent discount.*
No es verdad que el horario **cambie** la próxima semana.	*It isn't true that the schedule is changing next week.*
Ella **niega** que Juan **sea** su novio.	*She denies that Juan is her boyfriend.*

4. *Unreality:* expectations, indefiniteness, nonexistence

Busco a **alguien** que **pueda** hacerlo.

I'm looking for someone who can do it.

¿Hay **alguien** en la clase que **hable** alemán?

Is there anyone in the class who speaks German?

No hay **nadie** aquí que **sepa** su dirección.

There is nobody here who knows his address.

Formation of the present subjunctive

The present subjunctive is formed by dropping the **-o** from the stem of the first person singular of the present indicative and adding the following endings.

The Present Subjunctive of Regular Verbs

-ar *Verbs*	-er *Verbs*	-ir *Verbs*
trabajar	**comer**	**vivir**
trabaj**e**	com**a**	viv**a**
trabaj**es**	com**as**	viv**as**
trabaj**e**	com**a**	viv**a**
trabaj**emos**	com**amos**	viv**amos**
trabaj**éis**	com**áis**	viv**áis**
trabaj**en**	com**an**	viv**an**

 ATENCIÓN: Notice that the endings for -er **and** -ir **verbs are the same.**

The following table shows you how to form the first person singular of the present subjunctive from the infinitive of the verb.

Verb	First Person Singular (Indicative)	Stem	First Person Singular (Present Subjunctive)
habl**ar**	hablo	**habl-**	hable
aprend**er**	aprendo	**aprend-**	aprenda
escrib**ir**	escribo	**escrib-**	escriba
dec**ir**	digo	**dig-**	diga
hac**er**	hago	**hag-**	haga
tra**er**	traigo	**traig-**	traiga
ven**ir**	vengo	**veng-**	venga
conoc**er**	conozco	**conozc-**	conozca

Vamos a practicar

Quiz

Give the present subjunctive of the following verbs.

1. **yo:** comer, venir, hablar, hacer, salir, ponerse
2. **tú:** decir, ver, traer, trabajar, escribir, conocer
3. **él:** vivir, aprender, salir, estudiar, levantarse, hacer
4. **nosotros:** escribir, caminar, poner, desear, tener, afeitarse
5. **ellos:** salir, hacer, llevar, conocer, ver, bañarse

Subjunctive forms of stem-changing verbs Stem-changing **-ar** and **-er** verbs maintain the basic pattern of the present indicative. Their stems undergo the same changes in the present subjunctive.

recomendar *(to recommend)*		**recordar** *(to remember)*	
recomiende	recomendemos	recuerde	recordemos
recomiendes	recomendéis	recuerdes	recordéis
recomiende	recomienden	recuerde	recuerden
entender *(to understand)*		**mover** *(to move)*	
entienda	entendamos	mueva	movamos
entiendas	entendáis	muevas	mováis
entienda	entiendan	mueva	muevan

Stem-changing **-ir** verbs change the unstressed **e** to **i** and the unstressed **o** to **u** in the first person plural:

mentir *(to lie)*		**dormir** *(to sleep)*	
mienta	mintamos	duerma	durmamos
mientas	mintáis	duermas	durmáis
mienta	mientan	duerma	duerman

Subjunctive forms of irregular verbs

dar	estar	saber	ser	ir
dé	esté	sepa	sea	vaya
des	estés	sepas	seas	vayas
dé	esté	sepa	sea	vaya
demos	estemos	sepamos	seamos	vayamos
deis	estéis	sepáis	seáis	vayáis
den	estén	sepan	sean	vayan

■ The subjunctive of **hay** (impersonal form of **haber**) is **haya.**

Vamos a practicar

Quiz

Give the present subjunctive of the following verbs.

1. yo: dormir, mover, cerrar, sentir, ser
2. tú: mentir, volver, ir, dar, recordar
3. ella: estar, saber, perder, dormir, ser
4. nosotros: pensar, recordar, dar, morir, cerrar
5. ellos: ver, preferir, dar, ir, saber

❷ THE SUBJUNCTIVE WITH VERBS OF VOLITION
El subjuntivo usado con verbos de deseo

All impositions of will, as well as indirect or implied commands, require the subjunctive in subordinate clauses. The subject in the main clause must be different from the subject in the subordinate clause.

■ Some verbs of volition:

aconsejar	*to advise*	querer	
desear		recomendar	*to recommend*
mandar	*to order*	rogar	*to beg*
necesitar		sugerir	*to suggest*
pedir			

■ Note the sentence structure for the use of the subjunctive in Spanish.

Yo quiero	que	*Ud.* estudie.
main clause		subordinate clause
I want		*you* to study.

—¿Qué quieren hacer Uds. hoy? *"What do you want to do today?"*
—Queremos ir al aeropuerto para   *"We want to go to the airport to*
reservar los asientos para el   *reserve the seats for the Saturday*
vuelo del sábado.   *flight."*

—Quiero ir a Bahía Blanca   *"I want to go to Bahía Blanca this*
este fin de semana.   *weekend."*
—Entonces **te aconsejo** que   *"Then I advise you to buy the tickets*
compres los boletos cuanto   *as soon as possible."*
antes.
—Sí, voy a **pedirle** a Ernesto   *"Yes, I'm going to ask Ernesto to take*
que me **lleve** a la estación de   *me to the train station to buy them."*
trenes para comprarlos.
—**Te sugiero** que **viajes** por *"I suggest you travel at night."*
la noche.
—¿Por qué?   *"Why?"*
—Porque el tren de por la   *"Because the night train is faster."*
noche es más rápido.

ATENCIÓN: **Certain verbs of volition** (mandar, sugerir, aconsejar, **and** pedir) **are often preceded by an indirect object pronoun, which indicates the subject of the verb in the subjunctive:** Te sugiero que... *I suggest* **that** *you* **. . . ,** Le aconsejo que... *I advise you* **. . .**

—Nora **quiere** que la   *"Nora wants you to accompany*   Buenos Aires, Caracas,
acompañes a tomar el   *her to take the subway."*   México DF y algunas
subterráneo.   ciudades españolas
—No necesita tomar el   *"She doesn't need to take the*   tienen buenos sis-
subterráneo.   *subway.*   temas de metro que
Puede ir en taxi.   *She can go by taxi."*   son eficientes y
—Yo no puedo ir con Uds.   *"I can't go with you because my*   económicos.
porque mi hermano **quiere**   *brother wants me to go to the station*
que **vaya a** la estación a   *to get him a schedule."*
buscarle un itinerario.

ATENCIÓN: **If there is no change of subject, the infinitive is used.**

—¿Adónde quiere **ir** Ud.?
—Quiero **ir** al despacho de boletos.

Vamos a practicar

A Change the following sentences according to the new beginnings.

> **Modelo**
> Yo quiero buscar las maletas. Yo quiero que tú...
> Yo quiero que tú **busques**[1] las maletas.

1. Nosotros queremos comprar los boletos.
   Nosotros queremos que Uds....
2. Yo necesito reservar un asiento.
   Yo necesito que tú...
3. Ella desea ir a la estación de trenes.
   Ella desea que nosotros...
4. ¿Ud. quiere tomar el rápido?
   ¿Ud. quiere que ellos...?
5. Mis padres desean conseguir un itinerario.
   Mis padres desean que yo...
6. Oscar necesita estar allí a las diez.
   Oscar necesita que Ud....
7. Carlos quiere ir a buscar a su hermana.
   Carlos quiere que Marta...

B Use your imagination to complete the following sentences, using the infinitive or the subjunctive, as appropriate.

1. Yo le sugiero a mi amigo(a) que...
2. Ellos necesitan que tú...
3. Nosotros queremos...
4. Mis padres me ruegan que...
5. Yo necesito...
6. El (La) profesor(a) nos manda que...
7. Yo les recomiendo que...
8. Mi hermano(a) desea...
9. Yo te pido que...
10. Mi madre siempre me aconseja que...

---

[1]Verbs ending in **-car** change **c** to **qu** in the present subjunctive. For other verbs with spelling changes, see Appendix B.

C Following is what certain people want to do. Use the cues provided to suggest different alternatives.

MODELO Yo quiero tomar el metro. (un taxi)
Yo **te sugiero** que **tomes** un taxi.

1. Nosotros pensamos hacer las maletas mañana. (hoy)
2. Elsa quiere reservar los asientos para el lunes. (el martes)
3. Mis padres quieren viajar en tren. (en avión)
4. Daniel piensa ir a Córdoba. (Buenos Aires)
5. Yo quiero acompañar a Rosa. (Nora)
6. Yo pienso darle los boletos a Marta. (Laura)

3 THE ABSOLUTE SUPERLATIVE
El superlativo absoluto

In Spanish, there are two ways of expressing a high degree of a given quality without comparing one person or thing to another.

■ By modifying the adjective with an adverb **(muy, sumamente).**

—¿Cómo estuvo el vuelo?   *"How was the flight?"*
—Estuvo **muy** aburrido y fue   *"It was very boring and*
   sumamente largo.   *extremely long."*

■ By adding the suffix **-ísimo (-a, -os, -as)** to the adjective. This form is known as the absolute superlative. If the word ends in a vowel, the vowel is dropped before adding the suffix. Notice that the **í** of the suffix always has a written accent.

alt**o**	alt-	**ísimo**	alt**ísimo**
ocupad**a**	ocupad-	**ísima**	ocupad**ísima**
lent**os**	lent-	**ísimos**	lent**ísimos**
buen**as**	buen-	**ísimas**	buen**ísimas**
difícil	difícil-	**ísimo**	dificil**ísimo**
ric**a**	riqu-[1]	**ísima**	riqu**ísima**
larg**os**	largu[1]	**ísimos**	largu**ísimos**

_____
[1]This is an orthographic change.

En Buenos Aires, como en otras grandes ciudades del mundo hispano, la polución es un problema grave (*serious*) debido al gran número de automóviles.

—¿Fuiste a Buenos Aires el verano pasado?
—Sí, es una ciudad **bellísima,** pero no es fácil conducir allí. ¡Es **dificilísimo**! Hay **muchísimo** tráfico. Por eso hay tanta polución.

"Did you go to Buenos Aires last summer?"
"Yes, it is a very beautiful city, but it is not easy to drive there. It is extremely difficult! There is a lot of traffic. That's why there is so much pollution."

—¿Pueden ir al aeropuerto con nosotros?
—No, estamos **ocupadísimas.**

"Can you go to the airport with us?"
"No, we are extremely busy."

Vamos a practicar

Quiz

Change the underlined words in the following sentences to the absolute superlative.

1. Mi novia es <u>muy bella</u>.
2. Mi novio es <u>sumamente alto</u>.
3. Ellos están <u>muy ocupados</u>.
4. Es <u>muy fácil</u> llegar a la estación de trenes.
5. Ellas son <u>muy buenas</u>.
6. La cajera está <u>sumamente ocupada</u>.
7. Ellos son <u>muy lentos</u>.
8. Las clases son <u>sumamente difíciles</u> allí.
9. Ella está <u>sumamente aburrida</u>.
10. El tren es <u>muy rápido</u>.

Palabras y más palabras   Match the questions in column **A** with the answers in column **B**.

A	B
1. ¿Vas a viajar en tren? _____	a. Que vayas hoy mismo.
2. ¿Qué descuento te dieron? _____	b. ¡Es muy lento!
3. ¿Cuándo vas a reservar _____ el asiento? _____	c. Al despacho de boletos.
4. ¿Qué me recomiendas? _____	d. Sí, te ruego que lo hagas en seguida.
5. ¿Hay mucho tráfico allí? _____	e. No sé. No tengo el itinerario.
6. ¿Por qué no viajan en ese tren? _____	f. Cuanto antes.
7. ¿Se siente mal? _____	g. Sí, por eso hay tanta polución.
	h. Sí, no lo niego.

8. ¿Adónde fueron? _____
9. ¿A qué hora sale el rápido? _____

10. ¿Quieres que llame a Rosa? _____
11. Tú comes mucho, ¿no? _____
12. ¿Cómo es Elsa? _____

i. Sí, y espero conseguir boleto en el expreso.
j. Muy buena.
k. Sí, está mareada.
l. El diez por ciento.

En estas situaciones What would you say in the following situations?

1. Your friends are going to Buenos Aires. Tell them to leave as soon as possible if they don't want to miss the plane.
2. Someone plans to go to Europe. Advise him/her to go somewhere else.
3. Your friend is going to travel by train. Give him/her a few suggestions about what to do to prepare for the train trip.
4. Mention three things you hope to do this weekend.
5. Use the absolute superlative to describe your best friend or favorite movie star.

PARA ESCUCHAR Y ENTENDER

The following material is to be used with the In-Text Audio CDs.

I. Práctica

A Quiero que...
Say what Carmen wants everybody to do, using the present subjunctive and the cues provided. Repeat the correct answer after the speaker's confirmation. Listen to the model.

4–10

> **MODELO**   ¿Qué quiere Carmen que yo haga? (reservar el asiento)
> **Quiere que Ud. reserve el asiento.**

1. (comprar los boletos)
2. (ir a la estación de trenes)
3. (buscar el horario)
4. (darle un descuento)
5. (estar aquí a las dos)

6. (pedir un itinerario)
7. (viajar en el rápido)
8. (venir cuanto antes)
9. (cerrar la puerta)
10. (volver mañana)

B El superlativo absoluto

4–11   Rephrase each sentence, changing **muy** + *adjective* to the absolute superlative. Repeat the correct answer after the speaker's confirmation. Listen to the model.

> MODELO   Mi novio es muy alto.
> **Mi novio es altísimo.**

II. ¿Qué dicen?

1 ¿Lógico o ilógico?

4–12   The speaker will make some statements. Circle **L (lógico)** if the statement is logical and **I (ilógico)** if it is illogical. The speaker will verify your response.

1. L I	**3.** L I	**5.** L I	**7.** L I
2. L I	**4.** L I	**6.** L I	**8.** L I

2 ¿Verdadero o falso?

4–13   Listen carefully to the narration. Listen to it at least twice.

(Narración)

4–14   Now the speaker will make some statements about the narration you just heard. Tell whether each statement is true **(verdadero)** or false **(falso).** The speaker will confirm the correct answer.

3 Teresa y Verónica

4–15   Listen carefully to the dialogue. Listen to it at least twice.

(Diálogo 1)

4–16   Now the speaker will make some statements about the dialogue you just heard. Tell whether each statement is true **(verdadero)** or false **(falso).** The speaker will confirm the correct answer.

4 Anita y Roberto

4-17   Listen carefully to the dialogue. Listen to it at least twice.

(Diálogo 2)

4-18   Now the speaker will ask you some questions about the dialogue you just heard. Answer each question, omitting the subject. The speaker will confirm the correct answer. Repeat the correct answer.

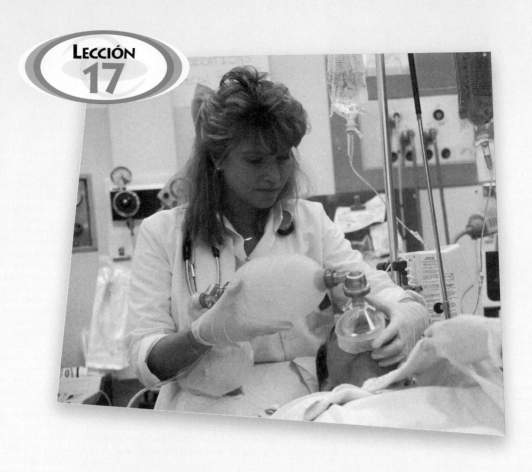

LECCIÓN 17

OBJECTIVES

Structures
1. The subjunctive to express emotion
2. The subjunctive with some impersonal expressions
3. Formation of adverbs

Communication
You will learn vocabulary related to hospital care in emergencies.

Search

Country highlighted: Uruguay

U ruguay, con una superficie (*area*) igual a la del estado de Washington, es el país de habla hispana más pequeño de la América del Sur. El estuario (*estuary*) del Río de la Plata, junto a la capital, Montevideo, es el centro estratégico de un intercambio (*interchange*) comercial creciente (*growing*). Sus playas, en el Atlántico, dan motivo (*give cause*) a grandes centros turísticos, entre ellos la ciudad balneario (*resort*) de Punta del Este.

Más del 80 por ciento de la tierra se usa para la agricultura, pero el país se ha industrializado rápidamente gracias a la electricidad a bajo costo que producen sus plantas hidroeléctricas.

En Montevideo, se concentra casi la mitad (*half*) de la población, y también la mayor parte de las actividades culturales, económicas y administrativas del país.

RESOURCES

Wherever you see the following icons additional resources are available:

 Internet
Go to **www.college.hmco.com/languages/spanish/students/** for additional practice on the topic.

 Student CD-ROM
Go to the **Video Grammar Tutor** for help with understanding the grammar topic at hand.

Go to the **In-Text Audio CDs** for more practice.

273

VOCABULARIO

Audio

COGNADOS

la ambulancia
el (la) dentista
la emergencia
especial
general
la medicina
necesario(a)
el (la) paciente
el (la) paramédico(a)
la penicilina
posible
probable
reciente

NOMBRES

el consultorio   *doctor's office*
el dolor   *pain, ache*
el (la) farmacéutico(a)   *pharmacist*
la inyección   *shot, injection*
las muletas   *crutches*
la pierna   *leg*
la radiografía   *X-ray*
la sala   *ward*
la sala de emergencia   *emergency room*
la sala de rayos X   *X-ray room*
el tobillo   *ankle*

VERBOS

alegrarse   *to be glad*
caerse (yo me caigo)   *to fall*
cuidar   *to take care (of)*
enyesar   *to put a cast on*
fracturarse, romperse   *to break*
pasar   *to happen*
sentir (e:ie)   *to regret, to be sorry*
temer   *to fear, to be afraid*
torcerse   *to twist*

ADJETIVOS

claro(a)   *clear*
cuidadoso(a)   *careful*

OTRAS PALABRAS Y EXPRESIONES

conviene   *it is advisable*
en este momento   *at this moment*
es difícil   *it's unlikely*
es una lástima   *it's a pity*
es mejor   *it's better*
es seguro   *it is certain*
ojalá   *I hope*
poner una inyección   *to give a shot*
puede ser   *it may be*
todos los días   *every day*
ya   *already*

 1 THE SUBJUNCTIVE TO EXPRESS EMOTION
El subjuntivo para expresar emoción

In Spanish, the subjunctive is always used in a subordinate clause when the verb in the main clause expresses any kind of emotion, such as fear, joy, pity, hope, pleasure, surprise, anger, regret, and sorrow.

■ Some verbs of emotion:

alegrarse (de) *to be glad*
esperar *to hope*
sentir (e:ie) *to regret, to be sorry*
temer *to fear*

—¿Quieres hablar con tu médico?

"Do you want to speak with your doctor?"

—Sí, pero **temo** que no **esté** en su consultorio en este momento.

"Yes, but I'm afraid he's not in his office at this moment."

—¿Hubo un accidente?
—Sí, **espero** que los paramédicos **vengan** en seguida.

"Was there an accident?"
"Yes, I hope the paramedics come right away."

—¿Qué le pasó a Andrés?
—Se cayó en la escalera y **temo** que **tenga** la pierna fracturada.

"What happened to Andrés?"
"He fell down the stairs and I'm afraid his leg is broken."

—**Siento** que no **puedas** ir con nosotros a ver a tus padrinos.
—No puedo ir porque tengo mucho dolor de cabeza.

"I'm sorry you can't go with us to see your godparents."
"I can't go because I have a bad headache."

—¿Vas a llamar una ambulancia?
—Sí, porque **temo** que no **podamos** llevar a Carmen al hospital en el coche.

"Are you going to call an ambulance?"
"Yes, because I'm afraid we can't take Carmen to the hospital in the car."

—El médico dice que ya estoy bien.
—**Me alegro** de que no **tengas** ningún problema.

"The doctor says I'm fine."
"I'm glad that you don't have any problems."

ATENCIÓN: The subject of the subordinate clause must be different from that of the main clause for the subjunctive to be used. If there is no change of subject, the infinitive is used instead.

—¿Vas a ir al hospital?
—Sí, pero **temo** no **encontrar** al médico en su consultorio porque es tardísimo.

"Are you going to go to the hospital?"
"Yes, but I'm afraid I won't find the doctor in his office because it's extremely late."

En muchos países hispanos existen las llamadas casas de socorro, donde se ofrecen los primeros auxilios (*first aid*) y cuidados (*care*) médicos urgentes. En general, son gratis.

—Mi sobrino tuvo un accidente y sus padres no están en Montevideo en este momento.
—¿Los llamaste?
—No, pero **espero poder** comunicarme con ellos esta noche.

"My nephew had an accident and his parents are not in Montevideo at this moment."
"Did you call them?"
"No, but I hope I can get in touch with them tonight."

Vamos a practicar

Quiz

A Complete the dialogues, using the infinitive or the present subjunctive as appropriate. Then act them out with a partner.

1. —Temo no _____ (poder) llevarte al hospital.

   —Espero que Ana _____ (poder) llevarme.

2. —Esperamos _____ (hablar) con el médico hoy.

   —Temo que él no _____ (estar) en su consultorio hasta mañana.

3. —Hoy no tengo que ir al hospital.

   —Me alegro de que (tú) no _____ (tener) que trabajar hoy.

4. —Mi mamá tiene mucho dolor de cabeza.

   —Siento que (ella) no _____ (sentirse) bien.

5. —Me alegro de _____ (ver) que los paramédicos ya están aquí.

   —Yo también, pero temo que _____ (ser) muy tarde.

B Use your imagination to complete the following sentences with either the present subjunctive or the infinitive, as appropriate.

1. Yo espero que mi médico...
2. Nosotros nos alegramos de...
3. Yo temo...
4. Siento que Uds....
5. Ellos sienten no...
6. Yo me alegro de que mis padres...
7. Nosotros tememos que...
8. Mis amigos se alegran de que yo...

❷ THE SUBJUNCTIVE WITH SOME IMPERSONAL EXPRESSIONS
El subjuntivo con algunas expresiones impersonales

In Spanish, some impersonal expressions that convey emotion, uncertainty, unreality, or an indirect or implied command are followed by a verb in the subjunctive. This occurs only when the verb of the subordinate clause has an expressed subject. The most common impersonal expressions include the following.

conviene	*it is advisable*	**es mejor**	*it is better*
es difícil	*it is unlikely*	**es necesario**	*it is necessary*
es importante	*it is important*	**ojalá**	*if only...! or I hope...*
es (im)posible	*it is (im)possible*	**puede ser**	*it may be*
es (una) lástima	*it is a pity*		

—El farmacéutico dice que **es necesario** que te **pongan** una inyección de penicilina.
—Yo soy alérgico a la penicilina.

"The pharmacist says that it's necessary that they give you a shot of penicillin."
"I'm allergic to penicillin."

> Con frecuencia los farmacéuticos recomiendan medicinas y ponen inyecciones.

—¿Cuándo quiere el médico que Luis tome la medicina?
—**Es mejor** que **empiece** a tomarla ahora mismo.

"When does the doctor want Luis to take the medicine?"
"It's better that he start to take it right now."

—¿Carlos tuvo un accidente?
—Sí, **ojalá que** el Dr. Lascano **esté** en la sala de emergencia porque él es su médico.

"Did Carlos have an accident?"
"Yes, I hope Dr. Lascano is in the emergency room because he is his doctor."

—¿Dónde está Ramiro?
—**Es probable** que **esté** en la sala de rayos X porque se torció el tobillo y tienen que hacerle una radiografía.

"Where is Ramiro?"
"It is probable that he is in the X-ray room because he twisted his ankle and they have to do an X-ray."

—Silvia se rompió la pierna y no podrá ir con nosotros al baile.

"Silvia broke her leg and she won't be able to go to the dance with us."

—**Es una lástima** que **tenga** que   *"It's a pity that she has to stay*
quedarse en casa.   *home."*

—Le enyesaron la pierna a   *"They put a cast on Quique's leg.*
Quique. Necesita **usar**   *He needs to use crutches to go to*
muletas para ir a trabajar.   *work."*

—**Es difícil** que él **vaya** a trabajar   *"It's unlikely that he'll go to work*
con una pierna rota.   *with a broken leg."*

ATENCIÓN: **When the impersonal expression implies certainty, the indicative is used.**

—¿Traen a los pacientes hoy?   *"Are they bringing the patients*
                                               today?"
—Sí, **es seguro** que los **traen** hoy.   *"Yes, it is certain that they are*
                                               bringing them today."

When a sentence is completely impersonal (that is, when no subject is stated), the expressions on page 277 are followed by the infinitive.

—¿Qué pasó?   *"What happened?"*
—Arturo tuvo un accidente.   *"Arturo had an accident."*
—Conviene **llevarlo** al hospital   *"It is advisable to take him to the*
ahora mismo.   *hospital right now."*

Vamos a practicar

Quiz

A Complete the following sentences using the infinitive, the indicative, or the subjunctive.

1. Conviene que ustedes _____ (tomar) la medicina ahora.

2. Es imposible _____ (ir) al dentista a esta hora.

3. Es mejor que ellos lo _____ (llevar) a la sala de emergencia.

4. Ojalá que el farmacéutico _____ (venir) pronto.

5. Es seguro que ella _____ (necesitar) una inyección de penicilina.

6. Es difícil que él _____ (conseguir) las muletas aquí.

7. Puede ser que la enfermera (*nurse*) _____ (tener) las radiografías.

8. Es importante que ella _____ (aprender) a poner inyecciones.

B Use your imagination to complete the following sentences with either the subjunctive or the infinitive, as appropriate.

1. Conviene...
2. Puede ser que mi médico...
3. Ojalá que mis padres...
4. Es difícil que yo...
5. Es importante...
6. Es una lástima que mis amigos...
7. Es imposible...
8. Es mejor que nosotros...

❸ FORMATION OF ADVERBS
Formación de adverbios

> **Adverb** a word that modifies a verb, an adjective, or another adverb. It answers the questions "How?", "When?", "Where?": She walked **slowly.** She'll be here **tomorrow.** She is **here.**

Most Spanish adverbs are formed by adding **-mente** (the equivalent of *-ly* in English) to the adjective.

especial	*special*	especial**mente**	*specially, especially*
reciente	*recent*	reciente**mente**	*recently*
probable	*probable*	probable**mente**	*probably*
general	*general*	general**mente**	*generally*

- If the adjective ends in **-o,** the ending changes to **-a** before adding **-mente.**

lent**o**	*slow*	lent**amente**	*slowly*
rápid**o**	*rapid*	rápid**amente**	*rapidly*
clar**o**	*clear*	clar**amente**	*clearly*

- If two or more adverbs are used together, both change the **-o** to **-a,** but only the last adverb takes the **-mente** ending.

lent**a** y cuidados**amente**   *slowly and carefully*

■ If the adjective has a written accent mark, the corresponding adverb retains it.

fácil   fácilmente

—¿Quién va a cuidar al   *"Who is going to take care*
  paciente?   *of the patient?"*
—**Probablemente,** su esposa.   *"Probably, his wife."*

—¿Has ido al dentista   *"Have you gone to the dentist*
  recientemente?   *recently?"*
—No, porque he tenido que   *"No, because I have had*
  trabajar todos los días.   *to work every day."*

—Rafael iba manejando **lenta**   *"Rafael was driving slowly*
  y **cuidadosamente** porque   *and carefully because he was*
  llevaba al niño al hospital.   *taking the child to the*
                                        hospital."

—Sí, porque **generalmente**   *"Yes, because he generally*
  maneja muy rápido.   *drives very fast."*

> En la mayoría de los países de habla hispana, los hospitales son gratis (*free*) y subvencionados por el gobierno. Hay clínicas privadas para la gente que no quiere ir a un hospital público.

Vamos a practicar

Complete the following sentences, using appropriate adverbs.

1. El médico me habló _____ y _____, pero yo no entendí nada.
2. _____ ellos van a ir al hospital hoy.
3. _____ ella cuida a los niños.
4. Ella se torció el tobillo _____.
5. Elba camina _____ porque usa muletas.
6. Trajo la penicilina _____ para mí.
7. Mi abuela siempre maneja _____ y _____.

Palabras y más palabras Match the questions in column **A** with the answers in column **B**.

A	B
1. ¿Paco tuvo un accidente? _____	**a.** Sí, se la van a enyesar.
2. ¿Ana se cayó en la escalera? _____	**b.** Sí, lo llevamos a la sala de rayos X.
3. ¿Se fracturó la pierna? _____	
4. ¿Tienes tiempo para ir a la farmacia? _____	**c.** Sí, y vinieron los paramédicos.
5. ¿Hubo un accidente? _____	**d.** Todos los días.
6. ¿Le van a hacer una radiografía? _____	**e.** Me puso una inyección.
	f. Sí, y se rompió la pierna.
7. ¿Qué le pasó a Daniel? _____	**g.** Penicilina.
8. ¿Qué hizo la enfermera? _____	**h.** Con un paciente.
9. ¿Cuándo cuidas tú a los niños? _____	**i.** Sí, lo llevaron al hospital.
	j. Porque tengo mucho dolor de cabeza.
10. ¿Con quién está el dentista? _____	**k.** Se torció el tobillo.
11. ¿Por qué tomas aspirinas? _____	**l.** No, en este momento estoy ocupada.
12. ¿Qué compraste en la farmacia? _____	

En estas situaciones What would you say in the following situations? What might the other people say?

1. You took your friend to the hospital because he fell down. Ask the doctor if he broke his leg or twisted his ankle.
2. You are sick. Ask the doctor if he's going to give you a shot.
3. You are going to call three friends: Eva, Marité, and Fernando. Eva broke her leg. Tell her what is necessary for her to do. Marité is in the hospital. Tell her you hope she'll feel better. Fernando wants to come visit you in May. It's unlikely that you'll be home at that time.

PARA ESCUCHAR Y ENTENDER

The following material is to be used with the In-Text Audio CDs.

I. Práctica

A Expresando emoción

4–19

Restate each of the following sentences, inserting the cue at the beginning and making any necessary changes. Repeat the correct answer after the speaker's confirmation. Listen to the model.

> **MODELO**   Rosa está mejor. (Espero)
> **Espero que Rosa esté mejor.**

1. (Temo)	**5.** (Espero)
2. (Espero)	**6.** (Me alegro)
3. (Siento)	**7.** (Espero)
4. (Temo)	**8.** (Sentimos)

B Expresiones impersonales

4–20

Restate each of the following sentences, inserting the cue at the beginning and making any necessary changes. Repeat the correct answer after the speaker's confirmation. Listen to the model.

> **MODELO**   Él conduce muy rápido. (Es difícil)
> **Es difícil que él conduzca muy rápido.**

1. (No conviene)	**5.** (Puede ser)
2. (Es necesario)	**6.** (Ojalá)
3. (Es imposible)	**7.** (Es una lástima)
4. (Es mejor)	**8.** (Es importante)

C Adverbios

4–21

Give the adverb that corresponds to each adjective. Repeat the correct answer after the speaker's confirmation. Listen to the model.

> **MODELO**   especial
> **especialmente**

II. ¿Qué dicen?

1 ¿Lógico o ilógico?

4-22

The speaker will make some statements. Circle **L (lógico)** if the statement is logical and **I (ilógico)** if it is illogical. The speaker will verify your response.

1. L I	**3.** L I	**5.** L I	**7.** L I
2. L I	**4.** L I	**6.** L I	**8.** L I

2 Eva y Carlos

4-23

Listen carefully to the dialogue. Listen to it at least twice.

(Diálogo 1)

4-24   Now the speaker will make some statements about the dialogue you just heard. Tell whether each statement is true **(verdadero)** or false **(falso).** The speaker will confirm the correct answer.

3 Fernando y Amalia

4-25

Listen carefully to the dialogue. Listen to it at least twice.

(Diálogo 2)

4-26   Now the speaker will make some statements about the dialogue you just heard. Tell whether each statement is true **(verdadero)** or false **(falso).** The speaker will confirm the correct answer.

4 En la sala de emergencia

4-27   Listen carefully to the dialogue. Listen to it at least twice.

(Diálogo 3)

4-28   Now the speaker will ask you some questions about the dialogue you just heard. Answer each question, omitting the subject. The speaker will confirm the correct answer. Repeat the correct answer.

LECCIÓN 18

OBJECTIVES

Structures

1. The subjunctive to express doubt, disbelief, and denial
2. The subjunctive to express indefiniteness and nonexistence
3. Diminutive suffixes

Communication

You will learn vocabulary related to college life.

Search

Nationality highlighted: Los puertorriqueños

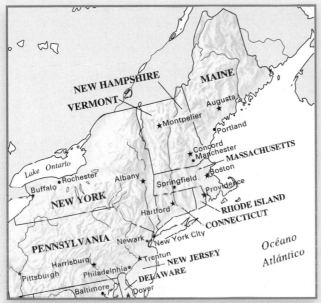

En la ciudad de Nueva York hay más de dos millones de hispanos, la mayoría de ellos puertorriqueños. Allí residen más puertorriqueños que en San Juan, la capital de Puerto Rico.

Desde la Segunda Guerra Mundial (*Second World War*) los puertorriqueños vinieron a Nueva York en busca de trabajo. En los últimos años muchos han ido subiendo (*rising*) en la escala social. Aunque la mayoría (el 70 por ciento) sigue viviendo en Nueva York, hoy hay puertorriqueños en todos los estados de la Unión.

En los últimos veinte años ha venido a los Estados Unidos un importante número de profesionales: abogados, médicos, profesores y gente de negocios, que encuentran buenas oportunidades de trabajo porque son bilingües.

Muchos puertorriqueños se han destacado en diferentes campos (*fields*): en la política, congresistas como Nydia Velázquez y José Serrano; en el cine, Jennifer López, Rita Moreno y Rosie Pérez; y en la música, Ricky Martin y Marc Anthony, entre otros muchos.

RESOURCES

Wherever you see the following icons additional resources are available:

Internet

Go to **www.college.hmco.com/languages/spanish/students/** for additional practice on the topic.

Student
CD-ROM

Go to the **Video Grammar Tutor** for help with understanding the grammar topic at hand.

Go to the **In-Text Audio CDs** for more practice.

VOCABULARIO

COGNADOS

bilingüe
la literatura
la psicología
el semestre
la sociología

la matrícula   *tuition*
la Navidad   *Christmas*
la nota   *grade*
el promedio   *grade point average*
la química   *chemistry*
el requisito   *requirement*

NOMBRES

el árbol   *tree*
la asignatura, la materia   *subject*
la beca   *scholarship*
la biblioteca   *library*
la conferencia   *lecture*
el (la) consejero(a)   *adviser*
la contabilidad   *accounting*
el (la) contador(a)   *accountant*
la especialización   *major*
el examen final   *final exam*
el examen parcial   *midterm exam*
la física   *physics*
el horario de clases   *class schedule*

VERBOS

dudar   *to doubt*
graduarse   *to graduate*
mantener   *to maintain*
matricularse   *to register*

ADJETIVO

seguro   *sure*

OTRAS PALABRAS Y EXPRESIONES

irle bien a uno(a)   *to do well*
sacar una nota   *to get a grade*

1 THE SUBJUNCTIVE TO EXPRESS DOUBT, DISBELIEF, AND DENIAL
El subjuntivo para expresar duda, incredulidad y negación

In Spanish, the subjunctive mood is always used in a subordinate clause when the main clause expresses doubt, uncertainty, or disbelief.

■   Doubt or uncertainty

—¿Vas a hablar con tu
consejero hoy?
—Sí, pero **dudo** que me **diga**
cuáles son los requisitos
generales que debo tomar.

*"Are you going to talk with your
adviser today?"*
*"Yes, but I doubt that he will tell
me what the general requirements
that I have to take are."*

—¿Puedes llevar a Teresa a la biblioteca? **Dudo** que ella **pueda** ir sola.

"Can you take Teresa to the library? I doubt that she can go by herself."

—Sí, la llevo en seguida.

"Yes, I'll take her right away."

—Mañana tengo dos exámenes finales, uno en química y otro en física. **Dudo** que me **vaya** bien.

"Tomorrow I have two final exams, one in chemistry and the other in physics. I doubt that I'll do well."

—Entonces no podrás ir a la conferencia porque tendrás que estudiar.

"Then you won't be able to go to the lecture because you will have to study."

ATENCIÓN: In the affirmative, the verb dudar takes the subjunctive in the subordinate clause even when there is no change of subject.

—¿Puedes ir conmigo a la clase de literatura?

"Can you go with me to the literature class?"

—**(Yo) dudo** que **(yo) pueda** ir contigo hoy.

"I doubt that I can go with you today."

When the speaker expresses no doubt and is certain of the reality, the indicative is used.

—Marcos necesita dinero para pagar la matrícula.

"Marcos needs money to pay tuition."

—**No dudo** que sus padres se lo **darán.**

"I don't doubt that his parents will give it to him."

—¿**Estás seguro** de que hoy **es** el examen parcial?

"Are you sure that the midterm exam is today?"

—Sí, porque el profesor me lo dijo ayer.

"Yes, because the professor told me (about it) yesterday."

■ Disbelief

The verb **creer** (*to believe, to think*) is followed by the subjunctive when used in negative sentences in which it expresses disbelief.

—Carlos dice que va a sacar una buena nota en el examen.

"Carlos says that he is going to get a good grade on the test."

—**No creo** que **saque** una buena nota porque nunca estudia.

"I don't think he'll get a good grade because he never studies."

—¿No vas a tomar psicología
y sociología este semestre?

—**No creo** que **necesite** esas
asignaturas. Además, **no
creo** que me **den** la beca.

—**Creo** que mi amiga Rosa
quiere venir a Nueva York
a visitarme.

—¿Va a necesitar pasaporte?

—No, porque los puertorriqueños
no necesitan pasaporte
para viajar a Estados Unidos.

*"Aren't you going to take psychology
and sociology this semester?"*

*"I don't think I need those subjects.
Besides, I don't think they will give
me the scholarship."*

*"I think my friend Rosa wants to
come to New York to visit me."*

"Does she need a passport?"

*"No, because Puerto Ricans don't
need a passport to travel to United
States."*

> A diferencia de otros grupos hispanos, los puertorriqueños son ciudadanos esta-
> dounidenses (*U.S. citizens*) y pueden entrar en los Estados Unidos sin necesitar visa o
> pasaporte. En 1898 la isla de Puerto Rico pasó a ser territorio estadounidense. Puerto
> Rico es hoy un estado libre asociado (*free associated state*) a los Estados Unidos.

■ Denial

When the main clause denies what is said in the subordinate clause, the
subjunctive is used.

—Es muy buen estudiante;
mantiene un promedio de A.

—**Es verdad** que **es** buen
estudiante, pero **no es verdad**
que **mantenga** ese promedio.

*"He is a very good student; he
maintains an A average."*

*"It's true that he is a good student,
but it's not true that he maintains
that G.P.A."*

**ATENCIÓN: When the main clause confirms rather than denies what is
said in the subordinate clause, the indicative is used.** Es verdad que es
buen estudiante.

Quiz

Vamos a practicar

A Complete the following dialogues, using the present indicative or the
present subjunctive of the verbs in parentheses. Then act them out with a
partner.

1. —¿Tus padres pueden llevarme a la universidad?

    —Estoy seguro de que _____ (poder) llevarte, pero dudo que
    _____ (ir) ahora.

2. —Yo creo que Fernando _____ (necesitar) tomar sociología y psicología.

—No creo que él _____ (querer) tomar esas asignaturas.

3. —¿Adónde fue Marta?

—Creo que _____ (estar) en la biblioteca.

4. —Yo estoy segura de que la literatura _____ (ser) un requisito.

—No es verdad que _____ (ser) un requisito. Dudo que tú _____ (tener) que tomarla.

5. —Dudo que mis padres me _____ (dar) dinero para la matrícula y no creo que yo _____ (conseguir) una beca.

—No dudo que tú _____ (poder) conseguirla porque mantienes un buen promedio.

B Use your imagination to complete the following sentences with either the subjunctive or the indicative, as appropriate.

1. Yo estoy seguro de que mis padres...
2. Dudo que la casa del profesor...
3. Es verdad que yo...
4. No estoy seguro de que mi amigo...
5. No es verdad que mi familia...
6. No creo que mi nota en esta clase...
7. No dudo que mis amigos...
8. Creo que el profesor...

2 THE SUBJUNCTIVE TO EXPRESS INDEFINITENESS AND NONEXISTENCE

El subjuntivo para expresar lo indefinido y lo no existente

The subjunctive is always used when a subordinate clause refers to someone or something that is indefinite, unspecified, or nonexistent.

—Quiero matricularme hoy. ¿**Hay alguien** aquí que **tenga** el horario de clases para este semestre?

"I want to register today. Is there anyone here who has the class schedule for this semester?"

—No, aquí **no hay nadie** que lo **tenga.**

"No, there is nobody here who has it."

—El profesor Vega **busca una**
secretaria que **sea** bilingüe.

—No conozco **a nadie** que **sea**
bilingüe y **quiera** trabajar aquí.

*"Professor Vega is looking for a
secretary who is bilingual."*

*"I don't know anybody who is
bilingual and wants to work here."*

ATENCIÓN: **If the subordinate clause refers to existent, definite, or
specific persons or things, the indicative is used.**

Aquí **hay alguien** que lo **tiene.**
Conozco a **alguien** que **es** bilingüe.

—Tú te gradúas este año, ¿no?
¿Cuál es tu especialización?

—Contabilidad. ¿**Conoces a
alguien** que **necesite**
un contador?

—No.

*"You are graduating this year,
aren't you? What is your major?"*

*"Accounting. Do you know someone
who needs an accountant?"*

"No."

En la mayoría de las universidades hispanas no existe el concepto de "*major*" usado en
los Estados Unidos. Los estudiantes españoles y latinoamericanos toman muy pocas
clases optativas (*electives*), ya que la mayoría comienza a especializarse a partir de su
primer año en la universidad.

Vamos a practicar

Quiz

A Complete the following sentences using the present subjunctive or
the present indicative of the verbs in parentheses.

1. ¿Hay alguien que _____ (sacar) una buena nota en esta clase?

2. No hay nadie que _____ (saber) la fecha del examen final.

3. ¿Hay alguien aquí que no _____ (tener) dinero para pagar la
matrícula?

4. Buscan a alguien que _____ (poder) enseñar química y física.

5. No conozco a nadie que _____ (mantener) un promedio de
A, pero conozco a varios estudiantes que _____ (mantener)
un promedio de B.

6. No hay nadie que _____ (ir) a la biblioteca a esta hora, pero
hay muchas personas que _____ (ir) más temprano.

7. Tengo una secretaria que _____ (ser) bilingüe, pero necesito
una que _____ (saber) contabilidad.

8. Estoy seguro de que no hay nadie que _____ (querer) ir a esa
conferencia.

B Use your imagination to complete the following sentences with either the subjunctive or the indicative, as appropriate.

1. Yo quiero una casa que...
2. No hay ningún profesor que...
3. En mi familia no hay nadie que...
4. Yo vivo en una casa que...
5. Conozco a una chica (un chico) que...
6. En mi clase de español hay muchos estudiantes que...
7. En la ciudad donde yo vivo hay muchas personas que...
8. Yo no conozco a nadie que...

3 DIMINUTIVE SUFFIXES
Los sufijos diminutivos

To express the idea of small size, and also to denote affection, special suffixes are used in Spanish. The most common suffixes are **-ito(a)** and **-cito(a)**. There are no set rules for forming the diminutive, but usually if the word ends in **-a** or **-o**, the vowel is dropped and **-ito(a)** is added.

niño	niñ + **ito** =	**niñito**	(*little boy*)
niña	niñ + **ita** =	**niñita**	(*little girl*)
abuelo	abuel + **ito** =	**abuelito**	(*grandpa*)
Ana	An + **ita** =	**Anita**	(*Annie*)

- If the word ends in a consonant other than **-n** or **-r**, the suffix **-ito(a)** is added.

árbol + **ito** =	**arbolito**	(*little tree*)
Luis + **ito** =	**Luisito**	(*Louie*)

- If the word ends in **-e, -n,** or **-r,** the suffix **-cito(a)** is added.

coche + **cito** =	**cochecito**	(*little car*)
mujer + **cita** =	**mujercita**	(*little woman*)
Carmen + **cita** = **Carmencita**		(*Carmen*)

—Hola, **abuelito.** ¿Me trajiste el **arbolito** de Navidad?

"*Hello, grandpa. Did you bring me the little Christmas tree?*"

—Sí, **Tomasito.**

"*Yes, Tommy.*"

—Me gusta tu **cochecito.**

"*I like your little car.*"

—Gracias, **Carmencita.**

"*Thanks, Carmen.*"

En Puerto Rico, como en todos los países de habla hispana, se miman mucho a los niños (*children are very pampered*). Cuando se habla de un niño, se usa mucho el diminutivo. Por ejemplo: si el niño está sentado, se dice que está "sentadito".

Vamos a practicar

Give the diminutive form of each of the following words.

1. primo
2. escuela
3. árbol
4. Raúl
5. coche
6. hermana
7. dolor
8. Adán
9. Adela
10. mamá

Palabras y más palabras   Circle the word or phrase that best completes each sentence.

1. No tengo que pagar la matrícula porque me dieron una (beca / nota).
2. Quiere ser contador. Su especialización es (química / contabilidad).
3. El semestre empieza la semana próxima. Tengo que (matricularme / graduarme).
4. Estudiamos para el examen, en la (conferencia / biblioteca).
5. Para sacar una buena nota en el (horario / semestre) necesito estudiar mucho.
6. Para saber qué clases debo tomar, voy a hablar con mi (médico / consejero).
7. Dudo que le vaya bien en esa clase porque nunca (mantiene / estudia).

En estas situaciones   What would you say in the following situations?

1. Ask a friend how he/she did in the final exam.
2. Ask Julio, a student from Puerto Rico, what his major is and when he is going to graduate. Ask him also what grade point average he maintains.
3. Your friend Susana never studies. Tell her that you doubt she can get a good grade in the midterm exam.
4. Ask a group of students if there is anybody who has the class schedule for next semester.

PARA ESCUCHAR Y ENTENDER

The following material is to be used with the In-Text Audio CDs.

I. Práctica

5–2

A Dudo que...

Restate each of the following sentences, inserting the cue at the beginning and making any necessary changes. Repeat the correct answer after the speaker's confirmation. Listen to the model.

> **MODELO**   No dudo que el profesor viene hoy (Dudo)
> **Dudo que el profesor venga hoy.**

1. (No estoy seguro)
2. (No creo)
3. (Es verdad)
4. (Tenemos)
5. (Dudamos)
6. (Hay alguien)
7. (Creen)
8. (Estamos seguros)
9. (No hay nadie)
10. (No es verdad)

5–3

B Sufijos diminutivos

The speaker will say some nouns. Change each one to the diminutive form.

II. ¿Qué dicen?

5–4

1 ¿Lógico o ilógico?

The speaker will make some statements. Circle **L (lógico)** if the statement is logical and **I (ilógico)** if it is illogical. The speaker will verify your response.

1. L I   3. L I   5. L I   7. L I
2. L I   4. L I   6. L I   8. L I

2 ¿Verdadero o falso?

5–5   Listen carefully to the narration. Listen to it at least twice.

(Narración)

5–6   Now the speaker will make some statements about the narration you just heard. Tell whether each statement is true (**verdadero**) or false (**falso**). The speaker will confirm the correct answer.

3 Rita y Sergio

5–7   Listen carefully to the dialogue. Listen to it at least twice.

(Diálogo 1)

5–8   Now the speaker will make some statements about the dialogue you just heard. Tell whether each statement is true (**verdadero**) or false (**falso**). The speaker will confirm the correct answer.

4 Ester y Tomás

5–9   Listen carefully to the dialogue. Listen to it at least twice.

(Diálogo 2)

5–10   Now the speaker will ask you some questions about the dialogue you just heard. Answer each question, omitting the subject. The speaker will confirm the correct answer. Repeat the correct answer.

LECCIÓN 19

Objectives

Structures
1. The subjunctive after certain conjunctions
2. The present perfect subjunctive
3. Uses of the present perfect subjunctive

Communication
You will learn vocabulary related to health problems and visits to the doctor's office.

Nationality highlighted: Los méxicoamericanos

El 63 por ciento de todos los "hispanos" residentes en los EE.UU. provienen (*come*) de México. Unos vivían en Texas, Nuevo México, California y otros estados antes de que pasaran estos territorios de México a los Estados Unidos como resultado de la guerra (*war*) entre los dos países. Otros llegaron impulsados (*driven*) por la falta (*lack*) de trabajo o los bajos salarios de su país. Muchos simplemente atravesaron la frontera (*crossed the border*) y, últimamente, su presencia en este país ha sido motivo (*cause*) de controversia. Sin embargo, la fuerza laboral barata que estos emigrantes han proporcionado (*furnished*), ha sido factor importantísimo en el desarrollo (*development*) de la agricultura en este país.

El grado (*degree*) de asimilación a la cultura americana de los méxicoamericanos es muy diverso, pero la mayoría conserva su lengua, sus tradiciones, su unidad familiar y sus conceptos morales, y se adapta a los usos (*customs*) de este país en relación con su trabajo y sus deberes (*duties*) cívicos. Muchos méxicoamericanos se han destacado (*have stood out*) en diferentes campos (*fields*); en la política: Cruz Bustamante, Vicegobernador de California y Loreta Sánchez, representante; en el cine: Eduardo James Olmos, Paul Rodríguez, Constance Marie y Carmen Zapata; en la música: Vicki Carr, Los Lobos; en la educación: France Córdova, presidenta de la Universidad de California en Riverside. Muchos han ganado honores en las fuerzas armadas de este país.

RESOURCES

Wherever you see the following icons additional resources are available:

Go to **www.college.hmco.com/languages/spanish/students/** for additional practice on the topic.

Internet

Go to the **Video Grammar Tutor** for help with understanding the grammar topic at hand.

Student CD-ROM

Go to the **In-Text Audio CDs** for more practice.

297

VOCABULARIO

Audio

COGNADOS

americano(a)
horrible
el resultado
el termómetro
el testamento

NOMBRES

el (la) abogado(a)   *lawyer*
el análisis   *test*
la autopista   *freeway*
el (la) ayudante   *assistant*
el catarro   *cold*
el chequeo   *checkup*
el (la) cirujano(a)   *surgeon*
la fiebre   *fever*
la gripe   *flu*
el jarabe   *syrup*
el (la) oculista   *eye doctor*
la operación, la cirugía   *surgery*
el (la) pasajero(a)   *passenger*
la pastilla   *pill*
el peso   *weight*

VERBOS

bajar   *to go down, to decrease*
chocar   *to collide*
sobrevivir   *to survive*
toser   *to cough*

OTRAS PALABRAS Y EXPRESIONES

a menos que   *unless*
antes de que   *before*
con tal que   *provided that*
en caso de que   *in case*
en cuanto, tan pronto como   *as
     soon as*
hacer ejercicio   *to exercise*
hasta que   *until*
para que   *in order that*
ponerse a dieta   *to go on a diet*
sin que   *without*

1 THE SUBJUNCTIVE AFTER CERTAIN CONJUNCTIONS
El subjuntivo después de ciertas conjunciones

The subjunctive is used after conjunctions of time when the main clause refers to the future or is a command.

■   Some conjunctions of time:

tan pronto como	*as soon as*
en cuanto	*as soon as*
hasta que	*until*
cuando	*when*

—Eva, ¿cuándo va a llamarte
el médico?
—Me llamará **tan pronto como
sepa** el resultado de los análisis.

*"Eva, when is the doctor going to
call you?"*
*"He will call me as soon as he finds
out the results of the tests."*

—Carlos, ¿a qué hora van a
empezar la operación?
—La van a empezar **en cuanto
llegue** el ayudante de la cirujana.

*"Carlos, at what time are they going
to begin the surgery?"*
*"They're going to begin it as soon as
the surgeon's assistant arrives."*

—Tomás, ¿cuándo vamos a salir
para el hospital?
—No podemos salir **hasta que**
el carro **esté** arreglado.

*"Tomás, when are we going
to leave for the hospital?"*
*"We can't leave until
the car is fixed."*

—**Cuando llegue** Marta, dígale
que **compre** el jarabe y un
termómetro.
—Muy bien. Se lo diré
cuando venga.

*"When Marta arrives,
tell her to buy the syrup
and a thermometer."*
*"Very well. I'll tell her
when she comes."*

> En las grandes ciudades hispanas, la medicina está muy adelantada (*advanced*), pero en muchos pueblos (*towns*) remotos no hay médicos ni hospitales. En ese caso, mucha gente recurre a (*turn to*) los servicios de un curandero (*healer*). Muchas mujeres tienen sus bebés con la ayuda de una partera (*midwife*).

**ATENCIÓN: If the action already happened or if there is no
indication of a future action, the indicative is used after the
conjunction of time.**

—¿A qué hora van a empezar
la operación?
—Siempre empiezan **en cuanto
llegan** los cirujanos.

*"At what time are they going to
begin the surgery?"*
*"They always begin as soon as the
surgeons arrive."*

—¿Qué haces con el niño cuando
tú tienes que trabajar?
—**Cuando** yo **trabajo,** mi mamá
viene a cuidarlo.

*"What do you do with the child
when you have to work?"*
*"When I work, my mother comes to
take care of him."*

—La Sra. Fuentes siempre espera
hasta que llega el Dr. Paz
porque él habla español.
—¿Él es México?
—No, es méxicoamericano.

*"Mrs. Fuentes always waits until
Dr. Paz arrives because he speaks
Spanish."*
"Is he from Mexico?"
"No, he is Mexican-American."

■ There are certain conjunctions that, by their very meaning, imply uncertainty or conditional fulfillment; they are therefore always followed by the subjunctive. Here are some of them.

a menos que	*unless*	**en caso de que**	*in case*
antes de que	*before*	**para que**	*in order that*
con tal que	*provided that*	**sin que**	*without*

—¿Va Ud. a firmar el testamento hoy?
—No puedo firmarlo **sin que** mi abogado lo **lea.**

"Are you going to sign the will today?"
"I can't sign it without my lawyer reading it."

—Estás tosiendo mucho. ¿Tienes catarro?
—Yo creo que es gripe. Voy a ir al médico **para que** me **haga** un buen chequeo.

"You are coughing a lot. Do you have a cold?"
"I think that it is the flu. I'm going to go to the doctor so that he can give me a good checkup."

—¿Vas a tomar las pastillas esta noche?
—Sí, voy a tomarlas a **menos que** me **baje** la fiebre.

"Are you going to take the pills tonight?"
"Yes, I'm going to take them unless the fever goes down."

Vamos a practicar

A Complete the following dialogues, using the present indicative or the present subjunctive of the verbs in parentheses. Then act them out with a partner.

1. —¿Cuándo vas a volver a la oficina?
   —En cuanto me _____ (bajar) la fiebre y me _____ (sentir) mejor.

2. —¿Cuándo te va a llamar Jorge?
   —No me va a llamar hasta que el doctor le _____ (dar) el resultado de los análisis.

3. —¿Qué vas a hacer?
   —Voy a llamar a Tito para que me _____ (traer) el jarabe cuando _____ (venir) esta tarde.

4. —Todos los días, yo llamo a mamá tan pronto como _____ (llegar) a casa.

    —Cuando (tú) la _____ (llamar) hoy, dile que me mande las pastillas.

5. —¿Vas a comprar el termómetro?

    —No puedo comprarlo a menos que tú me _____ (llevar) a la farmacia.

6. —¿Te vas a ir de vacaciones?

    —No puedo irme antes de que el cirujano _____ (decidir) si necesito la operación o no.

    —Yo puedo quedarme contigo en caso de que (tú) me _____ (necesitar).

7. —¿Por qué tomas estas pastillas?

    —Porque son muy buenas. Siempre me siento mejor en cuanto las _____ (tomar)

8.   Tengo que salir de casa sin que los niños me _____ (ver).

    —Sí, porque cuando tú _____ (irse), ellos siempre lloran (*cry*).

B Use your imagination to complete the following sentences with the present indicative or the present subjunctive, as appropriate.

1. No te bajará la fiebre a menos que...
2. El cirujano va a comenzar la operación en cuanto...
3. Ella siempre me llama tan pronto como...
4. Todas las noches lo espero hasta que...
5. Voy a limpiar la casa en caso de que...
6. Carlos siempre llama a su abogado cuando...
7. No puedo ir al hospital antes de que...
8. No puedo comprarte el jarabe sin que tú...
9. Voy a ir al médico para que...
10. Yo no te voy a llamar hasta que...

② THE PRESENT PERFECT SUBJUNCTIVE
El presente perfecto de subjuntivo

The present perfect subjunctive is formed with the present subjunctive of the auxiliary verb **haber** and the past participle of the main verb.

The Present Perfect Subjunctive			
	Present Subjunctive of haber	+	*Past Participle of the Main Verb*
yo	haya		hablado
tú	hayas		comido
Ud. él ella	haya		vivido
nosotros	hayamos		hecho
vosotros	hayáis		visto
Uds. ellos ellas	hayan		puesto

Vamos a practicar

Quiz

Conjugate the following verbs in the present perfect subjunctive for each subject given.

   1. yo: hacer, venir, comer, levantarse
   2. tú: trabajar, poner, decir, acostarse
   3. ella: escribir, cerrar, abrir, sentarse
   4. nosotros: romper, hablar, llegar, vestirse
   5. ellos: morir, vender, alquilar, bañarse

❸ USES OF THE PRESENT PERFECT SUBJUNCTIVE
Usos del presente perfecto de subjuntivo

The present perfect subjunctive is used in the same way as the present perfect tense in English, but only in sentences that require the subjunctive in the subordinate clause. It describes events that have ended prior to the time indicated in the main clause.

—¿Ya han pagado Uds. la
  cuenta del oculista?
—No recuerdo... no,
  no creo que la **hayamos
  pagado** todavía.

*"Have you already paid the eye
  doctor's bill?"*
*"I don't remember... No, I don't
  think we've paid it yet."*

—Hubo un accidente en la autopista. Chocaron dos autobuses, y **temo** que **hayan muerto** todos los pasajeros.
—¡Qué horrible![1] **Ojalá** que algunos **hayan sobrevivido.**

"*There was an accident on the freeway. Two buses collided and I fear that all the passengers (have) died.*"
"*How horrible! I hope that some (of them) (have) survived.*"

En las ciudades hispanas, la gente camina mucho todos los días, una actividad excelente para mantenerse en forma. Generalmente no suelen hacer un régimen de ejercicio, pero en general, los hispanos "hacen footing" (*jog*) por los parques o van a los gimnasios para tomar clases de ejercicios aeróbicos.

—Inés se ha puesto a dieta.
—Sí, pero **no creo** que **haya perdido** mucho peso porque nunca hace ejercicio.

"*Inés has gone on a diet.*"
"*Yes, but I don't think she has lost a lot of weight because she never exercises.*"

Vamos a practicar

Quiz

A Complete the following dialogues, using the present perfect subjunctive. Then act them out with a partner.

1. —¿Crees que el cirujano ha terminado ya la operación?
   —No, no creo que la _____ (terminar).

2. —Dicen que Mario se ha puesto a dieta.
   —Dudo que se _____ (poner) a dieta, porque él no necesita perder peso. Además, él siempre hace ejercicio.

3. —Ha habido (*There has been*) un accidente en la autopista. Chocaron un ómnibus y un coche.
   —Ojalá que no _____ (morir) nadie.
   —Temo que los pasajeros del coche no _____ (sobrevivir).
   —¡Qué horrible!

4. —Gloria ha ido a la oculista.
   —Me alegro de que _____ (decidir) ir, porque no ve muy bien.

5. —¿Hay alguien aquí que _____ (estar) en México este verano?
   —No, aquí no hay nadie que _____ (ir) a México.

6. —¿El Sr. Vega ya ha hecho el testamento?
   —No, no creo que lo _____ (hacer) todavía.

---

[1]The Spanish equivalent of *how* + adjective is **qué +** adjective.

B Use your imagination to complete the following sentences, using the present perfect subjunctive.

1. Yo me alegro de que mis padres...
2. Ojalá que tú...
3. Yo no creo que mi médico...
4. Mi familia espera que yo...
5. El (La) profesor(a) espera que nosotros...
6. Yo siento que Uds....
7. En mi familia no hay nadie que...
8. Yo dudo que mi hermano(a)...

Palabras y más palabras Complete the following exchanges, using the vocabulary learned in this lesson. Then act them out with a partner. You may use a vocabulary word more than once.

1. —¿Cuándo sabrás el _____ de los análisis?

   —En _____ me llame el médico.

2. —¿Hubo un accidente?

   —Sí, fue horrible. No _____ nadie.

3. —¿Qué hiciste para perder _____?

   —Hice ejercicio y me puse a _____.

4. —¿Para qué le das aspirina?

   —Para que le baje la _____.

5. —¿Qué pasó?

   —_____ un coche y un ómnibus en la _____.

6. —No veo bien.

   —Pues ve al _____.

7. —¿A quién espera el cirujano?

   —Espera a su _____ para poder empezar la _____.

8. —¿Qué va a comprar en la farmacia?

   —Un jarabe, un _____ y unas _____.

9. —Lupe tiene mucha _____. La voy a llevar al médico.

   —¿Crees que tiene catarro o _____?

10. —No me siento bien.

    —Ve al médico para que te haga un _____.

En estas situaciones What would you say in the following situations? What would the other person say?

1. Your friend isn't feeling well. Suggest that he/she goes to the doctor so he/she can give your friend a good checkup.
2. You know someone who wants to lose weight. Tell him/her that he/she must go on a diet and exercise more.
3. Explain what you are going to do as soon as classes are over.
4. There has been an accident. Express hope that no one has died.

PARA ESCUCHAR Y ENTENDER

The following material is to be used with the In-Text Audio CDs.

I. Práctica

 A El subjuntivo después de ciertas conjunciones

5–11 Restate each of the following sentences, inserting the cue at the beginning and making any necessary changes. Repeat the correct answer after the speaker's confirmation. Listen to the model.

> **Modelo** Siempre me llama tan pronto como llega. (Me va a llamar)
> **Me va a llamar tan pronto como llegue.**

1. (Los voy a llamar)
2. (Voy a comprar)
3. (Ella va a venir)
4. (No voy a poder hacer nada)
5. (Van a traer)
6. (Vamos a estar aquí)

 B El pretérito perfecto de subjuntivo

5–12 Restate each of the following sentences, inserting the cue at the beginning and using the present perfect subjunctive. Make any other necessary changes. Repeat the correct answer after the speaker's confirmation. Listen to the model.

> **Modelo** El doctor ha llegado. (Espero)
> **Espero que el doctor haya llegado.**

1. (Espero)
2. (Siento)
3. (No creo)
4. (No es verdad)
5. (Dudo)
6. (No es verdad)
7. (No es cierto)
8. (Me alegro de)

II. ¿Qué dicen?

1 ¿Lógico o ilógico?

5–13   The speaker will make some statements. Circle **L (lógico)** if the statement is logical and **I (ilógico)** if it is illogical. The speaker will verify your response.

1. L I	**3.** L I	**5.** L I	**7.** L I
2. L I	**4.** L I	**6.** L I	**8.** L I

2 Tomás y Julio

5–14   Listen carefully to the dialogue. Listen to it at least twice.

(Diálogo 1)

5–15   Now the speaker will make some statements about the dialogue you just heard. Tell whether each statement is true (**verdadero**) or false (**falso**). The speaker will confirm the correct answer.

3 Sonia y Alfredo

5–16   Listen carefully to the dialogue. Listen to it at least twice.

(Diálogo 2)

5–17   Now the speaker will make some statements about the dialogue you just heard. Tell whether each statement is true (**verdadero**) or false (**falso**). The speaker will confirm the correct answer.

A Rita y Daniel

5–18   Listen carefully to the dialogue. Listen to it at least twice.

(Diálogo 3)

5–19   Now the speaker will ask you some questions about the dialogue you just heard. Answer each question, omitting the subject. The speaker will confirm the correct answer. Repeat the correct answer.

LECCIÓN 20

OBJECTIVES

Structures
1. The imperfect subjunctive
2. Uses of the imperfect subjunctive
3. *If* clauses

Communication
You will learn vocabulary related to running errands.

Nationality highlighted: Los cubanoamericanos

En 1959, fecha en que la revolución castrista llegó al poder (*power*) en Cuba, comenzó la invasión cubana en Miami. Las confiscaciones de bienes (*property*) y la supresión de libertades impuestas por Castro obligaron a la élite del país a emigrar, y los Estados Unidos le abrieron las puertas a este segmento de la población. Este grupo de cubanos transformó la pequeña ciudad turística que era Miami en 1959, en la gran metrópoli industrial y comercial actual (*current*). Desde luego, como la puerta de entrada quedó abierta a todos los que huían (*flee*) del comunismo, en los años transcurridos (*that have elapsed*) desde 1959, se han sumado (*have been added*) a la élite inicial cubanos de todos los niveles económicos, sociales y culturales. Actualmente los cubanos controlan no sólo la vida económica de la ciudad, sino la política.

Los cubanos son el 5 por ciento de los hispanos de este país, y como buena parte de ellos vinieron por razones políticas, no económicas, son los emigrantes hispanos más conservadores, con mayor nivel de escolaridad y mayor ingreso (*income*) per cápita. Entre los más conocidos podemos destacar (*highlight*), en la política: Rafael Díaz Balart e Iliana Ross, representantes; en el cine: Andy García y Cameron Díaz; y en la música: Jon Secada, Gloria Estefan y Celia Cruz.

RESOURCES

Wherever you see the following icons additional resources are available:

Go to **www.college.hmco.com/languages/spanish/students/** for additional practice on the topic.

Go to the **Video Grammar Tutor** for help with understanding the grammar topic at hand.

Go to the **In-Text Audio CDs** for more practice.

VOCABULARIO

Audio

COGNADOS

el consulado
el crédito
la fotocopia

NOMBRES

la **billetera**   *wallet*
el **correo**   *post office*
la **cortina**   *curtain*
la **diligencia**   *errand*
la **entrevista**   *interview*
el **informe**   *report*
el **(la) jefe(a)**   *boss, chief*
el **paquete**   *package*
los **parientes**   *relatives*
el **préstamo**   *loan*
el **talonario de cheques**   *checkbook*
el **teléfono celular**   *cellphone*

VERBOS

**apurarse, darse
   prisa**   *to hurry*
asistir (a)   *to attend*
devolver (o:ue)   *to return (something),
   to give back*
grabar   *to tape, to record*
preocuparse   *to worry*
recoger   *to pick up*

OTRAS PALABRAS Y EXPRESIONES

como   *since*
echar al correo   *to mail*
hacer diligencias   *to do errands*
pedir prestado(a)   *to borrow*
perderse algo   *to miss (out)*
un montón de   *a lot of*

  1 THE IMPERFECT SUBJUNCTIVE
El imperfecto de subjuntivo

The Imperfect Subjunctive

Verb	Preterit, Third Person Plural	Stem	Imperfect Subjunctive	
hablar	hablaron	**habla-**	que yo habla-	**ra**
comer	comieron	**comie-**	que tú comie-	**ras**
vivir	vivieron	**vivie-**	que Ud. vivie-	**ra**
traer	trajeron	**traje-**	que él traje-	**ra**
ir	fueron	**fue-**	que ella fue-	**ra**
saber	supieron	**supie-**	que nosotros supié-	**ramos**
dar	dieron	**die-**	que vosotros die-	**rais**
decir	dijeron	**dije-**	que Uds. dije-	**ran**
poner	pusieron	**pusie-**	que ellos pusie-	**ran**
estar	estuvieron	**estuvie-**	que ellas estuvie-	**ran**

The imperfect subjunctive is the past tense of the subjunctive. It is formed in the same way for all verbs, regular and irregular. The **-ron** ending of the third person plural of the preterit is dropped and the following endings are added to the stem: **-ra, -ras, -ra, -ramos, -rais, -ran.**[1]

■ Notice the written accent mark in the first person plural form.

Vamos a practicar

Quiz

Give the imperfect subjunctive of the following verbs.

1. yo:	bajar, aprender, abrir, cerrar, estar, acostarse
2. tú:	salir, sentir, temer, recordar, venir, ponerse
3. Ud.:	llevar, romper, morir, revisar, volar, alegrarse
4. nosotros:	esperar, traer, pedir, volver, servir, vestirse
5. ellos:	tener, ser, dar, estar, poder, irse

❷ USES OF THE IMPERFECT SUBJUNCTIVE
Usos del imperfecto de subjuntivo

■ The imperfect subjunctive is always used in a subordinate clause when the verb of the main clause is in the past and requires the subjunctive mood.

—¿Qué te sugirió él?

—Me **sugirió** que **pidiera** un préstamo en el banco.

—¿Lo pediste?

—No, porque como no tengo crédito **temí** que no me lo **dieran.**

"What did he suggest to you?"

"He suggested that I ask for a loan at the bank."

"Did you ask for it?"

"No, because since I don't have credit I was afraid that they wouldn't give it to me."

—Mamá me **pidió** que **comprara** estampillas y que **echara** estas cartas al correo. Son todas para sus parientes en Cuba.

—A mí me **dijo** que **fuera** a la tintorería para recoger las cortinas.

"Mom asked me to buy stamps and to mail these letters. They are all for her relatives in Cuba."

"She told me to go to the cleaners to pick up the curtains."

---

[1]See Appendix B: Verbs, for the **-se** endings of the imperfect subjunctive, which are less frequently used.

—Y a papá le **pidió** que
  hiciera otras diligencias.

*"And she asked Dad to run other
  errands."*

—Mi tía me **pidió** que le
  grabara el programa de Cristina.
—Ella nunca se lo pierde.

*"My aunt asked me to tape Cristina's
  program."*
"She never misses it."

—El jefe me **dio** el informe
  para que **hiciera** fotocopias y las **llevara** al consulado
  americano.
—¿Ya lo hiciste?
—No, porque también me **dijo**
  que **escribiera** un montón
  de cartas.

*"The boss gave me the report so that
  I could make photocopies and take
  them to the American consulate."*

"Did you do it already?"
*"No, because he also told me to write
  a lot of letters."*

■ The imperfect subjunctive is also used when the verb of the main
  clause is in the present, but the subordinate clause refers to the past.

—Es una lástima que no **pudieras**
  asistir a la reunión ayer.
—No pude ir porque tuve que
  ir a una entrevista.

*"It's a pity that you weren't able to
  attend the meeting yesterday."*
*"I couldn't go because I had to go
  to an interview."*

■ The imperfect subjunctive form of **querer (quisiera)** is used as a
  polite form of request.

—**Quisiera** pedirle un favor.

"I would like to ask you a favor."

Vamos a practicar

A Complete the following dialogues using the imperfect subjunctive.
Then act them out with a partner.

1. —Anita, te dije que _____ (hacer) fotocopias de este informe.

   —No pude porque papá me pidió que _____ (ir) a la oficina
   de correos.

2. —Mamá quería que yo _____ (recoger) las cortinas en la tintorería.

   —A mí me pidió que _____ (hacer) un montón de diligencias.

3. —Es una lástima que Julio no _____ (poder) ir a la entrevista
   ayer.

   —No pudo ir porque su jefe le pidió que _____ (asistir) a una
   junta.

4. —Siento que ellos no te _____ (dar) el préstamo.

—Era difícil que me lo _____ (dar) porque no tengo buen crédito.

5. —Alicia nos pidió que _____ (comprar) estampillas y que _____ (echar) unas cartas al correo.

—¡Pero mamá quería que (nosotros) _____ (ir) con ella al consulado americano!

6. —Alina nos pidió que le _____ (grabar) su programa favorito.

—Y a los chicos les rogó que _____ (ir) con ella a esperar a sus parientes en el aeropuerto.

B Use your imagination to complete the following sentences, using the imperfect subjunctive.

1. Siento que ayer tú no...

2. Yo les pedí a mis amigos que...

3. Mis padres querían que yo...

4. El profesor nos dijo que...

5. Yo quería que mi hermano(a)...

6. Yo me alegré de que Uds....

3 *IF* CLAUSES
Oraciones condicionales

In Spanish, the imperfect subjunctive is used in a clause introduced by **si** (*if*) when it refers to statements considered contrary to fact, hypothetical, or unlikely to happen. The resultant clause usually has a verb in the conditional.

Si yo fuera Ud...	*If I were you...*
—**Si** yo **tuviera** dinero, iría de vacaciones con Uds.	"*If I had money, I would go on vacation with you.*"
—¿No se lo puedes pedir prestado a tu padre?	"*Can't you borrow it from your father?*"
—No, porque **si** mi padre me lo **prestara,** tendría que devolvérselo antes de septiembre, y yo necesito el dinero para pagar la matrícula.	"*No, because if my father were to lend it to me,[1] I would have to give it back to him before September, and I need the money to pay for registration.*"

---

[1]Many colloquial English speakers use the simple past tense to express a contrary-to-fact or hypothetical situation, e.g., "*... if my father **lent** it to me.*"

—**Si tuviéramos** tiempo, podríamos llevar estos paquetes al correo ahora.

"*If we had time, we could take these packages to the post office now.*"

—No te preocupes. Podemos llevarlos mañana.

"*Don't worry. We can take them tomorrow.*"

—No puedo comprar la computadora porque no tengo mi talonario de cheques.

"*I can't buy the computer because I don't have my checkbook.*"

—**Si** yo **fuera** tú, usaría una tarjeta de crédito.

"*If I were you, I would use a credit card.*"

—Tienes razón. Si tengo mi MasterCard en la billetera, voy a usarla.

"*You're right. If I have my Master-Card in my wallet; I am going to use it.*"

ATENCIÓN: **When an** *if* **clause is not contrary to fact or hypothetical, or when there is a possibility that the situation it describes will happen, the indicative is used.**

Voy a comprar un teléfono celular **si** mi padre me **da** el dinero.

"*I'm going to buy a cell phone if my father gives me the money.*"

Dile a mamá que **si se apura,** puedo llevarla a la Calle Ocho.

"*Tell Mom that if she hurries up, I can take her to Eighth Street.*"

> A partir de 1959, la Calle Ocho en Miami se convirtió en el centro de los negocios y de la vida de los cubanos refugiados. Muchos empezaron a llamarla "la pequeña Habana". Pronto empezaron a llegar emigrantes de toda América Latina y hoy la Calle 8 es una pequeña babel de dialectos hispanos.

■ The present subjunctive is **never** used with an *if* clause.

Vamos a practicar

A Complete the following dialogues, using the imperfect subjunctive. Then act them out with a partner.

1. —Si yo _____ (tener) dinero, le compraría una computadora y un teléfono celular a Pepe.

   —Si yo _____ (ser) tú, no le compraría nada.

2. —Si Estrella me _____ (devolver) el dinero que le presté, yo podría pagar mis cuentas.

—Estoy segura de que si ella _____ (poder), te lo devolvería.

3. —Ernesto se preocupa mucho por sus hijos.

—Yo también me preocuparía si mis hijos _____ (ser) como los de él.

4. —Si Carolina _____ (venir) hoy, podríamos ir al consulado juntas.

—Si nosotras no _____ (trabajar) hoy, iríamos contigo.

5. —Si tú _____ (tener) un examen y un amigo te _____ (pedir) que _____ (hacer) un montón de diligencias, ¿qué harías?

—Le diría que no.

B Use your imagination to complete the following sentences, using either the imperfect subjunctive or the present indicative, as appropriate.

1. Yo llevaría el paquete al correo si...
2. Ella te compraría una billetera si...
3. Nosotros pagaríamos con un cheque si...
4. Haré las fotocopias hoy si...
5. Ellos van a asistir a la reunión si...
6. ¿Qué harías tú si... ?
7. Mi papá pediría un préstamo si...
8. Te voy a devolver el dinero si...

Palabras y más palabras Circle the word or phrase that best completes each sentence.

1. No tengo dinero. Se lo voy a pedir (prestado / preocupado) a mi tío.
2. Ella (devuelve / asiste) a la universidad.
3. Tengo que ir a la tintorería para (comprar / recoger) mis pantalones.
4. Voy a (echar / bajar) estas cartas al correo.
5. Estoy muy ocupada. Tengo que (hacer / chocar) muchas diligencias.
6. Voy al banco para pedir un (paquete / préstamo) porque necesito dinero.
7. No tengo mi (talonario / informe) de cheques.
8. Compré (billeteras / cortinas) para las ventanas de mi cuarto.
9. Fui al (consulado / correo) americano para recoger mi pasaporte.
10. Ella (se sienta / se preocupa) mucho por sus hijos.
11. Grábame el programa porque no me lo quiero (apurar / perder).
12. No puedo llamarla porque no tengo mi (billetera / teléfono celular) conmigo.

En estas situaciones What would you say in the following situations?

1. You are going with a friend. Tell him/her to hurry up because you have to run a lot of errands. Mention three or four errands.
2. Mention three things people asked you to do.
3. Mention four things you are going to buy if you have more money.
4. Talk about a few things you could do if you had more time.

PARA ESCUCHAR Y ENTENDER

The following material is to be used with the In-Text Audio CDs.

I. Práctica

5–20

A El imperfecto de subjuntivo
Restate each of the following sentences, inserting the cue at the beginning and making any necessary changes. Repeat the correct answer after the speaker's confirmation. Listen to the model.

> **MODELOS**   Ella quiere que yo vaya con él. (Ella quería)
> **Ella quería que yo fuera con él.**

1. (Fue una lástima)	5. (No había nadie)
2. (No creí)	6. (Necesitaba)
3. (Esperaba)	7. (No quería)
4. (Dudábamos)	8. (No creían)

5–21

B Oraciones condicionales
Restate each of the following sentences, inserting the cue at the beginning and making any necessary changes. Repeat the correct answer after the speaker's confirmation. Listen to the model.

> **MODELO**   Iré si tengo tiempo. (Iría)
> **Iría si tuviera tiempo.**

1. (Le hablaría)	5. (Vendríamos)
2. (Compraríamos)	6. (Me alegraría)
3. (Lo harían)	7. (Lo compraría)
4. (Se lo diría)	8. (Lo haríamos)

II. ¿Qué dicen?

1 ¿Lógico o ilógico?

5–22 The speaker will make some statements. Circle **L (lógico)** if the statement is logical and **I (ilógico)** if it is illogical. The speaker will verify your response.

1. L I	**3.** L I	**5.** L I	**7.** L I
2. L I	**4.** L I	**6.** L I	**8.** L I

2 ¿Verdadero o falso?

5–23 Listen carefully to the narration. Listen to it at least twice.

(Narración)

5–24 Now the speaker will make some statements about the narration you just heard. Tell whether each statement is true (**verdadero**) or false (**falso**). The speaker will confirm the correct answer.

3 Tito y su papá

5 25 Listen carefully to the dialogue. Listen to it at least twice.

(Diálogo 1)

5–26 Now the speaker will make some statements about the dialogue you just heard. Tell whether each statement is true (**verdadero**) or false (**falso**). The speaker will confirm the correct answer.

4 Tere y José

5–27 Listen carefully to the dialogue. Listen to it at least twice.

(Diálogo 2)

5–28 Now the speaker will ask you some questions about the dialogue you just heard. Answer each question, omitting the subject. The speaker will confirm the correct answer. Repeat the correct answer.

¿CUÁNTO SABE USTED AHORA?

LECCIÓN 16

A The present subjunctive

Complete the following, using the Spanish equivalent of the verbs in parentheses in the present subjunctive. Follow the model.

MODELO   ...que yo _____ (*speak*)
...que yo **hable**

1. ...que nosotros _____ (*close*)

2. ...que ellos _____ (*go*)

3. ...que tú _____ (*open*)

4. ...que Pablo _____ (*recommend*)

5. ...que Ud. _____ (*leave*)

6. ...que yo _____ (*return*)

7. ...que Uds. _____ (*want*)

8. ...que ella _____ (*understand*)

9. ...que nosotros _____ (*have*)

10. ...que las chicas _____ (*put*)

11. ...que tú _____ (*bring*)

12. ...que los estudiantes _____ (*give*)

13. ...que yo _____ (*be:* **estar**)

14. ...que Teresa _____ (*be:* **ser**)

15. ...que Uds. _____ (*know:* **saber**)

B The subjunctive with verbs of volition

Give the Spanish equivalent of the words in parentheses.

1. Yo _____ al club con Teresa, pero mamá _____ al médico. (*want to go / wants me to accompany her*)

2. No sé que hacer. ¿_____, Anita? (*What do you suggest that I do*)

3. Si tú _____ al despacho de boletos, yo _____ con Aníbal. (*need to go / advise you to go*)

4. Si Uds. _____ el tren, _____ cuanto antes.
(*don't want to miss* / *I suggest that you leave*)

5. Yo le voy a pedir a Raúl _____ los boletos esta tarde.
(*to buy*)

6. Mamá _____ ahora, pero yo no tengo tiempo.
(*wants me to pack*)

C The absolute superlative

Change the following to the absolute superlative.

1. sumamente difícil
2. muy lenta
3. sumamente buenas
4. muy alto

5. muy largo
6. sumamente rápido
7. muy inteligentes
8. sumamente fáciles

D Vocabulario

Complete the following sentences, using words learned in **Lección 16.**

1. ¡Son las cinco! Tienes que salir cuanto _____.

2. Me dieron un _____ del diez por _____.

3. Quiero reservar un _____ para el vuelo a Mérida.

4. Todos los trenes son muy lentos, menos (*except for*) el _____.

5. Vamos a estar en la _____ de trenes a las diez.

6. Alberto dice que ella es muy bonita. ¡Yo no lo _____!

LECCIÓN 17

A The subjunctive to express emotion

Give the Spanish equivalent of the words in parentheses.

1. Espero que el médico _____ la inyección. (*gives him*)

2. Temo que el consultorio _____. (*is closed*)

3. Espero que _____ a la sala de emergencia. (*they take him*)

4. Temo que ella _____ a los niños. (*can't take care*)

5. Me alegro de que ella _____ al dentista hoy. (*is going*)

6. Sentimos que ellos _____ en el hospital. (*have to stay*)

B **The subjunctive with some impersonal expressions**

Complete the following sentences, using the present subjunctive or the infinitive, as appropriate.

1. Conviene que ella _____ (ver) al médico hoy.
2. Es difícil que mi médico _____ (poder) verme mañana.
3. Es importante _____ (saber) lo que pasó.
4. Es posible que ellos me _____ (poner) una inyección.
5. Es lástima que ella no _____ (tener) la medicina.
6. Yo creo que es mejor no _____ (ir) al hospital hoy.
7. Es necesario _____ (esperar) a los paramédicos.
8. Ojalá que él _____ (sentirse) mejor.

C **Formation of adverbs**

Complete the following sentences, using the Spanish equivalent of the words in parentheses.

1. Ella vino _____ para verte. (*especially*)
2. Fui al médico _____. (*recently*)
3. Yo hablé _____ y _____, y los pacientes me entendieron. (*slowly / clearly*)
4. Nosotros _____ nos levantamos a las seis. (*generally*)
5. Ellos todo lo hacen muy _____. (*easily*)

D **Vocabulary**

Complete the following sentences, using words learned in **Lección 17.**

1. Lo llevaron al hospital en una _____.
2. Se rompió la pierna. Va a necesitar _____ para caminar.
3. Lo llevaron a la _____ de emergencia.
4. El doctor está en su _____.
5. Lo llevaron a la sala de rayos X para hacerle una _____.
6. Le van a _____ una inyección.
7. Yo me rompí el brazo; me lo van a _____.
8. En este _____ llegan los paramédicos.

LECCIÓN 18

A The subjunctive to express doubt, disbelief, and denial

Complete the following exchanges, using the present subjunctive or the present indicative of the verbs given.

1. —Creo que Julio _____ (estar) tomando cinco asignaturas.

   —Dudo que él _____ (poder) sacar buenas notas.

2. —Ana es muy buena estudiante. Estoy segura de que _____ (mantener) un promedio de A.

   —Es verdad que ella _____ (ser) buena estudiante, pero no creo que _____ (mantener) ese promedio.

3. —El profesor Varela enseña psicología y química.

   —No es verdad que él _____ (enseñar) química.

B The subjunctive to express indefiniteness and nonexistence

Rephrase these sentences according to the new beginnings.

1. Tengo un estudiante que es de México.
   No tengo ningún estudiante...

2. Hay alguien que puede llevarlo a la biblioteca.
   No hay nadie...

3. Aquí hay una secretaria que es bilingüe.
   Aquí no hay ninguna secretaria...

4. Hay dos personas aquí que saben contabilidad.
   Busco a alguien...

5. Necesito a alguien que pueda dar una conferencia.
   Hay una profesora...

C Diminutive suffixes

Give the diminutive form of the following words.

1. Carmen
2. árbol
3. niños
4. café
5. Juan
6. favor
7. piernas
8. Ana
9. hermana
10. noche

D Vocabulario

Complete the following sentences, using words learned in **Lección 18.**

1. La contabilidad es mi _____ favorita.
2. El examen _____ es en octubre y el examen _____ es en diciembre.
3. Me alegro de que saques buenas _____ en la clase.
4. No puedo tomar clases. No tengo dinero para pagar la _____.
5. Estudiamos las ideas de Isaac Newton en nuestra clase de _____.
6. Mi _____ quiere que tome una clase de física.

LECCIÓN 19

A The subjunctive after certain conjunctions

Complete the following sentences, using the Spanish equivalent of the words in parentheses.

1. No va a hacer testamento hasta que _____. *(her lawyer comes)*
2. Yo siempre espero hasta que mi ayudante _____ el resultado. *(brings me)*
3. Yo podré ir a trabajar en cuanto me _____. *(the fever goes down)*
4. Cuando él _____ el resultado de los análisis, se va a alegrar. *(knows)*
5. No sobrevivirán a menos que _____ al hospital inmediatamente. *(they take them)*
6. En cuanto el cirujano _____ al hospital, siempre habla con sus ayudantes. *(arrives)*
7. No te sentirás mejor a menos que _____ estas pastillas. *(you take)*
8. Voy a comprar aspirinas en caso de que Adela _____. *(has a fever)*

B The present perfect subjunctive

Give the present perfect subjunctive of the verbs given.

1. ...que yo _____ (llegar)
2. ...que Uds. _____ (volver)

3. ...que Teresa _____ (ir)

4. ...que tú _____ (decir)

5. ...que nosotros _____ (hacer)

6. ...que Ud. _____ (preferir)

7. ...que Carlos _____ (abrir)

8. ...que los niños _____ (poner)

C Uses of the present perfect subjunctive

Rephrase the following sentences according to the new beginnings.

1. Nosotros hemos hecho el trabajo.

   Ellos no creen que nosotros...

2. Yo he estado enfermo.

   Ella duda que yo...

3. Han muerto muchos.

   No es verdad que...

4. Ha ido a México.

   No hay nadie que...

5. Tú le has escrito una carta.

   Ella no cree que tú...

6. Ellos han hablado con la enfermera.

   Espero que...

7. Uds. no han visto a sus pacientes.

   Siento que Uds....

8. Ana y yo hemos ido a su consultorio.

   No es cierto...

D Vocabulario

Complete the following sentences, using words learned in **Lección 19.**

1. Los _____ ya están en el tren.

2. Necesito el _____ para ver si tiene fiebre.

3. Hubo un accidente en la _____.

4. Te traje un _____ porque estás tosiendo mucho.

5. Tengo que salir _____ de que lleguen los chicos.

6. Para bajar de peso me voy a poner a _____ y voy a hacer _____.

7. No sé si tengo catarro o _____.

8. El médico me va a hacer un buen _____.

9. No veo bien. Tengo que ir al _____.

10. ¿Tienes el _____ de los análisis?

LECCIÓN 20

A The imperfect subjunctive

Give the imperfect subjunctive of the verbs given.

1. ...que ellos _____ (asistir)

2. ...que tú _____ (ser)

3. ...que nosotros _____ (devolver)

4. ...que Estela _____ (ir)

5. ...que yo _____ (recoger)

6. ...que Roberto _____ (poder)

7. ...que Ud. _____ (querer)

8. ...que Uds. _____ (dar)

9. ...que Luis y yo _____ (hacer)

10. ...que las niñas _____ (traer)

B Uses of the imperfect subjunctive

Rephrase the following sentences according to the new beginnings.

1. Yo tuve que trabajar.
   No era verdad que yo...

2. Nosotros pusimos el dinero en el banco.
   Ella quería que nosotros...

3. Tú fuiste al correo.
   Tu papá te dijo que...

4. Ellos hicieron las diligencias.
   La Sra. Rojas quería que ellos...

5. Ud. llevó el paquete.
   Yo quería que Ud....

6. Uds. hablaron con el jefe.
   Nosotros esperábamos que Uds....

7. María estuvo enferma.

  Yo sentí mucho que María...

8. Esteban perdió la billetera.

  Yo temía que Esteban...

C *If* clauses

Complete the following sentences, using the Spanish equivalent of the words in parentheses.

1. _____, le diré que tú la necesitas. *(If I see her)*

2. _____, no haría eso. *(If I were you)*

3. _____, iría contigo. *(If she had time)*

4. _____, podré comprar las cortinas. *(If he gives me the money)*

5. _____, llegaríamos mañana. *(If we went by car)*

6. _____, te va a traer el dinero. *(If she can come)*

7. _____, podríamos ir con ellos, Anita. *(If you wanted to)*

8. Iré al banco _____. *(if they go with me)*

D Vocabulario

Complete the following sentences, using words learned in **Lección 20.**

1. Voy a poner el dinero en la _____.

2. Te voy a _____ el dinero que te pedí _____ la semana pasada.

3. Voy a escribir un _____ para mi clase de historia.

4. No tengo dinero para comprar el coche. Voy a pedir un _____.

5. ¿Tienes tu _____ de cheques?

6. Ellos _____ a la Universidad de Salamanca.

7. Tengo un _____ de cartas para _____ al correo.

8. Compré un teléfono _____.

9. Voy a _____ mi programa favorito porque no me lo quiero _____.

10. ¡Es tarde! ¡Tienes que _____ prisa!

INTRODUCTION TO SPANISH SOUNDS AND THE ALPHABET

Sections marked with a Web-audio icon are recorded on the website that supplements this text. Repeat each Spanish word after the speaker, imitating as closely as possible the correct pronunciation.

The Alphabet

LETTER	NAME	LETTER	NAME	LETTER	NAME	LETTER	NAME
a	a	h	hache	ñ	eñe	t	te
b	be	i	i	o	o	u	u
c	ce	j	jota	p	pe	v	ve
d	de	k	ka	q	cu	w	doble ve
e	e	l	ele	r	ere	x	equis
f	efe	m	eme	rr	erre	y	i griega
g	ge	n	ene	s	ese	z	zeta

Audio

The Vowels

1. The Spanish **a** has a sound similar to the English *a* in the word *father*. Repeat:

   Ana   casa   banana   mala   dama   mata

2. The Spanish **e** is pronounced like the English *e* in the word *eight*. Repeat:

   este   René   teme   deme   entre   bebe

3. The Spanish **i** is pronounced like the English *ee* in the word *see*. Repeat:

   sí   difícil   Mimí   ir   dividir   Fifí

4. The Spanish **o** is similar to the English *o* in the word *no,* but without the glide. Repeat:

   solo   poco   como   toco   con   monólogo

5. The Spanish **u** is similar to the English *ue* sound in the word *Sue.* Repeat:

Lulú	un	su	universo	murciélago

The Consonants

1. The Spanish **p** is pronounced like the English *p* in the word *spot.* Repeat:

pan	papá	Pepe	pila	poco	pude

2. The Spanish **c** in front of **a, o, u, l,** or **r** sounds similar to the English *k.* Repeat:

casa	como	cuna	clima	crimen	cromo

3. The Spanish **q** is only used in the combinations **que** and **qui** in which the **u** is silent, and also has a sound similar to the English *k.* Repeat:

que	queso	Quique	quinto	quema	quiso

4. The Spanish **t** is pronounced like the English *t* in the word *stop.* Repeat:

toma	mata	tela	tipo	atún	Tito

5. The Spanish **d** at the beginning of an utterance or after **n** or **l** sounds somewhat similar to the English *d* in the word *David.* Repeat:

día	dedo	duelo	anda	Aldo

In all other positions, the **d** has a sound similar to the English *th* in the word *they.* Repeat:

medida	todo	nada	Ana dice	Eva duda

6. The Spanish **g** also has two sounds. At the beginning of an utterance and in all other positions, except before **e** or **i,** the Spanish **g** sounds similar to the English *g* in the word *sugar.* Repeat:

goma	gato	tengo	lago	algo	aguja

In the combinations **gue** and **gui,** the **u** is silent. Repeat:

Águeda	guineo	guiso	ligue	la guía

7. The Spanish **j,** and **g** before **e** or **i,** sounds similar to the English *h* in the word *home.* Repeat:

   jamás   juego   jota   Julio   gente   Genaro   gime

8. The Spanish **b** and the **v** have no difference in sound. Both are pronounced alike. At the beginning of the utterance or after **m** or **n,** they sound similar to the English *b* in the word *obey.* Repeat:

   Beto   vaga   bote   vela   también   un vaso

   Between vowels, they are pronounced with the lips barely closed. Repeat:

   sábado   yo voy   sabe   Ávalos   Eso vale

9. In most Spanish-speaking countries, the **y** and the **ll** are similar to the English *y* in the word *yet.* Repeat:

   yo   llama   yema   lleno   ya   lluvia   llega

10. The Spanish **r (ere)** is pronounced like the English *tt* in the word *gutter.* Repeat:

    cara   pero   arena   carie   Laredo   Aruba

    The Spanish **r** in an initial position and after **l, n,** or **s,** and **rr (erre)** in the middle of a word are pronounced with a strong trill. Repeat:

    Rita   Rosa   torre   ruina   Enrique   Israel
    perro   parra   rubio   alrededor   derrama

11. The Spanish **s** sound is represented in most of the Spanish-speaking world by the letters **s, z,** and **c** before **e** or **i.** The sound is very similar to the English sibilant *s* in the word *sink.* Repeat:

    sale   sitio   solo   seda   suelo
    zapato   cerveza   ciudad   cena

    In most of Spain, the **z,** and **c** before **e** or **i,** is pronounced like the English *th* in the word *think.* Repeat:

    zarzuela   cielo   docena

12. The letter **h** is silent in Spanish. Repeat:

hilo   Hugo   ahora   Hilda   almohada   hermano

13. The Spanish **ch** is pronounced like the English *ch* in the word *chief.* Repeat:

muchacho   chico   coche   chueco   chaparro

14. The Spanish **f** is identical in sound to the English *f.* Repeat:

famoso   feo   difícil   fuego   foto

15. The Spanish **l** is pronounced like the English *l* in the word *lean.* Repeat:

dolor   ángel   fácil   sueldo   salgo   chaval

16. The Spanish **m** is pronounced like the English *m* in the word *mother.* Repeat:

mamá   moda   multa   médico   mima

17. In most cases, the Spanish **n** has a sound similar to the English *n.* Repeat:

nada   norte   nunca   entra   nene

The sound of the Spanish **n** is often affected by the sounds that occur around it. When it appears before **b, v,** or **p,** it is pronounced like the English *m.* Repeat:

invierno   tan bueno   un vaso   un bebé   un perro

18. The Spanish **ñ (eñe)** has a sound similar to the English *ny* in the word *canyon.* Repeat:

muñeca   leña   año   señorita   piña   señor

19. The Spanish **x** has two pronunciations, depending on its position. Between vowels, the sound is similar to the English *ks.* Repeat:

examen   boxeo   exigente   éxito

Before a consonant, the Spanish **x** sounds like the English *s*. Repeat:

expreso   excusa   exquisito   extraño

Linking

Audio

In spoken Spanish, the various words in a phrase or sentence are not pronounced as isolated elements, but are combined. This is called *linking*.

1. The final consonant of a word is pronounced together with the initial vowel of the following word. Repeat:

   Carlos anda   un ángel   el otoño   unos estudiantes

2. The final vowel of a word is pronounced together with the initial vowel of the following word. Repeat:

   su esposo   la hermana   ardua empresa   la invita

3. When the final vowel of a word and the initial vowel of the following word are identical, they are pronounced slightly longer than one vowel. Repeat:

   Ana alcanza   me espera   mi hijo   lo olvida

   The same rule applies when two identical vowels appear within a word. Repeat:

   cooperación   crees   leemos   coordinación

4. When the final consonant of a word and the initial consonant of the following word are the same, they are pronounced as one consonant with slightly longer-than-normal duration. Repeat:

   el lado   un novio   Carlos salta   tienes sed   al leer

Rhythm

Rhythm is the variation of sound intensity that we usually associate with music. Spanish and English each regulate these variations in speech differently, because they have different patterns of syllable length. In Spanish the length of the stressed and unstressed syllables remains almost the same, while in English stressed syllables are considerably longer than unstressed ones. Pronounce the following Spanish words, enunciating each syllable clearly.

es-tu-dian-te	bue-no	Úr-su-la
com-po-si-ción	di-fí-cil	ki-ló-me-tro
po-li-cí-a	Pa-ra-guay	

Because the length of the Spanish syllables remains constant, the greater the number of syllables in a given word or phrase, the longer the phrase will be.

Intonation

Intonation is the rise and fall of pitch in the delivery of a phrase or a sentence. In general, Spanish pitch tends to change less than English, giving the impression that the language is less emphatic.

As a rule, the intonation for normal statements in Spanish starts in a low tone, raises to a higher one on the first stressed syllable, maintains that tone until the last stressed syllable, and then goes back to the initial low tone, with still another drop at the very end.

Tu amigo viene mañana.	José come pan.
Ada está en casa.	Carlos toma café.

Syllable Formation in Spanish

General rules for dividing words into syllables are as follows.

Vowels

1. A vowel or a vowel combination can constitute a syllable.

a-lum-no	a-bue-la	Eu-ro-pa

2. Diphthongs and triphthongs are considered single vowels and cannot be divided.

bai-le	puen-te	Dia-na	es-tu-diáis	an-ti-guo

3. Two strong vowels (**a, e, o**) do not form a diphthong and are separated into two syllables.

em-ple-ar	vol-te-ar	lo-a

4. A written accent on a weak vowel (**i** or **u**) breaks the diphthong, thus the vowels are separated into two syllables.

    trí-o   dú-o   Ma-rí-a

Consonants

1. A single consonant forms a syllable with the vowel that follows it.

    po-der   ma-no   mi-nu-to

    NOTE: **rr** is considered a single consonant: **pe-rro.**

2. When two consonants appear between two vowels, they are separated into two syllables.

    al-fa-be-to   cam-pe-ón   me-ter-se   mo-les-tia

    EXCEPTION: When a consonant cluster composed of **b, c, d, f, g, p,** or **t** with **l** or **r** appears between two vowels, the cluster joins the following vowel: **so-bre, o-tros, ca-ble, te-lé-gra-fo.**

3. When three consonants appear between two vowels, only the last one goes with the following vowel.

    ins-pec-tor   trans-por-te   trans-for-mar

    EXCEPTION: When there is a cluster of three consonants in the combinations described in rule 2, the first consonant joins the preceding vowel and the cluster joins the following vowel: **es-cri-bir, ex-tran-je-ro, im-plo-rar, es-tre-cho.**

Accentuation

In Spanish, all words are stressed according to specific rules. Words that do not follow the rules must have a written accent to indicate the change of stress. The basic rules for accentuation are as follows.

1. Words ending in a vowel, **n,** or **s** are stressed on the next-to-the-last syllable.

    hi-jo   **ca**-lle   **me**-sa   fa-**mo**-sos
    flo-**re**-cen   **pla**-ya   **ve**-ces

2. Words ending in a consonant, except **n** or **s,** are stressed on the last syllable.

ma-**yor**   a-**mor**   tro-pi-**cal**   na-**riz**   re-**loj**   co-rre-**dor**

3. All words that do not follow these rules must have the written accent.

ca-**fé**	**lá**-piz	**mú**-si-ca	sa-**lón**
án-gel	**lí**-qui-do	fran-**cés**	**Víc**-tor
sim-**pá**-ti-co	rin-**cón**	a-**zú**-car	**dár**-se-lo
sa-**lió**	**dé**-bil	e-**xá**-me-nes	**dí**-me-lo

4. Pronouns and adverbs of interrogation and exclamation have a written accent to distinguish them from relative pronouns.

—¿**Qué** comes?   *"What are you eating?"*
—La pera que él no comió.   *"The pear that he did not eat."*

—¿**Quién** está ahí?   *"Who is there?"*
—El hombre a quien tú llamaste. *"The man whom you called."*

—¿**Dónde** está?   *"Where is he?"*
—En el lugar donde trabaja.   *"At the place where he works."*

5. Words that have the same spelling but different meanings take a written accent to differentiate one from the other.

el	*the*	él	*he, him*	te	*you*	té	*tea*
mi	*my*	mí	*me*	si	*if*	sí	*yes*
tu	*your*	tú	*you*	mas	*but*	más	*more*

APPENDIX B VERBS

Regular Verbs

Model -ar, -er, -ir verbs

INFINITIVE		
amar (*to love*)	**comer** (*to eat*)	**vivir** (*to live*)

GERUND		
amando (*loving*)	**comiendo** (*eating*)	**viviendo** (*living*)

PAST PARTICIPLE		
amado (*loved*)	**comido** (*eaten*)	**vivido** (*lived*)

SIMPLE TENSES
Indicative Mood

PRESENT		
(*I love*)	(*I eat*)	(*I live*)
am**o**	com**o**	viv**o**
am**as**	com**es**	viv**es**
am**a**	com**e**	viv**e**
am**amos**	com**emos**	viv**imos**
am**áis**[1]	com**éis**	viv**ís**
am**an**	com**en**	viv**en**

IMPERFECT		
(*I used to love*)	(*I used to eat*)	(*I used to live*)
am**aba**	com**ía**	viv**ía**
am**abas**	com**ías**	viv**ías**
am**aba**	com**ía**	viv**ía**
am**ábamos**	com**íamos**	viv**íamos**
am**abais**	com**íais**	viv**íais**
am**aban**	com**ían**	viv**ían**

---

[1] Vosotros **amáis:** The **vosotros** form of the verb is used primarily in Spain. This form has not been used in this text.

PRETERIT

(I love)	*(I ate)*	*(I lived)*
amé	comí	viví
amaste	comiste	viviste
amó	comió	vivió
amamos	comimos	vivimos
amasteis	comisteis	vivisteis
amaron	comieron	vivieron

FUTURE

(I will love)	*(I will eat)*	*(I will live)*
amaré	comeré	viviré
amarás	comerás	vivirás
amará	comerá	vivirá
amaremos	comeremos	viviremos
amaréis	comeréis	viviréis
amarán	comerán	vivirán

CONDITIONAL

(I would love)	*(I would eat)*	*(I would live)*
amaría	comería	viviría
amarías	comerías	vivirías
amaría	comería	viviría
amaríamos	comeríamos	viviríamos
amaríais	comeríais	viviríais
amarían	comerían	vivirían

Subjunctive Mood

PRESENT

([that] I [may] love)	*([that] I [may] eat)*	*([that] I [may] live)*
ame	coma	viva
ames	comas	vivas
ame	coma	viva
amemos	comamos	vivamos
améis	comáis	viváis
amen	coman	vivan

IMPERFECT (two forms: -ra, -se)

([that] I [might] love)	([that] I [might] eat)	([that] I [might] live)
amara(-ase)	comiera(-iese)	viviera(-iese)
amaras(-ases)	comieras(-ieses)	vivieras(-ieses)
amara(-ase)	comiera(-iese)	viviera(-iese)
amáramos	comiéramos	viviéramos
(-ásemos)	(-iésemos)	(-iésemos)
amarais(-aseis)	comierais(-ieseis)	vivierais(-ieseis)
amaran(-asen)	comieran(-iesen)	vivieran(-iesen)

Imperative Mood (Command Forms)

(love)	(eat)	(live)
ama (tú)	come (tú)	vive (tú)
ame (Ud.)	coma (Ud.)	viva (Ud.)
amemos (nosotros)	comamos (nosotros)	vivamos (nosotros)
amad (vosotros)	comed (vosotros)	vivid (vosotros)
amen (Uds.)	coman (Uds.)	vivan (Uds.)

COMPOUND TENSES

PERFECT INFINITIVE

haber amado	haber comido	haber vivido

PERFECT PARTICIPLE

habiendo amado	habiendo comido	habiendo vivido

Indicative Mood

PRESENT PERFECT

(I have loved)	(I have eaten)	(I have lived)
he amado	he comido	he vivido
has amado	has comido	has vivido
ha amado	ha comido	ha vivido
hemos amado	hemos comido	hemos vivido
habéis amado	habéis comido	habéis vivido
han amado	han comido	han vivido

PLUPERFECT

(*I had loved*)	(*I had eaten*)	(*I had lived*)
había amado	había comido	había vivido
habías amado	habías comido	habías vivido
había amado	había comido	había vivido
habíamos amado	habíamos comido	habíamos vivido
habíais amado	habíais comido	habíais vivido
habían amado	habían comido	habían vivido

FUTURE PERFECT

(*I will have loved*)	(*I will have eaten*)	(*I will have lived*)
habré amado	habré comido	habré vivido
habrás amado	habrás comido	habrás vivido
habrá amado	habrá comido	habrá vivido
habremos amado	habremos comido	habremos vivido
habréis amado	habréis comido	habréis vivido
habrán amado	habrán comido	habrán vivido

CONDITIONAL PERFECT

(*I would have loved*)	(*I would have eaten*)	(*I would have lived*)
habría amado	habría comido	habría vivido
habrías amado	habrías comido	habrías vivido
habría amado	habría comido	habría vivido
habríamos amado	habríamos comido	habríamos vivido
habríais amado	habríais comido	habríais vivido
habrían amado	habrían comido	habrían vivido

Subjunctive Mood

PRESENT PERFECT

(*[that] I [may] have loved*)	(*[that] I [may] have eaten*)	(*[that] I [may] have lived*)
haya amado	haya comido	haya vivido
hayas amado	hayas comido	hayas vivido
haya amado	haya comido	haya vivido
hayamos amado	hayamos comido	hayamos vivido
hayáis amado	hayáis comido	hayáis vivido
hayan amado	hayan comido	hayan vivido

PLUPERFECT (two forms: -ra, -se)		
([*that*] *I* [*might*] *have loved*)	([*that*] *I* [*might*] *have eaten*)	([*that*] *I* [*might*] *have lived*)
hubiera(-iese) amado	hubiera(-iese) comido	hubiera(-iese) vivido
hubieras(-ieses) amado	hubieras(-ieses) comido	hubieras(-ieses) vivido
hubiera(-iese) amado	hubiera(-iese) comido	hubiera(-iese) vivido
hubiéramos(-iésemos) amado	hubiéramos(-iésemos) comido	hubiéramos(-iésemos) vivido
hubierais(-ieseis) amado	hubicrais(-ieseis) comido	hubierais(-ieseis) vivido
hubieran(-iesen) amado	hubieran(-iesen) comido	hubieran(-iesen) vivido

Stem-Changing Verbs

The -ar and -er stem-changing verbs

Stem-changing verbs are those that have a change in the root of the verb. Verbs that end in -ar and -er change the stressed vowel **e** to **ie**, and the stressed **o** to **ue**. These changes occur in all persons, except the first and second persons plural of the present indicative, present subjunctive, and command.

INFINITIVE	PRESENT INDICATIVE	IMPERATIVE	PRESENT SUBJUNCTIVE
cerrar	cierro	—	cierre
(*to close*)	cierras	cierra	cierres
	cierra	(Ud.) cierre	cierre
	cerramos	cerremos	cerremos
	cerráis	cerrad	cerréis
	cierran	(Uds.) cierren	cierren

INFINITIVE	PRESENT INDICATIVE	IMPERATIVE	PRESENT SUBJUNCTIVE
perder (*to lose*)	pierdo	—	pierda
	pierdes	pierde	pierdas
	pierde	(Ud.) pierda	pierda
	perdemos	perdamos	perdamos
	perdéis	perded	perdáis
	pierden	(Uds.) pierdan	pierdan
contar (*to count, to tell*)	cuento	—	cuente
	cuentas	cuenta	cuentes
	cuenta	(Ud.) cuente	cuente
	contamos	contemos	contemos
	contáis	contad	contéis
	cuentan	(Uds.) cuenten	cuenten
volver (*to return*)	vuelvo	—	vuelva
	vuelves	vuelve	vuelvas
	vuelve	(Ud.) vuelva	vuelva
	volvemos	volvamos	volvamos
	volvéis	volved	volváis
	vuelven	(Uds.) vuelvan	vuelvan

Verbs that follow the same pattern include the following.

acertar   *to guess right*
acordarse   *to remember*
acostar(se)   *to go to bed*
almorzar   *to have lunch*
atravesar   *to go through*
cegar   *to blind*
cocer   *to cook*
colgar   *to hang*
comenzar   *to begin*
confesar   *to confess*
costar   *to cost*
demostrar   *to demonstrate, to show*
despertar(se)   *to wake up*
empezar   *to begin*
encender   *to light, to turn on*
encontrar   *to find*

entender   *to understand*
llover   *to rain*
mostrar   *to show*
mover   *to move*
negar   *to deny*
nevar   *to snow*
pensar   *to think, to plan*
probar   *to prove, to taste*
recordar   *to remember*
resolver   *to decide on*
rogar   *to beg*
sentar(se)   *to sit down*
soler   *to be in the habit of*
soñar   *to dream*
tender   *to stretch, to unfold*
torcer   *to twist*

The -ir *stem-changing verbs*

There are two types of stem-changing verbs that end in **-ir:** one type changes stressed **e** to **ie** in some tenses and to **i** in others, and stressed **o** to **ue** or **u;** the second type always changes stressed **e** to **i** in the irregular forms of the verb.

Type 1	**e:ie**	or	**i**
	-ir:		
	o:ue	or	**u**

These changes occur as follows.

Present Indicative: all persons except the first and second plural change **e** to **ie** and **o** to **ue.** *Preterit:* third person, singular and plural, changes **e** to **i** and **o** to **u.** *Present Subjunctive:* all persons change **e** to **ie** and **o** to **ue,** except the first and second persons plural, which change **e** to **i** and **o** to **u.** *Imperfect Subjunctive:* all persons change **e** to **i** and **o** to **u.** *Imperative:* all persons except the second person plural change **e** to **ie** and **o** to **ue;** first person plural changes **e** to **i** and **o** to **u.** *Present Participle:* changes **e** to **i** and **o** to **u.**

	Indicative		*Imperative*	*Subjunctive*	
INFINITIVE	PRESENT	PRETERIT		PRESENT	IMPERFECT
sentir	siento	sentí	—	sienta	sintiera(iese)
(*to feel*)	sientes	sentiste	siente	sientas	sintieras
	siente	sintió	(Ud.) sienta	sienta	sintiera
PRESENT	sentimos	sentimos	sintamos	sintamos	sintiéramos
PARTICIPLE	sentís	sentisteis	sentid	sintáis	sintierais
sintiendo	sienten	sintieron	(Uds.) sientan	sientan	sintieran
dormir	duermo	dormí	—	duerma	durmiera(-iese)
(*to sleep*)	duermes	dormiste	duerme	duermas	durmieras
	duerme	durmió	(Ud.) duerma	duerma	durmiera
PRESENT	dormimos	dormimos	durmamos	durmamos	durmiéramos
PARTICIPLE	dormís	dormisteis	dormid	durmáis	durmierais
durmiendo	duermen	durmieron	(Uds.) duerman	duerman	durmieran

Other verbs that follow the same pattern include the following.

advertir	*to warn*	**herir**	*to wound, to hurt*
arrepentir(se)	*to repent*	**mentir**	*to lie*
consentir	*to consent, to pamper*	**morir**	*to die*
convertir(se)	*to turn into*	**preferir**	*to prefer*
discernir	*to discern*	**referir**	*to refer*
divertir(se)	*to amuse oneself*	**sugerir**	*to suggest*

Type II **-ir: e:i**

The verbs in this second category are irregular in the same tenses as those of the first type. The only difference is that they only have one change: **e:i** in all irregular persons.

	Indicative		Imperative		Subjunctive	
INFINITIVE	PRESENT	PRETERIT			PRESENT	IMPERFECT
pedir	pido	pedí	—		pida	pidiera(-iese)
(*to ask for,*	pides	pediste		pide	pidas	pidieras
to request)	pide	pidió	(Ud.)	pida	pida	pidiera
PRESENT	pedimos	pedimos		pidamos	pidamos	pidiéramos
PARTICIPLE	pedís	pedisteis		pedid	pidáis	pidierais
pidiendo	piden	pidieron	(Uds.)	pidan	pidan	pidieran

Verbs that follow this pattern include the following.

competir	*to compete*	**reír(se)**	*to laugh*
concebir	*to conceive*	**reñir**	*to fight*
despedir(se)	*to say good-bye*	**repetir**	*to repeat*
elegir	*to choose*	**seguir**	*to follow*
impedir	*to prevent*	**servir**	*to serve*
perseguir	*to pursue*	**vestir(se)**	*to dress*

Orthographic-Changing Verbs

Some verbs undergo a change in the spelling of the stem in certain tenses, in order to maintain the original sound of the final consonant. The most common verbs of this type are those with the consonants **g** and **c**.

Remember that **g** and **c** have a soft sound in front of **e** or **i** and a hard sound in front of **a, o,** or **u.** In order to maintain the soft sound in front of **a, o,** and **u, g** and **c** change to **j** and **z,** respectively. And in order to maintain the hard sound of **g** and **c** in front of **e** and **i, u** is added to the **g (gu)** and **c** changes to **qu.**

The following important verbs undergo spelling changes in the tenses listed below.

1. Verbs ending in **-gar** change **g** to **gu** before **e** in the first person of the preterit and in all persons of the present subjunctive.

   pagar (*to pay*)
   Preterit: pagué, pagaste, pagó, etc.
   Pres. Subj.: pague, pagues, pague, paguemos, paguéis, paguen

   Verbs that follow the same pattern: **colgar, jugar, llegar, navegar, negar, regar, rogar.**

2. Verbs ending in **-ger** and **-gir** change **g** to **j** before **o** and **a** in the first person of the present indicative and in all persons of the present subjunctive.

   proteger (*to protect*)
   Pres. Ind.: protejo, proteges, protege, etc.
   Pres. Subj.: proteja, protejas, proteja, protejamos, protejáis, protejan

   Verbs that follow the same pattern: **coger, corregir, dirigir, elegir, escoger, exigir, recoger.**

3. Verbs ending in **-guar** change **gu** to **gü** before **e** in the first person of the preterit and in all persons of the present subjunctive.

   averiguar (*to find out*)
   Preterit: averigüé, averiguaste, averiguó, etc.
   Pres. Subj.: averigüe, averigües, averigüe, averigüemos, averigüéis, averigüen

   The verb **apaciguar** follows the same pattern.

4. Verbs ending in **-guir** change **gu** to **g** before **o** and **a** in the first person of the present indicative and in all persons of the present subjunctive.

conseguir (*to get*)
Pres. Ind.:   consigo, consigues, consigue, etc.
Pres. Subj.:   consiga, consigas, consiga, consigamos, consigáis,
        consigan

Verbs that follow the same pattern: **distinguir, perseguir, proseguir, seguir.**

5. Verbs ending in **-car** change **c** to **qu** before **e** in the first person of the preterit and in all persons of the present subjunctive.

tocar (*to touch, to play* [*a musical instrument*])
Preterit: toqué, tocaste, tocó, etc.
Pres. Subj.:   toque, toques, toque, toquemos, toquéis, toquen

Verbs that follow the same pattern: **atacar, buscar, comunicar, explicar, indicar, pescar, sacar.**

6. Verbs ending in **-cer** and **-cir** preceded by a consonant change **c** to **z** before **o** and **a** in the first person of the present indicative and in all persons of the present subjunctive.

torcer (*to twist*)
Pres. Ind.:   tuerzo, tuerces, tuerce, etc.
Pres. Subj.:   tuerza, tuerzas, tuerza, torzamos, torzáis, tuerzan

Verbs that follow the same pattern: **convencer, esparcir, vencer.**

7. Verbs ending in **-cer** and **-cir** preceded by a vowel change **c** to **zc** before **o** and **a** in the first person of the present indicative and in all persons of the present subjunctive.

conocer (*to know, to be acquainted with*)
Pres. Ind.:   conozco, conoces, conoce, etc.
Pres. Subj.:   conozca, conozcas, conozca, conozcamos, conozcáis,
        conozcan

Verbs that follow the same pattern: **agradecer, aparecer, carecer, entristecer, establecer, lucir, nacer, obedecer, ofrecer, padecer, parecer, pertenecer, reconocer, relucir.**

8. Verbs ending in **-zar** change **z** to **c** before **e** in the first person of the preterit and in all persons of the present subjunctive.

rezar (*to pray*)
Preterit: recé, rezaste, rezó, etc.
Pres. Subj.: rece, reces, rece, recemos, recéis, recen

Verbs that follow the same pattern: **abrazar, alcanzar, almorzar, comenzar, cruzar, empezar, forzar, gozar.**

9. Verbs ending in **-eer** change the unstressed **i** to **y** between vowels in the third person singular and plural of the preterit, in all persons of the imperfect subjunctive, and in the present participle.

creer (*to believe*)
Preterit: creí, creíste, creyó, creímos, creísteis, creyeron
Imp. Subj.: creyera(ese), creyeras, creyera, creyéramos, creyerais, creyeran
Pres. Part.: creyendo

Leer and **poseer** follow the same pattern.

10. Verbs ending in **-uir** change the unstressed **i** to **y** between vowels (except **-quir,** which has the silent **u**) in the following tenses and persons.

huir (*to escape, to flee*)
Pres. Part.: huyendo
Past Part.: huido
Pres. Ind.: huyo, huyes, huye, huimos, huís, huyen
Preterit: huí, huiste, huyó, huimos, huisteis, huyeron
Imperative: huye, huya, huyamos, huid, huyan
Pres. Subj.: huya, huyas, huya, huyamos, huyáis, huyan
Imp. Subj.: huyera(ese), huyeras, huyera, huyéramos, huyerais, huyeran

Verbs that follow the same pattern: **atribuir, concluir, constituir, construir, contribuir, destituir, destruir, disminuir, distribuir, excluir, incluir, influir, instruir, restituir, sustituir.**

11. Verbs ending in **-eír** lose one **e** in the third person singular and plural of the preterit, in all persons of the imperfect subjunctive, and in the present participle.

reír(se) (*to laugh*)
Preterit: reí, reíste, rió, reímos, reísteis, rieron
Imp. Subj.: riera(ese), rieras, riera, riéramos, rierais, rieran
Pres. Part.: riendo

Freír and **sonreír** follow the same pattern.

12. Verbs ending in **-iar** add a written accent to the **i,** except in the first and second persons plural of the present indicative and subjunctive.

fiar(se) (*to trust*)
Pres. Ind.:   fío, fías, fía, fiamos, fiáis, fían
Pres. Subj.: fíe, fíes, fíe, fiemos, fiéis, fíen

Verbs that follow the same pattern: **ampliar, criar, desviar, enfriar, enviar, esquiar, guiar, telegrafiar, vaciar, variar.**

13. Verbs ending in **-uar** (except **-guar**) add a written accent to the **u,** except in the first and second persons plural of the present indicative and subjunctive.

actuar (*to act*)
Pres. Ind.:   actúo, actúas, actúa, actuamos, actuáis, actúan
Pres. Subj.: actúe, actúes, actúe, actuemos, actuéis, actúen

Verbs that follow the same pattern: **acentuar, continuar, efectuar, exceptuar, graduar, habituar, insinuar, situar.**

14. Verbs ending in **-ñir** remove the **i** of the diphthongs **ie** and **ió** in the third person singular and plural of the preterit and in all persons of the imperfect subjunctive. They also change the **e** of the stem to **i** in the same persons.

teñir (*to dye*)
Preterit: teñí, teñiste, **tiñó**, teñimos, teñisteis, **tiñeron**
Imp. Subj.: **tiñera(ese), tiñeras, tiñera, tiñéramos, tiñerais, tiñeran**

Verbs that follow the same pattern: **ceñir, constreñir, desteñir, estreñir, reñir.**

Some Common Irregular Verbs

Only those tenses with irregular forms are given below.

adquirir (*to acquire*)

Pres. Ind.:	adquiero, adquieres, adquiere, adquirimos, adquirís, adquieren
Pres. Subj.:	adquiera, adquieras, adquiera, adquiramos, adquiráis, adquieran
Imperative:	adquiere, adquiera, adquiramos, adquirid, adquieran

andar (*to walk*)

Preterit:	anduve, anduviste, anduvo, anduvimos, anduvisteis, anduvieron
Imp. Subj.:	anduviera (anduviese), anduvieras, anduviera, anduviéramos, anduvierais, anduvieran

avergonzarse (*to be ashamed, to be embarrassed*)

Pres. Ind.:	me avergüenzo, te avergüenzas, se avergüenza, nos avergonzamos, os avergonzáis, se avergüenzan
Pres. Subj.:	me avergüence, te avergüences, se avergüence, nos avergoncemos, os avergoncéis, se avergüencen
Imperative:	avergüénzate, avergüéncese, avergoncémonos, avergonzaos, avergüéncense

caber (*to fit, to have enough room*)

Pres. Ind.:	quepo, cabes, cabe, cabemos, cabéis, caben
Preterit:	cupe, cupiste, cupo, cupimos, cupisteis, cupieron
Future:	cabré, cabrás, cabrá, cabremos, cabréis, cabrán
Conditional:	cabría, cabrías, cabría, cabríamos, cabríais, cabrían
Imperative:	cabe, quepa, quepamos, cabed, quepan
Pres. Subj.:	quepa, quepas, quepa, quepamos, quepáis, quepan
Imp. Subj.:	cupiera (cupiese), cupieras, cupiera, cupiéramos, cupierais, cupieran

caer (*to fall*)

Pres. Ind.:	caigo, caes, cae, caemos, caéis, caen
Preterit:	caí, caíste, cayó, caímos, caísteis, cayeron
Imperative:	cae, caiga, caigamos, caed, caigan
Pres. Subj.:	caiga, caigas, caiga, caigamos, caigáis, caigan
Imp. Subj.:	cayera (cayese), cayeras, cayera, cayéramos, cayerais, cayeran
Past Part.:	caído

conducir (*to guide, to drive*)

Pres. Ind.:	conduzco, conduces, conduce, conducimos, conducís, conducen
Preterit:	conduje, condujiste, condujo, condujimos, condujisteis, condujeron
Imperative:	conduce, conduzca, conduzcamos, conducid, conduzcan
Pres. Subj.:	conduzca, conduzcas, conduzca, conduzcamos, conduzcáis, conduzcan
Imp. Subj.:	condujera (condujese), condujeras, condujera, condujéramos, condujerais, condujeran

(All verbs ending in **-ducir** follow this pattern.)

convenir (*to agree*) See **venir.**

dar (*to give*)

Pres. Ind.:	doy, das, da, damos, dais, dan
Preterit:	di, diste, dio, dimos, disteis, dieron
Imperative:	da, dé, demos, dad, den
Pres. Subj.:	dé, des, dé, demos, deis, den
Imp. Subj.:	diera (diese), dieras, diera, diéramos, dierais, dieran

decir (*to say, to tell*)

Pres. Ind.:	digo, dices, dice, decimos, decís, dicen
Preterit:	dije, dijiste, dijo, dijimos, dijisteis, dijeron
Future:	diré, dirás, dirá, diremos, diréis, dirán
Conditional:	diría, dirías, diría, diríamos, diríais, dirían
Imperative:	di, diga, digamos, decid, digan
Pres. Subj.:	diga, digas, diga, digamos, digáis, digan
Imp. Subj.:	dijera (dijese), dijeras, dijera, dijéramos, dijerais, dijeran
Pres. Part.:	diciendo
Past Part.:	dicho

detener (*to stop, to hold, to arrest*) See **tener.**

entretener (*to entertain, to amuse*) See **tener.**

errar (*to err, to miss*)

Pres. Ind.:	yerro, yerras, yerra, erramos, erráis, yerran
Imperative:	yerra, yerre, erremos, errad, yerren
Pres. Subj.:	yerre, yerres, yerre, erremos, erréis, yerren

estar (*to be*)

Pres. Ind.:	estoy, estás, está, estamos, estáis, están
Preterit:	estuve, estuviste, estuvo, estuvimos, estuvisteis, estuvieron

Imperative:	está, esté, estemos, estad, estén
Pres. Subj.:	esté, estés, esté, estemos, estéis, estén
Imp. Subj.:	estuviera (estuviese), estuvieras, estuviera, estuviéramos, estuvierais, estuvieran

haber (*to have*)

Pres. Ind.:	he, has, ha, hemos, habéis, han
Preterit:	hube, hubiste, hubo, hubimos, hubisteis, hubieron
Future:	habré, habrás, habrá, habremos, habréis, habrán
Conditional:	habría, habrías, habría, habríamos, habríais, habrían
Imperative:	he, haya, hayamos, habed, hayan
Pres. Subj.:	haya, hayas, haya, hayamos, hayáis, hayan
Imp. Subj.:	hubiera (hubiese), hubieras, hubiera, hubiéramos, hubierais, hubieran

hacer (*to do, to make*)

Pres. Ind.:	hago, haces, hace, hacemos, hacéis, hacen
Preterit:	hice, hiciste, hizo, hicimos, hicisteis, hicieron
Future:	haré, harás, hará, haremos, haréis, harán
Conditional:	haría, harías, haría, haríamos, haríais, harían
Imperative:	haz, haga, hagamos, haced, hagan
Pres. Subj.:	haga, hagas, haga, hagamos, hagáis, hagan
Imp. Subj.:	hiciera (hiciese), hicieras, hiciera, hiciéramos, hicierais, hicieran
Past Part.:	hecho

imponer (*to impose, to deposit*) See **poner.**

introducir (*to introduce, to insert, to gain access*) See **conducir.**

ir (*to go*)

Pres. Ind.:	voy, vas, va, vamos, vais, van
Imp. Ind.:	iba, ibas, iba, íbamos, ibais, iban
Preterit:	fui, fuiste, fue, fuimos, fuisteis, fueron
Imperative:	ve, vaya, vayamos, id, vayan
Pres. Subj.:	vaya, vayas, vaya, vayamos, vayáis, vayan
Imp. Subj.:	fuera (fuese), fueras, fuera, fuéramos, fuerais, fueran

jugar (*to play*)

Pres. Ind.:	juego, juegas, juega, jugamos, jugáis, juegan
Imperative:	juega, juegue, juguemos, jugad, jueguen
Pres. Subj.:	juegue, juegues, juegue, juguemos, juguéis, jueguen

obtener (*to obtain*) See **tener.**

oír (*to hear*)

Pres. Ind.:	oigo, oyes, oye, oímos, oís, oyen
Preterit:	oí, oíste, oyó, oímos, oísteis, oyeron
Imperative:	oye, oiga, oigamos, oíd, oigan
Pres. Subj.:	oiga, oigas, oiga, oigamos, oigáis, oigan
Imp. Subj.:	oyera (oyese), oyeras, oyera, oyéramos, oyerais, oyeran
Pres. Part.:	oyendo
Past Part.:	oído

oler (*to smell*)

Pres. Ind.:	huelo, hueles, huele, olemos, oléis, huelen
Imperative:	huele, huela, olamos, oled, huelan
Pres. Subj.:	huela, huelas, huela, olamos, oláis, huelan

poder (*to be able*)

Pres. Ind.:	puedo, puedes, puede, podemos, podéis, pueden
Preterit:	pude, pudiste, pudo, pudimos, pudisteis, pudieron
Future:	podré, podrás, podrá, podremos, podréis, podrán
Conditional:	podría, podrías, podría, podríamos, podríais, podrían
Imperative:	puede, pueda, podamos, poded, puedan
Pres. Subj.:	pueda, puedas, pueda, podamos, podáis, puedan
Imp. Subj.:	pudiera (pudiese), pudieras, pudiera, pudiéramos, pudierais, pudieran
Pres. Part.:	pudiendo

poner (*to place, to put*)

Pres. Ind.:	pongo, pones, pone, ponemos, ponéis, ponen
Preterit:	puse, pusiste, puso, pusimos, pusisteis, pusieron
Future:	pondré, pondrás, pondrá, pondremos, pondréis, pondrán
Conditional:	pondría, pondrías, pondría, pondríamos, pondríais, pondrían
Imperative:	pon, ponga, pongamos, poned, pongan
Pres. Subj.:	ponga, pongas, ponga, pongamos, pongáis, pongan
Imp. Subj.:	pusiera (pusiese), pusieras, pusiera, pusiéramos, pusierais, pusieran
Past Part.:	puesto

querer (*to want, to wish, to like*)

Pres. Ind.:	quiero, quieres, quiere, queremos, queréis, quieren
Preterit:	quise, quisiste, quiso, quisimos, quisisteis, quisieron
Future:	querré, querrás, querrá, querremos, querréis, querrán
Conditional:	querría, querrías, querría, querríamos, querríais, querrían

Imperative: quiere, quiera, queramos, quered, quieran
Pres. Subj.:   quiera, quieras, quiera, queramos, queráis, quieran
Imp. Subj.:   quisiera (quisiese), quisieras, quisiera, quisiéramos,
                 quisierais, quisieran

resolver (*to decide on*)
Past Part.:   resuelto

saber (*to know*)
Pres. Ind.:   sé, sabes, sabe, sabemos, sabéis, saben
Preterit: supe, supiste, supo, supimos, supisteis, supieron
Future: sabré, sabrás, sabrá, sabremos, sabréis, sabrán
Conditional: sabría, sabrías, sabría, sabríamos, sabríais, sabrían
Imperative: sabe, sepa, sepamos, sabed, sepan
Pres. Subj.:   sepa, sepas, sepa, sepamos, sepáis, sepan
Imp. Subj.:   supiera (supiese), supieras, supiera, supiéramos,
                 supierais, supieran

salir (*to leave, to go out*)
Pres. Ind.:   salgo, sales, sale, salimos, salís, salen
Future: saldré, saldrás, saldrá, saldremos, saldréis, saldrán
Conditional: saldría, saldrías, saldría, saldríamos, saldríais, saldrían
Imperative: sal, salga, salgamos, salid, salgan
Pres. Subj.:   salga, salgas, salga, salgamos, salgáis, salgan

ser (*to be*)
Pres. Ind.:   soy, eres, es, somos, sois, son
Imp. Ind.:   era, eras, era, éramos, erais, eran
Preterit: fui, fuiste, fue, fuimos, fuisteis, fueron
Imperative: sé, sea, seamos, sed, sean
Pres. Subj.:   sea, seas, sea, seamos, seáis, sean
Imp. Subj.:   fuera (fuese), fueras, fuera, fuéramos, fuerais, fueran

suponer (*to assume*) See **poner.**

tener (*to have*)
Pres. Ind.:   tengo, tienes, tiene, tenemos, tenéis, tienen
Preterit: tuve, tuviste, tuvo, tuvimos, tuvisteis, tuvieron
Future: tendré, tendrás, tendrá, tendremos, tendréis, tendrán
Conditional: tendría, tendrías, tendría, tendríamos, tendríais,
                 tendrían
Imperative: ten, tenga, tengamos, tened, tengan
Pres. Subj.:   tenga, tengas, tenga, tengamos, tengáis, tengan
Imp. Subj.:   tuviera (tuviese), tuvieras, tuviera, tuviéramos,
                 tuvierais, tuvieran

traducir (*to translate*) See **conducir.**

traer (*to bring*)

Pres. Ind.:	traigo, traes, trae, traemos, traéis, traen
Preterit:	traje, trajiste, trajo, trajimos, trajisteis, trajeron
Imperative:	trae, traiga, traigamos, traed, traigan
Pres. Subj.:	traiga, traigas, traiga, traigamos, traigáis, traigan
Imp. Subj.:	trajera (trajese), trajeras, trajera, trajéramos, trajerais, trajeran
Pres. Part.:	trayendo
Past Part.:	traído

valer (*to be worth*)

Pres. Ind.:	valgo, vales, vale, valemos, valéis, valen
Future:	valdré, valdrás, valdrá, valdremos, valdréis, valdrán
Conditional:	valdría, valdrías, valdría, valdríamos, valdríais, valdrían
Imperative:	vale, valga, valgamos, valed, valgan
Pres. Subj.:	valga, valgas, valga, valgamos, valgáis, valgan

venir (*to come*)

Pres. Ind.:	vengo, vienes, viene, venimos, venís, vienen
Preterit:	vine, viniste, vino, vinimos, vinisteis, vinieron
Future:	vendré, vendrás, vendrá, vendremos, vendréis, vendrán
Conditional:	vendría, vendrías, vendría, vendríamos, vendríais, vendrían
Imperative:	ven, venga, vengamos, venid, vengan
Pres. Subj.:	venga, vengas, venga, vengamos, vengáis, vengan
Imp. Subj.:	viniera (viniese), vinieras, viniera, viniéramos, vinierais, vinieran
Pres. Part.:	viniendo

ver (*to see*)

Pres. Ind.:	veo, ves, ve, vemos, veis, ven
Imp. Ind.:	veía, veías, veía, veíamos, veíais, veían
Preterit:	vi, viste, vio, vimos, visteis, vieron
Imperative:	ve, vea, veamos, ved, vean
Pres. Subj.:	vea, veas, vea, veamos, veáis, vean
Imp. Subj.:	viera (viese), vieras, viera, viéramos, vierais, vieran
Past. Part.:	visto

volver (*to return*)

Past Part.:	vuelto

Spanish–English Vocabulary

The number following each vocabulary item indicates the lesson in which it first appears. The following abbreviations are used.

adj.	adjective	*Méx.*	México
f.	feminine noun	*pl.*	plural
fam.	familiar	*pron.*	pronoun
form.	formal	*sing.*	singular
m.	masculine noun		

A

a to, 3; at, 1; in, 15
— **casa** home, 6
— **la derecha** to the right, 9
— **la izquierda** to the left, 9
— **menos que** unless, 19
— **menudo** often, 2
¿— **qué hora...?** at what time?, 1
¿— **quién?** to whom?, 2
abierto(a) open, 14
abogado(a) (*m., f.*) lawyer, 19
abrigo (*m.*) coat, 10
abril April, PI
abrir to open, 2
abuela (*f.*) grandmother, 3
abuelo (*m.*) grandfather, 3
aburrido(a) boring, bored, 11
accidente (*m.*) accident, 11
aceite (*m.*) oil, 14
aconsejar to advise, 16
acordarse (o:ue) (de) to remember, 9
acostar (o:ue) to put to bed, 9
acostarse to go to bed, to lie down, 9
acumulador (*m.*) battery, 14
adiós good-bye, PI
¿**adónde?** where to?, 3
aeropuerto (*m.*) airport, 12
afeitarse to shave (oneself), 9
agencia (*f.*) agency
— **de alquiler de automóviles** (*f.*) car rental agency, 15
— **de viajes** (*f.*) travel agency, 7
agente de viajes (*m., f.*) travel agent, 7
agosto August, PI
ahora now, 3
— **mismo** right now, 9

aire acondicionado (*m.*) air conditioning, 4
alberca (*f.*) swimming pool (*Méx.*), 4
alcohólico(a) alcoholic, 6
alegrarse (de) to be glad, 17
alemán (alemana) German, 1
algo something, anything, 6
alguien someone, anyone, 6
algún any, some, 6
alguna vez ever, 6
algunas veces sometimes, 6
alguno(a) any, some, 6
algunos(as) (*pl.*) any, some, 6
almorzar (o:ue) to have lunch, 6
almuerzo (*m.*) lunch, 5
alquilar to rent, 15
alto(a) tall, 3
allá over there, 8
allí there, 6
amarillo(a) yellow, PI
ambulancia (*f.*) ambulance, 17
americano(a) American, 20
amigo(a) (*m., f.*) friend, 2
amistad (*f.*) friendship, PII
amor (*m.*) love
análisis (*m.*) test (analysis), 19
anaranjado(a) orange, PI
anillo (*m.*) ring, 13
— **de compromiso** (*m.*) engagement ring, 13
anoche last night, 10
anteayer the day before yesterday, 12
antes de before, 9
antes de que before, 19
año(s) year(s), PI
apagar to turn off, 11
apellido (*m.*) surname, PI
— **de soltera** (*m.*) maiden name, PI
aprender to learn, 2

apurarse to hurry, 20
aquel(los), aquella(s) (*adj.*) that, those (distant), 8
aquél(los), aquélla(s) (*pron.*) that (one), those (distant), 8
aquello (*neuter pron.*) that, 8
aquí here, 2
árbol (*m.*) tree, 18
aretes (*m. pl.*) earrings, 13
argentino(a) Argentinian, 3
arreglar to fix, 14
arroz (*m.*) rice, 11
— **con pollo** (*m.*) chicken with rice, 11
asado(a) roasted, baked, 2
ascensor (*m.*) elevator, 13
asiento (*m.*) seat, PI
asignatura (*f.*) subject, 18
asistir to attend, 20
aspiradora (*f.*) vacuum cleaner, 10
aspirina (*f.*) aspirin, 8
atender (e:ie) to wait on, to attend to, 9
auto (*m.*) car, automobile, 3
autobús (*m.*) bus, 2
automático(a) automatic, 15
automóvil (*m.*) car, automobile, 3
autopista (*f.*) freeway, 19
avenida (*f.*) avenue, 7
avión (*m.*) airplane, 7
ayer yesterday, 10
ayudante (*m., f.*) assistant, 19
ayudar to help, 10
azul blue, PI

B

bajar to go down, to decrease, 19
banco (*m.*) bank, 6

bañar(se) to bathe (oneself), 9
baño (*m.*) bathroom, 9
barato(a) inexpensive, 4
barco (*m.*) ship, 15
barrer to sweep, 10
básquetbol (*m.*) basketball, 8
basura (*f.*) trash, 11
batería (*f.*) battery, 14
beber to drink, 2
bebida (*f.*) drink, 2
beca (*f.*) scholarship, 18
bello(a) beautiful, 16
biblioteca (*f.*) library, 18
bicicleta (*f.*) bicycle, 8
bien well, fine, PI
    muy —, ¿y usted? very
        well, and you?, PI
    no muy — not very well, PI
bilingüe (*adj.*) bilingual, 18
billete (*m.*) ticket, 7
billetera (*f.*) wallet, 20
blanco(a) white, PI
boleto (*m.*) ticket, 16
bolsa de dormir (*f.*) sleeping
    bag, 8
bonito(a) pretty, 3
bote (*m.*) can (*Méx.*), 10
botella (*f.*) bottle, 2
botiquín (*m.*) medicine
    cabinet, 9
buenas noches good evening
    (good night), PI
buenas tardes good
    afternoon, PI
bueno(a) good, 2; kind, 16
buenos días good morning
    (good day), PI
¡Buen viaje! Bon voyage!, 7
buscar to look for, to pick up,
    to get, 16

C

caballo (*m.*) horse, 8
cabeza (*f.*) head, 8
café brown, PI; (*m.*) coffee, 2
cafetera (*f.*) coffeepot, 11
cafetería (*f.*) cafeteria, 1
cajero(a) (*m., f.*) cashier, 15
    — automático automatic
        teller machine (ATM), 15
calculadora (*f.*) calculator, 17
caliente hot, 2
calle (*f.*) street, PI
cama (*f.*) bed, 6
camarero(a) (*m., f.*) waiter,
    waitress, 2
cambiar to change, 14
    — un cheque to cash a
        check, 15

caminar to walk, 11
camisón (*m.*) nightgown, 13
cancelar to cancel, 7
cansado(a) tired, 3
cárcel (*f.*) jail, 5
carne (*f.*) meat, 7
caro(a) expensive, 4
carro (*m.*) car, automobile, 3
carta (*f.*) letter, 6
cartera (*f.*) purse, 12
casa (*f.*) house, PII
casado(a) married, PI
casi almost, 14
    — nunca hardly ever, 11
catálogo (*m.*) catalogue, 12
catarro (*m.*) cold, 19
catorce fourteen, PI
cena (*f.*) dinner, 5
centro comercial (*m.*) mall, 12
cepillo (*m.*) brush, 9
cerca de near to, 6
cero zero, PI
cerrado(a) closed, 14
cerrar (e:ie) to close, 5
cerveza (*f.*) beer, 1
champán (*m.*) champagne, 1
champú (*m.*) shampoo, 9
chaqueta (*f.*) jacket, 13
cheque (*m.*) check, 6
chequear to check, 15
chequeo (*m.*) checkup, 19
chica (*f.*) girl, young woman, 2
chico (*m.*) boy, young man, 2
chocar to collide, 19
chocolate (*m.*) chocolate, 2
cien, ciento one hundred, PII
cinco five, PI
cincuenta fifty, PII
cine (*m.*) movie theater,
    movies, 5
cirugía (*f.*) surgery, 19
cirujano(a) (*m., f.*) surgeon, 19
ciudad (*f.*) city, PI
claro(a) clear, 17
clase (*f.*) class, 4
clima (*m.*) climate, PII
club (*m.*) club, 3
    — automovilístico (*m.*)
        auto club, 14
cobija (*f.*) blanket, 6
cobrar to charge, 15
cocina (*f.*) kitchen, 10
cocinar to cook, 10
cocinero(a) (*m., f.*) cook, 11
coche (*m.*) car, automobile, 3
colchón (*m.*) mattress, 6
collar (*m.*) necklace, 13
comenzar (e:ie) to begin, to
    start, 5
comer to eat, 2
comida (*f.*) meal, food, 1

como since, 20
¿cómo? how?, 3
    ¿— es? what is he (she, it)
        like?, 3
    ¿— está usted? how are
        you?, PI
    ¿— se dice...? how do you
        say...?, 6
    ¿— se escribe...? how do
        you spell...?, PI
comprar to buy, 5
computadora (*f.*) computer, 12
con with, 2
    ¿— quién? with whom?, 2
    — tal que provided that, 19
    — vista al mar with an
        ocean view, 6
concierto (*m.*) concert, 5
conducir to drive, 7
conferencia (*f.*) lecture, 18
confirmar to confirm, 7
conocer to know, to be familiar
    with, 7; to meet (for the first
    time), 13
conseguir (e:i) to obtain, to
    get, 7
consejero(a) (*m., f.*) adviser, 18
consulado (*m.*) consulate, 20
consultorio (*m.*) doctor's
    office, 17
contabilidad (*f.*) accounting, 18
contador(a) (*m., f.*)
    accountant, 18
contrato (*m.*) contract, 17
conversación (*f.*) conversation,
    PII
conviene it is advisable, 17
corbata (*f.*) tie, 13
correo (*m.*) post office, 20
cortar(se) to cut (oneself), 9
cortina (*f.*) curtain, 20
corto(a) short, 9
cosa (*f.*) thing, 11
costar (o:ue) to cost, 6
crédito (*m.*) credit, 20
creer to think, to believe, 4
criado(a) (*m., f.*) servant, 10
¿cuál(es)? what?, which
    (one)?, 3
cuando when, 19
¿cuándo? when?, 5
¿cuánto(a)? how much?, 5
    — antes as soon as
        possible, 16
    ¿— tiempo? how long?, 11
    ¿— tiempo hace que...?
        how long ago...?, 13
¿cuántos(as)? how many?, 1
cuarenta forty, PII
cuarto (*m.*) room, 4
cuarto(a) (*adj.*) fourth, 5

cuatro four, PI
cubrir to cover, 14
cuchara (*f.*) spoon, 1
cuenta (*f.*) bill, check, 1; account, 15
cuidadoso(a) careful, 17
cuidar to take care, 17
cuñada (*f.*) sister-in-law, 3
cuñado (*m.*) brother-in-law, 3

D

dar to give, 3
darse prisa to hurry, 20
de of, from, PII
  — **cambios mecánicos** a car with a standard shift, 15
  ¿— **dónde es...?** where is... from?, PII
  — **memoria** by heart, 7
  — **nada** you're welcome, PI
  ¿— **quién?** whose?, 2
  — **vez en cuando** once in a while, 12
debajo (de) underneath, 11
deber (+ *inf.*) must, to have to, should, 2
decidir to decide, 2
décimo(a) tenth, 5
decir (e:i) to say, 5; to tell, 6
decisión (*f.*) decision, PII
dentista (*m., f.*) dentist, 17
depositar to deposit, 15
desayunar to have breakfast, 5
desayuno (*m.*) breakfast, 5
descuento (*m.*) discount, 16
desear to want, to wish, 1
despedirse (e:i) to say good-bye, 11
despertarse (e:ie) to wake up, 9
después later, 6; afterwards, 12
devolver (o:ue) to return (something), to give back, 20
día (*m.*) day, PI
diario (*m.*) newspaper, 6
diciembre December, PI
diecinueve nineteen, PI
dieciocho eighteen, PI
dieciséis sixteen, PI
diecisiete seventeen, PI
diez ten, PI
difícil difficult, 16
diligencia (*f.*) errand, 20
dinero (*m.*) money, PII
dirección (*f.*) address, PI
divertirse (e:ie) to have a good time, 11
divorciado(a) divorced, PI
doblar to turn, 9

doce twelve, PI
doctor(a) (*m., f.*) M.D., doctor, PI
dólar (*m.*) dollar, 3
doler (o:ue) to hurt, to ache, 8
dolor (*m.*) pain, 17
domicilio (*m.*) address, PI
domingo (*m.*) Sunday, PI
¿dónde? where?, PII
dormir (o:ue) to sleep, 5
dormirse (o:ue) to fall asleep, 9
dormitorio (*m.*) bedroom, 9
dos two, PI
doscientos two hundred, PII
dudar to doubt, 18
dueño(a) (*m., f.*) owner, 4

E

echar al correo to mail, 20
edad (*f.*) age, PI
educación (*f.*) education, 5
el the (*m.*), PII
él he, 1; him, 6
elegante elegant, 13
elegir (e:i) to choose, to select, 11
ella she, 1; her, 6
ellas they (*f.*), 1; them (*f.*), 6
ellos they (*m.*), 1; them (*m.*), 6
embajada (*f.*) embassy, 7
emergencia (*f.*) emergency, 17
empezar (e:ie) to begin, to start, 5
empleado(a) (*m., f.*) clerk, attendant, 14
en in, at, 1; inside, over, 15
  — **casa** at home, 12
  — **caso de que** in case, 19
  — **cuanto** as soon as, 19
  — **esa época** in those days, 12
  — **este momento** at this moment, 18
  seguida right away, 14
encontrarse (o:ue) (con) to meet (for an appointment), 12
enero January, PI
enfermero(a) (*m., f.*) nurse, PI
enfermo(a) sick, 3
ensalada (*f.*) salad, 7
enseñar to teach, 11
entender (e:ie) to understand, 5
entonces then, in that case, 7
entrada (*f.*) ticket (for an event), 8
entrar to enter, to come in, 10
entrenador(a) (*m., f.*) trainer, coach, 8
entrevista (*f.*) interview, 20
enviar to send, 8
enyesar to put a cast on, 18

escalera (*f.*) stairs, 13
  — **mecánica** (*f.*) escalator, 13
escaparate (*m.*) store window, 12
escoba (*f.*) broom, 10
escribir to write, 2
  — **a computadora** to type, 12
escuela (*f.*) school, 5
ese(os), esa(as) (*adj.*) that, those (nearby), 8
ése(os), ésa(as) (*pron.*) that (one), those (nearby), 8
eso (*neuter pron.*) that, 8
espaguetis (*m. pl.*) spaghetti, 10
España Spain, 7
español (*m.*) Spanish (language), PII
español(a) Spanish person, 1
especial special, 17
especialización (*f.*) major, 18
espejo (*m.*) mirror, 9
esperar to wait (for), 3; to hope, 16
esposa (*f.*) wife, 4
esposo (*m.*) husband, 4
esquiar to ski, 8
esquíes (*m. pl.*) skis, 8
esquís (*m. pl.*) skis, 8
esta noche tonight, 5
está nublado it's cloudy, 10
estación de servicio (*f.*) gas station, 14
estación de trenes (*f.*) train station, 16
estado civil (*m.*) marital status, PI
Estados Unidos (*m. pl.*) United States, 3
estampilla (*f.*) stamp, 6
estar to be, 3
este(a) this, 6
este(os), esta(s) (*adj.*) this, these, 8
éste(os), ésta(s) (*pron.*) this (one), these, 8
esto (*neuter pron.*) this, 8
estudiante (*m., f.*) student, 3
estudiar to study, 1
examen (*m.*) exam, 15
  — **final** (*m.*) final exam, 18
  — **parcial** (*m.*) midterm exam, 18
excursión (*f.*) excursion, 6
expreso (*m.*) express train, 16
extranjero(a) foreign, 7

F

fácil easy, 16
falso(a) false
familia (*f.*) family, 3
farmacia (*f.*) pharmacy, 6

favor (*m.*)   favor, 11
febrero   February, PI
fecha (*f.*)   date, PI
— **de nacimiento** (*f.*)   date of birth, PI
feliz   happy, 1
femenino(a)   feminine, PI
ferretería (*f.*)   hardware store, 13
fiebre (*f.*)   fever, 19
fiesta (*f.*)   party, 2
fin de semana (*m.*)   weekend, 16
firmar   to sign, 17
física (*f.*)   physics, 18
folleto turístico (*m.*)   tourist brochure, 7
fotocopia (*f.*)   photocopy, 20
fracturarse   to break (a bone), 17
francés (*m.*)   French (language), 1
francés (francesa)   French, 1
frazada (*f.*)   blanket, 6
fregadero (*m.*)   sink, 11
freno (*m.*)   brake, 14
frío(a)   cold, 2
frito(a)   fried, 2
funcionar   to work, to function, 13

G

galería de arte (*f.*)   art gallery, 13
gasolina (*f.*)   gasoline, 14
gasolinera (*f.*)   gas station, 14
general   general, 17
generalmente   generally, 9
gente (*f.*)   people
gerente (*m., f.*)   manager, 4
gimnasio (*m.*)   gym, 4
goma (*f.*)   tire, 14
— **pinchada** (*f.*)   flat tire, 14
grabar   to tape, 20
gracias   thank you, PI
graduarse   to graduate, 18
grande   big, large, 1
gripe (*f.*)   flu, 19
gris   gray, PI
grúa (*f.*)   tow truck, 14
guapo(a)   handsome, 1
guía (*m., f.*)   guide, 6
gustar   to like, to be pleasing, 8
gusto   pleasure, PI
el — **es mío**   the pleasure is mine, PI

H

habitación (*f.*)   room, 4
hablar   to speak, to talk, 1
hacer   to do; to make, 5
— **buen (mal) tiempo**   to be good (bad) weather, 10

— **(mucho) calor**   to be (very) hot, 10
— **diligencias**   to do errands, 20
— **ejercicio**   to exercise, 19
— **falta**   to need, to lack, 8
— **(mucho) frío**   to be (very) cold, 10
— **sol**   to be sunny, 10
— **(mucho) viento**   to be (very) windy, 10
hasta   until, 15
— **luego**   I'll see you later, PI
— **mañana**   I'll see you tomorrow, PI
— **que**   until, 19
hay   there is, there are, PII
helado(a)   frozen, iced, 7
hermana (*f.*)   sister, 3
hermano (*m.*)   brother, 3
hermoso(a)   beautiful, 15
hija (*f.*)   daughter, 2
hijo (*m.*)   son, 2
hijos (*m. pl.*)   children (son[s] and daugher[s]), 2
hola   hi, hello, PI
hombre (*m.*)   man, PII
hora (*f.*)   hour, 4
horario (*m.*)   schedule, 16
horrible   horrible, 19
hospital (*m.*)   hospital, 3
hotel (*m.*)   hotel, 3
hoy   today, PI
huevo (*m.*)   egg, 2

I

idea (*f.*)   idea, PII
idioma (*m.*)   language, PII
iglesia (*f.*)   church, 5
impaciente   impatient, 9
impermeable (*m.*)   raincoat, 10
importante   important, 5
imposible   impossible, 14
información (*f.*)   information, 7
informe (*m.*)   report, 20
inglés (*m.*)   English (language), 1
inglés (inglesa)   English, 1
inteligente   intelligent, 1
interesante   interesting, 11
invierno (*m.*)   winter, 10
invitado(a) (*m., f.*)   guest, 11
inyección (*f.*)   shot, injection, 17
ir   to go, 3
— **a esquiar**   to go skiing, 8
— **a pie**   to walk, to go on foot, 11
— **caminando**   to walk, to go on foot, 11

— **de compras**   to go shopping, 11
— **de vacaciones**   to go on vacation, 12
irle bien a uno(a)   to do well, 18
irse   to leave, to go away, 9
italiano (*m.*)   Italian (language), 1
itinerario (*m.*)   schedule, 16

J

jabón (*m.*)   soap, 5
jamás   never, 6
jarabe (*m.*)   syrup, 19
jefe(a) (*m., f.*)   boss, chief, 20
joyería (*f.*)   jewelry store, 12
jueves (*m.*)   Thursday, PI
jugar (u:ue)   to play (a game or sport), 8
julio   July, PI
junio   June, PI
junta (*f.*)   meeting, 11
juntos(as)   together, 12

L

la   the (*f.*), PII; her, it (*f.*), you (*form. f.*), 6
lámpara (*f.*)   lamp, PII
lápiz (*m.*)   pencil, PII
largo(a)   long, 16
las (*f. pl.*)   the, PII; them, you, 7
lástima (*f.*)   shame, pity, 17
lata (*f.*)   can, 10
lavadora (*f.*)   washing machine, 10
lavar(se)   to wash (oneself), 9
lavarse la cabeza   to wash one's hair, 9
le   (to) her, (to) him, (to) you (*form.*), 7
lección (*f.*)   lesson, PII
leche (*f.*)   milk, 2
leer   to read, 2
lengua (*f.*)   language, PII
lento(a)   slow, 16
levantar   to lift, to raise, 9
levantarse   to get up, 9
libertad (*f.*)   liberty, PII
librería (*f.*)   bookstore, 6
libro (*m.*)   book, PII
licuadora (*f.*)   blender, 11
límite (*m.*)   limit, 10
— **de velocidad** (*m.*)   speed limit, 10
limpiar   to clean, 10
limpiaparabrisas (*m.*)   windshield wiper, 14

liquidación (*f.*)   sale, 11
listo(a)   ready, 14
literatura (*f.*)   literature, 18
llamar   to call, 2
llamarse   to be named, 9
llanta (*f.*)   tire, 14
llave (*f.*)   key, 4
llegar   to arrive, 4
llenar   to fill, 14
llevar   to take (something or someone to someplace), 2
llover (o:ue)   to rain, 10
lluvia (*f.*)   rain, 10
lo   him, it (*m.*), you (*form. m.*), 6
    — siento   I'm sorry, PI
los   the (*m. pl.*), PII; them (*m.*), you (*m. pl.*), 6
los (las) dos   both, 10
lugar (*m.*)   place, 13
    — de interés (*m.*)   place of interest, 6
    — de nacimiento (*m.*)   place of birth, PI
    — donde trabaja (*m.*)   place of work, PI
lunes (*m.*)   Monday, PI
luz (*f.*)   light, PII

M

madera (*f.*)   wood, 3
madre (*f.*)   mom, mother, 3
mal   badly, 4
maleta (*f.*)   suitcase, 4
malo(a)   bad, 2
mamá (*f.*)   mom, mother, 3
mandar   to send, 8; to order, 16
manejar   to drive, 7
mano (*f.*)   hand, PII
manta (*f.*)   blanket, 6
mantel (*m.*)   tablecloth, 1
mantener   to maintain, 18
mañana (*f.*)   morning, 1; tomorrow, 3
máquina de afeitar (*f.*)   razor, 9
mar (*m.*)   ocean, 6
marca (*f.*)   brand, 11
mareado(a)   dizzy, 16
marrón   brown, PI
martes (*m.*)   Tuesday, PI
marzo   March, PI
más   more, 4
    — tarde   later, 6
masculino(a)   masculine, PI
materia (*f.*)   subject, 18
matrícula (*f.*)   tuition, 18
matricularse   to register, 18
mayo (*m.*)   May, PI
mayor   older; bigger, 4

me   me, 6; (to) me, 7; (to) myself, 8
    — gusta...   I like..., PI
mecánico(a) (*m., f.*)   mechanic, 14
media hora   half an hour, 11
mediano(a)   medium, 13
medianoche (*f.*)   midnight, 9
médico(a) (*m., f.*)   M.D., doctor, PII
mejor   better, 4
menor   younger; smaller, 4
menos   to, until (with time), 1; less, fewer, 4
mentir (e:ie)   to lie, 11
menú (*m.*)   menu, 2
mercado (*m.*)   market, 4
mes (*m.*)   month, 5
mesa (*f.*)   table, PII
metal (*m.*)   metal, 3
mexicano(a)   Mexican, 1
mi (*adj.*)   my, 3
mí (*pron.*)   me, 6
miércoles (*m.*)   Wednesday, PI
mil   thousand, 1
milla (*f.*)   mile, 10
mío(a) (*adj.*)   my, of mine, 9
mío(a) (*pron.*)   mine, 9
mirar   **to look at, 12**
    — vidrieras   to window shop, 12
mochila (*f.*)   backpack, 8
moda (*f.*)   fashion, 13
momento (*m.*)   moment, 9
montar a caballo   to ride a horse, 8
montar en bicicleta   to ride a bicycle, 8
morado(a)   purple, PI
morir (o:ue)   to die, 11
moto (*f.*)   motorcycle, 15
motocicleta (*f.*)   motorcycle, 15
motor (*m.*)   engine, 15
mozo (*m.*)   waiter, 2
muchacha (*f.*)   girl, young woman, 1
muchacho (*m.*)   boy, young man, 1
muchas gracias   thank you very much, PI
mucho   a lot, very much, 1
    — gusto   it's a pleasure to meet you, PI
mueblería (*f.*)   furniture store, 13
mujer (*f.*)   woman, PII
muleta (*f.*)   crutch, 17
museo (*m.*)   museum, 2
muy   very, 3

N

nacionalidad (*f.*)   nationality, PI
nada   nothing, 6

nadar   to swim, 7
nadie   nobody, no one, 6
Navidad (*f.*)   Christmas, 18
necesario(a)   necessary, 17
necesitar   to need, 1
negar (e:ie)   to deny, 16
negro(a)   black, PI
neumático (*m.*)   tire, 14
nevar (e:ie)   to snow, 10
ni... ni   neither... nor, 6
niebla (*f.*)   fog, 10
nieta (*f.*)   granddaughter, 13
nieto (*m.*)   grandson, 13
ningún   none, not any, 6
ninguno(a)   none, not any, 6
niño(a) (*m., f.*)   child, kid, 8
noche (*f.*)   evening, 1
nombre (*m.*)   name, PI
norteamericano(a)   North American (from the U.S.), PI
nos   us, 6; (to) us, 7; (to) ourselves, 9
nosotros(as)   we, 1; us, 6
nota (*f.*)   grade, 18
novela (*f.*)   novel, 7
noveno(a)   ninth, 5
noventa   ninety, PII
novia (*f.*)   girlfriend, 3
noviembre   November, PI
novio (*m.*)   boyfriend, 3
nublado(a)   cloudy, 10
nuestro(a) (*adj.*)   our, 2
nuestro(s), nuestra(s) (*pron.*)   ours, 9
nueve   nine, PI
nuevo(a)   new, 12
número (*m.*)   number, PI
    — de la licencia para conducir (manejar) (*m.*)   driver's license number, PI
    — de seguro social (*m.*)   social security number, PI
    — de teléfono (*m.*)   phone number, PI
nunca   never, 6

O

o   or, 2
o... o   either... or, 6
ochenta   eighty, PII
ocho   eight, PI
octavo(a)   eighth, 5
octubre   October, PI
oculista (*m., f.*)   eye doctor, 19
ocupación (*f.*)   occupation, PI
ocupado(a)   busy, 16
oficina (*f.*)   office, 5
    — de correos (*f.*)   post office, 6

— **de turismo** (*f.*)   tourist office, 7
ojalá   if only..., I hope, 17
ómnibus (*m.*)   bus, 2
once   eleven, PI
operación (*f.*)   surgery, 19
opuesto(a)   opposite
oro (*m.*)   gold, 13
os   to/for you (fam. pl., m./f.), 7
otoño (*m.*)   fall, 5
otra vez   again, 11
otro(a)   other, another, 4

P

paciencia (*f.*)   patience, 11
paciente (*m., f.*)   patient, 17
padre (*m.*)   dad, father, 3
padres (*m. pl.*)   parents, 3
pagar   to pay (for), 1
página deportiva (*f.*)   sports page, 8
país (*m.*)   country, 7
panadería (*f.*)   bakery, 13
pantalón (*m.*)   pants, 9
pantalones (*m. pl.*)   pants, 9
papa (*f.*)   potato, 2
papá (*m.*)   dad, father, 3
paquete (*m.*)   package, 20
par (*m.*)   pair, 12
para   to, in order to, 5; for, 6; by, 10
— **que**   in order that, 19
¿— **quién?**   for whom?, 8
parabrisas (*m.*)   windshield, 14
paraguas (*m. sing.*)   umbrella, 10
paramédico(a) (*m., f.*)   paramedic, 17
parar   to stop
parientes (*m.*)   relatives, 20
parque (*m.*)   park, 9
partido (*m.*)   game, match, 8
pasado(a)   past, last, 10
pasaje (*m.*)   ticket, 7
pasajero(a) (*m., f.*)   passenger, 19
pasaporte (*m.*)   passport, 7
pasar   to happen, 17
pasar (por)   to go by, 10
pase   come in, PI
pastel (*m.*)   pie, 2
pastilla (*f.*)   pill, 19
patata (*f.*)   potato (*Spain*), 2
patines (*m. pl.*)   skates, 8
pedir (e:i)   to ask, 5; to request, to order, 6
— **prestado**   to borrow, 20
peine (*m.*)   comb, 9
peligroso(a)   dangerous, 15
pelo (*m.*)   hair, 9

pelota (*f.*)   ball, 8
peluquería (*f.*)   beauty salon, beauty parlor, 9
peluquero(a) (*m., f.*)   hairdresser, 9
pensión (*f.*)   boarding house, 4
peor   worse, 4
pequeño(a)   small, little (size), 4
perder (e:ie)   to lose, 5
perderse algo   to miss out, 20
perfume (*m.*)   perfume, 9
periódico (*m.*)   newspaper, 6
pero   but, 1
perro (*m.*)   dog, 15
persona (*f.*)   person, 13
pescado (*m.*)   fish, 2
peso (*m.*)   weight, 19
pie (*m.*)   foot, 8
pierna (*f.*)   leg, 17
pieza de repuesto (*f.*)   spare part, 14
piscina (*f.*)   swimming pool, 4
piso (*m.*)   floor (story), 5; (surface), 11
plata (*f.*)   silver, 15
playa (*f.*)   beach, 6
pluma (*f.*)   pen, PII
poco(a)   little (quantity), 4
poder (o:ue)   to be able, 6
poema (*m.*)   poem, PII
pollo (*m.*)   chicken, 2
poner   to put, to place, 7
— **una inyección**   to give a shot, 18
ponerse   to put on, 9
— **a dieta**   to go on a diet, 19
por   around, along, by, for, through, 10
— **ciento**   percent, 16
— **favor**   please, PI
— **hora**   per hour, 10
— **noche**   per night, 6
¿— **qué?**   why?, 3
— **teléfono**   on the phone
porque   because, 3
portugués (*m.*)   Portuguese (language), 13
posible   possible, 17
postre (*m.*)   dessert, 7
precio (*m.*)   price, 15
preferir (e:ie)   to prefer, 5
preguntar   to ask a question, 8
preocuparse   to worry, 20
preparar   to prepare, 10
presidente(a) (*m., f.*)   president, 8
préstamo (*m.*)   loan, 20
prestar   to lend, 8
primavera (*f.*)   spring, 5
primero(a)   first, 5
primo(a) (*m., f.*)   cousin, 3

probable   probable, 17
probablemente   probably, 15
probador (*m.*)   fitting room, 12
probar (o:ue)   to try, to taste, 9
probarse (o:ue)   to try on, 9
problema (*m.*)   problem, PII
profesión (*f.*)   profession, 3
profesor(a) (*m., f.*)   professor, teacher, instructor, PI
programa (*m.*)   program, PII
progreso (*m.*)   progress, PII
promedio (*m.*)   grade point average, 18
pronto   soon, 17
próximo(a)   next, 5
psicología (*f.*)   psychology, 18
pueblo (*m.*)   town, 6
puerta (*f.*)   door, PII
— **de atrás** (*f.*)   back door, 10
pues   well, 12

Q

que   than, that, 4; which, 8
— **viene**   next, 6
¿qué?   what?, 1
¿— **tal?**   how's it going?, PI
¿— **tiempo hace hoy?**   what's the weather like today?, 10
¿— **hora es?**   what time is it?, 1
quedar   to be located, 7
quedarse   to stay, to remain, 12
querer (e:ie)   to want, 5
querido(a)   dear, 9
¿quién(es)?   who?, whom?, 2
química (*f.*)   chemistry, 18
quince   fifteen, PI
quinto(a)   fifth, 5
quitar   to take away, to remove, 9
quitarse   to take off (e.g., one's clothing), 9

R

radiografía (*f.*)   X-ray, 17
rápido (*m.*)   express train, 16
¡rápido!   quick!, 11
rápido(a)   fast, 16
raqueta de tenis (*f.*)   tennis racket, 8
recibir   to receive, 2
reciente   recent, 17
recientemente   recently, 14
recoger   to pick up, 20
recomendar (e:ie)   to recommend, 16
recordar (o:ue)   to remember, 6
refresco (*m.*)   soft drink, soda, 1

regalar to give (a present), 8
regalo (*m.*) present, gift, 6
reloj (*m.*) clock, watch, 15
remolcador (*m.*) tow truck, 14
repetir (e:i) to repeat, 7
requisito (*m.*) requirement, 18
reservación (*f.*) reservation, 7
reservar to reserve, 16
restaurante (*m.*) restaurant, 1
resultado (*m.*) result, 19
reunión (*f.*) meeting, 11
revisar to check, 15
revista (*f.*) magazine, 5
rogar (o:ue) to beg, 16
rojo(a) red, P1
romper to break, 14
romperse to break (i.e., a bone), 17
ropa (*f.*) clothes, clothing, 10
rosado(a) pink, P1

S

sábado (*m.*) Saturday, P1
saber to know how, to know a fact, 7
sacar una nota to get a grade, 18
sala (*f.*) ward, room, 17
— **de emergencia** (*f.*) emergency room, 17
— **de rayos X** (*f.*) X-ray room, 17
salir to go out, to leave, 7
salsa (*f.*) sauce, 10
se (to) himself, (to) herself, (to) yourself (*form.*), (to) yourselves, (to) themselves, 9
— **dice** one says, 6
secadora (*f.*) dryer, 11
secretario(a) (*m., f.*) secretary, PII
seguir (e:i) to continue, to follow, 7
— **derecho** to continue straight ahead, 9
según according to, 11
segundo(a) second, 5
seguro(a) sure, 18
seis six, PI
sello (*m.*) stamp, 6
semana (*f.*) week, 5
semestre (*m.*) semester, 18
sentar (e:ie) to sit, 9
sentarse (e:ie) to sit down, 9
sentir (e:ie) to regret, to be sorry, 17
sentirse (e:ie) to feel, 12
señor Mr., sir, gentleman, PI
señora Mrs., madam, lady, PI
señorita Miss, young lady, PI

separado(a) separated, PI
septiembre September, PI
séptimo(a) seventh, 5
ser to be, PII
— **difícil** to be unlikely, 17
— **importante** to be important, 17
— **imposible** to be impossible, 17
— **(una) lástima** to be a pity, 17
— **mejor** to be better, 17
— **necesario** to be necessary, 17
— **seguro** to be certain, 17
servilleta (*f.*) napkin, 1
servir (e:i) to serve, 5
sesenta sixty, PII
setenta seventy, PII
sexo (*m.*) sex, PI
sexto(a) sixth, 5
si if, 8
sí yes, 1
siempre always, 2
siete seven, PI
silla (*f.*) chair, PII
sin falta without fail, 15
sin que without, 19
sistema (*m.*) system, PII
sobre about, 13
sobrevivir to survive, 19
sobrina (*f.*) niece, 3
sobrino (*m.*) nephew, 3
sociología (*f.*) sociology, 18
solamente only, 1
solo(a) alone, 4
sólo only, 1
soltero(a) single, PI
sombrero (*m.*) hat, 12
sopa (*f.*) soup, 7
sortija (*f.*) ring, 13
su (*adj.*) his, her, its, your (*form.*), their, 2
suegra (*f.*) mother-in-law, 3
suegro (*m.*) father-in-law, 3
suerte (*f.*) luck, 7
suéter (*m.*) sweater, 10
sugerir (e:ie) to suggest, 16
sumamente extremely, highly, 16
supermercado (*m.*) supermarket, 10
supervisor(a) (*m., f.*) supervisor, 4
suyo(s), suya(s) (*pron.*) yours (*form.*), his, hers, theirs, 9

T

talla (*f.*) size, 13
tallarines (*m. pl.*) spaghetti, 10

taller (*m.*) repair shop, 14
talonario de cheques (*m.*) checkbook, 20
también also, too, 4
tampoco neither, 6
tan as, 4
— **pronto como** as soon as, 19
— **... como** as... as, 4
tanque (*m.*) tank, 14
tarde (*f.*) afternoon, 1; late, 2
tarjeta (*f.*) card, 9
— **de crédito** (*f.*) credit card, 9
taxi (*m.*) taxi, 2
te you (*fam.*), 6; (to) you, 7; (to) yourself, 8
¿— **gusta?** do you like...?, PI
té (*m.*) tea, 2
teatro (*m.*) theater, 5
teléfono (*m.*) telephone, PII
— **celular** (*m.*) cell phone, 20
telegrama (*m.*) telegram, PII
televisión (*f.*) television, PII
temer to fear, 17
temprano early, 2
tenedor (*m.*) fork, 1
tener to have, 4
— **... años (de edad)** to be... years old, 4
— **calor** to be hot, 4
— **cuidado** to be careful, 4
— **frío** to be cold, 4
— **hambre** to be hungry, 4
— **miedo** to be afraid, 4
— **paciencia** to be patient, 11
— **prisa** to be in a hurry, 4
— **que** (+ *inf.*) to have to, 4
— **razón** to be right, 4
— **sed** to be thirsty, 4
— **sueño** to be sleepy, 4
— **suerte** to be lucky, 7
tenis (*m.*) tennis, 8
tercero(a) third, 5
terminar to finish, 15
termómetro (*m.*) thermometer, 19
terraza (*m.*) terrace, 9
testamento (*m.*) will, 19
ti (*fam. sing.*) you, 6
tía (*f.*) aunt, 3
tiempo (*m.*) time, 18
tienda (*f.*) store, 4
— **de campaña** (*f.*) tent, 8
timbre (*m.*) stamp (*Méx.*), 6
tintorería (*f.*) dry cleaners, 9
tío (*m.*) uncle, 3
tipo (*m.*) type, 13
toalla (*f.*) towel, 5
tobillo (*m.*) ankle, 17
todavía yet, 9

ENGLISH–SPANISH VOCABULARY

A

a un(a), PI

a lot mucho, 1; **a lot of** un montón de, 20

about sobre, 13

accident accidente (*m.*), 11

according to según, 11

account cuenta (*f.*), 15

ache doler (o:ue), 8

address dirección (*f.*), domicilio (*m.*), PI

advise aconsejar, 16

adviser consejero(a) (*m., f.*), 18

afternoon tarde (*f.*), 1

afterwards después, 12

again otra vez, 11

age edad (*f.*), PI

air conditioning aire acondicionado (*m.*), 4

airplane avión (*m.*), 7

airport aeropuerto (*m.*), 12

alcoholic alcohólico(a), 6

all todo(a), 11
— **day long** todo el día, 12

almost casi, 14

alone solo(a), 4

along por, 10

already ya, 17

also también, 4

always siempre, 2

ambulance ambulancia (*f.*), 17

American americano(a), 20

an un(a), PI

ankle tobillo (*m.*), 17

another otro(a), 4

any algún, alguno(a), algunos(as), 6

anyone alguien, 6

anything algo, 6

April abril, PI

Argentinian argentino(a) (*m., f.*), 3

around por, 10

arrive llegar, 4

art gallery galería de arte (*f.*), 13

as tan, 4
— **soon as** en cuanto, tan pronto como, 19
— **soon as possible** cuanto antes, 16
— **... as** tan... como, 4

ask pedir (e:i), 5; preguntar, 8

aspirin aspirina (*f.*), 8

assistant ayudante (*m., f.*), 19

at a, en, 1
— **home** en casa, 12
— **this moment** en este momento, 18
— **what time?** ¿a qué hora ...?, 1

attend asistir, 20
— **to** atender (e:ie), 9

August agosto, PI

aunt tía (*f.*), 3

auto club club automovilístico (*m.*), 14

automatic automático(a), 15
— **teller machine (ATM)** cajero automático (*m.*), 15

automobile auto (*m.*), carro (*m.*), coche (*m.*), 3

autumn otoño (*m.*), 10

avenue avenida (*f.*), 7

B

back door puerta de atrás (*f.*), 10

backpack mochila (*f.*), 8

bad malo(a), 2

badly mal, 4

baked asado(a), 2

bakery panadería, (*f.*), 13

ball pelota (*f.*), 8

bank banco (*m.*), 6

basketball basquetbol (*m.*), 8

bathe (*oneself*) bañar(se), 9

bathing suit traje de baño (*m.*), 12

bathroom baño (*m.*), 9

battery acumulador (*m.*), batería (*f.*), 14

be ser, PII; estar, 3
— **...years old** tener ... años (de edad), 4
— **able** poder (o:ue), 6
— **afraid** tener miedo, 4
— **careful** tener cuidado, 4
— **cold** tener frío, 4; hacer frío, 10
— **familiar with** conocer, 7
— **glad** alegrarse (de), 17
— **good (bad) weather** hacer buen (mal) tiempo, 10
— **hot** tener calor, 4; hacer calor, 10
— **hungry** tener hambre, 4

— **in a hurry** tener prisa, 4
— **located** quedar, 7
— **named** llamarse, 9
— **patient** tener paciencia, 11
— **pleasing** gustar, 8
— **right** tener razón, 4
— **sleepy** tener sueño, 4
— **sorry** sentir (e:ie), 17
— **thirsty** tener sed, 4
— **(very) windy** hacer (mucho) viento, 10

beach playa (*f.*), 6

beautiful hermoso(a), 15; bello(a), 16

beauty salon peluquería (*f.*), 9

because porque, 3

bed cama (*f.*), 6

bedroom dormitorio (*m.*), 9

beer cerveza (*f.*), 1

before antes de, 9; antes de que, 19

beg rogar (o:ue), 16

begin comenzar (e:ie), empezar (e:ie), 5

believe creer, 4

best mejor, 4

better mejor, 4

bicycle bicicleta (*f.*), 8

big grande, 1

bill cuenta (*f.*), 1

black negro(a), PI

blanket cobija (*f.*), frazada (*f.*), manta (*f.*), 6

blender licuadora (*f.*), 11

blue azul, PI

boarding house pensión (*f.*), 4

book libro (*m.*), PII

bookstore librería (*f.*), 6

bored aburrido(a), 11

boring aburrido(a), 11

borrow pedir prestado, 20

boss jefe(a) (*m., f.*), 20

both los (las) dos, 10

bottle botella (*f.*), 2

boy chico (*m.*), muchacho (*m.*), 1

boyfriend novio (*m.*), 3

brake freno (*m.*), 14

brand marca (*f.*), 11

break romper, 14
— **a bone** fracturarse, romperse, 17

breakfast desayuno (*m.*), 5

bring traer, 5

broom escoba (*f.*), 10
brother hermano (*m.*), 3
brother-in-law cuñado (*m.*), 3
brown café, marrón, PI
brush cepillo (*m.*), 9
bus autobús (*m.*), ómnibus (*m*), 2
busy ocupado(a), 16
but pero, 1
buy comprar, 5
by para, por, 10
— **heart** de memoria, 7

C

cafeteria cafetería (*f.*), 1
calculator calculadora (*f.*), 17
call llamar, 2
can bote (*m.*) (*Méx.*), lata (*f.*), 10
cancel cancelar, 7
car auto (*m.*), automóvil (*m.*), carro (*m.*), coche (*m.*), 3
— **rental agency** agencia de alquiler de automóviles (*f.*), 15
card tarjeta (*f.*), 9
careful cuidadoso(a), 17
cash a check cambiar un cheque, 15
cashier cajero(a) (*m., f.*), 15
catalogue catálogo (*m.*), 12
chair silla (*f.*), PII
champagne champán (*m.*), 1
change cambiar, 14
charge cobrar, 15
check (*restaurant*) cuenta (*f.*), 1; (*bank*) cheque (*m.*), 6; chequear, revisar, 15
checkbook talonario de cheques (*m.*), 20
chemistry química (*f.*), 17
chicken pollo (*m.*), 2
— **with rice** arroz con pollo, 11
chief jefe(a) (*m., f.*), 20
child niño(a) (*m., f.*), 8
children (son[s] and daughter[s]) hijos (*m. pl.*), 2
chocolate chocolate (*m.*), 2
choose elegir (e:i), 11
Christmas Navidad (*f.*), 18
church iglesia (*f.*), 5
city ciudad (*f.*), PI
class clase (*f.*), 4
clean limpiar, 10
clear claro(a), 17
clerk empleado(a) (*m., f.*), 14
climate clima (*m.*), PII

clock reloj (*m.*), 15
close cerrar (e:ie), 5
closed cerrado(a), 14
clothes ropa (*f.*), 10
clothing ropa (*f.*), 10
cloudy nublado(a), 10
club club (*m.*), 3
coach entrenador(a) (*m., f.*), 8
coat abrigo (*m.*), 10
coffee café (*m.*), 2
coffeepot cafetera (*f.*), 11
cold frío(a), 2
collide chocar, 19
comb peine (*m.*), 9
come venir, 4
— **back** volver (o:ue), 6
— **in** pase, PI; entrar, 10
computer computadora (*f.*), 12
concert concierto (*m.*), 5
confirm confirmar, 7
consulate consulado (*m.*), 20
continue seguir (e:i), 7
— **straight ahead** seguir derecho, 9
contract contrato (*m.*), 17
conversation conversación (*f.*), PII
cook cocinar, 10; cocinero(a) (*m., f.*), 11
cost costar (o:ue), 6
cousin primo(a) (*m., f.*), 3
country país (*m.*), 7
cover cubrir, 14
credit crédito (*m.*), 20
— **card** tarjeta de crédito (*f.*), 9
crutch muleta (*f.*), 17
curtain cortina (*f.*), 20
cut cortar, 9

D

dad papá, 3
dangerous peligroso(a), 15
date fecha (*f.*), PI
— **of birth** fecha de nacimiento (*f.*), PI
daughter hija (*f.*), 2
day día (*m.*), PII
— **before yesterday** anteayer, 12
dear querido(a), 9
December diciembre, PI
decide decidir, 2
decision decisión (*f.*), PII
decrease bajar, 19
dentist dentista (*m., f.*), 17
deny negar (e:ie), 16

deposit depositar, 15
dessert postre (*m.*), 7
die morir (o:ue), 11
difficult difícil, 16
dinner cena (*f.*), 5
discount descuento (*m.*), 16
divorced divorciado(a), PI
dizzy mareado(a), 16
do hacer, 5
— **errands** hacer diligencias, 20
do you like...? ¿te gusta...?, PI
doctor's office consultorio (*m.*), 17
doctor doctor(a) (*m., f.*), médico(a) (*m., f.*), PI
dog perro (*m.*), 15
dollar dólar (*m.*), 3
door puerta (*f.*), PII
doubt dudar, 18
dress vestido (*m.*), 9
drink tomar, 1; bebida (*f.*), beber, 2
drive conducir, manejar, 7
driver's license number número de la licencia para conducir (manejar) (*m.*), PI
dry cleaners tintorería (*f.*), 9
dryer secadora (*f.*), 11

E

early temprano, 2
earrings aretes (*m. pl.*), 13
easy fácil, 16
eat comer, 2
education educación (*f.*), 5
egg huevo (*m.*), 2
eight ocho, PI
eighteen dieciocho, PI
eighth octavo(a), 5
eighty ochenta, PII
either... or o... o, 6
elegant elegante, 13
elevator ascensor (*m.*), 13
eleven once, PI
embassy embajada (*f.*), 7
emergency room sala de emergencia (*f.*), 17
emergency emergencia (*f.*), 17
empty vacío(a), 14
engagement ring anillo de compromiso (*m.*), 13
engine motor (*m.*), 15
English (*language*) inglés (*m.*), 1
English inglés(esa), 1
enter entrar, 10

errand   diligencia (*f.*), 20
escalator   escalera mecánica, 13
evening   noche (*f.*), 1
ever   alguna vez, 6
every   todos(as), 11
— **day**   todos los días, 18
exam   examen (*m.*), 15
excursion   excursión (*f.*), 6
exercise   hacer ejercicio, 19
expensive   caro(a), 4
express train   rápido (*m.*), expreso (*m.*), 16
extremely   sumamente, 16
eye doctor   oculista (*m., f.*), 19

F

fall   otoño (*f.*), 10
fall asleep   dormirse (o:ue), 9
family   familia (*f.*), 3
fashion   moda (*f.*), 13
fast   rápido(a), 16
father   padre, papá (*m.*), 3
father-in-law   suegro (*m.*), 3
favor   favor (*m.*), 11
fear   temer, 17
February   febrero, PI
feel   sentirse (e:ie), 12
feminine   femenino(a), PI
fever   fiebre (*f.*), 19
fewer   menos, 4
fifteen   quince, PI
fifth   quinto(a), 5
fifty   cincuenta, PII
fill   llenar, 14
final exam   examen final (*m.*), 18
fine   bien, PI
finish   terminar, 15
first   primero(a), 5
fish   pescado (*m.*), 2
fitting room   probador (*m.*), 12
five   cinco, PI
fix   arreglar, 14
flat tire   goma pinchada (*f.*), 14
flight   vuelo (*m.*), 7
floor (*story*)   piso (*m.*), 5; (*surface*), 11
fly   volar (o:ue), 6
fog   niebla (*f.*), 10
follow   seguir (e:i), 7
food   comida (*f.*), 1
foot   pie (*m.*), 8
for   para, 6; por, 10
— **whom**   ¿para quién?, 8
foreign   extranjero(a), 7
fork   tenedor (*m.*), 1
forty   cuarenta, PII
four   cuatro, PI

fourteen   catorce, PI
fourth   cuarto(a), 5
freeway   autopista (*f.*), 19
French (*language*)   francés (*f.*), 1
French   francés (francesa), 1
Friday   viernes, PI
fried   frito(a), 2
friend   amigo(a) (*m., f.*), 2
friendship   amistad (*f.*), PII
from   de, PII
frozen   helado(a), 7
function   funcionar, 13
furniture store   mueblería (*f.*), 13

G

game (*match*)   partido (*m.*), 8
garbage   basura (*f.*), 11
gas station   estación de servicio (*f.*), gasolinera (*f.*), 14
gasoline   gasolina (*f.*), 14
general   general, 17
generally   generalmente, 9
gentleman   señor, PI
German   alemán (alemana), 1
get   conseguir (e:i), 7; buscar, 16
— **a grade**   sacar una nota, 18
— **dressed**   vestirse (e:i), 9
— **up**   levantarse, 9
gift   regalo, 6
girl   chica (*f.*), muchacha (*f.*), 1
girlfriend   novia (*f.*), 3
give   dar, 3
— **a present**   regalar, 8
— **a shot**   poner una inyección, 18
— **back**   devolver (o:ue), 20
go   ir, 3
— **away**   irse, 9
— **by**   pasar (por), 10
— **down**   bajar, 19
— **on a diet**   ponerse a dieta, 19
— **on foot**   ir a pie, 11
— **on vacation**   ir de vacaciones, 12
— **out**   salir, 7
— **shopping**   ir de compras, 11
— **skiing**   ir a esquiar, 8
— **to bed**   acostarse (o:ue), 9
gold   oro (*m.*), 13
good   bueno(a), 2
— **afternoon**   buenas tardes, PI
— **evening** (*good night*)   buenas noches, PI
— **morning**   buenos días, PI
goodbye   adiós, PI
grade   nota (*f.*), 18
granddaughter   nieta (*f.*), 13

grandfather   abuelo (*m.*), 3
grandmother   abuela (*f.*), 3
grandson   nieto (*m.*), 13
gray   gris (*f.*), 1
green   verde, PI
guest   invitado(a) (*m., f.*), 11
guide   guía (*m.*), 6
gym   gimnasio (*m.*), 4

H

hair   pelo (*m.*), 9
— **dresser**   peluquero(a) (*m., f.*), 9
half an hour   media hora, 11
hand   mano (*f.*), PII
handsome   guapo(a), 1
happen   pasar, 17
happy   feliz, 1
hardly ever   casi nunca, 11
hardware store   ferretería (*f.*), 13
hat   sombrero (*m.*), 12
have   tener, 4
— **a good time**   divertirse (e:ie), 11
— **breakfast**   desayunar, 5
— **lunch**   almorzar (o:ue), 6
— **to**   deber (+ *inf.*), 2; tener que (+ *inf.*), 4
he   él, 1
head   cabeza (*f.*), 8
hello   hola, PI
help   ayudar, 10
her   su, 2; ella, 5; la, 6; le, 7
here   aquí, 2
hers   suyo(s), suya(s), 9
herself   se, 9
highly   sumamente, 16
him   él, 5; lo, 6; le, 7
himself   se, 9
his   su, 3; suyo(s), suya(s), 9
hope   esperar, 16
horrible   horrible, 19
horse   caballo (*m.*), 8
hospital   hospital (*m.*), 3
hot   caliente, 2
hotel   hotel (*m.*), 3
hour   hora (*f.*), 4
house   casa (*f.*), PII
household chores   trabajos de la casa (*m. pl.*), 11
how?   ¿cómo?, 3
— **are you?**   ¿cómo está usted?, PI
— **do you say...?**   ¿cómo se dice...?, 6
— **long ago...?**   ¿cuánto tiempo hace que...?, 13

— **long?** ¿cuánto tiempo?, 11
— **many?** ¿cuántos(as)?, 1
— **much?** ¿cuánto(a)?, 5
hurt doler (o:ue), 8
husband esposo (*m.*), 4

I

I yo, 1
I hope ojalá, 17
I like... me gusta..., PI
I'll say ya lo creo, 5
I'll see you later hasta luego, PI
I'll see you tomorrow hasta
　mañana, PI
I'm sorry lo siento, PI
iced helado(a), 7
idea idea (*f.*), PII
if si, 8
if only ojalá, 17
impatient impaciente, 9
important importante, 5
impossible imposible, 14
in a, 15; en, 1
— **case** en caso de que, 19
— **order that** para que, 19
— **order to** para, 5
— **that case** entonces, 7
— **those days** en esa época, 12
inexpensive barato(a), 4
information información (*f.*), 7
injection inyección (*f.*), 17
intelligent inteligente, 1
interesting interesante, 11
interview entrevista (*f.*), 20
it (*m., f.*) la, lo, 6
— **is a pity** es (una) lástima, 17
— **is advisable** conviene, 17
— **is better** es mejor, 17
— **is certain** es seguro, 17
— **is unlikely** es difícil, 17
— **may be** puede ser, 17
Italian (*language*) italiano (*m.*),
　1
its su(s) (*adj.*), 2

J

jacket chaqueta (*f.*), 13
jail cárcel (*f.*), 5
January enero, PI
jewelry store joyería (*f.*), 12
July julio, PI
June junio, PI

K

key llave (*f.*), 4

L

kid niño(a) (*m., f.*), 8
kind bueno(a), 16
kitchen cocina (*f.*), 10
know conocer, saber, 7

L

lady señora, PI
lack hacer falta, 8
lamp lámpara (*f.*), PII
language idioma (*m.*), lengua
　(*f.*), PII
large grande, 1
last pasado(a), 10
— **night** anoche, 10
late tarde, 2
lately últimamente, 14
later después, 6
lawyer abogado(a) (*m., f.*), 19
learn aprender, 2
leave salir, 7; irse, 9
lecture conferencia (*f.*), 17
leg pierna (*f.*), 17
lend prestar, 8
less menos, 4
lesson lección (*f.*), PII
letter carta (*f.*), 6
liberty libertad (*f.*), PII
library biblioteca (*f.*), 18
lie mentir (e:ie), 11
lie down acostarse (o:ue), 9
lift levantar, 9
light luz (*f.*), PII
like gustar, 8
limit límite (*m.*), 10
literature literatura (*f.*), 18
little poco(a) (*quantity*),
　pequeño(a) (*size*), 4
live vivir, 2
loan préstamo (*m.*), 20
long largo(a), 16
look at mirar, 12
look for buscar, 16
lose perder (e:ie), 5
love amor (*m.*)
luck suerte (*f.*), 7
lunch almuerzo (*m.*), 5

M

madam señora, PI
magazine revista (*f.*), 5
maiden name apellido de soltera
　(*m.*), PI
mail echar al correo, 20
make hacer, 5
mall centro comercial (*m.*), 12
man hombre (*m.*), PII

manager gerente (*m., f.*), 4
March marzo, PI
marital status estado civil
　(*m.*), PI
market mercado (*m.*), 4
married casado(a), PI
masculine masculino, PI
mattress colchón (*m.*), 6
May mayo, PI
me mí, 6; me, 6
meal comida (*f.*), 1
meat carne (*f.*), 7
mechanic mecánico(a) (*m., f.*), 14
medicine cabinet botiquín
　(*m.*), 9
medium mediano(a), 13
meet (*for an appointment*) encon-
　trarse (o:ue), 12; (*for the first
　time*) conocer, 13
meeting junta (*f.*), reunión (*f.*), 11
menu menú (*m.*), 2
metal metal (*m.*), 3
Mexican mexicano(a), 1
midnight medianoche (*f.*), 9
midterm exam examen parcial
　(*m.*), 18
mile milla (*f.*), 10
milk leche (*f.*), 2
mine mío(a), 9
mirror espejo (*m.*), 9
mom mamá, 3
moment momento (*m.*), 9
Monday lunes, PI
money dinero (*m.*), PII
month mes (*m.*), 5
more más, 4
morning mañana (*f.*), 1
mother madre (*f.*), 3
mother-in-law suegra (*f.*), 3
motorcycle moto (*f.*), 15; moto-
　cicleta (*f.*), 15
movie theater cine (*m.*), 5
movies cine (*m.*), 5
Mr. señor, PI
Mrs. señora, PI
much mucho, 2
museum museo (*m.*), 2
must deber (+ *inf.*), 2
my mi, 3; mío(a), 9
myself me, 8

N

name nombre (*m.*), PI
napkin servilleta (*f.*), 1
nationality nacionalidad
　(*f.*), PI
near to cerca de, 6
necessary necesario(a), 17

necklace collar (*m.*), 13
need necesitar, 1
neither tampoco, 6
neither... nor ni... ni, 6
nephew sobrino (*m.*), 3
never jamás, 6; nunca, 6
new nuevo(a), 12
newspaper diario (*m.*), periódico (*m.*), 6
next próximo(a), 5; que viene, 6
niece sobrina (*f.*), 3
nightgown camisón (*m.*), 13
nine nueve, PI
nineteen diecinueve, PI
ninety noventa, PII
ninth noveno(a), 5
no one nadie, 6
nobody nadie, 6
none ninguno(a), ningún, 6
North American (*from the U.S.*) norteamericano(a), PI
not any ningún, ninguno(a), 6
not very well no muy bien, PI
nothing nada, 6
novel novela (*f.*), 7
November noviembre, PI
now ahora, 3
number número (*m.*), PI
nurse enfermero(a) (*m., f.*), PI

O

obtain conseguir (e:i), 7
occupation ocupación (*f.*), PI
ocean mar (*m*), 6
October octubre, PI
of de, PII
of mine mío(a) (*adj.*), 9
office oficina (*f.*), 5
often a menudo, 2
oil aceite (*m.*), 14
older mayor, 4
once in a while de vez en cuando, 12
one uno, un(a), PI
one hundred cien, ciento, PII
one says se dice, 6
only solamente, 1
open abrir, 2; abierto(a), 14
or o, 2
orange anaranjado, PI
order mandar, 16; pedir (e:i), 6
other otro(a), 4
our nuestro(a) (*adj.*), 3
ours nuestro(s), nuestra(s), 9
ourselves nos, 9
over there allá, 8
owner dueño(a) (*m., f.*), 4

P

package paquete (*m.*), 20
pain dolor (*m.*), 18
pair par (*m.*), 12
pants pantalón (*m.*); pantalones (*m. pl.*), 9
paramedic paramédico(a) (*m., f.*), 18
parents padres (*m.*), 3
park parque (*m.*), 9
party fiesta (*f.*), 2
passenger pasajero(a) (*m., f.*), 19
passport pasaporte (*m.*), 7
past y (*with time expressions*), 1; pasado(a), 10
patience paciencia (*f.*), 11
patient paciente (*m., f.*), 18
pay (*for*) pagar, 1
pen pluma (*f.*), PII
pencil lápiz (*m.*), PII
people gente (*f.*)
percent por ciento, 16
per hour por hora, 10
per night por noche, 6
percent por ciento, 16
perfume perfume (*m.*), 9
person persona (*f.*), 13
pharmacy farmacia (*f.*), 6
phone number número de teléfono, PI
photocopy fotocopia (*f.*), 20
physics física (*f.*), 17
pick up buscar, 16; recoger, 20
pie pastel (*m.*), 2
pill pastilla (*f.*), 19
pink rosado, PI
place poner, 7; lugar (*m.*), 13
   — of birth lugar de nacimiento, PI
   — of interest lugar de interés, 6
   — of work lugar donde trabaja, PI
play (*a game or sport*) jugar(u:ue), 8
please por favor, PI
poem poema (*m.*), PII
Portuguese (*language*) portugués (*m.*), 13
possible posible, 17
post office oficina de correos (*f.*), 6; correo (*m.*), 20
potato papa (*f.*), patata (*f.*), 2
prefer preferir (e:ie), 5
prepare preparar, 10
present regalo (*m.*), 6
president presidente(a) (*m., f.*), 8
pretty bonito(a), 3

price precio (*m.*), 15
probable probable, 17
probably probablemente, 15
problem problema (*m.*), PII
profession profesión (*f.*), 3
program programa (*m.*), PII
progress progreso (*m.*), PII
provided that con tal que, 19
psychology psicología (*f.*), 18
purple morado, PI
purse cartera (*f.*), 12
put poner, 7
   — a cast on enyesar, 18
   — on ponerse, 9
   — to bed acostar (o:ue), 9

R

rain llover (o:ue); lluvia (*f.*), 10
raincoat impermeable (*m.*), 10
raise levantar, 9
razor máquina de afeitar (*f.*), 9
read leer, 2
ready listo(a), 14
receive recibir, 2
recent reciente, 17
recently recientemente, 14
recommend recomendar (e:ie), 16
red rojo, PI
red wine vino tinto (*m.*), 1
register matricularse, 18
regret sentir (e:ie), 17
remain quedarse, 12
remember recordar (o:ue), 6; acordarse (o:ue) (de), 9
remove quitar, 9
rent alquilar, 15
repair shop taller (*m.*), 14
repeat repetir (e:i), 1
report informe (*m.*), 20
request pedir (e:i), 6
requirement requisito (*m.*), 18
reservation reservación (*f.*), 7
reserve reservar, 16
restaurant restaurante (*m.*), 1
result resultado (*m.*), 16
return volver (o:ue), 6; (*something*) devolver (o:ue), 20
rice arroz (*m.*), 11
ride a bicycle montar en bicicleta, 8
ride a horse montar a caballo, 8
right away en seguida, 14
right now ahora mismo, 9
ring anillo (*m.*), sortija (*f.*), 13
roasted asado(a), 2
room cuarto (*m.*), habitación (*f.*), 4

S

salad ensalada (f.), 7
sale liquidación (f.), venta (f.), 11
Saturday sábado, PI
sauce salsa (f.), 10
say decir (e:i), 5
— goodbye despedirse (e:i), 11
schedule horario (m.), itinerario (m.), 16
scholarship beca (f.), 18
school escuela (f.), 5
seat asiento (m.), PI
second segundo(a), 5
secretary secretario(a) (m., f.), PII
see ver, 7
select elegir (e:i), 11
sell vender, 13
semestre semester (m.), 18
send mandar, enviar, 8
separated separado(a), PI
September septiembre, PI
servant criado(a) (m., f.), 10
serve servir (e:i), 5
seven siete, PI
seventeen diecisiete, PI
seventh séptimo(a), 5
seventy setenta, PII
several varios(as), 13
sex sexo, PI
shampoo champú (m.), 9
shave (oneself) afeitar(se), 9
she ella, 1
ship barco (m.), 15
shoe zapato (m.), 12
— store zapatería (f.), 12
short corto(a), 9
shot inyección (f.), 17
should deber (+ inf.), 2
sick enfermo(a), 3
sign firmar, 17
silver plata (f.), 15
since como, 20
single soltero(a), PI
sink fregadero (m.), 11
sir señor, PI
sister hermana (f.), 3
sister-in-law cuñada (f.), 3
sit sentar (e:ie), 9
— down sentarse (e:ie), 9
— down (take a seat) tome asiento, PI
six seis, PI
sixteen dieciséis, PI
sixth sexto(a), 5
sixty sesenta, PII
size talla (f.), 13

skates patines (m. pl.), 8
ski esquiar, 8
skis csquícs (m. pl.), esquís (m. pl.), 8
sleep dormir (o:ue), 5
sleeping bag bolsa de dormir (f.), 8
slow lento(a), 16
small pequeño(a), 4
smaller menor, 4
snow nevar (e:ie), 10
soap jabón (m.), 5
social security number número de seguro social, PI
soda refresco (m.), 1
soft drink refresco (m.), 1
some unos(as), PII; algunos(as) (pl.), algún, alguno(a), 6
someone alguien, 6
something algo, 6
sometimes algunas veces, 6
son hijo (m.), 2
soon pronto, 17
soup sopa (f.), 7
spaghetti espaguetis (m. pl.), tallarines (m. pl.), 10
Spanish (language) español (m.), PII
Spanish español(a), 1
spare part pieza de repuesto (f.), 14
speak hablar, 1
special especial, 17
speed limit límite de velocidad (m.), 10
speed velocidad (f.), 10
spoon cuchara (f.), 1
sports page página deportiva (f.), 8
spring primavera (f.), 5
stairs escalera (f.), 13
stamp timbre (m.) (Méx.), estampilla (f.), sello (m.), 6
start comenzar (e:ie), empezar (e:ie), 5
stay quedarse, 12
stop parar
store tienda (f.), 4
— window escaparate (m.), vidriera (f.), 12
street calle (f.), PI
student estudiante (m., f.), 3
study estudiar, 1
suggest sugerir (e:ie), 16
suit traje (m.), 13
suitcase maleta (f.), valija (f.), 4
summer verano (m.), 10
Sunday domingo, PI
supermarket supermercado (m.), 10

supervisor supervisor(a) (m., f.), 4
sure seguro(a), 18
surgeon cirujano(a) (m., f.), 19
surgery cirugía (f.), operación (f.), 19
surname apellido (m.), PI
survive sobrevivir, 19
sweater suéter (m.), 10
sweep barrer, 10
swim nadar, 7
swimming pool alberca (f.) (Méx.), piscina (f.), 4
syrup jarabe (m.), 19
system sistema (m.), PII

T

table mesa (f.), PII
tablecloth mantel (m.), 1
take tomar, 2; (something or someone to someplace) llevar, 2
— away quitar, 9
— care cuidar, 17
take off (i.e., one's clothing) quitarse, 9
talk hablar, 1
tall alto(a), 3
tank tanque (m.), 14
tape grabar, 20
taste probar (o:ue), 9
taxi taxi (m.), 2
tea té, 2
teach enseñar, 11
teacher profesor(a) (m., f.), PI
telegram telegrama (m.), PII
telephone teléfono (m.), PII
television televisión (f.), PII
tell decir (e:i), 6
ten diez, PI
tennis tenis (m.), 8
— racquet raqueta de tenis (f.), 8
tent tienda de campaña (f.), 8
tenth décimo(a), 5
terrace terraza (m.), 9
test (analysis) análisis (m.), 19
than que, 4
thank you gracias, PI
that aquel, aquella (adj.), 8; aquello (neuter pron.), 8; ese, esa (adj.), 8; eso (neuter pron.), 8; que, 4
that (one) aquél, aquélla (pron.), 8; ése, ésa (pron.), 8
the el, la, las, los, PII
the pleasure is mine el gusto es mío, PI

theater   teatro (*m.*), 5
their   su(s) (*adj.*), 2
theirs   suyo(s), suya(s) (*pron.*), 9
them   ellas, ellos, 6; las, los, 7; les, 8
themselves   se, 9
then   entonces, 7
there   allí, 6
  — are   hay, PII
  — is   hay, PII
thermometer   termómetro (*m.*), 19
these   estos, estas (*adj.*), 8
these (ones)   éstos, éstas (*pron.*), 8
they   ellas, ellos, 1
thing   cosa (*f.*), 11
think   creer, 4
third   tercero(a), 5
thirteen   trece, PI
thirty   treinta, PI
this   este(a), 6, (*adj.*), 8
this   esto (*neuter pron.*), 8
this (one)   éste, ésta (*pron.*), 8
those (distant)   aquellos, aquellas (*adj.*), 8
those (nearby)   esos, esas (*adj.*), 8
those (ones) (distant)   aquéllos, aquéllas (*pron.*), 8
those (ones) (nearby)   ésos, ésas (*pron.*), 8
thousand   mil, 1
three   tres, PI
through   por, 10
Thursday   jueves, PI
ticket   billete (*m.*), pasaje (*m.*), 7; entrada (*f.*), 8; boleto (*m.*), 16
tie   corbata (*f.*), 13
till   menos, 1
time (occasion)   vez (*f.*), 15; tiempo (*m.*), 18
tire   goma (*f.*), llanta (*f.*), neumático (*m.*), 14
tired   cansado(a), 3
to   menos, 1; a, 3; para, 5
  — the left   a la izquierda, 9
  — the right   a la derecha, 9
  — whom?   ¿a quién?, 2
toaster   tostadora (*f.*), 11
today   hoy, PI
together   juntos(as), 12
tomato   tomate (*m.*), 10
tomorrow   mañana, 3
tonight   esta noche, 5
too   también, 4
tour   excursión (*f.*), 6
tourist brochure   folleto turístico (*m.*), 7
tourist office   oficina de turismo, 7
tow truck   grúa (*f.*), remolcador (*m.*), 14

towel   toalla (*f.*), 5
town   pueblo (*m.*), 6
train   tren (*m.*), 15
  — station   estación de trenes (*f.*), 16
trainer   entrenador(a) (*m., f.*), 8
translate   traducir, 7
trash   basura (*f.*), 11
travel   viajar, 3
  — agency   agencia de viajes (*f.*), 7
  — agent   agente de viajes (*m., f.*), 7
tree   árbol (*m.*), 18
trip   viaje (*m.*), 7
truth   verdad (*f.*), 7
try   probar (o:ue), 9
try on   probarse (o:ue), 9
Tuesday   martes, PI
tuition   matrícula (*f.*), 18
turn   doblar, 9
  — off   apagar, 11
twelve   doce, PI
twenty   veinte, PI
twenty-eight   veintiocho, PI
twenty-five   veinticinco, PI
twenty-four   veinticuatro, PI
twenty-nine   veintinueve, PI
twenty-one   veintiuno, PI
twenty-seven   veintisiete, PI
twenty-six   veintiséis, PI
twenty-three   veintitrés, PI
twenty-two   veintidós, PI
twist   torcerse, 17
two   dos, PI
two hundred   doscientos, PII
type   tipo (*m.*), 13

U

umbrella   paraguas (*m. sing.*), 10
uncle   tío (*m.*), 3
underneath   debajo (de), 11
understand   entender (e:ie), 5
United States   Estados Unidos, 3
university   universidad (*f.*), PII
unless   a menos que, 19
until   hasta, 15; hasta que, 19
us   nos, 6; nosotros(as), 6
use   usar, 13

V

vacation   vacaciones (*f. pl.*), 5
vacuum cleaner   aspiradora (*f.*), 10
various   varios(as), 13
velocity   velocidad (*f.*), 10

very   muy, 3
  — much   mucho, 1
  — well, and you?   muy bien, ¿y usted?, PI
veterinarian   veterinario(a) (*m., f.*), 15
visit   visitar, 2

W

wait   (*for*) esperar, 3; (*on*) atender (e:ie), 9
waiter   camarero (*m.*), mozo (*m.*), 2
waitress   camarera (*f.*), 2
wake up   despertarse (e:ie), 9
walk   caminar, 11; ir caminando, ir a pie, 11
wallet   billetera (*f.*), 20
want   desear, 1; querer (e:ie), 5
ward room   sala (*f.*), 17
wash   lavar, 9
wash one's hair   lavarse la cabeza, 9
washing machine   lavadora (*f.*), 10
watch   reloj (*m.*), 15
we   nosotros(as), 1
Wednesday   miércoles, PI
week   semana (*f.*), 5
weekend   fin de semana (*m.*), 16
weight   peso (*m.*), 19
well   bien, PI; pues, 12
what?   ¿qué?, 1; ¿cuál(es)?, 3
  — is he (she, it) like?   ¿cómo es?, 3
  — time is it?   ¿qué hora es?, 1
  — is the weather like today?   ¿qué tiempo hace hoy?, 10
when   ¿cuándo?, 5; cuando, 19
where?   ¿dónde?, PII
where is... from?   ¿de dónde es...?, PII
where to?   ¿adónde?, 3
which   que, 8
which (one)?   ¿cuál(es)?, 3
white   blanco, PI
who?   ¿quién(es)?, 2
whom?   ¿quién(es)?, 2
whose?   ¿de quién?, 2
why?   ¿por qué?, 3
widowed   viudo(a) (*m., f.*), PI
wife   esposa (*f.*), 4
will   testamento (*m.*), 19
window   ventana (*f.*), 9
  — shop   mirar vidrieras, 12
windshield   parabrisas (*m.*), 14
  — wiper   limpiaparabrisas (*m.*), 14

wine   vino (*m.*), 1
winter   invierno (*m.*), 10
with   con, 2
    — whom?   ¿con quién?, 2
without   sin que, 19
    — fail   sin falta, 15
woman   mujer (*f.*), PII
wood   madera (*f.*), 3
work   trabajar, 1; (*i.e., a machine*)
    funcionar, 13
worry   preocuparse, 20
worse   peor, 4
write   escribir, 2

X

X-ray   radiografía (*f.*), 17
    — room   sala de rayos X (*f.*), 17

Y

year(s)   año(s) (*m.*), PI
yellow   amarillo, PI
yes   sí, 1
yesterday   ayer, 10
yet   todavía, 9
you   tú, usted, ustedes, 1; ti, 6; te,
    la, las, lo, los, 6; le, les, te, 7
young man   chico (*m.*), mucha-
    cho (*m.*), 2
young woman   chica (*f.*),
    muchacha (*f.*), 2

younger   menor, 4
your   tu (*fam. adj.*), su (*form.
    adj.*), 3
yours   tuyo(s), tuya(s) (*fam.
    pron.*), 9; suyo(s), suya(s) (*form.
    pron.*), 9
yourself   te, se, 9
yourselves   se, 9

Z

zero   cero, PI

INDEX